War Sermons

Edited by

Gilles Teulié and Laurence Lux-sterritt

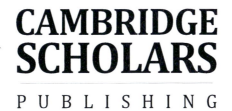

CAMBRIDGE
SCHOLARS
PUBLISHING

BL
65
.W2
W3827
2009

War Sermons, Edited by Gilles Teulié and Laurence Lux-sterritt

This book first published 2009

Cambridge Scholars Publishing

12 Back Chapman Street, Newcastle upon Tyne, NE6 2XX, UK

British Library Cataloguing in Publication Data
A catalogue record for this book is available from the British Library

ISBN (10): 1-4438-0546-7, ISBN (13): 978-1-4438-0546-9

TABLE OF CONTENTS

INTRODUCTION

GILLES TEULIE & LAURENCE LUX-STERRITT

That war is more than justified, that it is of solemn obligation, when required by the direct command of God is unquestionable.[1]

Some twenty-seven centuries ago, the Chinese military theoretician Sun Zu warned rulers that lack of popular support in times of war might herald their untimely downfall. Throughout history, monarchs asserted the legitimacy of their rule of divine right in order to secure their people's allegiance and to avoid any dissension with regards to their martial command. A ruler's authority was not to be questioned by commoners, and neither were his decisions to wage war. In order to embark upon military campaigns with the full support of public opinion, leaders often stressed the collusion of the political and the religious spheres to justify involvement. They depicted their wars as holy and sacred; they were not merely pleasing to the gods, they were also the expression of their divine will, and their direct intervention would guarantee victory on the battlefield. As illustrated by Roman generals' performing of pre-battle religious ceremonies to secure the gods' good will and by the Aztecs' sacrifices of war prisoners as tokens of gratitude for the divinities' help, mankind has always resorted to some form of spirituality in times of conflict. According to Azar Gat, such ritual ties led to the cohesion of a group of individuals who therefore could use their solidarity to oppose others;[2] subsequently:

[i]n war, the gods, temples, and cults constituted at one and the same time an entity to which appeals for help could be made, a sacred part of the shared culture for the defence and glory of which people could be easily aroused, and, indeed, a semi-independent source of warfare for the satisfaction of the gods' own special requirements, such as a human sacrifice. This powerful projection of the community in the supernatural

---

[1] Rev. Thomas T. Stone, *Sermons on War*. Boston: Pierce and Williams, 1829, 8.
[2] Azar Gat, *War in Human Civilization*. Oxford: OUP, 2006, 55.

sphere thus constituted as potent an instrument of and motivation for war
as did other –more 'real'- tangible or symbolic factors.[3]

Thus, war came to be considered not only as spiritually acceptable, but
also a means of personal improvement; combat could become a process of
redemption for soldiers who, through the selfless and ultimate sacrifice of
their lives, gained eternal life in the afterlife.

From the very beginnings of Christianity, the incompatibility of the act
of killing with the message of love expressed in the Gospels was tackled
by theologians willing to reconcile the masses with this apparent
contradiction. The importance devoted by the primitive Church to non-
violence was close to Christ's message of love and peace. Origen (185-
253), one of the Fathers of the Church, argued in his *Contra Celsum* that
no reason could ever justify the drawing of one's sword. Yet others like
Athanasius of Alexandria (296-373) or Ambrose of Milan (338-397), on
the contrary, believed that killing an enemy on the battlefield was
permitted and paved the way for future efforts at legitimising war violence
in certain circumstances. During the slow process of Christianisation
which followed Constantine's Edict of Milan (313), the defence of the
empire against invaders quickly became a Christian duty; in the context of
the Barbarian invasions facing Rome in the 5th century onwards,
Augustine of Hippo was prompted to delineate the concept of "Just War".
In his *City of God*, he expressed the idea that peace was order and war was
evil; however, he also admitted that in the context of the invasions, waging
war was necessary to bring order back to God's creation. Figures as
diverse as Isidore of Seville (560-636), champion of the Hispanic
resistance to barbarism, or the Benedictine monk Gratian (359-383),
author of the *Decretum Gratiani* (1150), justified war as a means of
retribution through which injustice may be avenged. During this period,
little distinction was made between the notion of just war and that of holy
war; indeed, although great efforts were made to promote the Crusades,
the spiritual unease of warriors forced to slay fellow soldiers had to be
taken into account. Likewise, the Crusades witnessed blurring of the
boundaries between military and religious activities, as embodied by the
various military orders which created the unique status of monk-soldiers
such as the order of the Hospital of St John (the Hospitallers), the Teutonic
Knights of the Hospital of St Mary of Jerusalem (the Teutonic Knights) or
the famed order of the Poor Knights of Christ and the Temple of Solomon
(the Knights Templar) among others. At the heart of these Orders' *raison
d'être* was the dual characteristic conferred to their members: as monks,

---

[3]*Ibid.*, 433.

they would devote their lives to God while as soldiers they would safeguard pilgrims to Jerusalem. Their martial mission was therefore based on defensive wars, as underlined by the supporter of the order of the Temple, French Cistercian abbot Bernard de Clairvaux, who stated to Hugue de Payens, co-founder of the order in a famous letter (*Liber ad Milites Templi: De Laude Novae Militae*, 1135) that the Templars had a double protection: an armor of faith and another of steel.

It was in the 13th century, however, that the theory of just war (*jus ad bellum*, or the right to wage war) was finally developed in its fullest form by Thomas Aquinas (1225-1274) in his *Summa Theologica* (1266-1273).[4] According to him, a defensive war was always "just" whereas an offensive one could be justified only under three conditions: first, it should be waged by the legitimate and highest authority in the land (by kings, emperors or popes) and not be a private war. Secondly, it should be waged upon legitimate grounds, as justified retribution against the offence given by the enemy, and only as a last resort after exhausting all other means of pacification and justice. Thirdly and finally, the intentions behind the offensive spur should never be moved by personal interest but rather by a true moral concern for the common good.

One of the corollaries of the Protestant Reformation was a sharp decline of the notion of just war, since Reformers advocated a return to the pacifism of the primitive Church; following a different reasoning, Machiavelli's *The Art of War* (1520) also rejected the just cause theory, this time on the grounds that states need not justify their wars, so long as they obeyed their own political rules on the subject. Yet echoes from the medieval past remained, especially in the Counter-Reformation Church; in an effort to counteract the spread of Protestantism, the Spanish founder Ignatius of Loyola (1491-1556) created his Society of Jesus. Jesuits, although members of the regular clergy, were invested with a mission in the secular world; theirs was a work of conversion and conquest which was detailed in explicitly martial vocabulary in Loyola's own *Formula Instituti*. The Jesuits were 'to serve as a soldier of God, beneath the banner of the cross'; known as the 'Soldiers of Christ', they were acknowledged to be the foot soldiers of the Pope and playing a crucial role in the efforts of the counter-reformation in Europe and the Americas.

The just war theory was once more the object of polemic in the century of Enlightenment, since the philosophical shift towards reason was opposed to a theological discourse based on faith. Later on, the ideas of

---

[4] A subsequent concept will follow: the *Jus in Bello*, or what is permissible in times of war.

"just war" and of "crusade" were debated in the 19th century and dissident voices (such as those of the Society of Friends, or Quakers) claimed that God could not support warmongers. Yet, in Britain, advocates of the imperial triptych of the three Cs (Civilization, Christianity, Commerce) supported the concept of the "muscular Christian" and the nation's mood for war. Such a brand of Protestantism encouraged individuals to fight a good war against the various guises of evil, be they personal (the inner struggle) or social in nature. For many, the civilizing mission, underpinned by the Christian ethos to evangelise, justified and legitimised war.

In the twentieth century, the fast-changing nature of warfare could not but provoke new reflections: thus, the idealized vision of war which had flourished since the 19th century met with disillusion in the 1920s. National churches had supported their state in the sustained efforts of World War I, but as the full scale of the devastation became clearer, they often questioned whether such horrors could ever be truly warranted. In the aftermath of the first global modern conflict, the promotion of pacifism took hold of consciences and many Christians were preaching peace in the 1930s, while totalitarian countries were establishing their power. Yet some clerics such as Kenneth Oliver, considered war as a lesser evil than Nazism: "I decided I could not stand aside and that if my services were required as a chaplain, I must go. War was evil, but submitting to a tyranny that threatened to enslave the whole of Europe was a far worse evil".[5]

In the context of total conflicts such as the Second World War, the notion of just war became more obsolete and was replaced by that of ideological wars in which two ideologically-defined blocks faced each other. The nuclear bombs launched on Hiroshima and Nagasaki triggered new reflection on the changing face of war, as Michael Walzer noted: "A new kind of war was born at Hiroshima and what we were given was a first glimpse at its deadliness".[6] With the atomic bomb, traditional warfare appeared outdated and armed conflicts bore the certainty of destruction on an unprecedented scale; thus, as nations became gradually aware of the deadly potential of the nuclear threat, they endeavoured to avoid military engagements whenever possible. The greater nations changed tactics for domination and, without jeopardising the defence of their own territory, began supporting relatively small-scale conflicts, often based on guerrilla warfare, in strategically important locations. In parallel, new types of war emerged, such as decolonisation wars, psychological wars, cold wars, or

---

[5] Kenneth Oliver, *Chaplain at War*. Chichester: Angel Press, 1986, 9.
[6] Michael Walzer, *Just and Unjust Wars A Moral Argument with historical Illustrations*. New York: Basic Books, 269.

wars against "terror". Interestingly enough, with the advent of global war against terrorism, the notion of a just war became actual once more: since the Gulf War of 1990 was both by claimed by the United Nations and accepted by Pope John Paul II as justified. Since then, some Western countries have defined other recent conflicts as "just"; the war in Iraq, for which the American President George W. Bush openly resorted to "crusade" rhetoric, testified that the spirit of the holy war had returned.

This collection of essays ponders upon the intricate relations between the military and the spiritual from the Middle Ages to the present day. In order to analyse human attitudes towards conflicts, it is necessary to dwell upon the nebulous area where the religious and political spheres interweave so tightly that they become virtually impossible to distinguish. Indeed, despite remaining the responsibility of the state, the political decision to go to war depends heavily on some spiritual underpinning since, without a moral, ethical, or religious justification, it stands for gratuitous violence and is often equated with aggression. In the last decades of the 20th century, the opinions of Church and State leaders have differed greatly on the necessity to wage war. Keith Robbins reminds us that: "[...], in relation to specific conflicts over the last quarter of a century, church leaderships have expressed scepticism if not outright hostility to British military activity overseas".[7]

Situated as they are at the intersection of religious and political awareness, war sermons are an invaluable source of information regarding societies in times of conflict. Indeed, whether favourable or hostile to the waging of war, preachers participated in the edification of their parishioners' opinion. The writing, delivering or reading of sermons shaped the mental process of peoples who sought their ministers' moral and spiritual guidance in times of crisis.[8] According to French theologian Laurent Gambarotto, writing about French Reformed Church pastors during the First World War, preachers were impregnated with a culture of war.[9] Through their sermons, preachers sometimes opposed their congregations' positive viewing of war; Rev. F.W. Aveling and Rev. G.

---

[7] Keith Robbins, "Onward Christian Soldiers? British Churches and War in the Nineteenth and Twentieth Century" in Gilles Teulié (ed.), *Religious Writings and War*, Montpellier, Les Carnets du Cerpac no 3, Montpellier UP, 177-197, (196, 197), 2006.

[8] Christiane D'Haussy (ed.), *English Sermons, Mirrors of Society*. Toulouse: Presses Universitaires du Mirail, 1995, 23

[9] Laurent Gambarotto, *Foi et Patrie. La prédication du protestantisme français pendant la Première Guerre Mondiale*. Genève : Labor et Fides, 1996, 415.

Critchley, for instance, both opposed the Anglo-Boer War (1899-1902) and became the objects of intimidation and collusion; they both received threats of physical violence and endured the smashing of their houses' windows, until the latter was finally driven to resign.[10] Yet most preachers acted in accordance with the public mood, and through their assent, they helped legitimise popular opinion on specific wars.

   This collection of essays inscribes itself within the renewed debate on the function of war, its representations and its rhetoric as generators of identity. Historians have already focused upon specific wars[11] or upon the sermons devoted to a particular religious group.[12] The purpose of our collection is somewhat different since it will trace, over the *longue durée*, the evolution of the rhetoric used from the pulpit to justify a divinely-ordained conflict or to condemn an unjust one. In the field of religious studies in the English-speaking world from the Middle Ages to the present day, an examination of the body of texts constituted by war sermons preached by Catholic or Anglican priests, Protestant pastors and ministers of other confessions, will throw considerable light on the evolution of ideologies. Sermons by their nature serve a multi-faceted function, they aim at the education, the edification and the exhortation of their congregations. As they commented upon events, homileticians and sermonists gave their audiences advice and moral guidelines; they combined the educational aspect of their sermons with exhortations which ranged from fund raising "to downright propaganda, when the influence of

---

[10] See Greg Cuthbertson, "Pricking the 'Nonconformist conscience': Religion against the South African War", in Donal Lowry (ed.), *The South African War Reappraised.* Manchester: Manchester UP, 2000, 169-185 (177).

[11] See Beverly Mayne Kienzle, *Cistercians, Heresy, and Crusade in Occitania 1145-1229: Preaching in the Lord's Vineyard.* Rochester NY: Boydell and Brewer, 2001; Christoph T. Maier, *Crusade, Propaganda and Ideology. Model Sermons for the Preaching of the Cross.* Cambridge: CUP, 2000; Charles Wilbanks, *The American Revolution and Righteous Community: Selected Sermons of Bishop Robert Smith.* Columbia, S.C.: University of South Carolina Press, 2007; William H. Duke, Jr., *For the Living in these Days. Responses to Terrorism. Sermons Preached by Virginia Baptist Ministers on the Sunday following the Septembre 11 Terrorist Attack.* Richmond VA: Centre for Baptist Heritage & Studies, University of Richmond, 2001; David B. Cheesbrough, *"God Ordained This War": War Sermons on the Sectional Crisis 1830-1865.* Columbia, SC: University of South Carolina Press, 1991; Unknown author, *Sermons on Slavery and the Civil War.* Ann Harbor: University of Michigan Library, 2001.

[12] See Marc Saperstein, *Jewish Preaching in Times of War, 1800-2001.* Oxford: The Littman Library of Jewish Civilization, 2007.

the sermon is used as a weapon for political or social indoctrination".[13]
This collection of essays will therefore attempt to decipher how ideologies
were elaborated and implemented, through time, in order to exhort people
to support wars. One of the essential keys to understanding the influence
played by war sermons is the justification of war through Scripture, which
cannot be dissociated from the notion of a just war and the way in which
that theory evolved. Thus, peace sermons in times of war, as well as those
using the metaphors of war and peace, are an integral part of this analysis
since they are as revealing of religious positions about armed conflicts as
sermons which supported war.

The following fourteen chapters are set in chronological order so as to
show the evolution of war sermons through the ages. As the power of the
Church increased in the Middle Ages, war in Europe became codified by
Christian nations. The creation of the Truce of God set a standard for lords
and knights and defined a religious framework for war. Clergymen came
to play an essential role in war, as proved by the creation in mid-12th
century of the "Bishop" as a chessman in the war game played by kings
and aristocrats and the subsequent use of chess war terminology in 13th
century sermons.[14] The military and the religious became so close that
sometimes there was no difference as intertwined when, during the third
crusade, the bishops of Lydda and Acre fought during the battle of Hattin
(July 1187). Thus, the collection opens with the troubled times of the
Crusades when, as Waltraud Verlaguet argues, sermons were an essential
component of the emergence of a European ideal and shaped modern
Western representations; at the core of the system which incited people to
start their military pilgrimage to Jerusalem, preachers adjusted their
rhetorical arguments in order to overcome the growing popular reticence
which met the frequent calls for crusades. In chapter two, Catherine
Hemet-Royer delves into the origin and evolution of medieval
"propaganda": focusing upon Thomas Bradwardine's preaching of his
Sermo Epinicius after the battle of Crécy, she demonstrates the importance
of thanksgiving sermons as tools to uplift the deflated morale of the
English troops. The writing of such war sermons was therefore, she
argues, an essential part of a court preacher's activity; through such
admonitions, clerics became an integral part of the war effort.

The Renaissance, and the Reformation in particular, heralded some
important changes in sermon-writing and, in chapter three, Leticia Alvarez

---

[13] Christiane D'Haussy (ed.), *English Sermons, Mirrors of Society*. Toulouse:
Presses Universitaires du Mirail, 1995, 23
[14] See James Robinson, *The Lewis Chessmen*. London: British Museum Press,
2004, 23.

Recio highlights the emerging specificity of English Protestant sermons, in which homiletic literature became increasingly central. These highly-politicised writings encapsulated the rhetoric elaborated to protect England, its Queen and its faith against their enemies, whether they came from overseas (Spain) or from within (English Catholics). From then on, Protestant pulpiteers perpetuated the art of sermon writing and preaching in England as a codified literary genre of crucial consequence even in the highest of spheres. Thus, in early modern England, sermons became a means for the nation to unite against a common enemy, and to grow stronger in its conviction that God favoured that chosen kingdom, that new Israel. In chapter four, through an analysis of the rhetoric of John Donne's sermons, Marie-Christine Munoz shows that the dichotomy of war and peace came to represent the symbolic fight of good against evil. Donne distanced himself from strictly political issues regarding his monarch's legitimacy in waging war and, rather, chose to address individuals Christians, through the evocation of their inner struggle to lead a good life. This was a battle of momentous import, a daily war against moral evil, the principles of which applied, of course, in the more tangible instance of military conflict: the Christian, in the end, had to choose a side, and to fight for a cause. Thus, in sermons about war, the frontiers between the religious and the military, between spiritual and physical war, are constantly breached; indeed, both the conceptual framework and the rhetorical tools used to refer to moral struggle or martial warfare have much in common, and participate of the same effort to tackle issues as absolute as good and evil. Marie L. Ahearn, referring to New England's Militia in the 18th century, commented upon the difficulty to distinguish between spiritual and military conflict: "Sometimes, in treating the dual theme of spiritual and temporal warfare, rhetorical distinctions blurred, and descriptions of spiritual war became interchangeable with war in this world; [...]."[15]

In Chapter five, Christine Ronchail studies the thanksgiving sermon of a French Reformed Church pastor celebrating the end of a conflict between two Protestant countries, England and the United Provinces. Although war sermons generally oppose a Christian nation to infidels, thus accounting for the obvious dichotomy between good and evil, this thanksgiving sermon, on the contrary, praises both sides, thereby raising the question of how two Protestant peoples can both benefit from the same divine support. Indeed, sermons focusing on the war effort were meant to emphasise the differences between opposing nations, to enhance the virtue

---

[15] Marie L. Ahearn, *The Rhetoric of War. Training Day, the Militia and the Military Sermon*. New York: Greenwood Press, 1989, 56.

of the civilised "us" whilst demonising the barbaric "them"; their purpose was clearly to exacerbate antagonism and galvanise the troops. Peace sermons, on the contrary, focused upon the similarities which made a peace treaty possible between nations which had been formerly opposed. Since peace was a sign of God's blessing, thanksgiving sermons showed that both sides were blessed, through peace, by divine grace. Peace was therefore construed as a sign of divine approval, as a reward bestowed upon two nations by the Almighty.

If the achievement of peace was understood as a clear sign of divine benevolence, war was, on the contrary, the symptom of God's wrath, a punishment sent upon all sinners. Through his analysis of rhetoric, Michael Rotenberg-Schwartz, in chapter six, shows that 18th century British sermons presented war as a God-sent punishment for the sins of society: using a wide range of Biblical references, they both justified defensive wars and commented upon the wrath of God against sinners. However, their theology was enriched by humanist trends which condemned brutality even in justified or divinely-ordained wars, thus heralding the pacifism of later years.

In the 18th century, an emerging notion of pacifism was concomitant with a desire to exhort European countries to federate their populations. Indeed, since the Middle Ages, sermons played an important role in the slow creation of national identities in European countries; this theme, introduced in chapter one, is analysed further in chapter seven, where Pasi Ihlainen's comparison of English and Prussian homilies demonstrates how 18th-century sermons contributed to the development of national awareness in both countries which, through religion and the preaching of war, developed a new sense of nationhood.

In chapter eight, Rémy Duthille sheds further light upon the transitional process which took place in the long 18th century, demonstrating the importance of fast sermons as a tool for dissenting preachers to contest the validity of the governments dealing with matters of war, while Anglican sermonists tended to be obedient supporters of the government's military policy. Through his sermons, a critic like Richard Price revealed the preoccupations of his time, in particular about new types of conflicts such the war of the American Revolution, in which a colony rose against its mother country. Though Price did not intend to defend the principle of revolution, he nonetheless advocated the right of resistance and the sovereignty of a people. The same spirit of resistance of the American people was key to the ideology which galvanised the opposing camps in the other conflict which shaped and defined modern America, the American Civil War. Massimo Rubboli, in chapter nine, tackles the problem which faced both Northern and Southern preachers: the justification of a civil war when "brothers fought against brothers". In such a traumatic context, new elements of justification had to be invented to replace the traditional arguments based on the Old Testament; the issues of independence and of slavery were at stake, and the concept of transgression was examined by the ministers of both sides, with sometimes surprisingly converging views about the common sins of the divided nations.

Thus, preachers naturally tackle political issues in their war sermons, and conversely, politicians, particularly in the United States, include the religious sphere in their speeches. The complementary nature of politics and religion was exemplified by statesmen such as Paul Kruger, President of the Republic of the Transvaal, who at the end of the 19th century spoke in the Parliament in Pretoria and preached on Sunday at his local Dutch Reformed church. Many political leaders well-versed in theology were keen on delivering speeches which, in their content, were akin to sermons. In chapter ten, Marie Beauchamps considers the "political sermons" of two American presidents, Abraham Lincoln and Woodrow Wilson in times of war. Written to serve national consciousness during two major conflicts (the American Civil War and First World War), those sermon-like speeches used and, and turn, perpetuated images and elements of the American Christian tradition. The war-like religious rhetoric of these two Presidents-turned-priests played an important part in the shaping of modern America's sense of identity.

A similarly glorified representation of war became increasingly embedded in the imperial mental process of newly industrialized countries across the Atlantic, especially so in the various wars opposing them to traditional "natives" from the 19th century onwards. Thus, sermons took on a certain entertainment value in Victorian England, and the nation's fondness for religious admonition was acknowledged and catered for in 1835 with the publication of a guidebook listing the London churches and preachers where one might hear the best sermons delivered.[16] Since the emergence of low cost prints enabled cheaper publications, there was a growing popular demand for the printing of sermons originally written to be delivered orally only. Hearing, reading, and discussing sermons thus became a favourite activity amongst sections of the Victorian population.[17] Thus, some outstanding preachers have marked both their contemporaries

---

[16] See Christiane D'Haussy (ed.), *English Sermons, Mirrors of Society*. Toulouse: Presses Universitaires du Mirail, 1995, 23

[17] Robert H. Ellison, *The Victorian Pulpit. Spoken and Written Sermons in Nineteenth Century Britain*. London : Associated University Press, 1998, 33.

and subsequent generations and, through the intellectual quality and the stirring verve of their sermons, they have gained a place in history.

Keith Robbins, in chapter 11 focuses on one such outstanding man. Hensley Henson, who preached in the late 19th and early 20th centuries, represents a landmark in the relationship between war sermons and the subject of war. Instead of rousing the troops to battle and justifying conflicts as expressions of God's will, such sermons came to reflect the general mood of disgust about war, and especially the First World War. Hensley Henson's sermons were undoubtedly patriotic, since they supported the general view that Germany was to blame for the ongoing bloodshed; however, Hensley transcended this simplistic and dual vision of good and evil. Far from inciting his flock's hatred towards their German foes, he attempted to show that the Germans were the victims of their leaders' propaganda. He continued preaching a sense of shared humanity during the Second World War before he finally retired.

Hensley witnessed the emergence of new media which enabled preachers to propagate their religious message on a larger scale. It was during the Second World War that the BBC developed its network and increased its broadcasts, including religious ones in which sermons about war played a significant part. Yet there were difficulties intrinsic to the preaching of sermons on radio broadcasts. In chapter twelve, Suzanne Bray takes a close look at William Temple, who became the voice of Britain's conscience despite a state censorship which was symptomatic of the growing distrust between the political and the spiritual spheres, especially with regards to the issue of controlling the media. Thus, Temple had to submit his sermons to the approval of political authorities before being allowed to broadcast; pacifist preachers were forbidden to speak on the radio and, in some instances, Temple himself was censored despite his position of Archbishop of Canterbury.

The presence of war sermons on BBC radio programmes has continued since the Second World War; in chapter thirteen, Serge Auffret brings to the fore what he calls "mini sermons" aired on the often controversial programme *Thoughts for the Day*, and particularly the slots relating to the sensitive issue of the American and British intervention and the war in Iraq. This chapter highlights how speakers on the show were carefully selected in order to comply with the BBC's strict policies about the equal representation of all races, faiths and socio-economic categories, and shows that a radio programme of this format differs from traditional war sermons since it allows the expression of a multiplicity of viewpoints, and acts as a platform for a lively debate.

Yet even in today's modern world, voicing a variety of opinions and allowing the free expression of dissidence in matters of religion and war remains challenging.   For all the evolutions and changes which have shaped the Western world since the Middle Ages, there remain some elements of continuity; thus, the final chapter of this volume concludes on the everlasting presence of the concept of Just War codified many centuries before, a concept which is till used in the context of modern war and which was a dominant theme in President Bush's campaign for the American war in Iraq. Through the sermons of some American Catholics priests, Anne Debray unveils the turmoil of people torn between their obedience to their Church, which advocated pacifism, and their allegiance to the state. In the events leading up to the war and once conflict was engaged, these dissident preachers expressed the untenable position of citizens whose faith could not be reconciled with their patriotism.

The links between State and Church, and between faith and war, are an intrinsic part of the historical mechanisms which influence a nation's relationship to warfare. Arguments used in the Crusades, or even earlier, are still current in the 21st century, and by their very nature, war sermons will always put military conflicts in relation with the divine, thereby perpetuating dogmas such as that of Just War or divine retribution. However, new types of wars have also prompted new forms of rhetoric meant to guide and convince an audience. This anthology on war sermons has spanned five centuries in the hope to provide a better understanding of the devices through which parishioners are led to form an opinion upon the legitimacy of a war; such varied articles set war sermons in a historical perspective which sheds a light on the genre of writing and delivering sermons on or about war throughout the centuries in Western countries.

CHAPTER ONE

CRUSADE SERMONS AS A FACTOR OF EUROPEAN UNITY

WALTRAUD VERLAGUET

The Crusades are a very special phenomenon in the history of the West. They took place at a crucial time when, over the two centuries of their influence, many changes and developments, alliances, successes and failures occurred. Leaving aside the specific political, economic and social motivations –avowed to a greater or lesser degree – which led up to the crusades, this paper will focus on a few chronological milestones, putting into perspective the war sermons of this period. Indeed, at that time, a singular intermingling of history, theology and poetry produced something new: the emergence of the idea of crusade, which evolved to become the flag bearer of the specific medieval worldview from which it grew.

The Origins

The history of the crusades begins, strictly speaking, with a sermon: that of Urban II at Clermont, France in 1095, when the association of war and holiness was sufficiently incongruous to necessitate justification. Yet the idea was not an absolute novelty but had ancient roots, which can be traced in the history of thought to at least three sources: the concept of a just war, the practice of pilgrimage and a feudal ideology. Even during the first centuries of Christianity, the question was asked whether a soldier could become a Christian and whether a Christian should be a soldier. As Christianity became a State religion, this question took on more importance, since the emperor was also the defender of Christendom. How could this demand be combined with the non-violence taught by Christianity?

Saint Augustine answered this conundrum by distinguishing between just and unjust wars;[1] he was later followed in Spain by Isidore of Seville (560-636), and in Germany, by Hraban Maur (776-856) who commented on the Book of Maccabees, comparing the persecution of the Jews under Antiochus IV to that of Christians in the Roman Empire. In a typological reading, Mattathias symbolised Christ, Antiochus the Antichrist, and the Maccabees prefigured the Christian army called to defend the people of God who were rewarded by the crown of martyrdom. At the same time in England, Aelfric used the same image and referred to Isidore of Seville to justify the war against the Scandinavians who were invading his country.[2] His bishop, Wulfstan, in his *Sermo Lupi ad Anglos*[3] announced the end of the world and the coming of the Antichrist to call for the defence of the realm and for justice. This was construed as the will of God. For Aelfric, armed defence in such circumstances should be compared to fighting the flames of Hell at the Last Judgement.

Thus, a shift in meaning appeared between a war permitted by God and a war desired by God; yet the notion of the defence of the *realm* was still absent in the 9th century when, as the suburbs of Rome were pillaged by the Saracens in 846, the Popes still spoke of defending the *Faith* by the sword. Leo IV proclaimed a "holy war" and affirmed that the soldiers who died in the fray merited eternal life, while John VIII made them martyrs and promised them absolution from sin.

War could therefore be just if it was waged in defence of the faith; however, for an expedition into a foreign land to be justified, another element must be present, and it is the notion of pilgrimage which serves as a cement for this singular connection between war and holiness. Significantly, the documents of the period do not refer to a "crusade" but use the vocabulary of the pilgrims. Since the beginning of Christianity, pilgrimages to the Holy Land have held great importance in the history of the Church. During the Middle Ages however, with the new ideology of feudalism, something changed in the way these places were considered.

As the political pole of power spread to integrate peoples whose customs and anthropology were different, the Emperor's status as the defender of Christianity mutated, giving an almost redemptive role to the

---

[1] His *De civitate dei* discusses different types of war. In Chapter XV of Book IV he writes: "Si ergo iusta gerendo belle, non impia, non iniqua." Cf. http://www.ac-nice.fr/philo/textes/Augustin-DeCivitateDei/.
[2] J. E. Cross, "Vernacular sermons in Old English", in Kienzle, Beverly Mayne, (ed.), *The Sermon.* Brepols: Turnhout, 2000, 583.
[3] *Ibid.*, 591.

Empire. Conflict management became a central point which determined the difficult balance between temporal and spiritual power. Certainly the military domain belonged by rights to the political lords. In order to safeguard its authority, the Church had to affirm its own prerogatives, on the one hand, by calling the Emperor to the defence of Christian lands, and on the other, by limiting the lords' freedom of action.

Thus, from the early Middle Ages, as Pope Gregory I already underlined in the 6th century, the Emperor's duty was to subjugate the pagans in order to convert them. In the 10th century, Widukind of Corvey described in his history of the Saxons the coronation of Otto the Great and reported the bishop as saying: "Take this sword and put to flight all the enemies of Christ... since you hold power in the Frankish realm by the will of God, in hope of an unshakeable peace for all Christians".[4]

Furthermore, the Church introduced ceasefires and rules limiting the violent acts of war, such as "God's peace" which protected non-belligerents – women and children, clerics, peasants and travellers – against any attack in time of war. The knights' honour code became progressively more Christian. Significantly, the 11th century saw the introduction of a blessing of swords, a highly symbolic gesture. Thus, the new world view of feudalism inevitably affected spirituality: from then on Christians understood their relationship with Christ as being a feudal one. Hence, the places where Christ had lived came to be considered as *His* land. When His country was under attack, their vassal faithfulness demanded their coming to His aid to defend His wealth. Bonizo of Sutri, at the end of the 11th century, theorised that those who were outside the Church may not possess what belonged to the Church, and that Christians were bound to defend their inheritance.[5]

In the 12th century it was the Cistercians above all who took charge of the preaching of the Crusades. This Order recruited among adults who very often had already had some military training. They were at the very heart of the symbiosis between spirituality and the chivalrous spirit. Bernard of Clairvaux, who drew up the Rule of the Templars, wrote in his tract *De laude novae militiae* that a Christian knight did not commit a sin

---

[4] "Accipe...hunc gladium, quo eicias omnes Christi adversarios ... auctoritate divina tibi tradita omni potestate totius imperii Francorum, ad firmissimam pacem omnium Christianorum." in Widukind von Corvey, *Res gestae Saxonicae – Die Sachsengeschichte, Stuttgart, Reclam*, 1981, 106 (my translation).

[5] "... quod qui extra ecclesiam sunt, nullo jure bona ecclesiae possunt possidere": in Friedrich-Wilhelm Wentzlaff-Eggebert, *Kreuzzugdichtung des Mittelalters. Studien zu ihrer geschichtlichen und dichterischen Wirklichkeit*. Berlin: Walter de Gruyter, 1960, 5.

when he killed an infidel, but on the contrary he avenged Christ which was all to his honour.[6] At the end of the 12th century, Henry of Strasburg defined the Crusade as a proper vassal obligation, appealing to the sense of honour of the knights.[7] Each vassal was rewarded for his service. According to the feudal logic of the law, God distributed fragments of salvation in the same way as the lord gave fiefdoms to his faithful retainers. Dipping into grace to attribute indulgences according to the merit of the servant appeared completely plausible, as will be discussed later. Let us remember for the moment that the initial question of whether a Christian had the *right* to take up arms had been transformed, during the Middle Ages, into quite another debate, regarding the circumstances in which a Christian had the *duty* to take up arms.

Chronology

The medieval climate of existential anguish created by apocalyptic effervescence was channelled by the reforms of the Church in the 10th and 11th centuries into religious fever, making eternal salvation in the hereafter appear as man's ultimate goal. When Byzantium called on Urban II for help against the Turks, all the ingredients were thus in place to launch the struggle.

The initiative for the Crusades came from Urban II himself, who preached about the first expedition at the Council of Clermont in 1095. Although the text of his speech is no longer extant, a number of chroniclers, like Foulque of Chartres, reported the tone of the message. Urban called for all other combats to cease in order to help the brethren in the faith against the infidels who were ravaging the Holy Places, promising remission of sins as a reward. He knew how to fire up the masses. The commitment not only of the nobles but also of the commoners surpassed all expectation. The military success of the first crusade accredited the theses which Urban II had expressed, and created a lasting stimulus in spite of the losses suffered later.

The later Popes delegated the order of preaching about the Holy Land campaign to papal legates, assisted by numerous preachers. Whereas the first crusade concerned only France and Italy, the second expanded the idea over the whole of Europe, as a result of Bernard of Clairvaux's efforts. Eugene III began this movement in 1145 with his Bull *Quantum*

---

[6] *Ibid.*, 23.
[7] Valmar Cramer, "Kreuzpredigt und Kreuzzugsgedanke von Bernard von Clairvaux bis Humbert von Romans", *Das Heilige Land in Vergangenheit und Gegenwart*, Heft, 17-20 (1939): 43-204. Quotation 90.

praedecessores nostri, which was sent to France and Italy; Bernard, named as papal legate for its publication, took the Bull to Germany and sent letters to the countries he could not get to. The expansion of the Cistercian order favoured the call to the Crusades, whilst Cistercian mystique gave it a deeper meaning.

Eugene III's Bull was structured in three parts[8], the form the later pronouncements would adopt. The first part was a narrative describing the sufferings endured by Christians in the Holy Land and the dishonour which the loss of the Holy Places meant to Christendom. In the second part Eugene exhorted his readers by taking up the traditional reference to the Book of Maccabees. The final part defined the privileges given to Crusaders. There, he marked himself out from other theologians and supported a highly emphasised interpretation of the power of the keys. For Abelard, for example, God absolved souls from punishment in the next world, whilst priests only had influence over the punishment inflicted by the Church: salvation was between God and the faithful. For Eugene III, on the other hand, it was between the Church and the faithful. As for Bernard of Clairvaux, he sought to reconcile the two, claiming that the power to bind or loose invested in the priest only became efficacious through penitence. In the framework of a feudal conception of faith, the contrition of the believer worked like the homage due to a lord from his vassal.

Bernard of Clairvaux preached at Vézelay in 1146. The texts of his sermons were later expurgated of the references to the Crusades as they were reworked in order to serve as examples for other occasions, but his letters have remained more explicit.[9] He added an important motif in comparison to Eugene III, that of the *tempus acceptabile*, the right time: according to him, the expedition to the Holy Land was a unique opportunity offered to sinners to gain salvation. The liberation of Jerusalem appeared almost secondary in comparison with the sanctification of the faithful. Consequently, the defeat of the second Crusade in 1148 led to a certain spiritual confusion: had God abandoned his own?

When Alexander III launched the third crusade in 1181, he argued that the defeats of the Christians in the Holy Land were the direct result of sin. This crusade was given the name of "the three kings" because of the

---

[8] Penny J. Cole, *The Preaching of the Crusades to the Holy Land, 1095-1270.* Cambridge: Cambridge University Press, 1991, 24 ; Valmar Cramer, "Kreuzpredigt und Kreuzzugsgedanke von Bernard von Clairvaux bis Humbert von Romans", 46.

[9] Beverly Mayne Kienzle (ed.), *The Sermon,* 272.

commitment of the rulers of England, France and Germany. After the fall of Jerusalem in 1187, Gregory VIII developed Bernard of Clairvaux's arguments for a *tempus acceptabile* in his Bull *Audita tremendi*, together with the reference to Mattathias. Equally, he emphasised the perennial character of Crusade. Henry of Alba, the great Cistercian preacher of this third expedition, developed this even further in his tract *De peregrinante civitate Dei*: here the earthly Jerusalem was lost because the Christians have lost the heavenly Jerusalem. He elaborated a complex symbolism of the Cross, at the same time an Ark of the Covenant and a ladder by means of which the believer may climb up to God.

Following Celestine III in 1195, Innocent III advocated the fourth Crusade. An energetic man, he was dismayed at the rout and the defeat which followed. In his Bull *Post miserabile* in 1198, and much more in *Quia major* in 1213, he strongly developed the idea of the crusade as a vassal duty; it was a Christian's obligation to free the Holy Land, and from then on, the idea of penitence remained secondary. This change of emphasis marked the preaching about the Crusades, and as a result, the Cistercians relinquished their pre-eminent role into the hands of new mendicant orders.

Innocent III's successor, Honorius III, completed the list of Bulls on the Crusades. He made use of the same vassal terminology and of the reference to Maccabees, but in his case penitence became a priority again. He introduced the example of Abraham, whom he called a "mystic", in order to appeal to crusaders to leave their countries and go to the land which was sanctified by the blood of Christ.[10] Among the great preachers of this first third of the 13th century, Philip of Oxford, whose tract *Ordinacio de praedicacione S. Crucis in Anglia* (1214) illustrated the new way of preaching which was beginning to be heard in the 13th century in the framework of scholastic education, with numerous allegories and *exempla*. For Philip, the indulgence accorded to the crusaders appeared more as a condition than a reward for the commitment of the warrior: he must be freed from all the weight of sin which may weigh him down so that he may depart for war.

Jacques of Vitry is also known not only as a preacher of the cross and for his participation in the fifth Crusade, but also for his commitment to recognising the beguine movement, in particular by his personal intercession to Honorius III. He brought together two aspects of the ideological synthesis of the Crusades in his own person. Jacques of Vitry

---

[10] "... in terram mystico exemplo Habre olim inclitam ac Christi sanguine consecratam". Quoted by Valmar Cramer, "Kreuzpredigt und Kreuzzugsgedanke von Bernard von Clairvaux bis Humbert von Romans", 113.

left an important body of sermons, several of which directly concern the crusaders" commitment:

> The Lord has indeed suffered the loss of his patrimony and wants to test (his) friends and find out if you are his faithful vassals. He who holds a fief from a liege lord is rightfully deprived of his fief if he abandons him, when he is involved in a war and his inheritance is taken away from him. You hold your body and soul and all that you have from the highest emperor who has you summoned today to come to his aid in battle, even if you are not bound by feudal law. He offers you such great payment that you ought to rush willingly, namely the remission of all sins with regard to punishment and guilt, and in addition eternal life.[11]

Jacques was very verbose about the spiritual benefits of the Crusades: for him, commitment to the war brought salvation not only to the combatant, but to his whole family. He also believed that this salvation was independent of the results of the combat, since the fact of enlisting was in itself sanctifying; this was an important proviso after the repeated defeats of the crusaders. Indeed, such military reverses had diminished the popular ardour for militant sermons calling to the Cross to such an extent that Jacques promised a reduction of 20 to 40 days in Purgatory for the mere fact of attending his preaching. He even argued against those who condemned armed combat by reference to the non-violence of the Gospels. It proved that they were ignorant of the real meaning of the Bible's teaching which, according to Jacques, was that armed combat was necessary and meritorious in the service of the Church.

After the diplomatic end of the sixth Crusade by Frederick II in 1229, a final wave of enlistment led to the last two expeditions in 1245 and 1270, in which Saint Louis participated. Among the preachers, Eudes of Châteauroux underlined the abolition of social status among the crusaders. Like Jacques of Vitry, he argued that combatants accumulated indulgences for their families. He used a new metaphor to express the passion with which the crusaders left their country to go to the Holy Land, comparing

---

[11] "Dominus quidem affligitur in patrimonii sui admissione et vult amicos probare et experiri si fideles eius vasalli estis. Qui enim a domino ligio tenent feodam, si desit illi dum inpugnatur et hereditas sua illi aufertur, merito feodo privatur. Vos autem corpus et animam et quicquid habetis a summo imperatore tenetis, qui vos hodie citari facit, ut ei in prelio succuratis, et licet iure feodi non teneremini. Tanta et talia stipendia offert vobis quod sponte currere deberetis, remissionem cunctorum scilicet peccatorum quantum ad penam et culpam et insuper vitam eternam." in Maier, *Crusade Propaganda and Ideology. Model Sermons for the Preaching of the Cross*, 98 (translated by Maier).

them to deer which left their territories during the mating season.[12] Another significant preacher, Humbert of Romans, went further in generalising the idea of the Crusade, claiming that every Christian was obliged to participate in this effort in one way or another, since the Crusade was a particular form of devotion: taking up one's cross thus came to signify sanctification.

The Ideology of the Crusades

The extension of the concept of the Crusade had significant impact upon the new world view, interweaving two different ways of thinking, that of spirituality and that of combat. The intermingling of both religious and military thinking had started to occur well before the Crusades, and was a logical consequence of the struggle for power between the temporal and the spiritual. With the Church taking over larger parts of every area of society, the christianisation of the knights' honour code found its counterpart in the militarisation of spirituality. We have already evoked the role of the Cistercians who, benefiting from a knightly and courtly education, easily used the metaphors of this sphere to give meaning to their devotional acts.

The liturgical celebration of the Cross also inspired the heraldry of flags and banners and the Cross became the flag of spiritual power over the world. Thus, through feudal ideology, military prowess took on a spiritual significance as feudal faithfulness to God. In the Benedictine Rule, the *militia Christi* designated spiritual warfare in the believer's heart. The pun between *militia* and *malitia*, the evil of the human heart, was often taken up by the preachers of the Crusades. In contrast, liturgical songs accompanied pilgrims and crusaders on their departure. Secular writings, chronicles, *chansons de geste* and the full range of the poetry of the Crusades made use of liturgical vocabulary.

Among the great epics of the 12th century, the *Kaiserchronik* was marked by this spiritualisation of the idea of chivalry, and idealised the figure of the Emperor: Charlemagne was thus shown as the hero in the struggle against paganism, a humble and good hero, while pagans were portrayed as in league with the Devil. Whilst the French version of the *Chanson de Roland* was more insistent on the idea of national greatness, the German version by the priest Conrad showed a Charlemagne who was

---

[12] "sic et hodie bendicit Dominus illos, qui pro amore eius velut cervi spirituales lustra dimittunt propria, id est terram, in qua nati fuerunt et nutriti.", in Penny J. Cole, *The Preaching of the Crusades,* 152.

Emperor of Christendom, fighting less for a military victory than for the conversion of pagan peoples. All the speeches in this poem were structured like sermons about the Crusades. Hartmann von der Aue, around 1200 described in his *Lied vom Glauben* (*Song of the Faith*) the virtues of the believer as those of the combatant: the *imitatio Christi* takes on the colours of a struggle where Christ himself carries the flag.

In the same way, the Benedictine Rule was linked with Cistercian spirituality which, in turn, influenced secular poetry. In the course of this evolution, the circle of those for whom it is destined has not ceased to grow. Whilst the Rule of Saint Benedict was addressed only to monks, the new devotion is for everyone. Everyone had had the opportunity to hear about the merits of the Crusades, not only in sermons but also in songs and recitations of poetry. Preachers began to address themselves to all: laity and monks, to people of every rank and every nationality.

Whereas until the 11th century sermons were destined essentially for monks, since the people mastered only the rudiments of an elementary Christian education, in the 12th century, as a result of the threat of heresy, of the schism within the Orthodox Church, and of the desire for reform in the Roman Church, an increase in preaching efforts led to the creation of new mendicant orders. Henceforth, any deviation from the strict line defined by the Roman Church was condemned. With the elaboration of the ideology of holy war, anything could become a crusade: the struggle against the Albigensians, against the Moors in Spain or against the pagan Slavs, or even against Christians who might oppose Rome, such as the Hohenstaufen.

Every country was implicated. The supra-national character of the religious orders, like that of the Roman Church in its entirety, contributed to making the appeal to holy war universal. Preachers crossed borders, combatants from various countries, speaking different languages, enlisted side by side in the same war. So, for example, English and French soldiers enlisted to reclaim Spain.[13]

Internal conflicts were called upon to cease, whilst the different countries' campaigns against external enemies were integrated in some way or another under the same banner of the Cross. Thus when Saint Bernard succeeded in winning the Emperor Conrad to his way of thinking in 1146, the latter was worried about his western borders. Suddenly the Diet of Frankfort decided, in the presence of Bernard, to defend the Empire against the Slavs. This war was thus considered as a necessary condition to make sure the Crusade went well. And quite logically,

---

[13] Giles Constable, "The Second Crusade as seen by Contemporaries", *Tradition 9* (1953): 213-279, 235.

soldiers were awarded the same indulgences as those who participated in the expedition to the Holy Land.[14] The Crusade against the Slavs was a part of *the* Crusade.

Another example shows the extension of the concept: an Anglo-Flemish expedition set out to follow the coast of Europe and gain the Holy Land by sea. En route, they were called upon by the King of Portugal to help him take back Lisbon from the Moors. Bishop Peter of Oporto, speaking in Latin and translated by interpreters into various languages, made a speech recorded by the English chronicler Osbern to convince crusaders that the struggle against the Moors was an integral part of the Crusade.

In fact the majority of the chroniclers of the period did not speak of expeditions or of armies in the plural. It was *the* Christian army, in the singular, which was engaged in the combat against the infidels. This consciousness of belonging to a common entity was also found in secular literature. Thus Conrad underlined in the German version of the Chanson de Roland that they were "all of one heart ... they are all called children of God".[15] All were called. Those unable to fight were called to supply wealth to finance those who could; for war was a costly business, each knight had to be equipped and look after his own needs. Tithes were levied to help cover costs. And those who could neither fight nor contribute were called to pray and to accomplish acts of devotion and of asceticism to support the crusaders morally and spiritually. Special sermons were addressed to those who stayed at home; women, children and any person who was not able to fight. A social and psychological pressure was thus brought to bear on all across Europe from the poorest to the noblest, calling for moral reform and spiritual warfare. Popes, bishops and preachers called for unity, for the cessation of any conflict other than that of taking up the cross, and particularly during the third Crusade when incessant rivalries between the Kings of France and England risked delaying the departure.

Laity and religious, men and women, combatants and non-combatants, every social class and every country were concerned. Moreover, the constitution of prayer communities, which included the dead, and the notion of vicarious suffering, caused a new form of spirituality to emerge

---

[14] Valmar Cramer, "Kreuzpredigt und Kreuzzugsgedanke von Bernard von Clairvaux bis Humbert von Romans", 45.

[15] Friedrich-Wilhelm Wentzlaff-Eggebert, *Kreuzzugdichtung des Mittelalters. Studien zu ihrer geschichtlichen und dichterischen Wirklichkeit*, 93.

which crossed every border, even that between the dead and the living.[16] The non-combatants won over through special devotion the spiritual support of those fighting, whilst the combatants won salvation for their families.[17] The generalisation of the vicarious sanctification of the living for the dead thus bound the whole of Christendom into one single community, beyond the borders of place and time.

Of course internal conflicts did not cease for all that. The political disagreements between various sovereigns are much to be blamed for the final failure of the Crusade project. But beyond this, and in spite of the struggles for power which continued to cross Europe, European unity was forged at the ideological level. It could be said that the Crusades played a central role in the crystallisation of the European ideal, if not *the* central role. The Western world view remained marked by the spirituality of this struggle.

Likewise, it is obvious that the preaching of the Cross did not transform all crusaders into saints. We know the stories of the terrible acts they committed on occasion. Pillage was the order of the day, and many economic and political motives were hidden behind the call to the Crusades. The German poet Walther von der Vogelweide denounced in very harsh terms the political ambitions of the papacy and the rapaciousness of the crusaders.[18] Yet even for him, taking up the cross was the touchstone of the knight's true worth. A shared sense of belonging was forged in the crucible of fighting under the sign of the cross and remained for centuries a mark of the singular interweaving of the values of combat and sanctification. It is not insignificant that today the field of economics, with its own secular spirituality, uses such terms as advertising "strategy" and "conquering" markets.

Therefore no-one could earn his salvation without participating, in one way or another, in this general effort of the Crusades which was the very essence of the demonstration of the *novo devotio*. "Devotion" comes from "*devovoe*" which designated first of all the commitment made by a vow, in the context of a sacrifice. It was used early on in the military context of sacrificing one's life. Henceforward, this sacrifice on the one hand was perceived as a form of martyrdom, and on the other referred to the whole of the believer's life, his gift of himself in faith.

---

[16] In the middle of the 11th century, Cluny inaugurated the festival of the dead: see J. Le Goff, *La Naissance du Purgatoire*. Paris: Gallimard, 1981, 170.
[17] Penny J. Cole, *The Preaching of the Crusades*, 137.
[18] Friedrich-Wilhelm Wentzlaff-Eggebert, *Kreuzzugdichtung des Mittelalters. Studien zu ihrer geschichtlichen und dichterischen Wirklichkeit*, 236.

Later Antiquity questioned whether a Christian could be a soldier, a question to which Augustine replied by elaborating the notion of a just war. The Middle Ages went further, asking in what circumstances a Christian should take up arms. At the end of this process, the conclusion was that a Christian's very nature was to fight. To show to what degree this chivalrous spirituality pervades the whole of the thought patterns of an era, I should like to conclude with a text from a context as far removed as possible from military preoccupations. It comes from the pen of Mechthild of Magdeburg, who was the first to write in the German language about personal mystical experiences. She lived as a beguine in the middle of the 13th century. Since the preaching of Jacques of Vitry, beguines had lived a form of semi-religious life which was recognised but ill-defined. The beguines testified in their writings to what could be called a courtly spirituality. Mechthild enjoyed a certain renown in her context, and she was frequently asked for as an intercessor. In her third book, she compared the struggle against temptation to the exploits of a knight:

> I interceded for a man, as I had been asked to do, that God should take away from him the desires of his body – even though they come without sin as long as they are not produced by ill-will. So our Lord said, "Be quiet! Would it please you if there were a knight, armed to the teeth and well trained and full of strength and skill, and who stayed without doing anything and neglected the honour of his lord and who lost the proper reward and the noble renown which comes from both, lord and knight, in the land? On the other hand: what would become of a man, who has not been trained for lack of armour, and who came to the tournament of a prince? He would quickly be put to death. This is why I must care for those who fall so easily. I make them fight like children so that they may win a garland of flowers as a reward. (III, XVIII).[19]

Works Cited

Cole, Penny J., *The Preaching of the Crusades to the Holy Land, 1095-1270*, Cambridge University Press 1991.

Constable, Giles, « the second Crusade as seen by contemporaries », in : *Tradition* 9 (1953) p. 213-279.

Cramer, Valmar, "Kreuzpredigt und Kreuzzugsgedanke von Bernhard von Clairvaux bis Humbert von Romans", *Das Heilige Land in Vergangenheit und Gegenwart,* Heft 17-20, 1939, p. 43-204.

Kienzle, Beverly Mayne (éd.), *The Sermon*, Turnhout : Brepols, 2000.

---

[19] Mechthild of Magdeburg, *La lumière fluente de la Divinité*, translated into French by Waltraud Verlaguet, Grenoble: Jérôme Millon, 2001, 97.

Maier, Christopher, *Crusade Propaganda and Ideology. Model Sermons for the Preaching of the Cross*, Cambridge University Press 2004.

Wentzlaff-Eggebert, *Kreuzzugsdichtung des Mittelalters. Studien zu ihrer geschichtlichen und dichterischen Wirklichkeit*, Berlin : Walter de Gruyter, 1960.

CHAPTER TWO

THOMAS BRADWARDINE'S VICTORY SERMON DURING THE HUNDRED YEARS WAR

CATHERINE ROYER-HEMET

In the millennium that is conventionally termed "the Middle Ages", the fourteenth century is occasionally referred to as "calamitous"[1] because of such dramatic occurrences as the Great Plague or the Peasants' revolt, to name but two. However, if attention is focused on England alone and on the period extending from 1337 to 1360, it seems hardly possible to retain such a pejorative adjective. These two dates, marking the onset of the Hundred Years War for the former and the signing of the Treaty of Bretigny-Calais for the latter, define a period generally deemed as "favourable" to England.[2]

Jean Favier wrote "The Hundred Years War has never lacked historians"[3], to which the seemingly endless series of monographs published on the period for decades and even centuries bears witness. Following this lead, this study will suggest that it did not lack propagandists either. It will first investigate the very nature of propaganda in that period and consider its authors, as well as the form it took, before focusing on the religious sermon as one specific means of conveying a propagandistic discourse.

Fourteenth-Century Propaganda: A Nameless Reality

Before dealing with the subject of propaganda in the 14th century, we

---

[1] Barbara Tuchman, *A Distant Mirror, This Calamitous Fourteenth Century*. Harmondsworth: Penguin Books, 1978.
[2] Michael Prestwich, *The Three Edwards. War and State in England, 1272-1377*. London: Routledge, 1980, 2nd ed. 2003, 166: "[...] astonishing successes".
[3] Jean Favier. *La guerre de cent ans*. Paris: Fayard, 1980, 615. (all translations are mine).

should consider the etymology of the word, especially since it simply did not exist then. The term was actually coined more than three centuries later with the creation of the *Congregatio de Propaganda Fide* by Pope Gregory XII. At that time, the meaning of "propaganda" was religious and derived from the Latin verb *propagare* which meant "to multiply specimens (of a plant for example), to cause to multiply or spread".[4] Most of the time, the Romans used the word in a context of gardening. So, from a horticultural background, the word obviously evolved into a political one, through linguistic mutations and owing to a number of historical circumstances until it reached the modern sense of the word, according to which we are told that propaganda is: "information, ideas, opinions or images, often only giving one part of an argument, which are broadcast, published or in some other way spread with the intention of influencing people's opinions."[5]

Today, owing to a number of historical precedents such as the two world conflicts of the 20th century, the word "propaganda" has come to be vested with a pejorative connotation. It goes without saying that propaganda became much more active with the arrival of the revolutionary technological invention of printing. Since there was no such thing as yet in the 14th century, looking at the propaganda of that time is doubly problematic, both linguistically as well as practically as far as the spreading of ideas was concerned. Nevertheless, the very concept and reality of propaganda were already at work. Though nameless, propaganda already existed. Modern historians of the period use the word when referring to the numerous publicity operations so as to spread the notion that the king's cause was right and worth fighting for. Moreover, a look at the map of France in 1360[6] (immediately after the signing of the Treaty of Bretigny-Calais, which granted the English sovereign all his territorial demands) reveals that, whatever propaganda had been used, it had worked out wonderfully and, at the same date, a keen contemporary observer could think that the war was over and that the English had won it.

If we acknowledge that propaganda, with or without a name, had long been in existence before it took on a linguistic reality, and that its birth coincides with what Claude Lefort dubs "the political fact"[7] - in other words the will of an individual or a group of individuals to dominate

---

[4] C.T. Onions, ed. *The Oxford Dictionary of English Etymology.* Oxford: Clarendon Press, 1996.

[5] *Cambridge Dictionary Online.* Cambridge University Press 2006.

[6] See map in appendix 1.

[7] Claude Lefort, « La propagande » in *Encyclopedia Universalis* CD-Rom Version 10.

others - then we can establish a list of common points between modern propaganda and that of the 14th century.

In order to illustrate Jowett and O'Donell's definition of the process of communication used in propaganda[8], this study will use a religious sermon which has crossed centuries under the name of *Sermo Epinicius* or "Victory Sermon"; preached by Thomas Bradwardine in the weeks following the battle of Crécy (August 1346) in which the English troops triumphed over the French, this sermon illustrates the efficiency of the propaganda set up by the English authorities was.

In their practical description, Jowett and O'Donnell start from an ordinary situation of communication, in which A sends a message to B. In the case of our sermon, A is our preacher from the pulpit, B is the audience facing him, namely King Edward III and his barons and knights and probably a number of soldiers who had contributed to the victory at Crécy. The two authors then list a number of other essential elements, namely a communicator, a message, a channel and an audience,[9] no less than four conditions to be respected, as they are in the case of the *Sermo Epinicius*, the message of which is one of thanksgiving to God for the victory at Crécy.

Of course, these parameters refer to an ordinary situation of communication. For it to don the cloak of propaganda, others must be added to that basic list, such as the particular circumstances surrounding the preaching of that sermon, the more or less obvious and stated purposes of the communicator and, last but not least, his competence and authority to deliver the message. The historical background connected with the *Sermo Epinicius* is complex insofar as it is multi-faceted, given the essentially religious atmosphere of the period and the fact that the Church was the only authority to regulate thinking. Thus, Alan Fletcher remarked that "[...] the Church [...] assumed the burden of interpreting the changes and chances of this fleeting world into meaningful patterns".[10] The English Church and the papacy had a stormy relationship, especially since throughout the first phase of the Hundred Years War, the residence of the papal *Curia* was at Avignon which was, on the whole, pro-French. Indeed, the English clergy must have found itself in the predicament of a double contradictory allegiance, to Rome on the one hand and to its temporal ruler on the other. The papacy in Avignon undoubtedly created an additional

---

[8] See Gareth S. Jowett and Victoria O'Donnell. *Propaganda and Persuasion.* Beverly Hills: Sage Publications, 1986, 14.
[9] *Idem.*
[10] Alan J. Fletcher. *Preaching and Politics in Late Medieval England.* Portland, Or.: Four Courts Press, 1998, 11.

bone of contention to an already strained relationship. Alan Fletcher described the Church as "[…] an institution with roots that were as much political as spiritual, and that had been sent down deep into the community"[11] and remarked that at no time in history was the Church above political turmoil.

Among the ranks of that clergy could be found some of the staunchest supporters of the king in the nascent conflict between France and England, which he called "our just quarrel".[12] The year 1346, known as *Annus Mirabilis*, the victorious year, culminated with the military success at Crécy-en-Ponthieu, a success which even the king himself did not expect. Two days after the battle, a decision was made to head for the town of Calais, where the English host must have arrived in the early days of September. Edward III and his advisers soon realised that, if Calais was to be taken, it would be after a siege of some duration, even though no-one at the time could have foreseen the eleven months of Calaisian resistance. The English settled down into what was to be a year-long environment and got organised, which meant building a wooden town for the besieging army; named "Villeneuve-la-Hardie", this was a proper town, erected around a standing church, St Peter's, a few kilometres to the south of Calais. Thanks to numerous scholarly works related to both Thomas Bradwardine's career and the *Sermo Epinicius*, it is possible to assert that the sermon was presumably preached from the pulpit of St Peter's in early November 1346.

The preaching of the *Sermo Epinicius*: to what ends?

What sort of sermon was it? According to the different categories of medieval sermons carefully listed in the formidable list compiled by Johannes Schneyer,[13] the *Sermo Epinicius* seems to evade precise classification. It was not a *sermo ad status*, since it was not aimed at an audience belonging to a distinct profession or social status, such as a monastic congregation. Nor was it a *sermo de sanctis*, or *de communi* as it did not celebrate a saint of the religious calendar. Furthermore, it was not a sermon *ad populum* insofar as the audience facing Bradwardine on that autumn day in the year 1346, though not really being exactly an elite, was nevertheless no ordinary one. Rather, it was a sermon of thanksgiving and

---

[11] *Idem.*

[12] Michael Prestwich. *Op. cit.*, 167.

[13] Johannes Schneyer. *Repertorium der Lateinischen Sermones des Mittlelalters.* 5 vols. (für die zeit von 1150-1350) (autoren : R-Schlub [W] Munster Westfalen: Aschendorffsche Verlagsbuchhandlung, 1970).

as such, a "circumstantial" one. The celebration was not only for the benefit of the Crécy victory but also for that against the Scots at Neville's Cross, the news of which had reached the king and his army in France in late October. Those two events were of such importance for the morale of the English troops that it was necessary to organize their official recognition. Yet, back in England, no request for a sermon of thanksgiving was recorded in the *Annals of St Paul's*,[14] despite the fact that the Cross at St Paul's was, from time almost immemorial, a much-favoured preaching place on such occasions. This lack may only be accounted for by the fact that such a task was being taken care of in France.

Helen Leith Spencer defines such circumstantial sermons as the *Sermo Epinicius* by stating that they were quite rare occurrences: "[...] the preachers are rarely topical [...]".[15] Thus, by definition, religious sermons were usually detached from earthly and ephemeral events and were supposed to begin with a quotation from the Holy Scriptures, which the Victory Sermon dutifully did; yet the rest of the text was inextricably linked with the contemporary historical background which surrounded both its conception and deliverance.

Besides, major studies[16] have established a number of similarities between the contents of the *Sermo Epinicius* and his greatest treatise, the *De Causa Dei contra Pelagium et de virtute causarum*, which he had completed a few years prior to the autumn of 1346. As a consequence, this reinforces the idea that the sermon was written with some urgency, which does not mean the preacher did not put into it all the care that may be imagined from a cleric such as Thomas Bradwardine.

This sermon was obviously intended for an audience that supported the English king's cause and whose members had, by and large, taken part in the military encounter at Crécy. So it was a sermon preached by an Englishman to Englishmen but not on English soil; rather on the land of the vanquished. Was this a mere coincidence or a deliberate strategic

---

[14] Henry Hart Milman. *Annals of St Paul's Cathedral.* London: John Murray, Albermarle Street, 1869, 69.

[15] Helen Leith Spencer in *The Sermon*, Beverly Mayne Kienzle, dir. Typologie des sources du Moyen Age occidental. Fasc. 81-83. Turhout-Belgium: Brepols, 2000, 634.

[16] Heiko Augustinus Oberman. *Thomas Bradwardine, a Fourteenth Century Augustinian. A Study of his Theology in its Historical Context.* Utrecht : Drukkerij en Uitgevers-Maatschappij, 1957. Pr. Hoffler, "Thomas Bradwardine's Victory Sermon in 1346" in A.I. Doyle, ed. *Studies in European History and Political Thought.* Aldershot: Ashgate, 2000. Edith Wilks Dolnikowski. *Thomas Bradwardine. A View of Time and a Vision of Eternity in Fourteenth-Century Thought.* Leiden : E.J. Brill, 1995.

initiative that aimed at giving more symbolical strength to the occasion? On the one hand, the sermon was preached in October whereas the Crécy victory had taken place two months earlier. Between those two dates, the English host had marched on Calais and then the decision had been made to besiege the town. Consequently, Thomas Bradwardine preached his sermon there and then for practical as well as political reasons. On the other hand, it was also eminently tactical to have a sermon preached for the celebration of a recent victory on the very spot of what the king expected to become another one, the surrender of Calais. The preaching of the *Sermo Epinicius* there and then cannot have been fortuitous; it must be understood as a deliberate enterprise of propaganda, owing to the fact that it was closely related to precise historical events, two military victories on the one hand, and the beginning of the siege of Calais on the other, and it used what can be called, at the risk of another anachronism, a means of mass communication, in this case a religious sermon, whose force of persuasion is widely acknowledged in both historical and theological circles.

One of the other reasons why this sermon seems to be atypical when compared to those that belonged to the same literary genre is related to a linguistic element. First of all, according to the *incipit* of the sermon, it was commanded by the sovereign himself ("*ad mandatum principi*") and preached in English ("*in Anglico primo dictus*").[17] The sermon presented a striking paradox: on the one hand, Edward III was, like all his Plantegenet predecessors on the English throne, a French-speaking person; on the other hand, Latin was the language of both intellectual thinking and writing, the language of "high abstract"[18] and above all, the language which was supposed to be used for the writing of sermons, since all the practical manuals aimed at helping preachers in their task, the *Artes Praedicandi,* were written in Latin as well. Yet, the *Sermo Epinicius* was first delivered in the vernacular.

Preaching *in vulgari,* particularly in the later part of the XIVth century – and here, the *Sermo Epinicius* may indeed appear as a forerunner of the trend – has long been assessed by scholars as evidence of the realisation from the part of preachers that they could convey whatever message they wanted to any audience much more easily if they did away with the

---

[17] Pr. Offler, *op. cit.* XIII. 16.
[18] J.A. Burrow. *Medieval Writers and their Work (Middle-English Literature and its Background).* Oxford: OUP, 1982, 87.

linguistic barrier of Latin. Preaching in the vernacular was preaching in the language of the people, the one they were able to understand.[19]

However, the text of the *Sermo Epinicius* has crossed time to reach us in a Latin version, written after it was delivered orally. Professor Offler questioned the nature of the connection between the two versions, pointing out that the Latin one is obviously a longer and much more sophisticated form of the vernacular one since, in it, biblical as well as philosophical quotations are plentiful. [20] Professor Offler questioned the plausibility of representing King Edward and his soldiers, however distinguished they might have been, in the conditions that were depicted earlier, listening to such a scholarly reading.

The decision to deliver that sermon in the vernacular was not made randomly. It corresponded to an educational wish on the part of the preacher to convey a precise message and, in this way, the *Sermo Epinicius* was emblematic of two tendencies that were emerging in that mid-14th century. The first one was linked with the symbolic strength of persuasion that was inherent to medieval preaching and all its characteristics. Here we find the connection with propaganda in the sense that "preaching" (*praedicare*) was synonymous of "spreading" or "communicating" (*propagare*). Thomas Bradwardine was, on that autumn day of 1346, delivering an official message. The second tendency was a linguistic one and bore witness to the slow evolution which was taking England along the path of a linguistic national awareness, the culminating point of which was epitomised in Edward III's decision in 1362 to have judiciary pleadings in English instead of French.[21] Thus the *Sermo Epinicius* hailed the growing inclination in the late Middle Ages in England to preach *in vulgari,* so as to achieve a better understanding on the part of audience. "The author speaks in order to be understood and possibly convince [...]".[22] This is made all the more relevant since the *Sermo Epinicius* was presumably first devised in Latin, the language of work for scholars such as Bradwardine, then delivered in English and finally laid in writing in Latin again for purposes of archival storage. Of course, we can only agree with Beverley Mayne Kienzle who remarked: "Lost are the emotions, gestures, voice modulations, crowd interaction,

---

[19] Gerald Owst. *Preaching in Medieval England. An Introduction to Sermon Manuscripts of the Period c. 1350-1450.* Cambridge : CUP, 1926, 225.

[20] Pr. Offler, *op. cit.* XIII, 4.

[21] S.B. Chrimes and A.L. Brown. *Select Documents of English Constitutional History (1307-1485).* London: Adam and Charles Black, 1961, 85.

[22] Jean Longère. *La prédication médiévale.* Paris : Etudes Augustiniennes, 1983, 12.

and other elements that constituted the sermon in its actual historical setting"[23]. Yet it is possible to glean some valuable information on the conditions of writing of the *Sermo Epinicius*.

Thomas Bradwardine: the ideal preacher or the ideal propagandist?

Thomas Bradwardine has become one of the major 14th-century references as a "thinker" in the broader sense of the word. Immediate posterity made Chaucer, as early as the end of the same century, list his name alongside with that of St Augustine in his *Nun's Priest Tale.*[24] Later, Wyclif paid homage to him in his writings and nowadays, he appears as an intellectual of a very high rank, who was known as such even in his lifetime. Compliments abound of his multi-faceted though short-lived career which barely covered a full decade but was crowned with resounding success, the culminating point being his translation to the highest ecclesiastical position in England, that of Archbishop of Canterbury in July 1349. Bradwardine can be described as a shooting star in the sky of that mid-14th century and very seldom indeed, can we find the shadow of a criticism concerning his intellectual righteousness.[25] Gordon Leff made some of the rare disparaging comments about the thinker by emphasizing his lack of indulgence towards God's creatures.[26]

Although the written Latin sermon that has survived was a more elaborate version than the speech delivered from the pulpit in the church of St Peter's, the overall message conveyed by that sermon was undoubtedly the same one: the military success of the English at Crécy over the French and at Neville's Cross over the Scots was a divine gift. In his Victory Sermon, the preacher devoted his energy and his eloquence to explaining why to his audience. He started his demonstration by respecting the first condition regulating all religious sermons, namely a scriptural quotation, in this case from St Paul's second epistle to the Corinthians: "Now thanks be to God, who always maketh us to triumph in Christ Jesus and manifesteth the odour of his knowledge by us in every place." [2.

---

[23] Beverley Mayne Kienzle, dir. *The Sermon.* Typologie des sources du Moyen Age occidental, Fasc. 81-83. Turnhout-Belgium: Brepols, 2000, 143.

[24] Geoffrey Chaucer. *The Canterbury Tales.* London : Penguin Books, 1969, 2nd ed. 1996, 196.

[25] Geoffrey Treasure, Gl Ed. *Who's who in British History - Beginnings to 1901-* Volume 1, 1998, 136.

[26] Gordon Leff, *Bradwardine and the Pelagians (A study of his 'De causa Dei' and its opponents).* Cambridge: CUP, 1957, 19.

Cor.2:14].[27] Then the development of the sermon obeyed a strict logical structure and exposed no less than seven false reasons which could be cited to account for the recent English victories. By examining them one by one, Bradwardine showed why they turned out to be invalid. For example, he talked about the influence of stars, sheer luck, human prowess and the soldiers' manliness. He methodically refuted all those reasons and eventually reached the conclusion that, because all of them were false, the only one that could be retained was that God simply willed those victories for the English and they must be grateful to Him. The doctrinal statement of the *Sermo Epinicius* was of course the divine deterministic conception that Bradwardine was known for advocating and which, on many occasions, he publicly had, both orally and in writing, prior to delivering that particular sermon.

In preaching the Victory Sermon, Bradwardine vented his own deep conviction that God pre-ordained everything in this world and His Will was to be found at the origin of every single event, such opinions as he had already publicised in his *De Cause Dei*, which began to be circulated a few years before the Crécy Victory. In the corpus of the sermon, he quoted St Paul again: "For it is God who worketh in you, both to will and to accomplish, according to his good will.." [Phil.2,13].[28]

For Thomas Bradwardine, it was essential to convey this precise message to the audience facing him: God had willed the two military victories for the English cause, He gave the English whatever means they needed to win and He must be praised for that. The preacher reinforced that idea by underlining the fact that those successes could not otherwise be accounted for since, even by contemporary standards, they were most surprising, in particular at Crécy where the French clearly outnumbered their enemies and thus, should have won.

Bradwardine, on that occasion of the *Sermo Epinicius*, managed to conciliate a number of important elements to convey the crucial idea that God willed everything on earth and such a major event as a military victory over the enemy must serve as a demonstration. He actually used a precise historical circumstance and turned it into a practical illustration of his theological convictions. It went without saying that he made the most of his status and moral authority in order to reach his goal, since he was chaplain and confessor of the king and he had been in his retinue

---

[27] « Deo autem gratias qui semper triumphat nos in Christo Iesu et odorem notitiae suae manifestat per nos in omni loco ». The Latin Vulgate.
http://www.latinvulgate.com/
[28] « Deus est enim qui operatur in vobis et velle et perficere pro bona voluntate ». The Latin Vulgate.

throughout the Crécy campaign. At the time of the *Sermo Epinicius*, Bradwardine was becoming an influential member of Edward III's political elite. Besides, his influence and aura among the soldiers is acknowledged by scholars.[29]

Thomas Bradwardine illustrated Jean-Paul Gourévitch's words: "[...] power subsists on a custom which places liege-men at key-positions."[30] In the Middle Ages, knowledge and power used to cohabit insofar as the *graduati*, those who had university degrees, were recruited in those shrines of learning, the *studium generali*. Once they were appointed to different posts of the state machinery, owing to either personal competence or patronage or both, they became what can be called nowadays the 'high civil servants'. They had the duties of preaching, pleading and healing.[31] As for Bradwardine, he benefited from the protection of the well-known and influential Richard de Bury who, from the onset of the young graduate's career at Oxford, noticed his outstanding intellectual capacities.

Thomas Bradwardine was a "modern" man by the standards of his time. He was well-placed to serve a monarch who was determined to push his luck as far as he could. Nevertheless, the theologian must have found it hard to establish a compromise between the demands of his religious faith and his doctrinal convictions on the one hand, the constraints of the clerical institution as a whole on the other, and, last but not least, the political ambitions of his master.

In her work about Thomas Bradwardine, Edith Dolnikowski highlighted the fact that his career was outstanding.[32] While serving as chaplain and confessor to the king, he was chosen alongside seven other envoys to go on a diplomatic mission on 22 October 1346 aiming at negotiating a truce with the French.[33] This particular occurrence took place a mere few days before the *Sermo Epinicius* was preached and shows what

---

[29] "To his apostolical labours among the English soldiers many attributed the success achieved." *The Catholic Encyclopedia.* Charles G., Herbermann, et al, eds. Vol. 14 (Simony-Tournély). New York : Robert Appleton Company, 1912, 693.

[30] Jean-Paul Gourévitch, *La propagande dans tous ses états*. Paris : Flammarion, 1981, 7.

[31] Jacques Verger, *Les gens de savoir en Europe à la fin du Moyen-Age*. Paris: PUF, 1997, 137.

[32] Edith Dolnikowski. "Thomas Bradwardine's *Sermo Epinicius*: some reflections on its political, theological and pastoral significance" in Jaqueline Hamesse, J., Kienzle, Beverly M., Stoudt, Debra L., Thayer, Anne T., eds. *Medieval Sermons and Society: Cloister, City, University*. Louvain-la-Neuve. 1998, 357.

[33] Heiko A. Oberman et James A. Weishepl. *Archives d'Histoire Doctrine et Littéraire du Moyen Age* (33ème année: 1958) Paris : Librairie philosophique J. Vrin. 1959, 300.

a busy man Bradwardine was. King Edward III's choice of a preacher was a clever one and he was undoubtedly well-advised in this regard. As a general rule, the monarch knew how to surround himself with educated and quick-witted councillors but in this particular case, he also knew that he could rely on a faithful and ardent royalist who staunchly defended, in the true Augustinian tradition, the fact that a plurality of rulers is no good thing and that, consequently, the wielding of power must reside in the hands of one man.[34]

Besides, the introduction to the sermon gave additional evidence of Bradwardine's undivided support to his sovereign: "*Dei Gracia Regis Anglie et Francie*"; "king of England and France by God's grace". Here the preacher acknowledged the official taking of the title by the English king which had taken place six years before in the Flemish town of Ghent. With those words, the dynastic claim of Edward III was no longer simply a claim, but became reality, a fact that was officially stated in front of an audience.

With the deliverance of the *Sermo Epinicius*, Thomas Bradwardine achieved a very clever combination of several official duties. First of all, he fulfilled his role as a civil servant; the king asked for a sermon to be preached and his servant complied with his wish. Then, he succeeded in allying his loyalty to his temporal master with that to the ecclesiastical institution of which he was a member and which was represented on that particular day by papal legates present in the audience. Finally, he engaged in his pastoral vocation by interpreting the deep meaning of the recent events and conveying the result of that interpretation to the congregation facing him. For a man like Thomas Bradwardine to become the champion of the king's warlike ambitions, there must have been powerful ideological stimuli. Three main factors may have influenced the theologian and led him to assume his stance publicly; two of those factors stemmed from the medieval tenets and the third one relied more on personal reasoning.

Thomas Bradwardine might have been aware of the paradox between the fifth commandment of the Mosaïc Law ("Thou shalt not kill") and the reality of the war. If biblical texts never offer an apology of war, they do not condemn it either. For a fourteenth-century theologian, the way had been paved by illustrious predecessors such as Augustine of Hippo, who had worked at depriving religious thought of all contradictions in this regard by concluding that worldly peace was impossible and, consequently, war must be tolerated; therefore, it had to be strictly regulated.

---

[34] Pr. Offler. *Op. cit.* XIII. 2.

With this in mind, Philippe Contamine asked the crucial question: "Was the Hundred Years War a just war?" Through his examination of the different criteria related to what has come to be called the "Just War Theory", he mentioned the person, the object, the cause, the spirit and the authority which were at stake in the case of a conflict such as the one in question. He did not forget to emphasize the fact that each side thought they were righteously fighting for their cause and publicly stated it with the support of lawyers and theologians. At the end of his analysis, the author very carefully reached his own conclusion regarding the Hundred Years War and declared that only a saint, someone righteous, was likely to wage a just war.[35] This assertion leads us to deal with the subject of medieval kingship at the time of the *Sermo Epinicius.*

Well ahead of the Crécy campaign, pro-king and pro-war propaganda had begun to appear in the sermons preached by some members of the high clergy, for example John Stratford, Archbishop of Canterbury, who, as early as 1327, had proclaimed that the war against the Scots was being waged in the name of faith, right and the country. Then, in 1337, he had openly supported the English king on the subject of his claim to the French crown.[36] Specialists have shown that a Western medieval king was, first and foremost, a Christian king who, because of the singleness of his role, became a *rex imago Dei*, a king resembling God.[37] Ernst Kantorowicz went further along this path by showing that, according to the writings of the so-called Norman Anonymous who dealt with the king's *persona mixta*, the two bodies of the king, a medieval sovereign was the "Anointed One", thus bearing resemblance with Christ.[38] Thanks to Professor Offler, we know that Thomas Bradwardine had deep-rooted royalist convictions. It is likely that, following the ideas of his time, he saw in Edward III the representative of Christ on earth, all the more as, in his treatise *De causa Dei*, he openly asserted his king's thaumaturgical powers, which was another aspect of the belief in the similarity between Christ as a healer and temporal rulers. Apart from the ideology of the just war and the belief in

---

[35] Philippe Contamine, « La guerre de cent ans fut-elle une guerre juste ? » in *Jeanne, d'Arc, une époque, un rayonnement.* Paris : Editions du CNRS, 1982, 21.

[36] Georges Minois. *L'Église et la guerre : de la Bible à l'ère atomique.* Paris : Fayard, 1994, 188.

[37] Jacques Le Goff in Anne J. Duggan, ed. *Kings and Kingship in Medieval Europe.* London: King's College London Centre for Late Antique and Medieval Studies, 1993, 2.

[38] Ernst Kantorowicz. *Les deux corps du roi (Essai sur la théologie politique au Moyen Age).* Paris : Gallimard, 1957, 2nd ed. 1989, 53-54.

the king's double identity, there may have been an additional reason which spurred Bradwardine on the path of propaganda in favour of his monarch.

Thomas Bradwardine was not only a scholar of exceptional calibre, he was also sharply aware of worldly affairs and his successive appointments to high positions within the state machinery bear witness to his will to make a career for himself. Let us not forget that he did not belong to any religious order and, being a member of the secular clergy, he obviously did not relish a secluded lifestyle. During the span of his short-lived but glorious public career, he made the most of all the opportunities available in his socio-professional circle, namely the patronage given by the famous bibliophile, Richard de Bury, bishop of Durham, to whom he owed his nomination in 1339 to the king's retinue. The wise and experienced counsel of de Bury was undoubtedly most useful to Bradwardine and was carefully followed, as the development of his career shows, but the future Archbishop of Canterbury was also guided by other examples which he chose to set himself. In this regard, Paul the apostle clearly played an important part as a role-model, as the numerous quotations from his Epistles in both the *Sermo Epinicius* and *De Causa Dei* reveal.

Did Bradwardine choose Saint Paul as his theological guide because he was not entirely satisfied with the four Gospels? Or was it because he knew about the life of Paul of Tarsus and was aware of his standing apart from the other apostles? Bradwardine had to go through a period of intellectual conflict which opposed him to his peers and made him a target of their criticism. This is only one among many similarities between the two characters which may account for the fact that the apostle was quoted in the *Sermo Epnicius* no less than nine times. There is little room for doubt as to the empathy our fourteenth-century theologian must have felt for Paul, since both of them were converts and educated men. Bradwardine may have seen in the similarity of their vocations another manifestation of the doctrine of predestination of which he was an ardent exponent.

Thus, it has been shown that in a given historical context, a particular sermon, the *Sermo Epinicius*, managed to produce what can be seen as an action of propaganda. This sermon was preached by a man who was representative of the socio-professional category to which he belonged, clerics of a high rank who sought to serve both their temporal ruler and the overall ecclesiastical institution based in Rome at a time when it was not easy to do so. Some historians are very careful not to use the word "propaganda" and prefer to refer to "favourable publicity". Nevertheless, there are many who acknowledge the role of the Church as a political platform in the Middle Ages with men belonging to the ecclesiastical hierarchy who voiced their opinions in favour of the reigning monarch and did so by preaching sermons which were the contemporary means of conveying a public message.

Episcopal registrars bear witness to the numerous requests for sermons *pro rege*, invitations to pray for the king and his enterprises. R.W. Jones speaks of involuntary political propaganda on the part of those who preached them.[39] In the case of Thomas Bradwradine, we can certainly argue in favour of a mixture combining professional integrity, theological righteousness as well as ideological idealism. Among his contemporary intellectual peers, John Stratford who preceded him at the see of Canterbury and Richard Fitzralph of Armagh, Archbishop of Ireland, also wrote sermons and preached them to captive audiences, eager to hear their messages. The strength of their convictions still transpires through the words of those sermons which it would be most interesting to compare with the *Sermo Epinicius*.

Works Cited

Burne, Alfred. *The Crécy War: a Military History of the Hundred Years War from 1337 to the Peace of Bretigny, 1360.* London: Eyre & Spottiswoode, 1955.

Catto J. I. and Ralph Evans, eds. The *History of the University of Oxford. Volume II: Late Medieval Oxford.* Oxford: Clarendon Press, 1992.

Chaucer, Geoffrey. *The Canterbury Tales, a selection.* London: Penguin Books, (1969) 1996.

Churchill, I.J. dir. *Dictionnaire d'Histoire et de Géographie Ecclésiastiques*, Tome X. Alfred Baudrillart, A. De Meyer et Et. Van Cauwenbergh. Paris : Librairie Letouzey et Ané, 1938.

Contamine, Philippe. « La théologie de la guerre à la fin du Moyen Age : la guerre de Cent Ans fut-elle une guerre juste ? » in *Jeanne d'Arc, une époque, un rayonnement.* Paris : Publications du CNRS, 1992.

Dolnikowski, Edith. "Thomas Bradwardine's *Sermo Epinicius* : some reflections on its political, theological and pastoral significance" in Hamesse, J., Kienzle, Beverly M., Stoudt, Debra L., Thayer, Anne T., eds. *Medieval Sermons and Society : Cloister, City, University.* Louvain-la-Neuve : 1998 ;

Ellul, Jacques. *Histoire de la propagande.* Que Sais-Je n° 1271 Paris : PUF, 1967.

---

[39] W.R. Jones. "The English Church and Royal Propaganda during the Hundred Years War" in *The Journal of British Studies*, Vol. 19, N°1 (Autumn 1979): 18-30.

Favier, Jean. *La guerre de cent ans.* Paris : Librairie Arthème Fayard, 1980.

Fletcher, Alan. *Preaching and Politics in Late Medieval England.* (Portland, Or.: Four Courts Press, 1998.

Gautier, Léon. *La Chevalerie.* Paris : Arthaud, 1959 ;

Glaire, J.F.. *La Sainte Bible selon la Vulgate.* Editions D.F.T.(1902) 2002.

Gourévitch, Jean-Paul. *La propagande dans tous ses états.* (Paris : Flammarion, 1981).

Le Goff, Jacques. in Anne J. Duggan, ed. *Kings and Kingship in Medieval Europe.* London: Centre for Late Antique and Medieval Studies, 1993.

Longère, Jean. *La prédication médiévale.* Paris : Etudes Augustiniennes, 1983.

Jones, W.R. « The English Church and Royal Propaganda during the Hundred Years War ». *The Journal of British Studies*, vol. 19, n° 1 (Autumn 1979).

Jowett, Gareth S. and Victoria O'DONNELL. *Propaganda and Persuasion.* (Beverley Hills: Sage Publications, 1986.

Kienzle, Beverly Mayne. *The Sermon.* Typologie des sources du Moyen Age occidental. Fasc. 81-83. Turnhout-Belgium: Brepols, 2000.

Milman, Henry Hart. *Annals of St. Paul's Cathedral.* London: John Murray, Albermarle Street, 1869.

Minois, Georges. *L'Église et la guerre: de la Bible à l'ère atomique.* Paris : Librairie Arthème Fayard, 1994.

Prestwich, Michael. *The Three Edwards. War and State in England, 1272-1377.* London: Routledge, 2ⁿᵈ ed., 2003.

Oberman, Heiko et James A. Weisheipl. *Archives d'Histoire Doctrinale et Littéraire du Moyen Age.* (33ᵉᵐᵉ année : 1958) Paris : Librairie Philosophique J. VRIN, 1959 .

Offler, Hilary Seton. A.I. Doyle, ed. *Church and Crown in the Fourteenth Century.* (Aldershot: Ashgate, 2000.

Ormrod, W.M. *The Reign of Edward III.* Stroud: Tempus Publishing Ltd., (1990) 2000.

Saville, Henri. ed. *Thomae Bradwardini Archiepiscopi Olim Cantuariensis: De Causa Dei Contra Pelagium et de Virtute Causarum ad suos Mertonenses.* (Londini: Ex officina Nortoniana Apud Ioannem Billium, M.D.C.XVIII).

Schneyer, Johannes. *Repertorium der Lateinischen Sermones des Mittelalters.* 5 vols. (für die zeit von 1150-1350) (autoren : R-Schlub [W]Munster Westfalen: Aschendorffsche Verlagsbuchhandlung, 1970.

Spencer, Helen Leith. in Beverly Mayne Kienzle, dir. *The Sermon.* Typologie des sources du Moyen Age occidental. Fasc. 81-83.Turnhout-Belgium: Brepols, 2000.

Sumption, Jonathan. *The Hundred Years War : Trial by Battle Vol. 1.* London: Faber & Faber, 1990.

Treasure, Geoffrey, ed. *Who's who in British History - Beginnings to 1901-* Vol. 1. (London, 1998.

Tuchman, Barbara W. *A Distant Mirror The calamitous 14th century.* Harmondsworth: Penguin Books, 1978.

Verger, Jacques. *Les gens de savoir en Europe à la fin du Moyen Age.* Paris : PUF, 1997.

Wehmeier, Sally, ed. *Oxford Advanced Learner's Dictionary.* Oxford: OUP, 2003.

Appendix 1

http://www.fordham.edu/halsall/maps/1360france.jpg

CHAPTER THREE

ENGLISH PROTESTANT SERMONS AT MOMENTS OF CRISIS: THE THREAT OF THE SPANISH ARMADA

LETICIA ÁLVAREZ-RECIO

Although sermons had been largely used as one more devotional practice in the late Middle Ages, it was at the end of the fifteenth century and throughout the sixteenth century with the growing influence of Humanism that this genre began to acquire a higher significance. The humanist concern with the preaching of the Gospel contributed to the development of homiletic literature in the Renaissance period, especially within the context of European Reformation and Counter-Reformation. Protestantism, in fact, provided the preachers with a relevance they had never enjoyed before, since, for the Reformed, "the sermon and the public preaching of the Scriptures were the sacred meeting-place between an imperfect humanity and the spirit of God".[1] Before then, preaching had been only one of many priestly functions; now, it was considered the priest's central and greatest duty.

England underwent a similar process since its separation from Rome. With the abrogation of the Mass and the auricular confession, preaching became the principal means through which the faithful could be shown the way to salvation and repent of their sins. Anglican priests became ministers and "ministers were preachers above all else".[2] The evolution of the sermon into a social and political event was just a question of time. Erasmus had emphasised each human being's obligation –no matter his

---

[1] Susan Wabuda, *Preaching during the English Reformation.* Cambridge: C.U.P., 2002, 13.

[2] Eric Josef Carlson, "The Boring of the Ear: Shaping the Pastoral Vision of Preaching in England, 1540-1640". *Preachers and People in the Reformation, and Early Modern Period.* Larissa Taylor (Ed.). Leida: Brill, 2001, 249-296, 255.

social condition– to understand the Word of God and act according to His laws. This was effectively exploited by the evangelical reformers, who promoted:

> the royal supremacy, through establishing the king as the final arbiter of doctrine. Until the Ecclesiastes was printed, the pulpit had hardly been used systematically to make political utterances, though intrusions of larger political events made occasional appearances in sermons... The political significance of the pulpit was remote and relatively unexplored, compared with the uses to which sermons and homilies were put under the terms of the royal supremacy.[3]

Thus, the sermon, which had been restricted to the court in the pre-Reformation period, became now a common practice for preachers of all sides who used it against one another as an instrument to discuss the future of the English Church. This explains its revival at the universities and in London from the early sixteenth century and the growing importance of training new orators according to the plain style recommended to affect wider and more socially diverse audiences.[4] The final step was the introduction of this genre into the printing marketplace during the second half of the Elizabethan period, a fact that made possible a larger dissemination of its didactic messages and which facilitated its appeal to a varied and increasingly literate public, usually concerned with contemporary problems.[5] In this sense, it is worth noting that most of the works printed in those years dealt with religious topics, which confirms the interest they aroused and the close link between the printing press and the doctrinal discussion between Catholics and Protestants.[6] Although the number of published sermons was considerably smaller than the pamphlets, the connection between both kinds of literature was explicit as both of them made use of the same rhetoric and, in most cases, shared the same purpose: to move their readers to act according to the authors' premises. According to Peter Lake and Michael Questier, who have studied the overlap between these two kinds of literature in Early Modern England,

---

[3] Wabuda, Preaching during the English Reformation, 90.

[4] *Ibid.*, 52-53.

[5] The publishing of sermons was a key novelty, as pre-Reformation orators only published their texts for use by other priests, but never intended them to be read by (or to) the audience at large. See Larissa Taylor, *Preachers and People in the Reformation and Early Modern Period.* Leiden: Brill, 2001, xi.

[6] On the connection between printing and religious literature, see Frances E. Dolan, *Whores of Babylon. Catholicism, Gender and Seventeenth Century Print Culture.* Ithaca: Cornell University Press, 1999.

"there [only] remained very considerable differences of tone and emphasis separating the treatments of such themes and narratives produced by the godly from those produced in Grub street or on the stage".[7] Both critics also point out the permanent dialogue and "on-going process of exchange and interpenetration" linking both worlds.[8] On the other hand, the pamphleteers and preachers' religious and political commitment explains why these two genres, which could be successfully used to support the *status quo*, may also have worked in the opposite way and become a problem for the authorities.

This was the case of Queen Elizabeth I, who started her rule with a general prohibition of all preaching in the country[9] and who witnessed a progressive decrease in the number of church dignitaries at court as her reign advanced. Her negligence in attending homilies and prayers, her removal of the sermon from the service and restriction on preaching in the shires and her own court were also well known and criticised.[10] However, the queen loved compliment and praise and the sermon could provide the preachers with a useful tool to commend her and attract her favour. Besides, in periods of crisis an homily could be used to confirm Elizabeth on a specific policy of which she might not be quite sure[11] or, in contrast, could work in a parallel and more subtle way to question certain decisions and suggest new lines of government at moments of crisis.

1588 was, most certainly, one of those critical years.[12] By then, the queen's excommunication, the arrival of the Jesuits, the plots against Elizabeth's life and, especially, the growing threat of an invasion had

---

[7] See Peter Lake and Michael Questier, *The Antichrist's Lewd Hat. Protestants, Papists and Players in Post-Reformation England.* New Haven: Yale U.P., 2002, 319.

[8] *Ibid.*, 326.

[9] See Edward Cardwell (Ed.), *Documentary Annals of the Reformed Church of England.* 2 Vols, Oxford, 1844, i, 208-210.

[10] For further information about preaching in the Elizabethan court, see Peter McCullough, *Sermons at Court. Politics and Religion in Elizabethan and Jacobean Preaching.* Cambridge: C.U.P, 1998.

[11] McCullough, *Sermons at Court*, 84.

[12] It is relevant, for instance, that the only time the queen attended a St Paul's Cross sermon, even though this was the most prestigious pulpit in the whole realm, occurred on 24 of November in 1588, since it was part of a general celebration for the victory over Spain. The sermon was delivered by John Piers, Bishop of Salisbury before the queen, the Council and the French ambassador. Unfortunately, no printed copy remains. See Miller MacLure (Ed.), *Register of Sermons Preached at Paul's Cross 1534-1642.* Ottawa: Dovehouse Editions, 1989, 66.

created a sense of paranoia against Catholic powers, and more concretely, against Spain. In 1588, when Philip's attack was more than a mere potential danger, writers on both sides got involved in a literary war that seemed to precede the actual confrontation that would come later. English Protestant priests did not lose the opportunity to arouse strong nationalistic feelings in their audience and encourage them to defend their country and the true church from any foreign invasion. The Spanish attack coincided too with a period of serious conflicts within the English Church, which began to be threatened not just by the followers of Rome, but also by Puritan groups who openly criticised it and demanded further religious reforms. In such difficult times, it is easy to understand the growing politicisation of the English sermon and its participation in the debate about contemporary problems.

This study will analyse four sermons preached and printed in the period from 1587 to 1589, shortly before, during and after the conflict with Spain. It will dwell upon the different strategies the authors used to promote such feelings in their readers and listeners, paying special attention to the political use they made of religious rhetoric. It will also try to connect these texts with the anti-Catholic and anti-Spanish language common in the pamphlet literature of the period in order to underline how all these writings formed a xenophobic discourse that attempted to dissipate or silence the deep internal divisions within English Protestantism. I have chosen both public and private sermons for my analysis, although the space where they were preached does not apparently reveal many differences in the use of such anti-Hispanic prejudices. In fact, all of them share the same object of attack and are equally poignant in their criticism. Nevertheless, Edmond Harris's *A Sermon Preached at Brocket Hall*,[13] which is addressed to a group of soldiers about to face the Spaniards in the battlefield, seems to be the most emphatic in its harangue against the enemy. The preacher's words in this regard are explicit from the beginning of the sermon:

> I thought good to choose out an other portion of Scripture,[14] agreeable to
> the present matter: especiallie considering howe some euill disposed

---

[13] The complete title is A Sermon Preached at Brocket Hall, Before the Right Worshipfull, Sir John Brocket, and other Gentlemen there Assembled for the Trayning of Soldiers. London, 1588. Unfortunately, we have no information about the preacher or the gentleman named Sir John Brocket, mentioned in the title.

[14] Harris's biblical reference is: "Dread not, neither bee afraid of them. The Lord your God which goeth before you he shall fight for you, according to all that he did in Egypt before your eyes" (Deut. 1.29-30). The use of quotations from the Bible was a rhetorical practice and constituted one of the main parts of the sermon.

persons goe about to weaken the hearts and hands of our countrimen, as though we were not able to encounter with our Popish and Spanish aduersaries that now threaten us with encomberance of warre in our owne land. (A3)

This same idea, however, is also present in the three public sermons, which insist on the proximity of the Spanish danger and the need to be prepared to face it. All of them were delivered in different towns – London, Oxford and Lydd (Kent) – which harboured practically no Catholic population,[15] so we may assume the presence of a socially varied audience sympathetic with the Protestant attacks on Spain and the followers of Rome. These texts are John Prime's[16] *The Consolations of David*[17], Isaac Colfe's[18] *A Sermon Preached on the Queenes Day*[19] and

---

William Perkin's *Arte of Prophecying* (1592), one of the most influential preaching manuals at the end of the sixteenth and seventeenth centuries, sums up the steps to write a good sermons: "1) To read the Text distinctly out of the Canonicall Scriptures. 2) To give the sense and understanding of it being read by the Scripture it selfe. 3) To collect a few and profitable points of doctrine out of the naturall sense. 4) To applie (if he haue the gift) the doctrines rightly collected to the life and manners of men, in a simple and plaine speech" (William Perkins, *The Arte of Prophecying: a Treatise Concerning the Sacred and Onely True Manner and Methode of Preaching*. Thomas Tuke (Trans.) [London, 1607], 148). For a detailed analysis on the style, organization and deliverance of sermons, the reader may consult M. A. Fraser Mitchell (Ed.). *English Pulpit Oratory from Andrewes to Tillotson. A Study of its Literary Aspects.* New York: Russell & Russell, 1962.

[15] For further information about the distribution of Catholics in England in the 16th century, see John Bossy's *The English Catholic Community 1570-1850.* New York: O.U.P., 1976.

[16] John Prime (1550-96). Church of England clergyman. According to the ODNB, "he established a reputation for aggressively protestant preaching". See Julian Lock. Prime, John (1549/50-1596). *Oxford Dictionary of National Biography*, ed. H. C. G. Matthew and Brian Harrison (Oxford: O.U.P., 2004), http://www.oxforddnb.com.fama.us.es:80/view/article/22792 (accessed February 2, 2006).

[17] *The Consolations of David Breefly Applied to Queene Elizabeth.* Oxford, 1588.

[18] Isaac Colfe (1558/9-1597). Church of England clergyman. In 1596, he gained the mastership of Kingsbridge Hospital in Canterbury and became one of the six preachers of the cathedral. This sermon is dedicated to the town of Lydd's authorities, whith whom he seemed to have a good relation. See Stephen Wright. Colfe, Isaac (1558/9-1597). *Oxford Dictionary of National Biography*, http://www.oxforddnb.com.fama.us.es:80/view/article/5901.

[19] *A Sermon Preached on the Queenes Day Being the 17 November 1587 at the Towne of Lidd in Kent.* London, 1588.

Thomas White's[20] *A Sermon Preached at Paules Crosse.*[21] Most of them were preached on the 17 of November of 1587, 1588 and 1589, respectively. This date, also known as the Accession Day, commemorated Elizabeth's accession to the English throne and her survival of the alleged Catholic dangers that surrounded her. It was a day to celebrate the English Protestants' deliverance from the power of Rome and by extension, the victory of imperial England over the Pope.[22] These three sermons made use of this festive occasion to praise the queen as the defender of the true faith and her nation as the heart of Christianity:

> Sathan would stoppe all the course of the word, but he cannot, for what Ground the gospel, the *Worde*, hath woon in the world (in spite of the God thereof) and all his followers, the Pope, the Turke, and other Tyrants, the Church everie where doeth witnesse; and with us, *Reioycing* and *Triumphing* this day, doth confesse, to the glorie and praise of God, saying that the truth is great, and hath preuailed, and praying that it may preuaile for euermore. *(A Sermon Preached at Paules Crosse*: 18)

With the threat and later victory over the Spanish Armada, this celebration acquired a special significance and began to be used not only as a way to inspire strength to the English people, but also to warn them to be on their guard against future dangers. The four sermons exemplify how religious and nationalistic feelings were invoked to provoke both military and political actions: their defence from the Spaniards as well as a much more rigid policy against those suspected of helping the enemy from within, the English Catholics and the Jesuits. The sermons address the English subjects, who are called first to repent and lead a godly life to ensure God's Providence: "[it is necessary] that we put away ungodliness farre from us, that wee repent us of our sinnes, and give our selues to holinesse of life, and a diligent following of the commaundements of God" (*A Sermon Preached at Brocket Hall*: C5-C6); and second, to obey and be loyal to their ruler: "(Good people) in all hartlesse imperfectiones, marke I pray you, that they who... dare not venture upon, nor enter into,

---

[20] Thomas White (1550-1624). Benefactor of Sion College (London). From 1588 to 1591, he acted as vicar of St Gregory by Paul. See Stephen Wright. White, Thomas (1550-1624). *Oxford Dictionary of National Biography*, http://www.oxforddnb.com.fama.us.es:80/view/article/29273.

[21] *A Sermon Preached at Paules Crosse the 17 of November A. 1589 in Ioyfull Remembrance and Thanksgiving unto God, for the Peaceable Yeres of her Maiesties Most Gratious Raigne Over Us.* London, 1589.

[22] For a detailed explanation of the relevance of the Accession Day in Elizabethan politics and culture, see Roy Strong, *The Cult of Elizabeth: Elizabethan Portraiture and Pageantry,* London: Thames & Hudson, 1977.

nor indeuour any good action of greatest duetie to God, Prince or Countrie, till all be sure in one side, are utterly reprooued by this ensample" (*The Consolations of David*: A6). In both cases, the subjects' responsibility is underlined as well as the negative consequences of any subversive or rebellious attitude for the general welfare.

The relation between the monarch and her subjects is interpreted in reciprocal terms, so the queen is enjoined to fulfil her duty as a protector and defender of the true church. The four sermons, in fact, agree on Elizabeth's need to apply harder measures against Catholics and reveal a certain critical tone against the queen's leniency in this regard: "Our Gracious Soueraigne, did suffer long, and too long, almost before shee tooke the Sword in hande, and stoode to her defence in the cause of the *Gospel*, against the *Enimies* thereof" (*A Sermon Preached at Paules Crosse*: 59).[23] The preachers appeal to the queen's responsibility to her people and emphasize her capacity to save or ruin them depending on whether she follows God's rules (that is, a strict Protestant programme) or not.

In this sense, the Prince's duty is clarified through different images that point out Elizabeth's ideal role as the supporter of the whole realm. John Prime compares her to the heart and the head of the body *(The Consolations of David*: B2) and alludes to Alciato's emblem 42, "The

---

[23] White's opinion would not be isolated as in 1580 there had already been a royal proclamation suppressing invasion rumours, with which the queen tried to calm her subjects by silencing those critical and admonitory voices: "The Queen's Majesty findeth the continuance, or rather increase, of the traitorous and malicious purposes and solicitations of such rebels and traitors as do live in foreign parts. . . And [who have] sought and practiced by all means possible to irritate all states against her majesty and the realm. . . Yet for a further demonstration of the increase of their rancour; they have caused to be devised in writings, and the same have published, that the *Pope, the King of Spain, and some other princes are accorded to make a great army to invade this realm of England* and other her Majesty's dominions, and to dispose of the crown, and the possessions of the subjects, and of the realm at their pleasure, *thereby intending to move the people of the realm to some murmuring*, as they imagine... " (my italics). Although Elizabeth insisted on England's readiness to face any foreign attack, she tried to maintain a suspiciously relaxed attitude –"... her highness hath never given just cause why any princes abroad should, contrary to their leagues with her, attempt anything prejudicial to her realms or countries" (Paul L. Hughes and James F Larkin (Eds.), *Tudor Royal Proclamations*. Vol.ii. *The Late Tudors (1553-1587)* [New Haven & London: Yale U.P., 1969], 469-470), which, no doubt, may have irritated many English Protestants. White's words reveal such uneasiness with the queen's policy.

most Steadfast Things cannot be Uprooted"[24] by linking Elizabeth to the image of the root: "If the root be quicke the branches grow: if the foundation be sure, all the building is the surer" (B2). Again, the virtues of "strength in constancy" which the emblem explains are not only applied to Elizabeth but demanded from her. The same idea prevails in other similes used by the same author, such as the rock –"You know who she is [Elizabeth] that built uppon the rocke, and you know who that rocke is" (B2) – or the anchor: "The Arke was framed for the waters, the Ship for the Sea, happy is the mariner that knoweth wher to cast Anker" (A5). Alciato reproduces a similar idea in his emblem 144 "The Good Prince": "When the sea is rough, the anchor holds the graceful ship steady so that it does not perish; and the dolphin comes to it for more steadiness so that the rage of the sea may do less harm. Thus, a lord should always be to his subjects what an anchor often is to sailors".[25] This makes clear the reference in Prime's sermon: the preacher is not just encouraging the people to obey their queen but indirectly asks her to behave as such an anchor for her subjects.

---

[24] In 1586 Geoffrey Whitney translated into English two different versions of this emblem from 1549 and 1551, which present the image of a strong oak that remains unmoveable against the sea. The epigram corresponding to the last one is significant to reproduce: "Even though Oceanus enrages himself so much that he explodes from the conceived fury, creating with his violence, fear throughout the world; and though by you, Turk, the Rhine is swallowed, you shall not set foot across the frontier as long as the invincible Charles holds the field; he, like the oak, does not move, even though its leaves are shaken by the wind" (Peter M. Daly (Ed.), *Andreas Alciatus. Emblems in Translations* [Toronto: University Press of Toronto, 1985]. The fact that, according to this version, the emblem is addressed to Charles I is relevant as Elizabeth used to portray herself as Charles's heir in order to emphasize the imperial nature of her government. Through the indirect reference to Alciato's work, Prime might also be emphasizing how the imperial program initiated under Henry VIII might be in danger unless the queen adopts a much more aggressive policy. In this sense, the use of the emblematic rhetoric in sermonic literature made it possible to introduce explicit or implicit messages that may appeal to different kinds and levels of listeners. For further information on the development of the imperial theme in the sixteenth century and the interrelation among the iconographical constructions of the different European monarchs, see Frances Yates. *Astraea. The Imperial Theme in the Sixteenth Century.* London, Boston: Routledge, Kegan Paul, 1975; and Lesley B. Cormack. "Britannia Rules the Waves?: Images of Empire in Elizabethan England". *Early Modern Literary Studies* 4.2/ Special Issue 3, September, 1998: 10. 1-20.

[25] Daly, Andreas Alciatus. *Emblems in Translation.*

At the same time, the appeal to union is constant and emphasizes the need of each single English subject to get involved in that common national project against the Spaniards:

> wee learne how perillous in each common wealth contention is betweene the subiects of the same: that it is even such as if the stones of one building should forsake their places and refuse their offices in keeping in and supporting of one another, and should divide themselves the one against the other, to the beating out and breaking of each other: wherby it must needes come to passe, that the house, yet bee it never so goodly and stately, never so firme and strong, must have a downfall and come to destruction. (*A Sermon Preached on the Queenes Day*: A7)

The orators also refer to the English Catholics, especially those who had gone abroad or were studying at the Jesuits' colleges, as they considered both places the main sites for training Englishmen in aversion to their mother country.[26] Thus, they tried to open their eyes so they could recognise their real enemies and come back to their logical and natural side, English Protestantism: "O foolish fugitives and Englishe Seminaries, seedemen of these tumults, what meane you, why seeke yee amity with euery straunger? Euen therefore God hath demonstratively taught you that your treacheries are wicked. Why goe you abroade? What want you at home? ... They are thine open enimies" (*The Consolations of David*: B7).[27]

---

[26] The Jesuits usually appear as the most dangerous influence in England and are made responsible for the foreign attacks the English nation had to suffer: "Our God is able to crosse, and cursse, all their plattes, and practises of warre, and other wretched meanes, especiallie of using wicked instruments to bring their purposes to passe; I meane not of our *Papists* onely: which ebbe, and flow, at home with tydings, as the *Tide*, but *Iesuites* more seruiceable than their *Generals*: which hunger after *Kings* heartes, *Counsellors* heades, *Captaines* handes, and *Prophets* tongues, as after meate... " (*A Sermon Preached at Paules Crosse*: 58-59). Both the Company of Jesus and the Pope are shown as the main threats for England's stability whereas Spain often remains in a secondary position. The anti-Pope or anti-jesuitical discourse exceeds thus the one against the Spaniards, who are portrayed as foolish followers of Romish Babylon: "For after the decay of the Romish supremacie they were inuented for this intent, that they might go from one King and kingdome to an other, stirring them to battaile against the decayers of their Babilon" (*A Sermon Preached at Brocket Hall*: B1).

[27] This message was also a common motif in pamphlet literature, which introduced the same topics with very similar nationalistic and preventive intentions. See, for instance,T. Tymme in his pamphlet *A Preparation againt the Prognosticated Dangers of this Yeare* (London, 1588): "let us imbrace christian unity and concord, the which also will make us invincible against all our enemies that seek to invade

Nevertheless, such an insistence on unity seems to reveal precisely the opposite: the lack of agreement among the English subjects about this policy.[28] In fact, there seems to be a certain anxiety about the alleged inferiority of the English people regarding the Spaniards and, especially, about the possible defecting of English Protestants to the Catholic side. This concern is more poignant in those sermons preached before the Armada invasion, as it can be inferred from Edmond Harris's words:

> ... there is somewhat that being cast in and muttered by Popish spirites or such like, may seeme to have some force and abilitie to discourage weakelings, whereunto for that purpose some aunswer is necessarie. First, they put in mens head that our enemies are politique, and therefore must needs preuayle... So brethren, let us assure our selves, that for as much as their whole policie tendeth to the aduancement of some wicked Absalom, the deposing of our faithful Soveraigne, and the working of wickednesse, the Lord will turne it into foolishnesse and destroy it. (A Sermon Preached at Brocket Hall: C3) (my italics)[29]

In this sense, they use their sermons to encourage those people and confirm them in their loyalty to God and their country:

> Now therefore as men that professe the Lord to be your only stay and trust, lift up your hearts, that it may bee knowne how you haue not professed in uaine, and that you are the true Souldiers of Christ Jesu, whom no force nor furniture of the enemie can feare, no rumours of warre can dismay, no hoastes of armed men can once abash or terrifie. (A4)

---

us" (B5). Other authors just allude to practical reasons: "the doubt to lose life, lands and goods, will cause us to agree" (An Exhortacion to all English Subiects, to Ione for the Defence of Queene Elizabeth and their Native Country [London, 1588], 2), a kind of justification which is, nevertheless, hardly ever present in the homilies.

[28] Thomas White dedicates a large part of his sermon to attack the radical attitude of some Puritan preachers, who alarm the country and provoke divisions within the English Church. He considers them false prophets and sets them at the same level as Catholics in their attempt to undermine English Protestantism: "And how euill a thing Contention is in the church, we have no need of forraine stories, of discourse to learne: our home maladies, and miseries can teach us, but too well: For Discorde, hath separated us one from another, for all good purposes. . . The old faction, which was, and yet remaineth still, is two fold, of the Anabaptists, and of the Papists, and these troubled our Church mightily... " (A Sermon Preached at Paules Crosse: 43-44).

[29] We also find the same fear in the pamphlets: "They [the Spaniards] hope perhaps to have, some helpe within this Ile" (An Exhortation: 1).

The war against Spain is interpreted as a religious duty any good Englishman had to fulfil out of piety and charity and any political or economic interest is carefully silenced:

> If the cause bee Gods, if the quarrell bee necessary, if thy calling suteable, if it bee a crosse that God layeth upon thee in a matter of faith and trueth, and requisite offices appertayning to pietie and charity, though it be a vale of daungers, Loe, David professeth he cannot, he will not yeelde, he will not feare, much less dispaire, and houer a loofe, or let all alone as men amazed and astonished in their feminine affections. (*The Consolations of David*: A6)

But this feeling of religious and moral obligation is generally mixed up with some anxiety about the superiority of the enemy, as the sermons after the Armada invasion also project the sense of menace present in the country when a second invasion was still possible:

> Although the Lorde in great mercie hath sowne our land both with men and cattle, he hath taught our handes to warre and our fingers to fight: he hath not bene to us an heath or a drie unfruitfull grounde, but hath blessed us plentifully with all things necessarie for our defence and the withstanding of our enemies. *Yet suppose that it were not so. Let it be that wee were but fewe and our adversaries many in number*, should that dismay us which professe the trueth? God forbid. (*A Sermon Preached at Brocket Hall*: B5) (my italics)[30]

England's weakness is partly made responsible for the introduction of some Catholic agents in the country with seriously destructive consequences. Although, once again, it is God's direct intervention through the war which has saved the nation from Spain and Rome, Prime implicitly condemns England's passivity and recklessness as she was unable to prevent such actions:

> Yet because this world is not the land of entire blessedness, euerlastingly to endure, sundry uncleane beasts haue entered, with ful entendment to staine the greene and fertle pastures wherein God hath placed her, and had done so (so it might haue beene) if God and his Christ, the great sheepehearde of our soules had not exerted his arme… (*The Consolations of David*: B3).

---

[30] The pamphleteer T. Tymme points out the same problem: "Let us altogether Ioyne handes as brethren against those abominable idolaters… who trust in their multitude, and presume altogether upon their strength: whereas the race doth no alwayes belong to the swift, nor the battaile to the strong" (B2).

This is the reason why, in general, all orators insist on the need to be cautious, never trusting a temporary victory over the Armada since the real war has no been won yet. In this regard, John Prime encourages his listeners not to be excessively optimistic and to get ready for future dangers: "And this is true wisedom indeede, in fa[ir?] weather to prouide for a tempest, in health to thinke of sicknesse, in prosperitye, peace and quietnesse, to forecast the worst, and with the wise Emite in sommer to lay up for the winter following" (A5).

Once the position of the English had been settled as the inferior party – at least discursively-, the preachers try to neutralise this fear by interpreting Spain's power in terms of pride and useless vainglory. Such superiority is presented as a mere lie, a false image the Spaniards tried to show but will finally be unable to maintain: "And so it fareth euer; when men comparingly set out themselues as Giantes, in theyr own conceites, though it be in causes of best account. Yet in the ende they come shorte of theyr reckoning" (*The Consolations of David*: A7).[31] The multiple references to biblical figures who, though apparently weaker and powerless, could vanquish their enemy thanks to God's help also work on this same line. David, the Old Testament King, is most frequently alluded to since his constancy and trust in God are shown as a model for English subjects to follow:

---

[31] Contemporary and later pamphlets and plays also portrayed the character of the Spaniard as arrogant and presumptuous, often comparing it with the peacock: "Signior being in the street, or any other publicke place his first gestures, are to bend the head, turne the eye, and peacock-like to behold himselfe if nothing be amisse" (H. W., *A Pageant of Spanish Humours wherin are Naturally Described and Lively Portrayed the Kinds and Quallities of a Signior of Spain* [London, 1599], B1). The Spaniard's attempt to show a strong appearance was seen as a way to hide his internal weakness: "[his] discourse is like to the Cipress tree, which being great and high bringeth foorth no fruite" (Robert Ashley, *A Comparison of the English and Spanish Nations Composed by a French Gentleman* [London, 1589], 25), an attitude which proves his absurd vanity and cowardice: "In a place of garrison, where nothing is to be done but bragging and domineering, then turn aloose, he will play his part, he esteems his skil, far to surpasse all others, but no sooner doth he heare the thundring rumor of *Los Enemigos*, or see them plant their Tents and standards with any advantage, before his residence, he is in a moment wholly metaphosed, his heart shrinkes like a peece of wet leather by the fire, all his Lyon like courage banished like smoake, for that from a Lyon he becomes a Hare, yet he will seeme to cloake it" (*A Pageant of Spanish Humours*, B2). Such a ridiculous description is frequent on stage or in the pamphlets, but it is less recurrent in the sermons, which may allude to such alleged vices of the enemy, but normally avoid any mocking references that could be considered improper for their context of deliverance.

In the 1.Sam.17. there was a notable combate towarde betweene Dauid and Goliath;... Goliath was a man of great stature, David but a little one; Goliath was was grimme and rough, David ruddie and tender; Goliah had armour and bootes of brasse, David could not bear any; Goliath was armed with a mightie shield and a speare like a Weauers beame, David had nothing but a sling and a stone and the brooke in it. When Saule sawe this unequalnesse in the match, he goeth about to withdrawe David from the combate, as one that in his iudgement was sure to fall before his enemie. David with an inuincible courage aunswereth againe in the presence of the King to prooue that the Lord would fight for him and give him the uictorie over his aduersarie... So in like manner... the triall which we haue had heretofore of Gods delivering of us from these and such like enemies ought to be so many assurances to all them that feare God, that the Lord will now also deliver us and destroy them... (*A Sermon Preached at Brocket Hall*: C1-C2)

Elizabeth's deliverance from Catholic dangers is, in fact, interpreted in the same providential way, which explains her comparison with this biblical king: "...God maketh it manifest to all the worlde, that himselfe was with her in all these tempests, and then the plat-forme was broken up, and the snare taken away, and a daughter of David had as great deliueraunces as euer David ...had..." (*The Consolations of David*: B3). These similes were not a novelty though, and these preachers were just siding with a traditional discourse that used to associate the different Tudor monarchs with Old Testament figures:

[David, the most relevant one,] serves primarily as a type for Henry VIII's claim to combine priestly with regal functions. David's image is particularly useful in portraying Henry as the intermediary between Heaven and Earth, because the Hebrew king was regarded by Christians as a prototype of the Messiah and thus as a salvatory symbol of the link between God and humanity... The iconographical conflict between ecclesiastical and secular power is resolved by conferring upon Henry VIII the Davidic and Christlike majesty associated with emperors during the Middle Ages.[32]

This same idea can be applied to Elizabeth, who is, therefore, shown as the inheritor of her father's imperial project. Her appeal to self-government and her rejection of any possible submission to Papal or Spanish rule are part of the Tudor imperial program begun by Henry VIII and developed under her brother Edward: "Happy did England thinke it selfe in the dayes of king Henry hir noble father: happy did it think itselfe

---

[32] John King, Tudor Royal Iconography. Literature and Art in an Age of Religious Crisis. Princeton: Princeton U.P., 1989, 59-60.

in the dayes of king Edward her godly brother: but yet neuer could it
repute it selfe so happy as it hath bene during the raigne of victorious
Queene Elyzabeth" (*A Sermon Preached on the Queenes Day*: C1).[33] By
alluding to Elizabeth's Protestant inheritance, the preachers try to silence
the still current attacks on her legitimacy by English Catholics, a question
which did not seem to be completely resolved and kept provoking some
anxiety among leading Protestants:

> These were the Councellers and Nobilitie of this Realme, in the dayes of
> Queene Mary her sister, who albeit they were the sworne assisters of the
> rightfull heire apparant to the Crown of this land: yea, and albeit they
> knewe by succession to be heires, and that not by extraordinarie
> annoynting as the kingdome of Israel came to David, but by naturall
> discent from her Father, and confirmed by the last will and testament of
> her Father of famous memorie king Henrie the eight, yet contrarie to law,
> contrarie to their oth, and contrarie unto conscience they refused her... (*A
> Sermon Preached on the Queenes Day*: B2)

However, these doubts are replaced by recurrent allusions to the
alleged tyranny and Catholic oppression under the Marian period. The
contrast between both sisters marks the autonomous nature of the
Elizabethan system and portrays the current queen as a new Astraea who
has brought back the Golden Age to the English country:

> ... Queen Mary left it [England] uexed with the insolence of the Spanish
> nation whom she brought in. Queene Elizabeth hath eased it, Mary left it in
> warre, Elizabeth hath gouerned it in peace: Mary left it in debt, Elizabeth
> hath discharged it: Mary left it in povertie, Elizabeth hath enriched it:

---

[33] Once again, the preachers echo the arguments that used to appear in
contemporary pamphlets, which, however, seemed to be more precise and
emphatic in this regard. William Chauncie, for example, uses a more demanding
tone in his pamphlet *The Rooting out of the Romishe Supremacie* (1580): "The
Noble Prince therfore, King Henry the eight, seeing and considering these
detestable enormities, and wicked usurpation of the Pope of Rome, did utterly
banish his counterfeit authority out of this realme of England... Which having him
selfe begun in part to doe, he had it confirmed with the consent of the whole
realme. . . to the great comfort of all his faithful subiectes, to the reviving of the
dignitie of his imperiall crowne, and most of all to the true honour and glory of the
Almightie. After this noble King, there succeede the godly worthie Prince his
sonne, King Edward... And of Late again (albeit) some interruption grewe in the
time of Queene Marie, Our Most vertuous and gratious Soveriegne, Queen
Elizabeth, following the godly steps of her noble father and brother, had it einacted
in her first parliament of the Bishoppe of Rome, and of all other foraine power, and
potentates, spiritual and temporall, should utterly be driven away" (127-128).

Mary left it weake, Elizabeth hath strengthened it... Mary banished true religion, Elizabeth hath restored it: Mary persecuted it, Elizabeth hath defended it: Mary cast it downe, Elizabeth hath aduanced it... (B8-C1)[34]

According to these preachers, it is her defence of the Protestant Church what ensures God's protection for her and her people and what makes her a vehicle through which God will favour England: "... hee that seeth not the finger of God to haue bene, and to be with Queen Elizabeth, seeth nothing and the brightnes of God shining upon her, and by her upon us, dooth dazell his sight, that he cannot see" (*The Consolations of David*: B4). The orators underline the close identification between Elizabeth and her subjects, both forming an interdependent unit never to be divided: "... it standeth us upon, which are the subiectes of this Common wealth to pray for the safety and prosperity of our Queene Elizabeth: for in the safety of Elizabeth consisteth ours: in her peace, ours, in her prosperity, ours: in her life, ours: in her death, ours: in her destruction, ours" (*A Sermon Preached on the Queenes Day*: D4). The war with Spain is interpreted as a providential sign which shows God's revenge on those who disobey him so England becomes a divine instrument to destroy the Pope, Spain and their supporters: "... if wee continue to hate her [the Whore of Babylon: Rome] still with all her whorish tromperies and superstitions, we shall be the meanes of the Lord to make her utterly desolate, by overthrowing these her onely defendants..." (*A Sermon Preached at Brocket Hall*: A8).[35] It is God who is acting against the

---

[34] The pamphlet literature of these years abounds in these images that evoke Elizabeth's restoration of the Golden Age – "let us from this hell of miseries cast backe our eyes uppon that heaven of blissefulnesse which wee doe enjoy at home, under the fortunate and happy government of our most excellent and incomparable soveraigne, there we shall finde an other estate of matters, all things flowing in plenty, peace, comfort, quietness, pleasure, and tranquilitie" (Lewis Lewkenor, *The Estate of the English Fugitives* [London, 1596], 121)– and compares the English country to a second Eden: "Peace and plentie flourishe in England. . . the Gospel of our saviour Christ is frankly freely and truly not only preached, but lovinglye imbraced by the Queene and her Subiectes. Saying then we are every way best and favoured from above: that the Lorde our mercifull God maketh England the Eden, a second paradise" (Robert Greene, *The Spanish Masquerado* [London, 1589], E4).

[35] The thanksgiving prayer appointed to be delivered in the churches soon after the defeat of the Armada went beyond and adopted a much more self-critical attitude towards the English nation. The Spanish invasion is interpreted as God's punishment for England's sins –"We cannot but confess, O Lord God, that the late terrible intended invasion of most cruel enemies was sent from thee, to the punishment of our sins, our pride, our covetousness, our excess in meat and drink,

Spaniards, not the English. Violence is justified as the result of the divine wrath against the unfaithful, who would be now punished for their sins:

> For it is notably knowne how much innocent blood the Pope our chiefe aduersarie, and his Lieutenant the Catholique King haue shed in Christendome... What then remaineth but that the Lorde now repay them againe, according to all that they haue done to his Saincts and children, and that the worde of the almightie be fulfilled on them, which saith, that he will make his arrowes dronke with their blood: which kinde of speech (beside other thinges) would not bee lightly ouerpassed by us, considering the bowe and the arrowe are weapons of defence, wherewith the Lorde hath armed our nation aboue the rest. (*A Sermon Preached at Brocket Hall*: A6-A7).

Nonetheless, such a violent and aggressive discourse could be partly problematic as it may contradict one of the main elements that conformed with the traditional description of Protestant England and Elizabeth as persecuted by oppressive Catholic forces: "When a Spanish Prince and an Italian Priest ruled England, when superstition, humane devises, will-worshippinges, and grosse idolatrie in a strange toung overruled al, then were our goods spoiled, our flesh martyred, our bodies burnt, and our ashes scattered, and our very soules sterved" (*The Consolations of David*: B5). The bloody references used previously to describe the English means against the enemy could affect and question such victimised depiction since they could underline its artificial basis. Some of the preachers, in fact, seem to be aware of the constructive nature of the Protestant discourse and unsuccessfully try to justify their position:

> Some will say peraduenture: why, the Papistes also and our enemies say as much for themselues, they boast how they are the Church of Christ, and Popedome Christes kingdome, wherefore nothing letteth but that this may serue their turnes as well as ours. The aunswer is easie (deerely beloued) Papistes are not of Christes kingdome. The reason is manifest, Christes kingdome is appoynted to subdue as al other, so the Romaine Monarchie

---

our security, our ingratitude, and our unthankfulness towards thee for so long peace, and other infinite blessings continually poured upon us" (John Strype (Ed.), *Annals of the Reformation and Establishment of Religion and other Various Occurrences in the Church of England during Queen Elizabeth's Happy Reign*, Vol. iii, part ii, New York: Burt Franklin, 1824, 28)– and the English victory as an opportunity offered them by God to mend their lives: ". . . O Heavenly Father, in thy justice to remember thy mercy towards us; turning our enemies from us, and that dreadful execution which they intended towards us, into a fatherly and most merciful admonition of us, to the amendment of our lives" (29).

and Empire whether the beast or image of the beast. (*A Sermon Preached at Brocket Hall*: B7)

Their arguments are taken from the same discourse they are trying to criticise, so they do not add any clear light on the problem and keep, instead, such doubts alive for more sceptical readers or listeners. Those contradictions are silenced and the audience can witness both opposite descriptions of Protestant England (as strong and aggressive on one hand, and persecuted on the other) used simultaneously to inspire strength to the English people and confirm their elected nature, an image which had already become a commonplace thanks to John Foxe's *Acts and Monuments* (1563).[36]

The preachers were just referring to a standardised image English Protestants had learned to identify with; this portrayal presented a binary description of both parties responding to the apocalyptic rhetoric that confronted the True Church of Christ with the False Church of Rome. In one of the sermons analysed, Edmund Harris makes use of traditional figures of the *Book of Revelation* –Gog, Magog (*A Sermon Preached at Brocket Hall*: B3), and the Whore of Babylon (A8)- to mark the ungodly nature of the Spanish and Catholic powers and prognosticates their final destructions, as happens in the biblical text:

> Ye see now we are come (deerely beloued) unto our owne time. The Gospell which lay hidde as it were till the yeere 1367 than began to shine foorth againe by the preaching of Wickleife, since that time which is but a shorte space in comparison the professors of the Gospell haue bene persecuted: now Gog and Magog make warre against the true professors of Christianitie... *We see then who are Gog and Magog, as also that our enemies which warre against us, that is to say, the Italians and the Spaniardes are a parte of them... Wherby is meant either that God will plague, punish and destroy them with most terrible iudgements from heaven...* (*A Sermon Preached at Brocket Hall*: B2-B3) (my italics)

The justification of violence is complemented by the references to Solomon, another Old Testament king who also remained as a model of royal behaviour for Tudor monarchs. Thomas White, for example, associates Elizabeth with him in order to emphasize the age of plenty and abundance she represents: "For *Salomons* Plentie who *gave Silver as stones in the streets of Hierusalem*, 2.Cron.1.15. I will not now compare England with Egypt, or with Canaan, but with England: *Elizabeth* with

---

[36] A hagiographic history of the English Church which soon became the most important work for English Protestantism together with the Bible.

Marie for Corn, with *Edward* for Coine, and with *Henrie* for quietnes..."
(*A Sermon Preached at Paules Crosse*: 53). John King explains how
Solomon prefigured the Queen's wisdom and wealth: "just as Solomon
prefigures Christ as a Prince of Peace, Elizabeth governs as a Christlike
Queen... The peacefulness of these godly monarchs results from the
restraint of power that can be always exercised in just warfare".[37] This last
point is extremely important since the struggle with Spain is always
presented as a defensive war in which Elizabeth must protect England and
Protestantism from foreign attacks –"for seeing they doe not come out
against our Soueraigne and against our Countrie for any Euill that they
have founde in them, but onely rise up to persecute us and to seeke our
soules for professing the trueth" (*A Sermon Preached at Brocket Hall*:
B4)–, the only means to restore peace and safety in the nation: "And unto
Tyrants warre is a felicitie, but unto good and *Christian Princes* a verie
necessitie: whose warres are nothing els, but the seeking of safetie and
peace*" (A Sermon Preached at Paules Crosse*: 59).[38]

Besides, this allusion could be reinterpreted as a possible criticism
against the queen for having reacted too late to the Catholic threat and as a
demand for a much stricter anti-Catholic policy. According to the texts,
the only possible way out is "an unfayned repentaunce, and a generall
conuersion, and certaine determination of the whole land to serue him
better than in former times" (*The Consolations of David*: B5-B6).
Although the words are addressed to the English subjects, the queen's
commitment with ensuring such a general repentance is essential since she
is the only one who, as God's deputy, could enforce it. The term
"unfayned" is not arbitrary either and seems to hide a certain criticism
against a general practice favoured by the queen, who allowed English
Catholics to convert externally to Protestantism and take the Oath of
Allegiance, while they continued observing the Catholic precepts in
private. Such a measure is discouraged and Elizabeth's attitude is
presented as insufficient and finally pernicious, as it promoted falseness
and secrecy in matters of religion.

Her comparison with Josiah and Hezekiah (A *Sermon Preaches at
Paules Crosse*: 54-57), both models of "purifying iconoclastically purging

---

[37] See John King, *Tudor Royal Iconography*, 256-7.
[38] We find a similar argument in contemporary pamphlets. Lewis Lewkenor, for
instance, describes Elizabeth's wars as "just, charitable and defensive" (121). In
this sense, a political and economic war is transformed into a religious crusade in
the discursive level.

monarchs"[39] could also be used by the authors to remind the queen of her duty towards the Reformed Religion, acknowledging the dangers that such a "tolerant" attitude could provoke. The fact that both Henry VIII and Edward VI had been compared to these two Old Testament figures during their reigns emphasises Elizabeth's need to continue the same Protestant line developed by her father and brother.

As a conclusion, the process of politicisation of the English Protestant sermon increased during the 1580s and 1590s and would reach its climax throughout the following century. The use of the Scriptures in order to justify the royal supremacy had been a constant feature in sermon literature from Henry VIII onwards, but as the century advanced, Protestant preachers began to take advantage of the pulpit and the press to spread their demands against religious toleration for Catholics. These, together with Spain, were portrayed as political instruments of the two main threats in contemporary Anglican imagination: the Pope and the Jesuits. Both powers were vilified and made responsible for the lack of safety and stability in the English country, a feeling which was projected not only in the homiletic literature of the period, but also in pamphlets and on the stage.

The growing prominence of certain radical groups who demanded much deeper reforms and questioned England's religious *status quo* contributed to the general state of confusion and disorder. No doubt the sermon genre was effectively used by these subversive sectors in the opposite direction, to provoke the government and increase the national crisis. The sermon, as the pamphlet, became then a useful instrument to participate in contemporary political and religious debate by criticising the current situation and proposing new lines of action, which can explain Elizabeth's dislike of such literature.

But Anglican and Puritan sermons seemed to agree in one basic thing: their resentful attitude towards Catholicism. Thus, this literature not only praised and eulogised the Head of the Church, but used such commendation to ask, and indirectly, press her to abandon any neutral attitude and take hold of the Protestant banner in England and Europe. The proposals could only put Elizabeth in a difficult position. The anti-Catholic or anti-Spanish discourses could arouse xenophobic feelings and to some extent, may have promoted some union among English Protestants, but were mainly used as vehicles to attack some royal measures as inefficient against the papal threat. Both the "Catholic" and

---

[39] Margaret Aston, *The King's Bedpost. Reformation and Iconography in a Tudor Group Portrait.* Cambridge: C.U.P., 1993, 113.

the "Spaniard" were exposed as scapegoats of Elizabeth's alleged mistakes.

Works Cited

Primary Sources

Anon. *An Exhortacion to all English Subiects, to Ioine for the Defence of Queene Elizabeth and their Native Country*. London, 1588.

Ashley, Robert. *A Comparison of the English and Spanish Nations Composed by a French Gentleman*. London, 1589.

Chauncie, William. *The Rooting out of the Romishe Supremacie*. London.

Colfe, Isaac. 1588. *A Sermon Preached on the Queenes Day Being the 17 November 1587 at the Towne of Lidd in Kent*. London, 1580.

Foxe, John. *Acts and Monumentes of the Church*. London, 1563.

Green, Robert. *The Spanish Masquerado*. London, 1589.

Harris, Edmond. *A Sermon Preached at Brocket Hall, Before the Right Worshipfull, Sir John Brocket, and other Gentlemen There Assembled for the Trayning of Souldiers*. London,1588.

H., W. *A Pageant of Spanish Humours wherin are Naturally Described and Lively Portrayed the Kinds and Quallities of a Signior of Spain*. London, 1599.

Lewkenor, Lewis. *The Estate of the English Fugitives*. London, 1596.

Perkins, William. *The Arte of Prophecying: A Treatise Concerning the Sacred and Onley True Manner and Methode of Preaching*. 1592. Trans. Thomas Tuke. London, 1607.

Prime, John. *The Consolations of David Breefly Applied to Queen Elizabeth: in a Sermon Preached in Oxford the 17th of November*. Oxford, 1588.

Tymme, Thomas. *A Preparation against the Prognosticated Dangers of this Yeare*. London 1588.

White, Thomas. *Sermon Preached at Paules Crosse the 17 of November An. 1589 in Ioyfull Remembrance and Thanksgiving unto God, for the Peaceable Yeres of her Maiesties Most Gratious Raigne over us, now 32*. London, 1589.

Secondary Sources

Aston, Margaret. *The King's Bedpost. Reformation and Iconography in a Tudor Group Portrait*. Cambridge: Cambridge University Press,1993.

Bossy, John. *The English Catholic Community 1570-1850*. New York: Oxford University Press,1976.

Cardwell, Edward. Ed. *Documentary Annals of the Reformed Church of England*. 2 Vols. Oxford: OUP,1842-4.

Carlson, Eric Josef. "The Boring of the Ear: Shaping the Pastoral Vision of Preaching in England, 1540-1640". In *Preachers and People in the Reformation, and Early Modern Period*. Ed. Larissa Taylor. Leida: Brill, 2001.

Cornmack, Lesley B. "Britannia Rules the Waves?: Images of Empire in Elizabethan England." *Early Modern Literary Studies* 4.2 (1998): 1-20.

Daly, Peter M. (Ed.). *Andreas Alciatus. Emblems in Translation*. Vol. ii. Toronto: University of Toronto Press, 1985.

Dolan, Frances E. *Whores of Babylon. Catholicism, Gender and Seventeenth Century Print Culture*. Ithaca: Cornell University Press, 1999.

Fraser Mitchell, M. A. Ed. *English Pulpit Oratory from Andrewes to Tillotson. A Study of its Literary Aspects*. New York: Russell & Russell, 1962.

Hughes, Paul L, and James F. Larkin. Eds. *Tudor Royal Proclamations*. Vol. ii. *The Late Tudors (1553-1587)*. New Haven & London: Yale University Press, 1969.

King, John N. *Tudor Royal Iconography. Literature and Art in an Age of Religious Crisis*. Princeton: Princeton University Press, 1989.

Lake, Peter, and Michael Questier. *The Antichrist's Lewd Hat. Protestants, Papists and Players in Post-Reformation England*. New Have: Yale University Press, 2002.

Lock, Julian. Prime, John (1549/50-1596). *Oxford Dictionary of National Biography*. Eds. H. C. G. Matthew and Brian Harrison. Oxford: OUP, 2004http:/www.oxforddnb.com.fama.us.es:80/view/article/22792.

McCullough, Peter. *Sermons at Court. Politics and Religion in Elizabethan and Jacobean Preaching*. Cambridge: Cambridge University Press, 1998.

Maclure, Miller. Ed. *Register of Sermons Preached at Paul's Cross 1534-1642*. Ottawa: Dovehouse, 1989.

Strong, Roy. *The Cult of Elizabeth*. London: Thames and Hudson, 1977.

Strype, John. Ed. *Annals of the Reformation and Establishment of Religion and other Various Occurrences in the Church of England during Queen Elizabeth's Happy Reign*. Vol. iii, part ii. New York: Burt Franklin, 1824.

Taylor, Larissa. Preachers and People in the Reformations and Early Modern Period. Leiden: Brill, 2001.

Wabuda, Susan. *Preaching during the English Reformation*. Cambridge: CUP, 2002.

Wright, Stephen.   Colfe, Isaac (1558/9-1597). *Oxford Dictionary of National Biography*. 2004-2005. Eds. H. C. G. Matthew and Brian Harrison Oxford: OUP, 2004.
    http:/www.oxforddnb.com.fama.us.es:80/view/article/5901.

White, Thomas (1550-1624). *Oxford Dictionary of National Biography*. 2004-2005. Eds. H. C. G. Matthew and Brian Harrison Oxford: OUP, 2004.
    http:/www.oxforddnb.com.fama.us.es:80/view/article/29273.

Yates, Frances A. *Astraea. The Imperial Theme in the Sixteenth Century*. London, Boston: Routledge, Kegan Paul, 1975.

CHAPTER FOUR

"*BELLUM SYMBOLUM MALI*": WAR & PEACE IN JOHN DONNE'S SERMONS OR THE STUDY OF A CONTEST

MARIE-CHRISTINE MUNOZ

Born in a family persecuted for its Catholic beliefs, to the extent of martyrdom with the execution of his uncle Thomas More in 1535, Donne apparently made the choice of religious conformity in 1615 when he became Deacon, Royal Chaplain and was made doctor in Divinity from Cambridge University. He then served the Church as Reader in Divinity at Lincoln's Inn till he was appointed Dean of St Paul's Cathedral in 1621. His religious position was clearly stated in his 1610 text entitled *Pseudo-Martyr : Wherein out of the Certaine Propositions and Gradations This Conclusion is Evicted, That Those Which Are of the Romane Religion in This Kingdome May and Ought to Take the Oath of Allegeance* (London : W. Burre, 1610), a text that caught the attention of James I and helped advance his favour at Court. In the pulpit Donne was particularly adamant that his freedom to write sermons according to his inspiration should be preserved and he refused to use the Elizabethan *Book of Homilies* (1547, rev. 1559, 1563) as a restrictive basis for his work: "God hath delivered us in a great measure... from this penury in preaching, we need not preach other Sermons, nor feed upon cold meat, in Homilies" (3:338). Therefore he might have cringed before the requirement that was made of him by James I in 1622 to justify a text entitled *Directions for Preachers*, intended to define and control the dogmatic content of sermons:

In future preachers were to confine themselves to topics covered by the Thirty-Nine Articles and the Book of Homilies, and Sunday afternoons were to be devoted to catechizing instead of to preaching. No one under the degree of bishop or dean was to 'preach in any popular auditory the deep points of Predestination, Election, Reprobation, or of the universality, efficacy, resistibility of God's grace'; no preacher of any rank was to 'meddle with matters of state and the differences between prince and people', and there was to be an end to 'railing against either papists or puritans'.[1]

On 15 September 1622 he preached on this text his first and longest sermon to be published under the title "A Sermon upon the XX. verse of the V. Chapter of the Booke of Iudges. Wherein occasion was justly [p.133] taken for the Publication of some Reasons, which his Sacred Majestie had been pleased to give, of those Directions for Preachers, which hee had formerly sent foorth". This sermon confirmed Donne's "readiness to uphold the royal policy and prerogative"[2], provided his own poetic freedom as a preacher was not too much hindered.

Though he probably witnessed the fall of Cadiz in 1596, when he joined the naval expedition of Robert Devereux, second Earl of Essex, Donne did not seem to develop an interest for warfare as a topic for preaching once he was appointed Dean of St Paul's. One may wonder why he never actually preached war sermons when his country was involved in the conflicts that divided the European kingdoms of his time. After the London Treaty of 1604 signalling the end of the war with Spain, Stuart England became involved in the Thirty Years' War when James's son in law was defeated at the Battle of the White Mountain in 1620, expelled from the throne of Bohemia to which he had been elected by the Protestant rebels of the Emperor, and then hounded from his homeland, the Palatinate, by Catholic troops. The king was expected to defend the cause of Protestantism in Europe. James thought it was essential to exercise control over the pulpit by checking his preachers when they tackled matters of state in their sermons. Though John Donne was adamant to maintain his theological freedom by enlarging the scope of his preaching beyond the limits of the prescribed Homilies, his position as a preacher of the Church of England had a political bearing on the references made to the foreign affairs of the kingdom, particularly when there were armed conflicts involved. John Donne's sermons always testified to a deep loyalty to his sovereign, be it James I or his successor Charles I. They repeatedly paid homage to the monarch by praising his ability to ensure peace in the kingdom as should any legitimate and competent ruler: "[…] As all we owe to God an acknowledgement of blessednesse, that we are born in a Christian Church, in a Reformed Church, in a Monarchy, in a Monarchy composed of Monarchies, and in the time of such a Monarch, as

---

[1] R. C. Bald, *John Donne: A Life*, Oxford: Clarendon Press, 1970, 433-34.
[2] *The Sermons of John Donne*, ed. George R. Potter & Evelyn M. Simpson, 10 vols, University of California Press: Berkeley & Los Angeles, 1953, 109.

is a Peace-maker, and a peace-preserver both at home and abroad."[3] Such political conformity had its limits for the extant body of sermons testifies to the fact that John Donne never wrote or preached war sermons as such. His interest lied primarily in the metaphoric reference to the theme of war as the embodiment of divine punishment against sin.

The multifarious faces of war and peace in Donne's sermons

In many of his sermons preached between 1615 and 1635 John Donne highlighted the ongoing contest between war and peace, using as scriptural references the several wars depicted in the Old Testament. He particularly drew from the prophetic books where Isaiah (13:34) or Ezechiel (38-39) for instance depicted war as the final contest between good and evil announcing the coming of a messianic figure. He thereby emphasized the terrifying nature of warfare as a deadly process, and dwelled on the theological dimension of the threat of war made to David interpreting it as the expression of God's scourge intended for sinful men:

> Now as the maledictions which were threatened to *David*, were presented to him by the Prophet in three formes, of warre, of famine, of pestilence ; so these blessings which are comprized in those three verses, may well be reduced to three things contrary to those three maledictions ; To the blessing of peace, contrary to *Davids* warre, *That there may be no invasion* ; To the blessing of plenty, contrary to *Davids* famine, *That our barnes may abound with all sorts of Corne* ; To the blessing of health, contrary to *David's* destroying sicknesse, *That our sonnes may grow up as plants in their youth.*[4]

War, famine and pestilence represented in scriptural terms the traditional series of plagues manifesting God's retributive justice as the expression of his holy wrath.

Relying on conventional representations of warfare, the evocation of war by the Holy Ghost, recalled by Donne in a later sermon upon 1 Cor 15.26, harped on the tremendous devastations of war and the impending human casualties:

---

[3] Vol. 3, Sermon 2, Preached at White-Hall, the 30. April 1620, Psal. 144.15. Being the first psalm for the day. "Blessed are the people that be so; yea blessed are the people, whose God is the Lord.", 8.

[4] *Ibid.*, 9.

And therefore the holy Ghost to intimate to us, that happy perfectnesse, which wee shall have at last, and not till then, chooses the Metaphor of an enemy, an enmity, to avert us from looking for true peace from any thing that presents it self in the way. Neither truly could the Holy Ghost imprint more horror by any word, then that which intimates war, as the word *enemy* does.[5]

The emotional bearing of such an evocation on the congregation must have been all the more powerful as Donne's contemporaries very probably heard in this description echoes of the dreadful fate of Troy, the universal archetype of the utter destruction of a civilization as a consequence of the devastating effects of war. The recollection of the words of the prophet Isaiah reinforced the radical interpretation of war as a social cataclysm causing the extermination of endless generations and even inducing the barrenness of the « wounded earth »:

But, when the Prophet *Isaiah* comes to the devastation, to the extermination of a war, he expresses it first thus ; *Where there were a thousand Vineyards at a cheape rate, all the land [shall] become briars and thornes* : That is much ; but there is more, *The earth shall be removed out of her place : that Land, that Nation, shall no more be called that Nation, nor that Land* : But, yet more then that too ; Not [p.6] onely, not that people, but no other shall ever inhabit it. *It shall never be inhabited from generation to generation, neither shall Shepheards be there*; Not onely no Merchant, nor Husbandman, but no depopulator: *none but Owles, and Ostriches, and Satyres,* […].[6]

The purpose of the preacher must have been to convey the idea that the prospect of a war, according to Scriptures, was of a terrifying nature for it would preclude all posterity for a civilization. Donne intended to conjure up an apocalyptic vision of the human predicament in times of war, from an anthropological standpoint. Not only was the trial of war to be withstood as a punishment for sin, it may in turn prove the very cause of sin by compelling individuals to commit acts of transgression out of sheer despair :

In a word, the horror of War is best discerned in the company he keeps, in his associates. And when the Prophet *Gad* brought *War* into the presence of *David*, there came with him *Famine*, and *Pestilence*. And when Famine entred, we see the effects ; It brought Mothers to eat their Children of a

---

[5] Vol.4. Preached at White-Hall, March 8 1621 [1621-1622], 1 Cor. 15.26: "The last enemie that shall be destroyed is death", 5.
[6] *Ibid.*, 5-6.

span long ; that is, as some Expositors take it, to take medicines to procure abortions, to cast their Children that they might have Children to eate.[7]

The terrifying prospects of cannibalism and infanticide were held against the sinners since they might turn into the very instrument of the complete destruction of their own breed.

These few examples of the depiction of the plague of war relied highly on the contrastive effect established when pitching the epitome of horror against what could not be anything but the acme of bliss, that is to say peace. The representations of the horrors of war according to the biblical paradigm, as shaped in these sermons, were intended to exacerbate the fears of the congregation and heighten the contrast with the bliss of godly peace. The purpose of the preacher was definitely prophylactic so that his flock would not yield to the manifold temptations of sin. Most of the time such a concern was coupled with an unrelenting interest in the rhetorical pattern used in the scriptural text, that was then regarded by the preacher as an archetype best suited to his own pastoral aim. Hence his repeated comments on the merits of metaphorical translations or contrastive approaches. With the customary acumen of a great poet, Donne commented in his sermon on 1 Cor. 15.26, preached before King James at Whitehall during Lent, in 1621, after his appointment as Dean of St Paul's, upon the appropriateness of the metaphoric choice made by the Holy Ghost in order to translate the abstract notion of evil into the familiar image of warfare: "[...] and enemie is the Metaphore which the holy Ghost hath taken here to express a want, a kind of imperfectnesse even in Heaven it selfe. *Bellum Symbolum Mali*. As peace is of all goodnesse, so warre is an emblem, a Hieroglyphique, of all misery."[8] He praised the accuracy of the device used in the biblical text for this metaphor translated into iconic terms ("emblem", "hieroglyphique") an unfathomable notion, so that thanks to the visual impression of the rendering it became easier for the audience to grasp the full meaning of the concept. The preacher consequently emphasized the importance of the commentary intended to provide an interpretation of the cryptic nature of the concept itself.

Similarly in his sermon about Psalm 144.15 Donne used a contrastive approach in order to weigh the merits of peace and war. War was vividly presented in contrast to « the blessing of peace » as a hideous and monstrous prospect, referring both to examples from the recent history of England and from the Biblical wars of the Old Testament. Such archetypes spoke of war in a very realistic manner, relying on historical accounts, by

---

[7] *Ibid.*, 6.
[8] *Ibid.*, 4.

showing that it could be the source of destruction of the nobility of a country:

> For the first temporall blessing of peace, we may consider the lovelinesse, the amiablenesse of that, if we looke upon the horror and gastlinesse of warre : either in *Effigie*, in that picture of warre which is drawn in every leafe of our own Chronicles, in the blood of so many Princes, and noble families, or if we look upon warre it selfe, at that distance where it cannot hurt us, as God had formerly kindled it amongst our neighbours, and as he hath transferred it now to remoter Nations, whilest we enjoy yet a Goshen in the midst of all those Egypts.[9]

Still using the same contrastive device so evocative of the idea of a contest, Donne pitched the devotees of war against the upholders of peace:

> [...] In all Kingdomes that border upon other Kingdomes, and in Islands which have no other border but the Sea, particular men, who by dwelling in those skirts and borders may make their profit of spoile, delight in hostility, and have an adversenesse and detestation of peace : but it is not so within : they who till the earth, and breed up cattell, and imploy their industry upon Gods creatures, according to Gods ordinance, feele the benefit and apprehend the sweetnesse, and pray for the continuance of peace.[10]

Those who benefited from warfare were labelled as parasites and sinners whereas the meek shepherds or countrymen who laboured devoutly were praised for their ability to cherish peace. The preacher's standpoint very explicitly condemned the upholders of war as sinful creatures standing on the Devil's side against the devout labourers. According to Donne's reading of the Scriptures, the correlative of peace in the Ancient Testament was prosperity, for the rightful could count abundance of worldly goods among their blessings: "This is the blessing, in which God so very very often expresses his gracious purpose upon his people, that he would give them peace; and peace with plenty; *O that my people had hearkned unto me !*, sayes God, *I would soone have humbled their enemies*, (there is their peace)". This was recognized as the *manna* of God, his reward: "*And I would have fed them with the fat of wheat, and with* [p.10] *the honey out of the Rocke*, and there is their plenty."[11] Obviously this reference to the nurturing figure of God could be

---

[9] Vol.3. Preached at White-Hall, the 30. April 1620, Psalm 144.15 "Blessed are the people that be so; yea blessed are the people, whose God is the Lord.", 9.
[10] *idem.*
[11] *idem.*

understood from a metaphoric standpoint as a reference to the notion of grace so debated after the proceedings of the synod of Dort.[12] The spectrum of metaphoric renderings of the understanding of peace in Donne's sermons also encompassed allusions to the field of architecture that recalled the type of organicist metaphor of the state so familiar to the Elizabethans and Jacobeans, as shown in Donne's sermon on 1 Cor 15.26, with the reference : "Let this Kingdome, where God hath blessed thee with a being, be the Gallery, the best roome of that house, and consider in the two walls of that Gallery, the Church and the State, the peace of a royall, and a religious Wisedome ;".[13] The gradual focus from the wider perspective of the state, and of political peace ensured thanks to the wisdom of the monarch, to a more intimate one, ranging from the Christian duties of the family and servants to the individual faith of the believer, surveyed the various levels of harmony induced by the peace of Christ : "Let thine own family be a Cabinet in this Gallery, and finde in all the boxes thereof, in the severall duties of Wife, and Children, and servants, the peace of vertue, and of the father and mother of all vertues, active discretion, passive obedience ; and then lastly, let thine owne bosome be the secret box, and reserve in this Cabinet, and find there the peace of conscience […]". The rhetorical device used by the preacher highlighted the hierarchical and orderly nature of such a human transposition of the "heavenly Jerusalem" adopting a threefold perspective. Even on a metaphorical level, human harmony was best translated by an orderly analogy, such as that of the social pyramid. This particular metaphorical rendering provided what Donne called "*visio pacis*", a heavenly vision of peace promised to mankind after resurrection: "in the best Gallerie of the best house that can be had, peace with the Creature, peace in the Church, peace in the State, peace in thy house, peace in thy heart, is a faire Modell, and a lovely designe even of the heavenly Jerusalem which is *Visio pacis*, where there is no object but peace."

Man's war against sin

In several of his sermons upon penitential Psalm 38 and upon 1 Cor. 15.26, Donne strove to depict as vividly as possible the never-ending human war against the supreme enemy, that is sin. He wished his listeners

---

[12] On the complex position of Donne regarding grace see Jeffrey Johnson, *The Theology of John Donne*, D. S. Brewer: Cambridge 1999, 122, 131-139.
[13] Vol.4. Preached at White-Hall, March 8 1621 [1621-1622], 1 Cor. 15.26: "The last enemie that shall be destroyed is death", 5.

to remember God's wrath against mankind after Adam's sin, even if it had
somehow abated after the sacrifice of Christ. Clearly his purpose was to
exhort his congregation to summon their spirits in order to eradicate this
lethal foe: "Antichrist alone is enemy enough; but never carry this
consideration beyond thy self. As long as there remains in thee one sin, or
the sinfull gain of that one sin, so long there is one enemy, and where there
is one enemy, there is no peace."[14] The promise of eternal peace had a
price for the repentant sinner since the process of resurrection eventually
completed by the war against death was described by Donne as a painful
experience implying a strife against sin : "You must weepe these tears,
tears of contrition, tears of mortification, before God will wipe all tears
from your eyes ; You must dye this death, this death of the righteous, the
death to sin, before this *last enemy, Death*, shalbe destroyed in you, and
you made partakers of everlasting life in soule and body too."[15] In this
allegory of human suffering and torment, encompassing the whole of
mankind in the wake of David, he referred repeatedly to the many
weapons used by the enemy as in a real war: "But these *Psalmes* were
made not only to vent *Davids* present holy passion, but to serve the
Church of God, to the worlds end. And therefore, change the person, and
wee shall finde a whole quiver of arrows."[16] He then proceeded to list the
various effects of the weapons used against the sinner: " [...] So that these
arrows which are lamented here, are all those miseries, which sinne hath
cast upon us ; *Labor*, and the childe of that, *Sicknesse*, and the off-spring
of that, *Death* ; And the *security* of conscience, and the *terrour* of
conscience ; the *searing* of the conscience, and the *over-tendernesse* of the
conscience"; Donne's customary reference to sickness leading to death
was then associated to the damaging effects of sin on the believer's
conscience. The metaphor of the arrow of sin allowed the preacher to map
out the different stages of the workings of sin on the human conscience:
"These arrows then in our Text, proceeding from *sin*, and sin proceeding
from *tentations*, and inducing *tribulations*, it shall advance your spirituall
edification most, to fixe your consideration upon those *fiery darts*, as they
are *tentations*, and as they are *tribulations*." The next stage in the
unravelling of the metaphor of the war against sin accounted for the very
physical wrestling of the sinner with his tormentors from the very
beginning of life. Relying on the same bellicose metaphor, Donne

---

[14] *Ibid.*, 7.

[15] *idem.*

[16] Vol.2, Sermon 1, Preached at Lincolns Inne, (1618?), Psal. 38.2 "For thine
arrowes stick fast in me, and thy hand presseth me sore", 7-8.

represented the penetration of sin in each individual as the shooting of an extremely swift arrow competing for pre-eminence with God's imprint:

> In the first minute that my soul is infus'd, the Image of God is imprinted in my soul ; so forward is God in my behalf, and so early does he visit me. But yet *Originall Sin* is there, as soon as that Image of God is there. My soul is capable of *God*, as soon as it is capable of *sin* ; and though sin doe not get the start of God, God does not get the start of sin neither. Powers, that dwell so far asunder, as *Heaven*, and *Hell*, *God*, and the *Devill*, meet in an instant in my soul, in the minute of my quickning, and the Image of *God*, and the Image of *Adam*, Originall sin, enter into me at once, in one and the same act. So swift is this arrow, *Originall sin*, from which all arrows of subsequent tentations are shot, as that God, who comes to my first minute of life, cannot come before death.[17]

The specificity of such a representation of man's fundamentally sinful predicament, from the very minute of conception, lay in the depiction of the workings of sin as a process beyond God's power. The arrow of sin defied God's influence by being so swift that it could not be hindered in its penetration. Donne's use of such an image here had some theological bearing since it suggested there might be some measure of helplessness in God that could be defeated by his own enemy. The representation of God conveyed by the preacher in this particular example seemed to question the concept of omnipotence generally attached to the Lord according to the reformed Creed.

Since those sermons were delivered by John Donne at Lincoln's Inn when he was reader in divinity, they were bound to reflect a conformist theology when dogmatic matter was at stake. Therefore the representation of Christ, as our universal Saviour, was carried out by the book, so to speak. Still Donne's stylistic emphasis on Christ's suffering was highly perceptible then for he chose to highlight the healing properties of the physical sacrifice of Christ. In the narrative development of the sermons, the character of Christ was cast as a universal surgeon, endowed with the ability to assuage human sufferings at last. The Passion was then presented as a proleptic model for the sufferings of the sinner repeatedly wounded by the onslaughts of his recurring sins and an analogy was drawn between those and the excruciating physical pains caused by the many torments inflicted to Jesus Christ during his Passion :

> How provident, how diligent a patience did our blessed Saviour bring to his Passion, who foreseeing that that would be our case, our sicknesse, to be first wounded with *single tentations*, and then to have even the wounds

---

[17] *Ibid.*, 11.

of our soul wounded again, by a daily reiterating of tentations in the same kinde, would provide us physick agreeable to our Disease, Chyrurgery comfortable to our wound, first to be *scourged* so, as that his holy body was torn with *wounds*, and then to have those *wounded again*, and often, with more violatings.[18]

The healing metaphor here was one of Donne's idiosyncrasies, to be found in numerous sermons as well as in his devotion treatise, *Devotions upon Emergent Occasions (*1623). It recalled the medieval *topos* of the King as thaumaturge, Jesus being of course here the king of kings. God himself was occasionally presented as a caring father willing to ensure the health of the body of his creatures. Relying again on the organicist metaphor previously noted, Donne referred to human health as the bodily correlative of peace.[19] Within the same organicist cluster of images, the conventional metaphor of the body politic wounded by war underlay the analogy between the state and the very body of the speaker, perceived as an emblem of the human predicament at large. The emphasis was clearly anthropological: "And, as the greatest misery of war, is, when our own Country is made the seat of the war; so it is of *affliction*, when *mine own Body* is made the subject thereof."[20] A similar anthropological concern is to be found in Donne's representation of the fight of the believer against temptation and death.

The war against temptation and death

Temptation was therefore presented as the face of the enemy to be fought relentlessly. Once again Donne resorted to the same *topos* in order to exhort the sinner to behave as a warrior shielded with the words of God; what he called "the *scriptum est*"[21] could be relied upon as a protection against the miseries induced by the onslaughts of temptation. In this same sermon on Psalm 38.2 John Donne proceeded to present the event of resurrection, promised to mankind by the sacrifice of Christ, as the result of the ongoing battle against sin. He underlined the permanence of choice by the Holy Ghost of a bellicose metaphor in order to depict the difficult process of resurrection for mankind:

---

[18] *idem.*
[19] Vol. 3, Sermon 2, Preached at White-Hall, the 30. Aprill 1620, Psal. 144.15. Being the first psalm for the day. "Blessed are the people that be so ; yea blessed are the people, whose God is the Lord.", 10.
[20] Vol.2, Sermon 1, Preached at Lincolns Inne, (1618?), Psal. 38.2 "For thine arrowes stick fast in me, and thy hand presseth me sore", 9.
[21] *Ibid.*, 13.

[...] the kingdom of Christ, which must be perfected, must be accomplished, (because all things must be subdued unto him) is not yet perfected, not accomplished yet. Why? What lacks it? It lacks the bodies of Men, which yet lie under the dominion of another. When we shall also see [p.2] by that Metaphor which the Holy Ghost chooseth to expresse that in, which is that there is *Hostis*, and so *Militia*, an enemie, and a warre, and therefore that Kingdome is not perfected, that he places perfect happinesse, and perfect glory, in perfect peace. [...] How truly a warfare is this life, if the Kingdome of Heaven it selfe, have not this peace in perfection?[22]

The promised bliss of the peace of resurrection for mankind still seemed hampered by the raging war against the enemy, that is sin, relentlessly striving to exert his domination over man. What is more, in this sermon, the preacher laid a definite emphasis on the place devoted to death in human life, inflating in a highly hyperbolic way the power and influence of this allegorised character: "Who then is this enemy? An enemy that may thus far thinke himselfe equall to God, that as no man ever saw God, and lived ; so no man ever saw this enemy and lived, for it is Death". The discrepancies between the two opponents were presented by the preacher as all the more striking as death seemed an almost omnipotent enemy to every single man:

> [...] An enemie that is so well victualled against man, as that he cannot want as long as there are men, for he feeds upon man himselfe. And so well armed against Man, as that he cannot want Munition, while there are men, for he fights with our weapons, our owne faculties, nay our calamities, yea our owne pleasures are our death. And therefore he is *Novissimus hostis*, saith the Text, *The last enemy*.[23]

The portrait drawn here highlighted the monstrous and terrifying nature of this enemy who preyed on the living from within, for it found sustenance on the very disposition to committing sins present in most human beings. From that point of view the expression "our own pleasures are our death" encapsulated the theological core of the commentary: sin was regarded as the cause of death in life, since it severed the bond between man and God, and beyond life since it could well preclude resurrection. The allegory fashioned by Donne in this sermon dramatized radically the inner fight within all sinners against a very intimate foe, gnawing at the insides of his victims–an evocation somehow reminiscent of medieval representations of death as we find them in "*danses*

---

[22] Vol.4. Preached at White-Hall, March 8 1621 [1621-1622], 1 Cor. 15.26: "The last enemie that shall be destroyed is death", 1.

[23] *Ibid.*, 2.

macabres" for instance. Donne then completed his frightening portrait of
death with a comparative study of man's other known enemies, in order to
establish the importance of the ultimate and definitive enemy against more
conventional enemies such as the figure of Satan: "We have other
Enemies; Satan about us, sin within us; but the power of both those, this
enemie shall destroy; but when they are destroyed, he shall retaine a
hostile, and triumphant dominion over us." The contest for domination
over man between the powers of temptation and those of evil could not
compete with the matchless powers of death who always proved victorious
in the end. One cannot but notice the extremely evocative and impressive
effect for a Church audience of such a vivid account carried through the
unravelling of the allegory of the war between evil, sin and death, where
theological notions were aptly translated into anthropological terms. Yet
the "paraphrase" of the biblical verse would not have been complete if
Donne had not commented upon the promise made to mankind by God
and Christ through the event of the resurrection of Christ, that is the
resurrection of mankind and its ultimate victory upon the "last enemy":
"But *Vsque quo Domine* ? How long O Lord? for ever ? No, *Abolebitur*:
wee see this Enemy all the way, and all the way we feele him ; but we
shall see him destroyed; *Abolebitur*. But how? or when ?" The rhetorical
choice of *accumulatio* underlined what could be interpreted by the
congregation as the emotion of the speaker (even if this was contrived), his
paramount anxiety and the urgency of the questioning, in order to mimic
what should be the angst of the believer. The direct address to God, the
union of the preacher and his flock in the pronoun "we", would have
increased the impression of familiarity for the listeners and probably
would have had a greater impact on their consciences: "[...] so at the
Resurrection of this body, I shall be able to say to the Angel of the great
Councell, the Son of God, Christ Jesus himselfe, I am of the same stuffe as
you, Body and body, Flesh and flesh, and therefore let me sit downe with
you, at the right hand of the Father in an everlasting security from this last
enemie, who is now destroyed, death."[24] The ultimate hope was to be
found in the promise of the Resurrection for the repentant believers. The
eagerness of the preacher to persuade his audience of this fundamental
theological point stemmed from the unrelenting repetition of the word
« resurrection » coupled with a ternary rhythm that reflected the threefold
dimension of the word itself:

> This destruction, this abolition of this last enemy, is by the Resurrection;
> for this Text is part of an argument for the Resurrection. [...] We had a

---

[24] *Ibid.*, 3.

Resurrection in prophecy; we have a Resurrection in the present working of Gods Spirit; we shall have a Resurrection in the finall consummation. [...] And this exhibites unto us a threefold occasion of advancing our devotion, in considering a threefold Resurrection: First, a Resurrection from dejections and calamities in this world, a Temporary Resurrection; Secondly, a Resurrection from sin, a Spirituall Resurrection; and then a Resurrection from the grave, a finall Resurrection.[25]

The pattern of the reasoning developed by the preacher was modelled on the gradation in intensity and importance of the different types of resurrection mentioned. He shifted from the material level of history to the spiritual level of the sinner's predicament and ultimately reached the final level that went beyond death itself, a Christ-like resurrection.

In an earlier sermon on Psalm 38.2 (1618 ?), Donne showed how God's mercy, which we may label God's peace, could eventually be granted to the repentant sinner. The preacher's part in such a process was to be accounted for as essential: "[...] the Preacher is but *saggitarius Dei*, the deliverer of Gods arrows; for Gods arrows are *sagittae Compunctionis*, arrows that draw bloud from the eyes ; Tears of repentance from *Mary Magdalen*, and from *Peter* ; And when from thee ?"[26] In his article "Preaching pastor versus custodian of order : Donne, Andrewes and the Jacobean church"[27] Daniel Doerksen very accurately points that against the Laudian position, Donne maintained an attachment to preaching reminiscent of William Perkins's exhortations in his *Arte of Prophecying* (1607).[28] He staged himself as God's instrument in delivering punishment and consolation at the same time through his sermon. The extolling virtues of the words of the preachers as well as their soothing quality were very conventionally presented in Donne's days as exerting a major influence on the congregation of sinners: "[...] The Psalm hath a *retrospect* too, it looks back to *Adam*, and to every particular man in his loines, and so, *Davids* case is our case, and all these arrowes stick in all us. But the Psalm and the text hath also a *prospect*, and hath a *propheticall* relation from *David* to

---

[25] *Ibid.*, 13.

[26] Vol.2, Sermon 1, Preached at Lincolns Inne, (1618?), Psal. 38.2 "For thine arrowes stick fast in me, and thy hand presseth me sore", 20.

[27] Daniel, Doerksen, "Preaching pastor versus custodian of order: Donne, Andrewes and the Jacobean Church", *Philological Quaterly*, Fall 1994, v73, n4, 417-430.

[28] On the influence of Perkins over Donne's prophesying see Raymond-Jean Frontain, "Donne's imperfect resurrection", *Papers on Language & Literature*, Fall 1990, vol. 26, Issue 4, 539-546.

our Saviour Christ Jesus." [29] The proleptic emphasis of the preacher on the sacrifice of Christ for the redemption of mankind upheld the idea of the ultimate victory of peace in Jesus Christ over sin.

More generally Donne's references to peace in his sermons upon the Psalms very often recalled the advent of Messiah and his sacrifice for the redemption of mankind. Christ was singled out as the *"Princeps Pacis"*, purveyor of spiritual peace if not temporal safety:

> One of Christs principall titles was, that he was *Princeps pacis*, and yet this Prince of peace sayes, *Non veni mittere pacem*, I came not to bring you peace, not such a peace as should bring them security against all warre. If a Ship take fire, though in the midst of the Sea, it consumes sooner, and more irrecoverably, then a thatched house upon Land : If God cast a fire-brand of warre, upon a State accustomed to peace, it burnes the more desperately, by their former security.[30]

In this particular excerpt the preacher warned his congregation about the essential distinction to be made between temporal and spiritual peace: the new Covenant established between God and man after Christ's sacrifice certainly did not imply that doomsday had come yet. Man was still intended to labour under the yoke of suffering till the Last Judgement and should certainly not bask in the assurance of salvation. Nevertheless in several of his sermons John Donne liked to dwell on the idea that the sacrifice of the son of God and his ensuing resurrection were the harbingers of universal peace for mankind, the ultimate victory over the enemy of death. His purpose was undoubtedly to exhort his congregation to repentance and faith in the promise of a better future for those who lived in faith and followed Christ's example–we notice here from a theological standpoint that Donne adhered to the dogma of *imitatio Christi*:

> [...] who shall answer us, if we aske, How beautifull is his face, who is the Author of this peace, when we shall see that in the glory of Heaven, the Center of all true peace? It was the inheritance of Christ Jesus upon the earth, he had it at his birth, he brought it with him, *Glory be to God on high, peace upon earth.* It was his purchase upon earth, *He made peace* (indeed he bought peace) *through the blood of his Crosse.* It was his Testament, when he went from earth; *Peace I leave with you, my peace I give unto you.* Divide [p.5] with him in that blessed Inheritance, partake

---

[29] *Ibid.*, 21.
[30] Vol. 3, Sermon 2, Preached at White-Hall, the 30. Aprill 1620, Psal. 144.15. Being the first psalm for the day. "Blessed are the people that be so; yea blessed are the people, whose God is the Lord.", 13.

with him in that blessed Purchase, enrich thy self with that blessed Legacy, his Peace.[31]

Peace was meant to be understood as the « inheritance », the « purchase », the "testament" of Christ for mankind, his legacy of hope of the ultimate victory of peace over warfare.

Whether John Donne came to terms with the anxieties of political and familial divided loyalties is a highly debated issue that must have had a bearing on his conception of warfare when he was in office as a much appreciated preacher. The influence of his preaching on such burning matters over his congregation would have been regarded as a political asset for the contemporary monarchs. Still the restricted selection of sermons surveyed in this article testifies to a different ideological stance on Donne's part, that is a strong emphasis on the spiritual strife between good and evil. Over a period of twenty years, his sermons harped upon the idea that the wars fought by devout Christians should be continuous and fierce for they were inner wars against evil. For twenty-first century readers of his sermons, the study of such a sample sheds a light on the wealth of metaphorical translations of what may be considered as a fairly conventional theological conception of spiritual warfare. John Donne's literary gift gives uncommon strength to his representations of the spiritual contest likely to exert a real spiritual influence on his parishioners and to lay a permanent cultural imprint on a more contemporary readership, presumably less concerned by theological issues. His writing will undoubtedly be remembered as a salient contribution to the spiritual crusades against evil launched by generations of preachers over the centuries.

Works Cited

Most of the quotations from John Donne's sermons belong to the online edition available through *Early English Books Online*.

Arshagouni Papazian, Mary, ed. *John Donne and the Protestant Reformation*. Detroit : Wayne State U P, 2003.

Bald, R. C. *John Donne : A Life*. Oxford : Clarendon P, 1970.

Carey, John. *John Donne : Life, Mind and Art*. London : Faber and Faber, 1981.

---

[31] Vol.4. Preached at White-Hall, March 8 1621 [1621-1622], 1 Cor. 15.26: "The last enemie that shall be destroyed is death", 4-5.

Flynn, Dennis. *John Donne and the Ancient Catholic Nobility.* Bloomington : Indiana U P, 1995.

Frontain, Raymond-Jean, Malpezzi, Frances, eds. *John Donne's Religious Imagination.* Canway, AR : UCA Press, 1995.

Jackson, Robert S. *John Donne's Christian Vocation.* Evanston, IL : Northwestern U P, 1970.

Johnson, Jeffrey. *The Theology of John Donne.* Cambridge : D. S. Brewer, 1999.

Lake, Peter. *Anglicans and Puritans ?: Presbyterianism and English Conforming Thought from Whitgift to Hooker.* London : Unwin Hyman, 1988.

MacLure, Millar. *The Paul's Cross Sermons, 1534-1642.* Toronto : U of Toront P, 1958.

Martz, Louis. *The Poetry of Meditation.* New Haven : Yale U P, 1954.

Mueller, William R. *John Donne : Preacher.* Princeton : Princeton U P, 1962.

Schleiner, Winfried. *The Imagery of John Donne's Sermons.* Providence, RI : Brown U P, 1970.

Shuger, Debora. *Habits of Thought in the English Renaissance.* Berkeley : U of California P, 1990.

Simpson, Evelyn, M. *John Donne's Sermons on the Psalms and Gospels.* Berkeley & Los Angeles : University of California Press, 1963, rpt 1991.

CHAPTER FIVE

RAIMOND GACHES' SERMON ON THE PEACE BETWEEN ENGLAND AND THE UNITED PROVINCES

CHRISTINE RONCHAIL

This article proposes a reading of a particular kind of war sermon in a particular context. The type of sermon chosen is a thanksgiving homily celebrating the peace treaty which marked the end of conflict between Protestant countries. The discourse was pronounced by a Calvinist minister in a Catholic setting: France. The man in question, a minister from provincial France, received his vocation from the Reformed Church of Paris, thus finding himself in a delicate personal situation. After examining the text in its context, bringing to the fore the key figures directly involved, and the overall construction of the sermon, we shall then move on to the ways in which the preacher tackles issues of war and peace in his sermon, and in particular his theological handling of the matter.

The date was June 2, 1654; the setting was the town house of Guillaume Boreel, ambassador of the United Provinces at the court of the king of France. The diplomat had invited the pastor Raimond Gaches to give a thanksgiving sermon to celebrate the recently signed peace treaty between England and the United Provinces, bringing an end to the first Anglo-Dutch war. In 1651, the English Parliament had made moves by suggesting to the United Provinces that they found a customs alliance. When the States General turned the offer down, the English Parliament voted the Navigation Act, on October 9. This stipulated that access to English ports was restricted "to ships owned by producing countries [of transported goods] and English ships, captained by an Englishman and with a crew made up of a majority of Englishmen."[1]

---

[1] Edmond Préclin, Victor-L. Tapié, *Le XVIIe siècle, monarchies centralisées (1610-1715).* Paris : PUF, 1949, 203.

The Anglo-Dutch war, sparked off by a quarrel over flags between the fleet commanded by Maarten Tromp on the one hand, and Robert Blake on the other, as well as by the Dutch refusal to pay taxes on fish caught off the Scottish coast, lasted for two years. The treaty of Westminster, signed on April 5, 1654, confirmed the total victory of England. The French king, Louis XIV, was absent from the capital. He had returned from Fontainebleau where the court frequently resided, but then left Paris again on May 30 to go to Reims, where he was crowned on June 7, 1654.

Guillaume or Willem Boreel (Middelburgh 1591 – Paris 1668) was an experienced diplomat, with particular knowledge of the Anglo-Dutch conflict. As Councillor and Grand Pensionary of the town of Amsterdam, he had been sent to England on an extraordinary mission in 1643. As commercial envoy, he had settled the conflict between the Dutch and English Indian companies before being appointed ambassador of the United Provinces in France from 1650. Curious by nature, he was keen on natural sciences—his correspondence includes an exchange of letters about the invention of the microscope—and was on familiar terms with Rembrandt, his neighbour in Amsterdam in 1636. Abraham and Bonaventure Elzevier dedicated their Ciceron[2] to him, and he corresponded with Caspar Barleus, a poet and theologian, also a professor at Leyden.

The man he chose to preach a sermon in his house was both a theologian and a poet. Little is known about Raimond (or Raymond) Gaches. He was born in Castres (France), and his father, Jacques Gaches was a lawyer and lieutenant-judge in the county of Lacaze. Raimond was the pastor in Castres until 1654 and a member of the Academy of Poetry. His poems and translations from Latin, the existence of which is documented in secondary sources, have been lost.[3] His publications consisted mostly of sermons, only eighteen of which have survived to this day, a relatively low number bearing in mind his long career, including fourteen years at Charenton.

His poetic talents gave an inspired, lyrical edge to his works. In one of his sermons, he addressed the congregation as follows: "...have lilies or roses grow in a fine living area, have the air perfumed by musk and amber,

---

[2] *M.Tulii Ciceronis Opera*, 10 vol. in 12, Lug. Batavor: Ex Officina Elzeviriana, 1642.
[3] Eugène et Emile Haag, *La France protestante ou vie des protestants français qui se sont faits un nom dans l'histoire*, 2ᵉ ed. revised by Henri Bordier, vol. VI. Paris : Sandoz-Fischbacher, 1877-1888, art. « Gaches ».

offering a host of fair sights to your eyes..."[4] He was rapidly noticed when he arrived in the capital, as Jean Rou noted in his memoirs:

> Amongst other things I know of the rumours surrounding M. Gaches when he came to begin his vocation, in the streets and amongst the ladyfolk above all, that his admirable allure, his sharp eyes, his white teeth, his fine hands and his Gascon accent greatly prepossessed in his favour.[5]

In 1654, Gaches received his vocation from the Consistory of Charenton, the place of exercise of the Paris Reformed Church.[6] The power and influence of the Church of Paris was such that the pastor had to prove himself first, which, for a Reformed minister, meant proving himself by preaching. Gaches thus set about his task with considerable vigour judging by his feast-day sermons from this period, which, excluding two cases, are those that have survived to this day. In circumstances such as these, the sermons were all the more polished and more largely attended. He preached successively on Easter Sunday, on April 5, 1654 (the dedication is to the Duchess de la Trémoille), the day of fasting on Friday 19 April, 1654, on the Monday of Pentecost, May 25, 1654 (dedicated to the princess of Turenne) and finally Thanksgiving on Monday June 2, 1654, dedicated to Guillaume Boreel. This last sermon in the series was, so the dedication informs us, specifically commissioned, written up in very little time and delivered to a pre-defined congregation.

The sermon was given in French to a public made up of carefully selected guests, the majority of whom were probably French-speaking, with a few surreptitiously added members of the Consistory of the Church of Paris, who were particularly attentive to the scope and terms of his discourse. Specific problems arise when one sets about analysing this type of text. The approach chosen here will be to study stylistic features from a theoretical angle, borrowing from discourse analysis.

---

[4] *Deuxième sermon sur la 2ᵉ épître de Pierre*; although undated, this sermon was most probably given in 1655.

[5] Jean Rou, *Mémoires inédits et opuscules,* published for the Société de l'Histoire du Protestantisme Français, using the manuscript conserved in the State Archives at the Hague by Francis Waddington. Paris/La Haye: Agence centrale de la Société/Nyhoff, 1857, vol. I, 170.

[6] Article XIV of the Edict of Nantes stipulated that Parisians could not worship within the capital, but had to be at least five leagues from Paris. It was possible to hold a service at the home of Guillaume Boreel since he was considered to be on foreign soil. England, Germany and Sweden likewise had resident ministers holding services in their embassies.

An essential feature of the sermon is its grounding in orality, using the word in performance. It hence draws on precise rules of discourse. The thanksgiving homily has a classical structure. It is a "French-style" sermon, the organisation of which within the Protestant Church, had not yet, in 1654, been systematised. The Parisian pastor Le Faucheur did not receive the necessary authorisation to publish and distribute his technical work[7] until 1656, thanks to the support of Valentin Conrart, secretary to the Académie Française and elder of Charenton, and Jean Claude's *Traité sur la composition d'un sermon*[8] [treatise on sermon composition] only appeared posthumously, in 1688.

Composition was thus guided by the only authority in terms of discourse that authors could refer to, meaning the rules of rhetoric. As far as sermons were concerned, codification had been established by François de Sales, Pierre de Bérulle and Vincent de Paul, who established rules henceforth followed by all Catholic sermonists. The men of letters making up the Reformed community of Charenton were in close contact with their Catholic counterparts. Like his Parisian colleague Drelincourt, Gaches was to be closely linked to Jean-François Senault (1601 – 1672), Superior of the Oratory, a foremost preacher at whose initiative a school of rhetoric was set up, and a friend of Valentin Conrart.[9]

The overall structure and organisation of the thanksgiving homily tended to follow Berulle's precepts. The sermon was constructed in four parts conforming to the rhetorical division of discourse. The exordium (introduction) was followed by a development (tractation) which unfolded into two sub-parts: the explanation or commentary followed by a reading from the Scriptures and the application. The application consisted in a development of textual meaning for the congregation to whom it is being presented. The sermon was brought to a close by a peroration.

The exordium had several functions. It prepared the minds of the listeners, setting up the fitting intellectual and spiritual framework. The pastor must, from the beginning, seek to please and command the attention of his congregation. To this end, he applied the classical rhetorical principle: *movere, placere, docere*. Unlike English sermons, described as

---

[7] Michel Le Faucheur, *Traité de l'action de l'orateur ou de la prononciation et du geste*. Paris, Augustin Courbé 1657.
[8] Jean Claude, *Traité sur la composition d'un sermon, in Œuvres posthumes de Mr Claude*. Amsterdam : Pierre Savouret, 1688.
[9] Alexandre Vinet, *Histoire de la prédication parmi les réformés de France au XVIIe siècle*. Paris : chez les Editeurs, rue de Rivoli 174, 1860, 291.

cold and distant,[10] the minister's words, and those of a Gascon in particular, were expected to demonstrate impassioned eloquence.

The exordium set up the sermon's horizon of expectation. The thanksgiving homily was given on a feast-day, and was carefully prepared. The preacher established an attitude of gratitude towards God, the father of his people, from his children to whom he listened despite their waywardness:

> You have come here, My Brothers, to present to the Lord, the same homage of holy acknowledgement, to join your hearts with those of so many true Christians who send up to the Heavens their thanks and praises.

This part closed by announcing clearly, or even insistently (as was the case here) the plan of the sermon to come, followed by a prayer. Such insistence demonstrated the need to preach effectively. The worshipper should be able to keep the structure of the text in mind so that the different stages of the sermon take effect.

This sermon had several interesting characteristics, in its internal workings most of all. One might have expected it to be merely a one-off text, written for one particular occasion. As a fact, Gaches prompted an overall reflection on the state of the world and the relations between Protestant countries, pondering at some length on peace. The sermon's scriptural inscription deserves mention. Gaches indeed took only the first part of verse 6, Psalm 122, the full text of which read: "Pray for the peace of Jerusalem; may your friends live in tranquillity".[11]

Bearing in mind the context, it is easy to understand what might have prompted him to leave out the second part of the verse, as we shall go on to see that "tranquillity" was not part of the Reformed ecclesial project. In general, sermons are backed up by a series of verses, a pericope, or even one or several chapters from the Scriptures, as was the case later, for example, in those of Jacques Saurin. The choice of extract in this case tends to suggest that it was very much a text taken as a pretext for more general considerations, and whose concision associated with the auditory effect of a plosive alliteration in the words "Pray for the peace" would

---

[10] Jean Claude, *op.cit.*

[11] The Biblical text given is translated directly from the French bible and the Hebrew. The 1611 King James version, used elsewhere here for the English translations, and the standard edition in England at the time, reads quite differently and does not contain the key words Gaches focuses on : "Pray for the peace of Jerusalem; they shall prosper that love thee."

enable the preacher to use the verse as a leitmotif, also giving his message a compelling rhythm.

Gaches used 44 direct and indirect biblical quotes, 37 of which were from the Old Testament, 7 from the New (the use of verse 6, Psalm 122 as a leitmotif has deliberately been discounted so as not to distort proportions). 29 quotes were used in the explanation and 15 in the application. More than half of these were taken from the histories and Psalms. While the preponderance of Psalms was typical of Reformed preaching in the seventeenth century,[12] that of the histories was not. Similarly, the balance between quotations from the two Testaments was inverted: scriptural usage tended in favour of the New Testament.

Gaches was expected to make an impact on his congregation. Preaching had a didactic role. The quest for efficiency is characteristic of sermons assuring the function that Jakobson called "conative" (which seeks to move or even influence the addressee). Beyond the overall structure borrowed from rhetorical discourse evoked earlier, he employed a whole arsenal of figures and tropes that would be the envy even of a Catholic sermonist of the day.

The overall frame of the speech set up a triangle of communication with the congregation: at its apex were the pronouns "me", "I", or the royal or inclusive "we", whilst at the base were found, on the one hand, "He" (God), "it or "she" (the Church) and on the other hand "you" (for the congregation).It was the "you" that acted as a pivot to destabilise the worshippers, so as better to reassure them later and ensure their progress.

Gaches constantly played on these positions, thus ensuring he never alienated the congregation. He presented himself now as their accuser, now as their peer, then slipped into a more neutral stance using impersonal structures. The sermon was of average length if one compares it to others preached at Charenton in the seventeenth century: using the same method as François Chevalier who, based on a corpus of eighty sermons, estimated the probable duration of a sermon according to the number of words, the thanksgiving sermon of Raymond Gaches can be estimated to have lasted about one hour and forty minutes. The duration of the sermon had little bearing on the compelling effect Gaches wished to have on his congregation. Indeed, the worshippers were accustomed, —one might even say "trained"— to listen to much longer sermons. In this case, however, the situation required that he demonstrate his great mastery of the homiletic arts and the excellence of his message enhanced by his knowing use of rhetorical questions:

---

[12] Françoise Chevalier, *La prédication protestante au XVIIe siècle*. Genève : Labor & Fides, 1994.

Because the Ark was in the fields, he dared not rest amongst his family, & when the Church of God of which the Ark was but the symbol, is buffeted by storms, how are we to take pleasure in rest? How shall we be capable of any feeling of joy? But what war, My Brothers; is there in the womb of the Earth gold enough to sustain the cost: Is there in the wilderness wood enough to build and repair so many ships? And will we find in the most peopled Towns men enough to fill them.

Gaches used anaphora to mark the rhythm of his message and retain his listeners' attention:

God cannot be vanquished but by prayer. Prayer alone stays His arm, prayer alone can bring on our delivery, prayer alone can grant us peace. Therefore, as our interests are inseparably bound to those of the Church, and as what counts for the Church must be to us even dearer than what touches us, we must shed tears in the presence of our Lord, we must ensure our moans and sighs reach up to Him, we must with profound humility and with extraordinary fervour do all we can to bring upon the Church the blessings of Heaven, in keeping with what the Prophet now exhorts us, Pray, he said, for the Peace of Jerusalem.

So as to mark the minds of his listeners more pointedly, he enumerated the terms "war" and "peace" in symmetry (five by five):

War fills houses with mourning, spills blood in torrents, burns towns to ashes, lays waste entire Provinces, & causes the ruin even of the most splendid empires; but peace on the contrary restores tranquillity & joy, brings happiness to Provinces and States, ensures trade between cities, rest within the family and life among individuals.

His prose was always highly visual, with preponderant use of red and black for a more striking imaginative effect, particularly in descriptions of war scenes, to which Gaches added touches of ekphrasis: "How appalling is the sight of a sea covered in fire and red with blood while the air is thick with smoke, while the heavy bulks of ships are swallowed down into the depths with the sorrowful souls who were closed within." Lastly, he played on the use of narrating tenses. He used the past (imperfect) to evoke the Jerusalem of biblical times, then slipped into the gnomic present when he portrayed the Church. In so doing, he also turned towards the future, outside temporality. This literary means enabled him to detach his speech from historical events and so attain his aim, which was to deliver a universal speech about war and peace. In this way he set up the sort of scenography that Bossuet expounded at length in his sermons from the Carême du Louvre in 1662. The explanation consisted, in fact, of a detailed commentary of the verse. The demonstration was constructed

around two themes: 1) The development of the analogy between
Jerusalem, chosen city of God and his prophet David as the city where the
name of the Lord is written,[13] and the Church, the people of God ("But
beneath the name of Ierusalem, we must hear, my brothers, the whole
Church of the Lord of which it was the symbol."). 2) Peace as the supreme
good covers "in general all sorts of goods" ("Peace is the foundation of all
the goods we possess... / [peace] restores tranquillity & joy, brings
happiness to Provinces and States, ensures trade between cities, rest within
the family and life among individuals.")

Gaches did not, however, stop at scriptural commentary. Rejoicing in
the newly restored peace, he embarked on a theological interpretation of
the conflict. In the application, the pastor tackled the question in three
stages: For some years, God had sent war across the whole of Europe,
Protestant countries included. There was thus no objective reason for
England and the United Provinces to be spared. Secondly, the author
homed in on the two countries. He affirmed that God's wrath was
particularly aimed at them, so it was normal that the war he sent should be
particularly horrible, causing great suffering. Lastly, if it was true that God
sent war, he was also the master of peace. He would show compassion, so
long as his people:

> ... shows itself willing, through humility, by repentance, by faith, & by the
> ardour of prayer, as if with so many victorious arms we were fighting
> against him, as if we were resisting his blows, & seeking to deflect, both
> above us and above our neighbours, the effects of his wrath.

In his first point, he evoked the conflict and the description allowed
him to present his vision of the world. He developed and drew on a series
of historical facts related to the political situation in Europe. He thus
summoned up a whole panorama of wars in Central Europe: Sweden
against Poland, the thirty-year war between Germany and Bohemia. He
also touched on the French situation via pointed allusions to the wars of
religion.

We can but be intrigued by his daring to tackle the issue of war. How
indeed could he mention a political situation when, for nearly forty years,
the king had forbidden pastors to expound their personal opinions on the
res politica in their sermons?[14] Had a certain implicit tolerance been
accorded by the king, or was Gaches benefiting from a certain freedom of
expression on the grounds that the sermon was being preached on "foreign

---

[13] 2 Chr 6, 6.
[14] The ruling dates back to the National Synod in Vitré in 1617.

soil" under the patronage of a high-ranking dignitary and an ally of France? Several elements doubtless came into play by way of an answer. As far as the position of Louis XIV was concerned, the king clearly allowed pastors to give vent to their opinions, so long as they did not go against his interests, and all the more if their ideas actively backed up his policies. One element which speaks in favour of this theory is the content of a sermon of thanksgiving pronounced and published in 1660, in which the same author took the liberty of evoking the political situation between France and Spain, in other words peace in the Pyrenees.

The 1654 sermon made explicit mention of the following: the repression of the Spanish Netherlands in the years 1567 – 1572 by the duke of Albe, the 1618 war in Bohemia, the conflict between Sweden and Poland in 1629, the French wars of religion which came to an end in the same year, and finally the end of the thirty-year war, which had come about six years previously. Conversely, it did not allude directly to the Fronde, the only recent conflict. Certain elements tend to suggest there might be a veiled reference in the description of civil wars. And last of all, it mentioned the existence of the Franco-Spanish war, but did not dwell on the matter. The Anglo-Dutch war had been particularly striking. It was the first conflict to take place exclusively at sea, with no land invasions, and with no intervention by land forces. Gaches' description is particularly forceful:

> War on land is horrible, but it must be confessed that it is a form of calm if it is compared to that terrible war that was waged on the sea. Is it not astonishment enough for man that the Ocean stirs up its waves, that the wind brings tempests, that sand banks & the tips of rocks threaten the ships? Must fire too be brought to the middle of the waves, so that men should burn in the heart of the waters? Of course the Sea is truly proud, the Winds are truly furious, the thunder is truly terrible, and lightning is truly impetuous, but an army of vessels is prouder than the sea, ruthless soldiers are more furious than the Winds; the blast of one hundred canons is more terrible than that of thunder, and those cannonballs which speed on their way with such violence, and which seem to fly with wings of flame, strike with more impetuosity than lightning.

One point deserves to be underlined: Gaches spoke neither of a vanquisher nor of the vanquished. And yet, he could not have been unaware that the treaty of Westminster had been signed. The *Gazette*, founded by Théophraste Renaudot, came out every Saturday and, by and large, information took eighteen days to reach the seat of the newspaper in Paris. The act had been signed on April 5, 1654 and the sermon was given fifty-eight days later. The only allusion to a vanquisher of sorts was a reference to Guillaume Boreel and his "Triumphant Fatherland", although the pastor could but have known the consequences of the treaty for the United Provinces. This was the only moment in the sermon when he spoke clearly of current affairs and left prudence aside.

Having established a general frame around his theme, he then went on to tackle the theological issues raised by the conflict between two Protestant countries. In theological terms, it was expected, and even desirable, that the infidel should attack the people of God. If the world were no longer in opposition with the Church, then it was the Church that had lost its true path. It was not acceptable for a Reformed Protestant, and even less for a minister, that the ungodly be integrated, or even assimilated.

The Church of God is incessantly threatened by surprises and attacks from Satan and his henchmen, the World and Hell have declared on it & an irreconcilable war, & without the protection of God, there is no alternative but that it must succumb to their violence and stratagems. The same cannot be said of a conflict between brothers:

> But, alas, it is indeed a strange thing when fellow citizens take up arms against others, when brothers kill each other, & when members of the same mystical Body of the Lord Jesus rip one another apart with detestable fury.

In the text, the Church was likened to Jerusalem, God's chosen city. It was made up of two peoples, England and the United Provinces which belonged to the same mystical body. In such a context, there could be neither vanquisher not vanquished, nor could the concept of a "just war" be employed. Not that Gaches abandoned the concept entirely, but he used it only for distant, non-Christian lands.

The task of the sermonist consisted in resolving the irksome matter of war between brothers, and the solution will be provided by a feat of theological reasoning. In Reformist thinking, there was a three-stage pattern governing the way things were faced with evil and sorrow in the world: creation (God created the world); the fall (man disobeyed God's rulings) and redemption (despite this transgression, God chose to forgive). The congregation saw itself as both the heir and the contemporary of the people of God, an interpretation guided by the preacher when he based his narrative on the analogy between the Church and Jerusalem, paraphrasing the Scriptures. In point of fact, the text was speaking of the faithful, his congregation. For a Reformed Protestant, the reference to Providence was a fundamental doctrinal concept. According to Calvin:

> ...all those who have heard it said from the mouth of Christ that the hairs on our heads are counted, (Matt 10, 30) will seek the cause later, and will

all be assured that events, whatever they may be, have been decreed by the secret council of God.[15]

In other words, everything came from God. If war was dividing brothers, it had been sent by God. In Calvin's eyes, Providence underlay everything: whatever happened had been willed by God. The key to suffering was that it was punishment sent by God; whatever happened in the world was providential by nature.

Gaches employed the entire charter of theological reasoning.[16] He explained and reminded the congregation that everything came from God whose wrath could be sparked off even against his own children. For this reason, although the sermon was of average length, he did not cut short the explanation so as better to show that divine punishment did not fall only on the enemies of Jerusalem (and therefore the Church) and the "infidel" but also on the people of God themselves. Intriguingly, certain features recalled fast-day sermons, when the congregation would expect to be castigated. Here Gaches was weeping for the bride of the Lord, the victim of her children's negligence. He personified the Church, using prosopopoeia, and drew parallels with biblical examples:

> When Rebecca felt her twins jostling in her belly, she cried out when the pain was strongest. If it be so, why am I thus? And the Church of the Lord Jesus, feeling its own children, who in its breast pursued their dangerous quarrels with so much spite and ill-will, might it not have said as its womb was torn, "If it be so, why am I thus?" Indeed there was much sorrow, & a loud voice of wailing was heard in Rama, when Rachel cried for her children and could not be consoled when they were no longer; Poor bride of the Lord Jesus, does it not suffice that your enemies persecute you? Must your own children add to your suffering, how many tears and how much blood have you shed during the horrors of so lamentable a war?

He extended the paradigm as far as presenting the Republic of United Provinces as the Daughter of Sion. The judgement of God had arrived, the preacher reproved the guilty. But a minister could not merely deliver a discourse of hopelessness; he must also draw lessons from the affliction. When sorrows came to the world, then as far as pastors were concerned, God was speaking, and it was their mission to translate his meaning into clear terms. The pedagogical aspect of affliction was a form of test, a punishment that would allow the true believer to gain in strength. For this reason, affliction was positive:

---

[15] Jean Calvin, *Institution chrétienne*, I, XVI, ii.
[16] Cf. Calvin, *op.cit.*

...& that on the contrary the condition of the Church on earth should be to be exposed to great calamities, although, when peace has been made with God, there is war with the world, and the purpose of afflictions is to render the Church more pure and more holy, just as the violence of the winds makes the air purer; nevertheless as piety has the promise of life now and life to come, & even the temporal prosperity of the Church being a virtue that we must obtain as far as we can, both by our wishes and by our cares.

As far as Gaches was concerned, God had sent war between two Protestant countries because they had not conformed to his expectation of them within the mystical body that was the Church. The end result of pedagogy by trial was that, once the afflictions were over, God called on men of virtue, princes capable of restoring peace, and poured blessings on his people.

...& if God has allowed war to be waged, he has also had magnanimous Princes be born amongst them, whose swords have been the terror of their enemies. The great God who was the Protector of the old state of Israel has been the Protector of these United Provinces; & we should appeal for His grace, so that in the future He might shower down his most precious blessings on them; may He make the strength of the Sceptre of Jesus-Christ, which is His Gospel, appear more and more. May He incline hearts to the obedience that should be rendered unto Him; May He make piety blossom within them; so that from the side of the earth He can secure the foundations of this Republic until the end of the world.

This was a case of collective punishment, concerning both the Church and the two nations. The preacher, who was responsible for his flock for whom he must vouch before God,[17] used the finest vector, which was the sermon, to address the faithful. In point of fact, he appealed to each individual member of the congregation, urging him to repent. He encouraged them to act as if the salvation of them all depended on the behaviour of each individual, for God would continue to send affliction if the faithful were not converted. The pastor would do all in his power to ensure the faithful remain mobilised, and offer them the way of prayer and supplication:

Come, ye Faithful, let us go to the breach before our God, he wills that by humility, by repentance, by faith and by the ardour of prayer, as if with so many victorious arms we were fighting against him, as if we were resisting

---

[17] Cf. Ez 3, chapter in which God defines the prophet's mission. In Calvinist theology, this mission is taken up by ministers.

his blows, & seeking to deflect, both above us and above our neighbours, the effects of his wrath.

To conclude, the preacher established and employed the analogy of the Republic of United Provinces: it was the Republic of Sion, the object of his peroration. Several reasons governed this choice, both theological and political. The theological motif was that the peroration enabled him to pursue his demonstration and reinforce it with a "conative" message; the political motif was that the United Provinces were, in 1654, allied with France, and Gaches would not toy with political power. The sermon was delivered in the home of Guillaume Boreel, and etiquette required that the pastor speak well of the sovereign state that offered him hospitality. There can be little doubting that had the sermon taken place in the British embassy, the conclusion would have been in the same vein, in favour of the British of course; in a context of a minima religious tolerance, however, there was every reason for the pastoral body to maintain favourable relations with those in power, and all the more since Gaches hoped to be taken on in Paris, which meant no backing could be taken lightly, especially coming from so well esteemed a figure as Guillaume Boreel.

Finally, although England was not in conflict with France, Cromwell was a regicide. It was not really thinkable for a French pastor, and so a loyalist, to make use of his name, especially since, at this era, the Lord Protector was hesitating between offering his support to Mazarin and concluding an alliance with Spain, the sworn enemy of both France and England.

Let us then unite both our hearts and our voices, to ask of God the happiness of this Republic, the confirmation of the peace and the rest and glory of one and the other of these flourishing states, that the war had divided and that the peace unites happily together.

The sermon, which was composed merely for the occasion, a simple thanksgiving service, allowed Raimond Gaches to display his rhetorical talents and to employ Calvinist theology even to the point of commenting on particularly delicate historical circumstances. In this trial, Gaches perfectly fulfilled his mission as Reformed minister who is answerable to God for his flock. At the end of the year, 1654, he joined the pastoral community in Charenton and spent the rest of his career, and indeed his life, in Paris.

Works Cited

Calvin, Jean, *Institutes of the Christian Religion*, 1536.

Chevalier, Françoise, *La prédication protestante au XVIIe siècle*, Genève : Labor & Fides, 1994.

Claude, Jean, *Traité sur la composition d'un sermon*, in *Œuvres posthumes de Mr Claude*, Amsterdam : Pierre Savouret, 1688.

Gaches, Raymond (or Raimond), *Action de graces pour la publication de la paix entre l'Angleterre et les Provinces Unies ou Sermon sur le Pseaume CXXII verset 6, prononcé dans l'Hostel de Monseigneur l'Ambassadeur des Provinces Unies le 2 juin 1654*, Charenton, Louis Vendosme, 1654, Library of the Society for the History of French Protestantism (Société de l'Histoire du Protestantisme Français), Ref. 26029 Res.

Haag, Eugène & Haag, Emile, *La France protestante ou vie des protestants français qui se sont faits un nom dans l'histoire*, 2e ed. revised by Henri Bordier, vol. VI, Paris : Sandoz-Fischbacher, 1877-1888, art. « Gaches ».

Jakobson, Roman: "Closing statements: Linguistics and poetics" in *Style in langage*, T.A Sebeok, New York, 1960.

Le Faucheur, Michel, *Traité de l'action de l'orateur ou de la prononciation et du geste*, Paris, Augustin Courbé 1657.

M.Tulii Ciceronis Opera, 10 vol. in 12, Lug. Batavor: Ex Officina Elzeviriana, 1642.

Préclin, Edmond, Tapié, Victor-L., *Le XVIIe siècle, monarchies centralisées (1610-1715)*, Paris : PUF, 1949.

Rou, Jean, *Mémoires inédits et opuscules*, published for the Société de l'Histoire du Protestantisme Français, using the manuscript conserved in the State Archives at the Hague by Francis Waddington, Paris/La Haye: Agence centrale de la Société/Nyhoff, 1857, vol. I.

Vinet, Alexandre, *Histoire de la prédication parmi les réformés de France au XVIIe siècle*, Paris : chez les Editeurs, rue de Rivoli 174, 1860.

CHAPTER SIX

SINNERS IN WAR, SINNERS IN VICTORY: ENGLISH WAR SERMONS, 1701-84

MICHAEL ROTENBERG-SCHWARTZ

Notwithstanding their popularity at the time of publication, eighteenth-century sermons have lain relatively neglected by scholars, probably because their overwhelming number is assumed to offer little more than tediousness of style and redundancy of content. Over the last twenty years, thanks particularly to J.C.D. Clark's *English Society*, sermons have garnered the attention of historians interested in assessing whether, and to what degree, Britain's socio-political culture had changed by the beginning of Victoria's reign.[1] When perused by these scholars, war sermons are read for what they have to say about forms of political authority and the relevance of the church in such matters, not for what they say about war and peace particularly. This will be the focus herein.[2] In fast-day and thanksgiving-day sermons alike, preachers interpret the causes and effects of war as fulfilment of the divine warning that no collective sin shall go unpunished. The sins named are occasionally political (for instance, disunity in the church, faction in Parliament), but usually feature the correlates of luxury that induce much cultural anxiety

---

[1] J.C.D. Clark, *English Society 1688-1832*. Cambridge: CUP, 1985. Focusing more on rhetoric and style, Rolf Lessenich's *Elements of Pulpit Oratory in Eighteenth-Century England*. Koln: Bohlau-Verlag, 1972, senses more doctrinal and political homogeneity in sermons than later accounts. See also: Robert Hole, *Pulpits, Politics and Public Order in England 1760-1832*. Cambridge: CUP, 1989; James E. Bradley, *Religion, Revolution and English Radicalism*. Cambridge: CUP, 2000; Tony Claydon, "The Sermon, the 'Public Sphere' and the Political Culture of Late Seventeenth-Century England" in *The English Sermon Revisited*, ed. Lori Anne Ferrell and Peter McCullough; Manchester; New York: Manchester UP, 2000.

[2] My reading offers more details than but has much in common with D. Napthine and W.A. Speck, "Clergymen and Conflict 1660-1763" *Studies in Church History* 20 (1983): 231-51.

throughout the century.[3] Whether in the midst of war, when the British are typically seen as justified, or in times of peace, sermons continually warn their audiences that if Britain continues to indulge in luxury it will not only be culpable for war and undeserving of peace but also will hasten its own destruction. In war sermons listeners are told that had they been more faithful and moral they would not be in this situation; in peace sermons they are warned that if they again backslide into sin another calamity will surely and soon befall them.

Preachers of the long eighteenth century are known for clarity but also a certain lack of originality. Milton, Fielding and others poke fun at preachers for their reliance on hack-oriented *vade mecums*. It is worth noting, however, that in their choice of prooftexts, eighteenth-century sermons offer a wide range of Biblical reference that often goes beyond what typical concordances may recommend. Consulting William Beveridge's *Thesaurus Theologicus* for Biblical proofs that war is lawful and providentially determined, for example, one is pointed to all of the following passages: Genesis 14.14; Numbers 31.2-3; Samuel 23.2; 1 Kings 2.14; Luke 3.14, 7.9; and Acts 10.1.[4] Additionally, *The Preacher's Directory* recommends the following for thanksgiving sermons on victory or deliverance from public calamity: Exodus 15.2, 15.26; Numbers 23.23; Deuteronomy 33.29; I Samuel 12.7, 12.24, 14.6, 17.47; Ezra 9.13-14; Esther 9.17; Psalm 18.4, 20.7, 47.9, 48.9, 95.1, 98.1, 118.15, 118.23, 126.3; Obadiah 17; and Luke I.74-5. It also offers the following citations for peace sermons: 1 Kings 4.25; 1 Chronicles 22.18; 2 Chronicles 20.30; Psalm 29.11, 46.9, 72.7, 147.14; Isaiah 2.4, 33.20, 65.25; Ezekiel 34.28; and Micah 4.4.[5]

These lists barely cover the possibilities. Of the sermons read for this essay, just the epigraphic citations alone show that preachers derived support from all over the Biblical canon. Those from the Old Testament

---

[3] Though I wish not to discount the importance of historical contextualisation, this essay describes a language that applies to sermons from every war, region, party, and sect in the period. There are individual exceptions, but they seem relatively generic. While Dissenters and oppositionists often vociferate against ministerial corruption, for example, Anglican preachers, or those from ascendant political parties, typically decry "murmuring" and advocate obedience. Obadiah Hughes, a Presbyterian, provides a wonderful exception when he includes test acts in a list of national sins (*Obedience to God the Best Security Against our Enemies* [London: 1742], 44).

[4] William Beveridge, *Thesaurus Theologicus: Or, A Complete System of Divinity* Vol. I. London: 1710, 225-26.

[5] [William Enfield], *The Preacher's Directory; or A Series of Subjects Proper for Public Discourses, with Texts Under Each Head*. London: 1771, 130-133.

cover: Genesis 9.14; Leviticus 18.25; Deuteronomy. 12.10-11, 20.1, 31.6, 33.29; Joshua 1.4, 7; Judges 20.28, 21.2-3, 21.6; 2 Sam. 2.26, 10.12; 1 Kings 8.44-5, 8.59; 2 Kings 20.19; Isaiah 2.4, 11.9, 11.13-4, 14.16-18, 25.9-10, 26.20, 40.31, 42.12, 57.19-21; Jeremiah 4.19, 4.21, 18.7-10, 29.7, 33.10-11, 36.7; Ezekiel 9.4; Joel 2.12-3; Jonah 3.4-5; Proverbs 14.34, 16.7, 16.20, 21.30-31; and 2 Chronicles 7.14, 15.2, 20.28-30. The prophets, especially Isaiah, get special attention here. But the most popular book by far is Psalms, from which the following lines are trotted out: Psalm 2.4, 20.5, 20.7, 29.10, 34.14, 44.9, 49.6, 50.15, 50.23, 60.10-2, 68.19, 83.10-2, 85.10, 97.1, 98.1, 103.10, 106.1, 106.21-3, 107.8, 107.43, 118.15; 118.24-5, 119.59, 120.5-7, and 145.8. Of course, some verses are more popular than others. Deuteronomy 23.9, for example, is the heading for nine war sermons throughout the century; Psalm 122.6-9 and Psalm 144.15 the headings for four each. The following appear as the heading twice: Deuteronomy 33.29, 2 Kings 9.22, Nahum 1.15, Psalm 29.11, 68.30, 85.8, 147.12-14, and 2 Chronicles 6.34-5, 9.8. Thus much for the Old Testament. New Testament epigraphs come from: Mathew 5.4, 24.6; Luke 19.41-42; John 14; Acts 7.26; Romans 1.21, 13.4, 14.13; Ephesians 6.13; Philippians 4.6; Colossians 4.2; 1 Timothy 2.2; Titus 3.1; and James 4.1-3. Colossians 3.15 appears three times as a heading, and Matthew 5.9, Luke 2.14, and Acts 24.2-3 appear twice each. This list is not exhaustive and, again, calls attention to only those verses used as epigraphs to war sermons. Of course, these and other verses are often alluded to within sermons. Offered so many possibilities from the Bible—to say nothing of the Church Fathers or secular history—war preachers perhaps had more work to do, and more to say, than satirists have heretofore acknowledged.

Though seemingly obvious in meaning, the terms "war" and "peace" are defined by preachers in a variety of ways. Presumably, all but the saintly daily experience the first kind, internal wars pitting religious conviction against sinful desire. Interpersonal wars, a second kind, are those pursued legally or in duels. The third kind is that generally understood by modern readers, but even this gets parsed into civil and international war. Many preachers introduce their sermons by surveying these possibilities and then narrowing their focus on either the civil or international. As it is typically considered war's opposite, peace gets similar, though inverse, definition. There exists the inner peace of pure faith; the peace of neighbourly interaction; and the peace of domestic quiet and sustainable international co-operation. Expressions of hope for "world" or "international" tranquillity often include only European or

Christian (itself narrowed to Protestant) unity.[6] Richard Watson, for example, believes that world peace as promised by the prophetic vision of Isaiah chapter 2 will come "when Christianity shall be universally received, rightly understood, and conscientiously practised."[7] Consequently, when considering the depredations of war, sermons often castigate Christians by comparing them to non-Christians or non-Europeans such as Native Americans or Muslims. At their most inclusive, preachers define global peace as a world harmonised by international trade. As most also recognize the likelihood of treaties and contractual obligations getting broken, preachers tend to describe world peace as a temporary condition, one that can only hint at the future that heaven holds in store. This may be realistic, but it is also a religious admission, for as Andrew Burnaby writes, to suppose all warring at a permanent end in this world is "to suppose human nature to be regenerated."[8] Burnaby goes on to state that human imperfection does not make any particular war, much less war in general, natural (he refutes the Hobbesian notion that man originally lived in a state of war), only extremely likely while passions run unchecked.

Generally speaking, then, sermons categorize war as an un-Christian activity. If the governing condition of European nations holds that none can subsist in safety but by the weapons of war, William Law asks in *An Humble, Earnest, and Affectionate Address to the Clergy*, "are not all Christian Kingdoms equally in the same *unchristian* State."[9] Earlier in the same piece Law reproaches more directly, saying that "to make Christians kill Christians for the Sake of Christ's Church, is [Satan's] highest *Triumph* over the highest *Mark*, which Christ has set upon those whom he has purchased by his Blood."[10] Chief among war's particular evils, he

---

[6] This may yet be seen as leaning towards peace. On the ability of religious affiliations to undermine easy commitments to strictly national identities, see Jeremy Black, "Confessional State or Elect Nation? Religion and Identity in Eighteenth-Century England," in *Protestantism and National Identity* ed. Tony Claydon and Ian McBride. Cambridge: CUP, 1998. The same essay notes, however, that toleration within nations arose so leaders could maximize all their resources (including people not affiliated with the state church) in waging war.

[7] Richard Watson, *A Sermon Preached before the University of Cambridge, on Friday, February 4th, 1780* 4th ed. Cambridge: 1780, 5.

[8] Andrew Burnaby, A Sermon Preached in Greenwich Church, on Thursday, July 29, 1784. London: 1784, 7.

[9] William Law, *An Humble, Earnest, and Affectionate Address to the Clergy* 2nd ed. London: 1764, 184. Though not a sermon, the text reflects sentiments often voiced in sermons. I refer to it for its amplification of such ideas, and for the importance of Law himself.

[10] *Ibid.*, 169.

continues, is the killing of Christian men before they understand revelation or undergo final confession.[11] Like Law's text, sermons often depict battlefields in a manner that highlights the antithetical nature of war's graphic violence to the message of Jesus's life. In a passage resembling countless others, for example, William Warburton describes "the dreadful ravages and many evils of war" (this time, the Seven Years' War) in the following imagery:

the throbs of a parent's heart; the sad long parting farewell of friends and relatives dear; the tedious marches; the acute sensation of hunger and thirst, amidst endless toil and fatigue; the coarsest food dealt forth with a penurious hand, when the scraps of a beggar would be considered as a banquet; the deep and ghastly wounds; the groans of the wounded, sufficient to pierce the nether millstone; the flowers of life, the glories of this world cut down, untimely and suddenly cut down, levelled with the dust, O how changed! breathless carcasses, and pale unless deluged in their own blood![12]

Such horrors are not always taken negatively. In a fast sermon at the beginning of the same war, John Chafy exhorts his listeners to let anger and wrath motivate them into fighting, and initiates this process by describing exactly those domestic horrors lamented by Warburton:

Let us alarm our Imaginations with all the grim Terrors of a War at our very Doors: Let us represent to our Minds the cruel Insolence of an Enemy trampling on the helpless Age of our venerable Parents; and wantonly rioting in the Virtue of deflower'd Virgins. Let us fancy to ourselves the horrid Prospect of his embruing his Hands in the Blood of innocent Infants, while their frantick Mothers (as the Wives of *Jewry* did to *Herod*'s Soldiers) throw out their fruitless Prayers to the unrelenting Murtherers, and scream for Mercy, which they are sure of not obtaining.[13]

Chafy goes on to state that if Britons are fated to lose the war, at least they should do so like the Roman senators who awaited the Gauls or the Jewish priests whom Pompey's soldiers could not terrify. As images of violence are thus not in themselves unequivocally anti-war, Warburton follows his sequence of horrors with a further description of a field in Germany: "That sun which in the morning beheld mighty hosts, bright in arms, terrible with banners, has before it set, beheld them scattered in

---

[11] *Ibid.*, 175-76.

[12] William Warburton, *A People's Prayer for Peace. A Sermon Preached at Northampton, February 13, 1761*. London: 1761, 24-5.

[13] John Chafy, *A Sermon, Preached at Broad-Chalk, in Wiltshire, on Friday the 11th of February, 1757*. Salisbury: 1757, 23-4.

flight, disarmed and smeared in the dust, or groaning in death; and the whole field has been an aceldema."[14] "Aceldama," a term literally meaning "field of blood," refers to the potter's field in the valley of Hinnom in which Judas Iscariot is said to have hung himself. Searching for an appropriate label for war in his peace sermon of 1713, William Bear also alludes to "Aceldama," associating with it another area in Hinnom:

> What shall I call it? An *Aceldama?* A Field of Blood? Or, rather the Valley of *Tophet?*…where the Lives of so many poor Wretches must be sacrificed to some cursed Idol of Ambition, Avarice or Envy, set up in the Heart of some wicked Prince, some haughty or cruel *Nimrod*, that hunts for the Prey, or thirsts for the Blood of other Nations…[15]

In the Bible, the valley of Tophet is a site of Baal and Moloch worship, where, according to Jeremiah 19.4, the Jews made human sacrifices to strange gods. By analogising a field of battle to locations of idol-worship and the field in which Jesus's betraying disciple committed suicide, Warburton and Bear imply the spiritual danger of engaging in war. Even so, Warburton goes on to explain that in thus describing war his intention is not to discourage men from engaging in the "just and honourable war in which we are engaged; the cause of liberty, of truth, of religion, and therefore the cause of God."[16]

Indeed, nearly every sermon from the century makes room for Augustinian "just war" theory. What puts war beyond reproach, of course, is provocation, an easy enough cause for preachers to show given ongoing presumptions of France's encroaching ambitions. Any war is just if it is defensive, as William Ayerst writes in a sermon of 1712:

> …tho' Christianity carries the Duties of Patience and Forbearance to a great Height, yet does it no where order us to give up ourselves a Prey to our Devourers, and cancels not that first Law of Nature, Self-Defence, which being confessedly allowable between Man and Man, must be so between Nation and Nation.[17]

Importantly, the right to self-defence is not limited to retaliatory acts, but includes pre-emptive strikes, as Walter Harte writes in 1739:

---

[14] Warburton, *People's Prayer*, 26.
[15] William Bear, *The Blessing of Peace. Set forth in a Sermon, Preached on Tuesday July the 7th, 1713*. Exon: 1713, 9.
[16] Warburton, *People's Prayer*, 28.
[17] William Ayerst, *The Duty and Motives of Praying for Peace (London: 1712), 7. See also William Fleetwood, A Sermon on the Fast-Day, January the Sixteenth, 1712/13*. London: 1712, 6.

"War...may be pronounced *just* and *lawful*, not only in times of actual invasion, but when we apprehend, and consequently are desirous to prevent such oppressions, as in the end must conclude in actual invasion."[18] Others write that war will be considered just so long as the contending parties have first tried to negotiate. For example, Richard Chapman writes that before war is declared, "there ought to be...some Overtures made for Peace by mutual Embassies...but then when such Overtures have been made, and to no purpose...why, doubtless, in such a Case, War is both Lawful and Just."[19] Convinced that such circumstances excuse war, Isaac Smithson carries the point further by arguing that the avoidance of armed conflict when excusable is in fact criminal.[20] Thus far, war seems justified by secular agents, and according to secular expectations. For most preachers, of course, religious and natural rights are mixed.

While preachers occasionally consider Grotian principles of international relations when pondering how to resolve broken treaties and quell princely ambitions, they usually resort almost immediately to heavenly justice. For example, in a justification of the War of Jenkins' Ear, George Smyth makes the right to self-defence a divinely inherited trait: "God's having implanted so deep in our Nature the Desire of preserving and defending ourselves, is a sufficient and plain Indication that he allows us the Use of all lawful Means in order to these Ends."[21] In a fast sermon of 1702, Henry Sacheverell takes note of a different heavenly attribution to dismiss secular rule. Premising that monarchical dignity is seated above the cognisance of law, he goes on to say there is no bar at which to arraign national disputes but the tribunal of God, which is the field of battle:

> where God Presides as the Great and Supream Lord and Judge of Life and Death, that gives Victory to Kings, and saves his servants from the Peril of the Sword, that sets up One and pulls down Another, and administers Justice by the sole Determination of His Will and Power.[22]

---

[18] Walter Harte, *The Reasonableness and Advantage of National Humiliations, upon the Approach of War.* Oxford: 1739-40, 16.

[19] Richard Chapman, *The Lawfulness of War in General, and Justness of the Present asserted.* London: 1704, 9.

[20] Isaac Smithson, *A Sermon, Occasioned by the Declaration of War Against France.* London: 1756, 17-8.

[21] George Smyth, *The Lawfulness of War; and the Duty of a People Entering into It.* London: 1740, 10.

[22] Henry Sacheverell, *A Defence of Her Majesty's Title to the Crown, and a Justification of Her Entring into a War with France and Spain.* London: 1710, 18.

Though negotiation with the sword transcends human law, in doing so it does not abrogate law altogether; rather it appeals to a higher one. Anticipating and dismissing Clausewitz's dictum that war is politics by other means, Chapman therefore explains that whereas citizens may have recourse to law, princes only have recourse to the sword because neither is subject to the other's law:

> Suppose, for Instance, That is a difference happens between any Subjects of a well-order'd, civiliz'd State, they have (or may have) immediate recourse to the Laws for its decision...Now the Case, we may observe, is much the same with respect to Princes; only with this difference. When Monarchs, or Princes quarrel, the Sword only is their Law: So that if War be in itself unlawful, then they can have no redress, when one injures or encroaches upon the other.[23]

Harte puts forth a different argument altogether, making the issue a search for truth. As people have rights that might be infringed, so too do kings; and since treaties are often trials of political skill conducted by self-interested judges, rather than inquiries into truth, wars are justified as "a sort of reference and appeal to the justice of God, who is the supreme arbitrator in these cases."[24]

Later in the century, preachers like Josiah Tucker cast doubt on so-called legitimate causes, associating them with self-interest and worldly desire for monetary or territorial expansion.[25] In a fast sermon of 1779, William Thom, a Scottish minister sympathetic to the American colonies, blames wars on kings and ministers who "are just big grown up children...with this particular difference, that instead of fighting the needless quarrels they have raised...they hound out their innocent subjects to battle."[26] At a different, less reductive moment, Thom astutely considers the manipulative potential of war, claiming it may be waged by ministers to distract attention from pressing domestic concerns: "sometimes wicked ministers of state engage their master in a war merely to screen themselves from condign punishment [or] to divert or stifle the clamour of an injured people against their covetous and bungling administration."[27] Even so, he

---

[23] Chapman, *Lawfulness of War*, 8-9.

[24] Harte, *Reasonableness and Advantage*, 18.

[25] Josiah Tucker, *The Case of Going to War, for the Sake of Procuring, Enlarging, or Securing of Trade*. London: 1763, 12-3. Though not a sermon, I refer to this work because it stands out in the period as a staunch anti-war tract.

[26] William Thom, *From whence come Wars? An Enquiry into the Origin, with a View of the Progress and Effects, of War*. Glasgow: 1782, 22.

[27] *Ibid.*, 8.

recognises that wars may be caused by the "violation of some sacred and perfect" rights.[28] Calling it an evil even when just, Newcome Cappe proposes and dismisses a litany of potential justifications (including dynastic ambition, economic prosperity, and the defence of a dubious or negligible right), by stating that "some of these things can in *no* circumstances warrant it, and none of them in *many*."[29] After denying that truth can ever be physically defended, he goes on to restrict just causes to one, oppression:

> What is it then by which war may be justified? Not by any pleas of truth, of the interest, propagation, honour, maintenance of truth…Truth does not want the patronage of the sword; the sword cannot serve her, and she would disdain such service…It is the actual or the threatened violation of the great common rights of men by which war must be justified. When the sword is drawn against oppression, the cause is the cause of God.[30]

Even in such instances, then, the religious paradigm obtains as a just cause for war.

As sermons equate secular with religious causes, they justify war with reference to the Bible itself. The Bible not only justifies war, but provides readers with exemplary military leaders who at times were commanded by God to attack an enemy. If the holiest of leaders were permitted to lead their nations to war, certainly others may follow their example. A related rationale argues that the Gospels' relative silence on professional soldiery implies that wars are permitted. Both arguments often appear side by side, as in Chapman's explanation that:

> …*Moses, Joshua* and *David* were Men of War, as well as of God, *Who taught their Hands to War, and their Fingers to Fight*: And the many Wars, Treaties and Alliances they enter'd into, by God's own appointment, are sufficient to convince us, That War was not in those times unlawful: And then next, as to the New Testament, we find no where therein any Prohibition of War, but rather an implicit Allowance thereof; as is very plain both from the Baptist's answer to the Soldier's Question, *And what shall we do?* where he does not tell 'em, that their Profession is in itself

---

[28] *Ibid.*, 12.

[29] In a different sermon just four years earlier, Cappe demonstrates the susceptibility of masses to the rhetoric of causes. Rather than describe who redefines such terms, there the words "ascribe" new meaning to themselves. Newcome Cappe, *A Sermon Preached on Friday the Fourth of February, MDCCLXXX*. York: 1780, 21.

[30] Newcome Cappe, *A Sermon Preached Thursday the Twenty-ninth of July, MDCCLXXXIV*. York: 1784, 12.

sinful, that they must quit their Posts, or desert their Colours. No, he only cautions 'em, *To do no Violence to any Man, nor accuse any falsely but to be content with their Wages.* A Caution indeed not improper for the Military Men of this Age: For tho' War be not in itself Sinful, yet they may make it so, by doing Violence, by being Cruel and Barbarous either before, or after, a Victory.[31]

Though he refers to ideals espoused by Matthew V (turn the other cheek) and Romans XVII (overcome evil with good), Ayerst also invokes as positive, and more realistic, influences such biblical warriors as Gideon, Barak, Samson, Jeptha, David, and Samuel.[32] Noting that Cornelius the centurion was the first gentile convert to Christianity, George Horne argues that the figure of a warrior and a Christian are not incompatible: "the General may still go forth, as of old, with the Prophet by his side. While the hands of Joshua are extended in the field, those of Moses may be elevated in prayer."[33]

Even with Biblical endorsement, sermons caution listeners neither to rely on nor to discredit God's assistance, lest they suffer unexpected defeat. An example of the former occurs in William Farmerie's fast sermon of 1710, in which people are reminded that even the ancient Jews, who were under God's direct protection, could not idly rely upon providence to save them, but had to levy men and order their armies:

> …therefore tis in vain for us to suspect, that Success and Victory will drop into our Mouths, unless we *pay our Tribute Penny for me, and thee,* contribute what we can towards it. The method of God's Providence is now settled, which is to work with second Causes, and therefore we must not expect to conquer our Enemies by our Prayers alone, or by any other spiritual Qualifications whatever they be; these must be done, tis true, but we must not leave the other undone.[34]

Like Farmerie's, John Denne's fast sermon of 1739 advocates preparedness, yet follows this with an opposite reminder not to forget God's influence:

> Men are seldom wanting to themselves…they are rather apt to *glory* and *trust* too much in their own *Wisdom* and *Might*; and the more they have of

---

[31] Chapman, *Lawfulness of War*, 7.

[32] Ayerst, *Duty and Motives*, 8.

[33] George Horne, *A Sermon Preached before the Honourable House of Commons.* Oxford: 1780, 5.

[34] William Farmerie, *God the Only Judge, and Our Only Hope in War.* London: 1710, 18.

both, the greater is their Danger of profanely thinking...either that all things come by Chance, or proceed from such a Necessity in *second* Causes, as excludes all Efficiency in the *first*...so that they never look up to God, implore his Aid and Favour, or rely for Success upon his *Providence*...[35]

Both pieces of advice recur in sermon after sermon, but the second predominates. Since providence decides who shall gain victory in war, John Shower reasons, "if God be on our side, we need not fear when Men rise up against us."[36]

A fear of God is a healthy thing, however, for as one can never anticipate which side God will choose, so too a nation ought never to assume that success signifies the rightness of its cause. At times, as Richard Fiddes writes, victory may be owing to the sinfulness of the enemy: "God may take occasions from the sins and impietys of a nation to punish it by what methods he pleases, and he often makes one wicked nation the instrument of his vengeance upon another, without any respect to the justice, or unlawfulness of the war of either Side."[37] Even if this case does not obtain, still victory should never be celebrated as an end in itself, for as John Conybeare declares in a thanksgiving sermon for the treaty of Aix-la-Chapelle, "Even a successful War is an Evil."[38] Likewise, Thomas Fothergill writes, "generally speaking even the Victors themselves are almost ruined thereby."[39] For one, victors are adversely affected by the deaths of soldiers—not only their own, John Butler notes, but their enemy's.[40] John Kennicott understands that the deaths of many preserve the lives of more, but rhetorically asks "is this a *pleasing* Contemplation?"[41] Other factors qualify victory as well, particularly economic ones. Joshua Toulmin, for example, focuses on the problems of depopulation and desolation, showing that a loss for one means a loss for

---

[35] John Denne, *The Only Sure Way to Success in War.* London: 1739-40, 10-1.

[36] John Shower, *A Fast-Sermon, on the Account of the Present War* 2nd ed. London: 1705, 22.

[37] Richard Fiddes, *A Sermon Preached on the Thanksgiving Day, December 3d, 1702.* York: 1703, 24. See also: William Thom, *Achan's Trespass in the Accursed Thing considered.* Glasgow: 1778, 7.

[38] John Conybeare, *True Patriotism.* London: 1749, 37.

[39] Thomas Fothergill, *The Desireableness of Peace, and the Duty of a Nation upon the Recovery of it.* Oxford: 1749, 7.

[40] John Butler, *A Sermon Preached Before the Honourable House of Commons, at the Church of St. Margaret's, Westminster, on Friday, December 13, 1776.* London: 1777, 6.

[41] Benjamin Kennicott, *The Duty of Thanksgiving for Peace in general, and the Reasonableness of Thanksgiving for Our Present Peace.* London: 1749, 11.

all. To this, he adds a final concern—namely, that one day the enemy may seek revenge. [42] Thom shares Toulmin's capacity to sense the misery of both sides in war: "in war the weaker side is miserable: and it commonly happens, that, in the course of the war, or, at least, in the issue of it, the stronger is miserable also." Noting that a kingdom seldom gains anything by war, either in terms of money or territory, he goes on to describe how victory facilitates both socio-economic decay and a cyclical repetition of armed conflict:

> The kingdom in striving to be victorious at an enormous expense, which it can ill bear, reduces itself to poverty and ruin,--and if at length it succeeds, those in the upper rank, may, for a while, enjoy a brutal and inglorious ease, whilst they wallow in luxury and debauchery, devouring that which, by the fortune of the war, hath fallen into their fangs; but when that is devoured, they commonly, like hungry dogs, fall to work again, and worry, and bite, and devour one another. In short, if a state hath been victorious, and hath conquered an extensive territory, it is but hastening the faster to its own downfall: either the subjects, great and small, will become absolute slaves under a despotic master, or else the empire, being too extensive, consisting of too many provinces, must crumble again into parts; parts amongst which all the horrible injustice, and all the horrible ills of war, are like to be acted over again, and suffered anew. [43]

This language bears a striking resemblance to the rise-and-fall narratives of history, very popular in the period, that blame national collapse on luxury and imperial overextension. Even more explicitly than Thom, Arnold King senses in present-day victory the historical signs of ultimate defeat: "The four great empires of the world were severally lost by their very greatness…if then kingdoms may be overturned by the progress of victory, it is evident…even the success of war may be the punishment!"[44] Because from a human perspective there is no way to tell victory from defeat, people must interpret every outcome as a manifestation of God's will and pray for the best.

Though they justify war itself, many sermons criticise the brutality of war as sinful. Sometimes this is implicit, as when Gideon Castelfranc gives thanks for Britons in Jamaica never having to prosecute the Seven

---

[42] Joshua Toulmin, *The American War Lamented*. London: 1776, 10.

[43] Thom, *From Whence*, 14, 16.

[44] Arnold King, *A Sermon Preached before the Right Honourable the Lord Mayor, the Aldermen, and Citizens of London, at the Cathedral Church of St. Paul, on Tuesday, April 25, 1749*. London: 1749, 10. For another list, this time with Biblical and secular exemplars, see: Newcome Cappe, *A Sermon Preached on the thirteenth of December*. York: 1776, 28.

Years' War, "either by perfidious breaches of our word; by such treacherous practices as the Law of Arms itself condemns; by inhuman cruelties; by assassinations; by tyrannical methods of forcing money into our coffers, and men into our service."[45] On the other hand, Chapman explicitly declares that, "tho' War be not in itself Sinful, yet they may make it so, by doing Violence, by being Cruel and Barbarous either before, or after, a Victory."[46] Modifying this point, many other writers admit that a war, justified though it may be at its inception, will become sinful if it is protracted beyond the moment when peace becomes attainable. Even when one side originally has a just claim to war, Thom writes, "soon after the war begins, it becomes difficult to say which of the belligerent parties is the most injurious, and deserves the greatest blame."[47] In his celebration of the Treaty of Utrecht—a peace to which Whigs bitterly objected—George Hooper contends that prolonging war is tantamount to challenging God directly: "to persist longer in [a war] than is necessary, is to change the Side, to begin to War against the Gospel; and by a bold Appeal to provoke the Almighty to judge for himself."[48] And Andrew Burnaby defines a just and righteous nation as one that makes war:

> with extreme reluctance, and always with hope and desire of speedily terminating it by a safe and honourable peace. They will make concessions, will give up and sacrifice many just claims and pretensions, to stop or prevent the effusion of human blood.[49]

Passages like these indicate a common concern that acts which fall outside the category of *jus in bello* be avoided. They also imply that wars should cease once goals have been achieved, lest people act on what Thomas Harris calls a "Spirit of Revenge," that desire for "the Destruction of the Countries and Kingdoms we war with," and thereby engage in sin.[50]

---

[45] Gideon Castelfranc, *A Sermon, Preached at the Parish Church of St. Andrew, on Friday the Second of September, 1763.* Kingston, Jamaica: 1763, 11.

[46] Chapman, *Lawfulness of War*, 7.

[47] Thom, *From Whence*, 12.

[48] George Hooper, *The Bishop of Bath and Wells's Thanksgiving-Sermon for the Peace.* London: 1713, 6. See also: Joseph Stennett, *A Sermon Preach'd at Little-Wild-Street on Tuesday, April 25, 1749.* London: 1749, 16; and Joseph Cornish, *The Miseries of War, and the Hope of Final and Universal Peace.* Taunton: 1784, 6-7.

[49] Burnaby, *A Sermon*, 8.

[50] Thomas Harris, *A Blow to France, or A Sermon Preach'd at the Meeting in Mill-Yard, in Good-man's-Fields; Nov. 22, 1709.* London: 1709, 20.

As they acknowledge its conduciveness to sinful behaviour, so too many sermons deem war itself sinful, even if just. For example, Bear writes that: "War at the *best*, is but a *Necessary Evil*: And the greatest *Victories*, obtain'd by the shedding of much Blood, are far from being *truly* Good or Glorious in themselves."[51] Later in the century, Robert Pool Finch recognises war's usefulness as an "instrument" to check injustice, avarice, and pride, but nevertheless sees it as "at best but disagreeable in itself, and frequently productive of the most fatal Evils."[52] Joseph Trapp sympathises with this view, calling war "the great fomenter of vice and wickedness," and specifying the corruptions endemic to military encampments.[53] Significantly, Trapp focuses on the Christians who perpetrate and perpetuate such offences. Calling war a "disgrace to Christianity," he goes on to wonder:

> that there should at *all* be any such Thing as *War*, among its Professors; were its Precepts duly obey'd, there would be nothing like it in these Parts of the World...that Christians should not only have Wars like other Nations, but more than other Nations; more Sharp, Cruel, and Bloody Wars, than any other People upon the Face of the Earth, directly contrary to the Genius and Tendency of the Religion they profess; is a most deplorable Scandal to that Religion, tho' no Argument against it.[54]

A similar, though oblique, approach is taken by Ayerst, when he compares contemporary Christian with Muslim society:

> Even the *Mahometans* themselves, whose very Religion was founded upon the Sword, seem of late Years more humanely inclined, and keep themselves freer from Dissensions among themselves, and Quarrels with their Neighbours, than those that pretend to be the Followers of the Gospel of Peace.[55]

This comparison derives its power from accepting yet flouting assumptions that Christian morality reigns supreme over the morals of others. Shower's sermon from earlier in the War of Spanish Succession,

---

[51] Bear, *Blessing of Peace*, 3.
[52] Robert Pool Finch, *A Sermon Preach'd in the Parish Church of St. Mary Woolnoth in Lombard Street, on Tuesday, April 25, 1749*. London: 1749, 13.
[53] Joseph Trapp, *A Sermon Preach'd at the Parish-Church of St. Martin in the Fields; January the 16th, 1711*. London: 1711, 12-3. Bear describes the negative impact of such camps on society at large.
[54] *Ibid.*, 10.
[55] Ayerst, *Duty and Motives*, 4.

which notices that Christianity is often used as a veil to justify imperial ambitions, sounds similar but is different:

> The Defence or Promotion of true Religion is sometimes made a Cover for Violence, Rapine and Murder. How many thousands of Indians and Infidels have been massacred by the Spaniards, to make room for Christianity, and to plant the Gospel among them? And how much innocent Blood hath been shed in Christendom, to reduce Hereticks to the Unity of the Roman Church, or punish their Obstinacy or Apostacy who would not return to it? And this under the pretence of Religion and Conscience, and a Zeal for Truth…Strange Christians, who think it their Duty to destroy all others, when and where they are able to do it, if the Pope do but require and encourage it for the Catholick Cause.[56]

Attacking Catholic false consciousness and playing on war-time hatred of Spain and France, Shower seems unaware that Anglicanism may similarly abuse. Then again, he spreads the blame fairly equally to all sinners when he notes that wars are "caused by *Armies* of *Iniquities* rather than of *Souldiers*."[57] As mentioned above, questions concerning British legitimacy will be asked later in the century, with particular regard to the American colonies and the slave trade. But even then it is common for many to differentiate true from false consciousness by distinguishing British from non-British sensibilities. For example, in 1784 Cappe declares: "The heart that mourns not over the existence, or rejoices not in the extinction of such miseries is a Barbarian's not a Briton's, a monster's, not a man's."[58] This invocation of Barbarians may be largely metaphorical, but Ayerst's and Burnaby's glances at Alexander the Great and Pyrrhus, the king of Epirus—both infamous exemplars of over-reaching conquerors—indicate ways in which profane history is brought in to illuminate religious thoughts on war.[59]

Among these thoughts is an occasional exploration of the origins of war as a human activity. While Trapp and Ayerst accept the responsibility of human agents, Warburton side-steps the issue by placing the burden on sin personified:

---

[56] Shower, *A Fast Sermon*, 8.

[57] *Ibid.*, 12. Thomas Penrose, on the other hand, reminds officers and militiamen of the county of Berks not to forget that "the best Success will ever attend those who are the best *Souldiers of Jesus Christ*." Here virtue is advocated, not assumed. Thomas Penrose, *The Practice of Religion and Virtue Recommended; especially in Times of Danger*. London: 1759, 19.

[58] Cappe, *A Sermon Preached Thursday*, 9.

[59] Ayerst, *Duty and Motives*, 13; Burnaby, *A Sermon*, 16.

War has been deemed a mysterious providence; How is it so, when its original is so easily traced, or universally known? Sin puts a cup of fury into the hands of Princes; Sin gives the sword to wound and slay its thousands, its millions; Sin spreads the horrid carnage, and even swells rivers with blood; it overturns fenced cities, and depopulates rich and powerful kingdoms.[60]

This is sober compared to Law's association of war with Satan.[61] Besides abstract sin or the devil himself, preachers typically trace aggression to base impulses such as ambition, pride, or lust. Of course, these passions are said to stem from the Fall. As Harte explains:

the first man, by rebelling against God, soon sowed the seeds of dissention in his own family, which sprung up and overspread the face of the whole earth. By withdrawing his allegiance from his Maker, he became a slave to his passions, to pride, avarice, and ambition, from whence arose violence, rapine, and War.[62]

As war is one of the dire effects of the fall, so J. Owen uses it as a descriptor of battle itself: "An *Eden* metamorphosed, not merely into a *wilderness*, but what is worse into a *field* of *blood!*" [63]

Once identified as the fruit of Adam's failure, war is placed under the category of divine punishment. William Dawes says this explicitly: "wars are generally sent by God, upon Nations, as Punishments for their Sins."[64] Sacheverell expresses the same, and adds this is true "whether [the war] succeeds well or ill."[65] And Bear reduces all causes to this one: "the Chief reason is because God himself hath a controversy with them…The Wicked (says the Psalmist) are but a sword in God's hand."[66] Cappe classes war "among the severest instruments of divine Discipline…with pestilence and famine, and by David pestilence was preferred before it."[67] And Richard Hurd admits that no national distress has ever been inflicted that was not

---

[60] Warburton, *People's Prayer*, 12.

[61] Law, *An Humble, Earnest*, 175.

[62] Harte, *Reasonableness and Advantage*, 20.

[63] J. Owen, *The Song of Deborah, apply'd to the Battle of Dettingen.* London: 1758, 25.

[64] William Dawes, *Times of War, Times for National Humiliation and Repentance* 2nd ed. London: 1707, 5. See also, Philip Barton, *The Nature and Advantages of a Religious Fast.* London: 1739, 11.

[65] Sacheverell, *A Defence*, 20.

[66] Bear, *Blessing of Peace*, 5.

[67] Cappe, *A Sermon Preached Thursday*, 9.

deserved.[68] Importantly, preachers represent war not as *a* punishment, but the only punishment available to God for castigating a wayward nation. While personal calamities aptly punish and correct individuals, Thomas Thompson writes: "When a Nation or Country suffers...to be sure this is the punishing Hand of God...for there is no punishing Bodies Politic but in this World."[69] Whereas individuals may be subject to punishment in both this and the afterlife, nations must always be punished presently because they have no afterlife.

Though sent as a punishment, war may conduce to good by encouraging sinners to return to God. Smyth expresses this sentiment: "the true reason of God's visiting a Nation...with war...is to correct and punish them for their sins, or to reclaim them from them, and teach them righteousness."[70] Under this rubric, every war hinges on the same determining factor: whether a nation ever comes together to repent its sins.[71] To a discussion of the rise and fall of Israel and Rome, William Smith adds a footnote that highlights the relevance of this sensibility to contemporary times:

> In regard to the Moderns, I shall only mention an answer...made by a French Officer, who during the wars between the two Nations, being asked by some English, flush'd with Conquest, 'when his Nation would gain such Victories over them,' calmly replied, 'when your sins are greater than ours.'[72]

Because eighteenth-century preachers tend to see war as a divine punishment, they conceive of penitence as the only one way to win. As the nation sins, so it falls; as it turns to righteousness, it will rise. After mouthing the words of a vain patriot who thinks that, "surely wealth and riches will bear us out, will gain us success and honour in the field," Farmerie retorts, "Alas, riches profit us nothing...if the lord be not with us."[73] Likewise, Philip Doddridge states that, "I think I may safely venture

---

[68] Richard Hurd, *A Sermon Preached before the Right Honourable the House of Lords, in the Abbey Church of Westminster, on Friday, December 13, 1776* 2nd ed. London: 1777, 9.

[69] Thomas Thompson, *A Discourse Relating to the Present Times, Addressed to the Serious Consideration of the Publi.* London: 1757, 12. See also, Sacheverell, *A Defence*, 30; and Toulmin, *American War*, 12.

[70] Smyth, *Lawfulness*, 23. See also: Chafy, *A Sermon*, 5.

[71] Penitence sometimes figures as more noble and beneficial than any military gain could be. See, for example: Thomas Scott, *The Reasonableness, Pleasure, and Benefit of National Thanksgiving.* Ipswich: 1759, 10.

[72] William Smith, *National Prosperity or Adversity dependent upon the virtuous or vicious State of a Nation.* London: 1740, 9.

[73] Farmerie, *God the Only*, 11.

to affirm that we can never form any just Expectation of continued success and prosperity in our Military Affairs, unless there be a zealous concern about a reformation in our manners."[74] Indeed, as preacher after preacher notes, penitence remains crucial notwithstanding the justness of the nation's cause.[75] Although a just cause may legitimize war, it can be trumped by moral laxity.

Significantly, even peace may endanger a careless nation, as Robert Drummond notes:

> Peace itself, but its very calmness and security may become the rankest source of vice, licentiousness and corruption…if we forget our God and abandon our virtue. A nation therefore will not appear, even to human policy, to be really and truly secure in its tranquillity, by being freed from the present alarms of War: except the people cultivate those principles, which are the natural preservatives of peace.[76]

His is not a unique position. Like Drummond, Stennett warns that Britain must exercise its virtue, justice, and fear of God, lest they abuse the gifts of peace and fall victim once again to the sword.[77] As passages like this show, eighteenth-century preachers treat peace as a contingent, fragile state, one that may enable sin as much as righteousness. J. Blackburn provides the rationale for such thinking:

> We see that successful Commerce brings Riches; that great Riches lead to Idleness and Corruption; and these to Slavery and Oppression: and that Success in War leads to Ambition; which, in the Prosecution, often impoverishes and ruins a Nation; or perhaps is carried on, to such an encrease of Dominion, that at last the Empire sinks, as it were oppress'd by its own Weight. While, on the other Hand, Observation will convince us, that loss of Victory, and want of Success, have often been the Means of securing those Liberties, and that Happiness, which Success would have put to the Hazard, if not intirely ruined.—The Truth is, we can form no certain Judgment in the Affair. For, after all our boasted Penetration, we are very short-sighted Creatures, and cannot penetrate into Futurity; nor see what the distant Consequences of Events may be; and, therefore,

---

[74] Philip Doddridge, *The Necessity of a General Reformation, in order to a well-grounded Hope of Success in War*. London: 1740, 12.

[75] See: Dawes, *Times of War*, 7; Sacheverell, *A Defence*, 29; Edward Cobden, *The Duty of a People Going Out to War*. London: 1744, 8.

[76] Robert Drummond, *A Sermon Preached before the House of Lords, in the Abbey Church of Westminster, on Tuesday April 25, 1749*. London: 1749, 8.

[77] Stennett, *A Sermon*, 13. See also: Joseph Partridge, *The Renovation of the Heart the only True and acceptable Fast*. Nantwich: 1778, 6-7.

cannot pronounce upon the Virtue of any Nation, or the Degree of divine Favour which it enjoys, either from its general Success, or want thereof.[78]

In the end, when it comes to war and peace, eighteenth-century sermons filter the world through the same lens: sin. While enlightened secularists such as Hume and Smith see jurisprudence, economics and reason as the keys to peace, preachers teach that only a holy nation can glory under heavenly protection. The ideal for preachers like Thomas Harris is for the nation to find satisfaction in a providentially defined balance:

> But this is one of the Vices of this Nation...we are apt to quarrel with Providence, for not granting us that Abundance, which...is better suspended, than granted. A Middling State, neither pinch'd with Straits on the one Hand, nor over flowing with Plenty on the other, is undoubtedly the best State for a Man, as a Creature corrupt.[79]

Victory does not bring an end to struggle, peace does—though not always that, for man as is a "creature corrupt." While to Jacob Jefferson and many others, peace is something first sustained at home through obedience to authority, to those like William Keate it is protected only by continuing to prepare for war:

> But if declining hostilities can scarcely secure us from the outrages of war; if the too anxious appearance of 'labouring for peace' be only the way more effectually to provoke offence, a dreadful and deplorable necessity it is, that peace never can be ensured, but by preparations for war; and the stronger the sinews, as they are called, of war are, the more flattering is the prospect of peace, and more permanent its establishment. In our case these sinews have been strained but too high, and however harsh and unwelcome be the truth, our distresses are to be ascribed, as much at least, to the forced exertions and unexampled success of a former war, as to the unfortunate events of that just concluded.[80]

What such passages reveal is an on-going cultural anxiety regarding Britain's standing as a nation—in itself, in comparison to Israel and other ancient empires, and most relevantly, in relation to the rest of an economically developing Europe. Literary scholars often think of Britain

---

[78] J. Blackburn, *Reflections on Government and Loyalty. A Sermon Preached at King John's Court, April 25, 1749*. London: 1749, 22.

[79] Harris, *A Blow*, 19.

[80] Jacob Jefferson, *The Blessings of Peace, and the Means of Preserving It*. Oxford: 1763, 20-9; William Keate, *Sermon Preached upon the Occasion, of the General Thanksgiving, for the Late Peace, July 29th, 1784*. Bath: 1784, 21-2.

at mid-century as supremely confident. During its first ascendant phase, however, preachers worried over what looked like Britain's impending doom.[81]

Works Cited

Ayerst, William. *The Duty and Motives of Praying for Peace*. London, 1712.

Barton, Philip. *The Nature and Advantages of a Religious Fast*. London, 1739.

Bear, William. *The Blessing of Peace. Set forth in a Sermon, Preached on Tuesday July the 7th, 1713*. Exon, 1713.

Beveridge, William. *Thesaurus Theologicus: Or, A Complete System of Divinity*. Vol. 1. London, 1710.

Black, Jeremy. "Confessional State or Elect Nation? Religion and Identity in Eighteenth-Century England." In *Protestantism and National Identity*, edited by Tony Claydon and Ian McBride. Cambridge: Cambridge University Press, 1998.

Blackburn, J. *Reflections on Government and Loyalty. A Sermon Preached at King John's Court, April 25, 1749*. London, 1749.

Bradley, James E. *Religion, Revolution and English Radicalism* Cambridge: Cambridge University Press, 2000.

Burnaby, Andrew. *A Sermon Preached in Greenwich Church, on Thursday, July 29, 1784*. London, 1784.

Butler, John. *A Sermon Preached Before the Honourable House of Commons, at the Church of St. Margaret's, Westminster, on Friday, December 13, 1776*. London, 1777.Cappe, Newcome. *A Sermon Preach'd at York, to a Congregation of Protestant Dissenters, on the 27th of November, 1757, just upon receiving the Account of the King of Prussia's Victory, on the Fifth of that Month*. York, 1757.

—. *A Sermon Preached on Friday the Fourth of February, MDCCLXXX*. York, 1780.

—. *A Sermon Preached on the thirteenth of December*. York, 1776.

—. *A Sermon Preached Thursday the Twenty-ninth of July, MDCCLXXXIV*. York, 1784.

---

[81] During the early, unsuccessful years of the Seven Years' War, Cappe laments, "Ah, Britain, God has left thee." Newcome Cappe, *A Sermon Preach'd at York, to a Congragation of Protestant Dissenters, on the 27th of November, 1757, just upon receiving the Account of the King of Prussia's Victory, on the Fifth of that Month*. York: 1757, 19.

Castelfranc, Gideon. *A Sermon, Preached at the Parish Church of St. Andrew, on Friday the Second of September, 1763*. Kingston, Jamaica, 1763.

Ceadel, Martin. *The Origins of War Prevention*. Oxford: Clarendon Press, 1996.

—. "Ten Distinctions for Peace Historians." In *The Pacifist Impulse in Historical Perspective*, edited by Harvey L. Dyck. Toronto: University of Toronto Press, 1996.

Chafy, John. *A Sermon, Preached at Broad-Chalk, in Wiltshire, on Friday the 11th of February, 1757*. Salisbury, 1757.

Chapman, Richard. *The Lawfulness of War in General, and Justness of the Present asserted*. London, 1704.

Chatfield, Charles. "Thinking about Peace in History." In *The Pacifist Impulse in Historical Perspective*, edited by Harvey L. Dyck. Toronto: University of Toronto Press, 1996.

Clark, J.C.D. *English Society 1688-1832*. Cambridge: Cambridge University Press, 1985.

Claydon, Tony. "The Sermon, the 'Public Sphere' and the Political Culture of Late Seventeenth-Century England." In *The English Sermon Revisited*, edited by Lori Anne Ferrell and Peter McCullough. Manchester; New York: Manchester University Press, 2000.

Cobden, Edward. *The Duty of a People Going Out to War*. London, 1744.

Conybeare, John. *True Patriotism*. London, 1749.

Cornish, Joseph. *The Miseries of War, and the Hope of Final and Universal Peace*. Taunton, 1784.

Dawes, William. *Times of War, Times for National Humiliation and Repentance*. 2nd ed. London, 1707.

Denne, John. *The Only Sure Way to Success in War*. London, 1739-40.

Doddridge, Philip. *The Necessity of a General Reformation, in order to a well-grounded Hope of Success in War*. London, 1740.

Drummond, Robert. *A Sermon Preached before the House of Lords, in the Abbey Church of Westminster, on Tuesday April 25, 1749*. London, 1749.

[Enfield, William.] *The Preacher's Directory; or A Series of Subjects Proper for Public Discourses, with Texts Under Each Head*. London, 1771.

Farmerie, William. *God the Only Judge, and Our Only Hope in War*. London, 1710.

Fiddes, Richard. *A Sermon Preached on the Thanksgiving Day, December 3d, 1702*. York, 1703.

Fleetwood, William. *A Sermon on the Fast-Day, January the Sixteenth, 1712/13*. London, 1712.

Fothergill, Thomas. *The Desireableness of Peace, and the Duty of a Nation upon the Recovery of it*. Oxford, 1749.

Ham, Robert. *The Right Way of Obtaining a Good and Safe Peace with our Enemies*. Exon, 1712.

Harris, Thomas. *A Blow to France, or A Sermon Preach'd at the Meeting in Mill-Yard, in Good-man's-Fields; Nov. 22, 1709*. London, 1709.

Harte, Walter. *The Reasonableness and Advantage of National Humiliations, upon the Approach of War*. Oxford, 1739-40.

Hole, Robert. *Pulpits, Politics and Public Order in England 1760-1832*. Cambridge: Cambridge University Press, 1989.

Hooper, George. *The Bishop of Bath and Wells's Thanksgiving-Sermon for the Peace*. London, 1713.

Horne, George. *A Sermon Preached before the Honourable House of Commons*. Oxford, 1780.

Howard, Michael. *War and the Liberal Conscience*. Camden: Rutgers University Press, 1978.

Hurd, Richard. *A Sermon Preached before the Right Honourable the House of Lords, in the Abbey Church of Westminster, on Friday, December 13, 1776*. 2nd ed. London, 1777.

Jefferson, Jacob. *The Blessings of Peace, and the Means of Preserving It*. Oxford, 1763.

Johnson, Samuel. *A Dictionary of the English Language*. 4th ed. London, 1773.

Keate, William. *Sermon Preached upon the Occasion, of the General Thanksgiving, for the Late Peace, July 29th, 1784*. Bath, 1784.

Kennicott, Benjamin. *The Duty of Thanksgiving for Peace in general, and the Reasonableness of Thanksgiving for Our Present Peace*. London, 1749.

King, Arnold. *A Sermon Preached before the Right Honourable the Lord Mayor, the Aldermen, and Citizens of London, at the Cathedral Church of St. Paul, on Tuesday, April 25, 1749*. London, 1749.

Law, William. *An Humble, Earnest, and Affectionate Address to the Clergy*. 2nd ed. London, 1764.

Lessenich, Rolf. *Elements of Pulpit Oratory in Eighteenth-Century England*. Koln: Bohlau-Verlag, 1972.

Morell, Thomas. *The Surest Grounds for Hopes of Success in War*. London, 1740. Napthine, D. and W.A. Speck. "Clergymen and Conflict 1660-1763." *Studies in Church History* 20 (1983): 231-51.

Owen, J. *The Song of Deborah, apply'd to the Battle of Dettingen.* London, 1758.

Partridge, Joseph. *The Renovation of the Heart the only True and acceptable Fast.* Nantwich, 1778.

Penrose, Thomas. *The Practice of Religion and Virtue Recommended; especially in Times of Danger.* London, 1759.

Piers, Henry. *Victory and Plenty, Great Subjects of Thanksgiving.* London, 1759.

Pool Finch, Robert. *A Sermon Preach'd in the Parish Church of St. Mary Woolnoth in Lombard Street, on Tuesday, April 25, 1749.* London, 1749.

Sacheverell, Henry. *A Defence of Her Majesty's Title to the Crown, and a Justification of Her Entring into a War with France and Spain.* London, 1710.

Scott, Thomas. *The Reasonableness, Pleasure, and Benefit of National Thanksgiving.* Ipswich, 1759.

Shower, John. *A Fast-Sermon, on the Account of the Present War.* London, 1705.

Smallridge, George. *A Sermon, Preached at the Royal Chapel at St. James's, on Wednesday, January the 16th, 1711-12.* London, 1712.

Smith, William. *National Prosperity or Adversity dependent upon the virtuous or vicious State of a Nation.* London, 1740.

Smithson, Isaac. *A Sermon, Occasioned by the Declaration of War Against France.* London, 1756.

Smyth, George. *The Lawfulness of War; and the Duty of a People Entering into It.* London, 1740.

Stennett, Joseph. *A Sermon Preach'd at Little-Wild-Street on Tuesday, April 25, 1749.* London, 1749.

Thom, William. *From whence come Wars? An Enquiry into the Origin, with a View of the Progress and Effects, of War.* Glasgow, 1782.

—. *Achan's Trespass in the Accursed Thing considered.* Glasgow, 1778.

Thompson, Thomas. *A Discourse Relating to the Present Times, Addressed to the Serious Consideration of the Public.* London, 1757.

Toulmin, Joshua. *The American War Lamented.* London, 1776.

Trapp, Joseph. *A Sermon Preach'd at the Parish-Church of St. Martin in the Fields; January the 16th, 1711.* London, 1711.

Tucker, Josiah. *The Case of Going to War, for the Sake of Procuring, Enlarging, or Securing of Trade.* London, 1763.

Warburton, William. *A People's Prayer for Peace. A Sermon Preached at Northampton, February 13, 1761.* London, 1761.

Watson, Richard. *A Sermon Preached before the University of Cambridge, on Friday, February 4th, 1780*. 4th ed. Cambridge, 1780.

CHAPTER SEVEN

PATRIOTISM IN MID-EIGHTEENTH-CENTURY ENGLISH AND PRUSSIAN WAR SERMONS

PASI IHALAINEN

Both during pre-modern and many modern military conflicts, religion has functioned as a basis for the construction of uniting identities for war-faring national communities. In ideological discussions related to such conflicts, the relationship between religion and national thought has often been quite intimate. The purpose of this paper is to analyse and compare the meanings attached to the concepts of "nation" and "fatherland" in mid-eighteenth-century English and Prussian war sermons. This period deserves specific attention, as the relationship between religion and national thought changed significantly during the age of the Enlightenment, leading to the rise of less theological and more secular national thought even within public religion.[1] The Seven Years' War, in particular, has also been seen as a watershed in the emergence of a new kind of an alliance between warfare and the ideology of the emerging modern nationalism.[2]

Not only in past texts, but also within the academic study of nationalism, the concepts of nation and nationalism have been given a wide range of

[1] Anthony D. Smith, *Chosen Peoples: Sacred Sources of National Identity* (Oxford 2003); Pasi Ihalainen, *Protestant Nations Redefined: Changing Perceptions of National Identity in the Rhetoric of English, Dutch and Swedish Public Churches, 1685–1772* (Leiden 2005). This article has been written within the projects "Three Varieties of the Protestant Enlightenment" and "Enlightened Loyalties", funded by the Academy of Finland. I am grateful to Jouko Nurmiainen, Patrik Winton and Charlotta Wolff for their comments on previous versions of this article.
[2] Jörn Leonhard, *Bellizismus und Nation. Kriegsdeutung und Nationsbestimmung in Europa und den Vereinigten Staaten 1750–1914* (München 2008), 175, 195. References are to an earlier unprinted version of the book accepted as *Habilitationsschrift* in Heidelberg in 2004.

definitions. Diverging national contexts have also given rise to different meanings in the vocabulary of national community. The emphasis here is on the empirical analysis of the conceptual construction of political or national community by the users of language themselves, and not on any modern theory on the emergence of nationalism, even though one of the prevalent theories has inspired the analysis. We must take into account both the traditional–often religion-based–"ethnic" uses of the concepts of nation and fatherland and the more modern–or at least more secular–uses of nation and fatherland which emerged over the course of the eighteenth century. The new uses would later include the notion of the active involvement of members of sovereign nations in the political process and lead to an ideology that truly deserves the title of "modern nationalism".

The process of change in the conceptions of national community is characterized here as the modernization of national thought. This modernization was in interesting ways connected with the secularisation of national ideologies propagated by the Protestant public churches. More modern forms of national thought can thus be identified even within traditional religion and not only in alternative areas of discourse.

My analysis here focuses on clerical definitions of political and national community in English and Prussian war sermons during the Austrian War of Succession (1740–48) and the Seven Years' War (1756–63). I have previously discussed the eighteenth-century clerical descriptions of national community not only in England but also in the Dutch Republic and Sweden in my book *Protestant Nations Redefined*, which demonstrates, among other things, the centrality of political sermons in the construction of national communities, the tendency of Israelite parallels of national community to become less direct, and the rise of non-theological vocabularies in clerical descriptions of community. The English sections of this chapter are based on observations presented more extensively in the book, though without a similar emphasis on war sermons. The Prussian sections aim at deepening the analysis of the wartime clerical constructions of political identity by providing a comparative perspective.[3] The extension of the comparative aspect enables us to search for source material which can be used to review Anthony D. Smith's recent suggestions that the feelings of the holiness of

---

[3] There are some good German examples of the comparative study of the English, French and German political cultures. See *The Transformation of Political Culture: England and Germany in the Late Eighteenth Century*, ed. Eckhart Hellmuth (Oxford 1990); Hans-Jürgen Lüsebrink, "Conceptual History and Conceptual Transfer: the Case of 'Nation' in Revolutionary France and Germany", *History of Concepts: Comparative Perspectives*, ed. Ian Hampsher-Monk et al. (Amsterdam 1998); Leonhard 2007.

the nation that are typical of modern nationalism are actually based on a secularised version of the ancient myths of chosen nations which were reformulated during the eighteenth century transition to modernity.[4] The English and Prussian cases demonstrate that the public churches provided conceptual constructions of national community that were entirely compatible with the gradual rise of more modern forms of national identification. The clergy began to increasingly present national community as an object of the sense of holiness and sometimes even to award its members a more active role in the formation of their future destiny. Interestingly, such clerical modernization of national thought could also occur during times of war.

Considering political sermons of the public churches one of the major media for propagating the official ideology of the state, I shall focus on the use of the concepts of nation and fatherland in sermons given during two military conflicts in which Britain and Prussia were both involved and which contributed to their rise to the status of great powers: the War of Austrian Succession and the Seven Years' War. Particularly the latter constituted a context for the expression of ideas that were patriotic in an increasingly secularized sense and even "nationalistic" in the sense that communities which understood themselves as nations were fighting each other.[5] A question of major interest is how the wars contributed to the conceptual redefinitions of national communities in two predominantly Protestant yet quite different states. Despite its pluralistic character, Britain has often been referred to as a rapidly modernizing "nation state" with an increasingly parliamentary government, while Prussia might be characterized as an absolutist "non-national state" in which modernization within the political system remained rather modest. In the Seven Years' War, Britain was fighting an essentially global and commercial war, whereas Prussia, surrounded by enemies, was fighting for her survival. Despite these and many other differences, the established churches functioned as media for the propagation of the official identity of the state in both countries.[6] No total confessional uniformity existed in either country, but the state did have a favoured church in both.

---

[4] Smith 2003, vii, 3–6, 10.

[5] This is particularly true of Britain and France, although patriotic language made progress in other countries as well. See Linda Colley, *Britons: Forging the Nation 1707–1837* (London 1992) and Edmond Dziembowski, *Un nouveau patriotisme français, 1750–1770: la France face à la puissance anglaise à l'époque de la guerre de Sept Ans* (Oxford 1998).

[6] See Eckhart Hellmuth, "Towards a Comparative Study of Political Culture: The Cases of Late Eighteenth-Century England and Germany", *The Transformation of*

In the case of England, we should focus on the Anglican sermons given to Parliament on national anniversaries, extraordinary fast days and major occasions of the monarchy as the clearest formulations of the ideology of the state. In the case of Prussia, no representative body to which sermons would have been regularly given existed, and many (perhaps most) of the interesting ones from the court were destroyed during World War II. Yet we do have a sufficient number left for a comparative analysis if we read all of the existing Lutheran and Reformed political sermons given by the leading clerics during the two wars.[7] Lutheran sermons represent the established church and the Reformed sermons the influential minority religion professed by the Royal Family and even much of the administration of the Lutheran Church itself.[8]

Two distinct themes will illustrate both the continuity and the change in the language used to describe national communities in war sermons. I shall analyze the relevance of what can be called the Israelite "prototype" of national and political community in these texts. I shall then compare the rise of non-theological languages in the creation of identity–patriotism derived from classical and non-Christian sources, the rhetoric of defending freedom, and the discourse on an economically understood nation. Both a transition within the traditional language of national community and the emergence of new vocabularies will thus be discussed.

The comparison brings up at least three noteworthy features in the modernization of Protestant national thought in the mid-eighteenth century. Firstly, the pace of change in the conceptualisations of national communities varied from country to country and led to rather different

---

Political Culture, 1, 26; Philip G. Dwyer, "Introduction: The Rise of Prussia", The Rise of Prussia 1700–1830, ed. Philip G. Dwyer (Harlow 2000), 4; Hans-Martin Blitz, Aus Liebe zum Vaterland. Die deutsche Nation im 18. Jahrhundert (Hamburg 2000), 172–3; Leonhard 2004, 175–203; Ihalainen 2005, 41–5.
[7] Printed political sermons given by prominent Prussian clergymen available in the State and University Library of Berlin, the Duke August Library in Wolfenbüttel and the University Library of Göttingen have been consulted. The Prussian authorities seem to have lost some of their interest in publishing war sermons after the victories of 1758, as the war was becoming ever more threatening.
[8] In 1740, the number of inhabitants in Prussia was 2.3 million, of which 90% were Lutheran, 3% Reformed and 7% Catholic. The monarch favoured Calvinists when appointing members of the council directing the Lutheran Church. Günter Birtsch, "The Christian Subject: The Worldly Mind of Prussian Protestant Theologians in the Late Enlightenment Period", The Transformation of Political Culture, 312; Walther Hubatsch, Friedrich der Große und die preußische Verwaltung (Köln 1973), 195; Christopher Clark, "Piety, Politics and Society: Pietism in Eighteenth-Century Prussia", The Rise of Prussia, 71.

understandings of the communities depending on particular circumstances. Secondly, each Protestant national community cherished a conception of divinity of its own, to which it could appeal and through the actions of which it could define itself in times of crisis. The relationship of the community with God, however, was changing. As a consequence, thirdly, the more secular veneration of nation or state, independent of direct divine interventions, was becoming possible. This secularisation of national community, which was a result of the newly formulated classical philosophy and economic expansion among other factors, was characteristic of the British political culture in general and its public religion, Anglicanism, in particular. In the Prussian case, a new more secular concept of the monarchy contributed to the modernization of patriotism.

Conceptual Distinctions between Israel and Britain

While the post-1688 regimes had made some use of the idea of England as a favoured nation, particularly Israelite parallels had steadily been losing popularity since the 1720s in Anglican descriptions of the national community. Alternative ways of conceptualising the community were taken into use so that the last explicitly Israelite metaphors of national community to be found in eighteenth-century English parliamentary sermons date from 1742. This revival of traditional parallels may reflect the unsuccessful war with Spain and the danger of Britain becoming involved in the European war to defend Hanover. The first war sermons thus reflect a conservative reaction but the later ones are much more up-to-date in their use of language.

In 1742, William Stukeley called England "our Zion" and noted its special status as "a most powerful nation" which God had freed from popery. He pointed out that England had been given a favourable geographical position and a uniquely free religious and political system.[9] William Webster interpreted the country as being "a favoured People of God" resembling the Jews, a people who had been given a mission to defend the true faith. Webster took an international point of view, however, suggesting that God wished to be "a Benefactor, not only to this Nation, but to the Liberties of Europe, and the whole Protestant cause". He argued that, because of her unique economic resources, England was more capable of advancing the cause of Christianity than any other nation. In

---

[9] William Stukeley, *National judgments . . . A Sermon . . . Commons . . . On the 30th Day of January, 1741–2. . .* (London 1742), 4, 22.

this sense, England seemed intended to be "his Chosen Nation" (a rare instance of the use of the exact term), a nation distinguished from other nations. Yet Webster saw this chosenness as conditional: God acted in a similar way towards all religious nations and might even choose another nation to be his favourite if the English failed to live religious lives. Divine interventions were no longer as miraculous as they had been at the time of ancient Israel and, as far as England was concerned, did not need to be, as the country was already so clearly favoured.[10] Webster's references to the special position and economic resources of England suggest that, despite the current neutrality of Britain, ideological preparations for an intervention in the War of Austrian Succession were being made. Isaac Maddox, in turn, considered the fate of the Jewish nation to be an illustration of divine actions towards "all other great communities" and discussed the nations of Judah and Britain side by side. The strength of the Israelite understanding of the English past is also apparent in a prayer to the "God of Israel" as the preserver of British liberties.[11]

After this revival of Israelite metaphors on the eve of the War of Austrian Succession, several preachers began to express doubts as to the justification of the far-reaching identification of England or Britain with Israel. In 1744, Matthew Hutton denounced the way in which "the Jewish History, the Prophecies and Circumstances relating to that peculiar State" had been used during the English republic "as if they had solely respected the Affairs of Great Britain".[12] In 1746, James Tunstall pointed out that though Israel could to some extent serve as a model for all nations, God had a covenant-like relationship with all nations. As a consequence, "we of this nation have not the like assurance of express promise" for temporal prosperity of the kind granted to Israel.[13] Thomas Hayter declared it a serious mistake to maintain "that any particular nation could be chosen" by God but for reasons applicable to all nations. According to Hayter, God was a "common Parent of the Universe" and could therefore not be a "respecter of . . . nations".[14] This rejection of the idea of a special chosenness of England illustrates the way in which the concept of nation was being redefined within Anglican thought even while the nation was at war with France. By 1750, England (or Britain for that matter) was no

---

[10] William Webster, *A Sermon . . . Commons . . . May 29. 1742* (London [1742]), dedication, 6, 16ff.
[11] Isaac Maddox, *A Sermon . . . Lords . . . May 29. 1742* (London 1742), passim.
[12] Matthew Hutton, *A Sermon . . . Lords . . . Jan. 30, 1734–44* (London 1744), 18.
[13] James Tunstall, *A Sermon . . . Commons . . . May 29, 1746* (London 1746) 4, 11.
[14] Thomas Hayter, *A Sermon . . . Commons . . . June 11, 1746* (London 1746), 6–7.

longer interpreted as an entirely Israel-like chosen nation, even by the highest representatives of the Anglican Church. The time of the War of Austrian Succession was thus marked with a clearer conceptual distinction between Britain as a national community and the Israel of the Old Testament.

The outbreak of the Seven Years' War also initially intensified the use of Israelite language in some Anglican sermons. Even during this time of war, however, none of the consulted *Anglican* preachers spoke about a "British Israel". There was no established concept of a "British Israel" that was comparable to the concepts of "the Dutch Israel", "the Swedish Israel" and even "the Prussian Israel". A search of the *Eighteenth Century Collections Online* demonstrates that no explicit use of the term "British Israel" occurred outside a few dissenting sermons as far as printed literature is concerned. Anglican preachers used less direct means to draw parallels between the chosen people of Israel and the Britons than their brethren on the Continent, which reflects the decreasing relevance of the analogy. In 1757, John Egerton distinguished the modern era, during which there had been no need for Providence to demonstrate its power so forcefully, from the biblical period, during which God had made interventions "in [sic] behalf of his chosen people". Yet he saw Britain as a nation which enjoyed constant providential blessings "in a peculiar manner, and in their fullest extent." He warned the Britons against counting excessively on their own powers "as a people" and urged them to count on divine protection for "his land" and "his people".[15] As the military victories leading to the global supremacy were celebrated in November 1759, the special status of ancient Israel was emphasized and the nation of Israel was seen as an example to be followed rather than as a nation entirely like Britain. James Johnson noted about Israel that:[16]

[T]hat people was under a *particular* Providence, and *peculiar* Administration; yet, if *that* method of God's proceeding with the Jews, as a nation, had not been founded in reason and justice, . . . And therefore, examples from that history, . . . , are, upon *that very* account, of greater weight and authority. . . . Their national glory and reputation *always* sunk as their idolatry and irreligion prevailed, and *revived* by their repentance, and reformation. . . . *We* have happily experienced his protecting power and goodness, in such a series of Mercies, . . . , as is hardly to be paralleled

---

[15] John Egerton, *A Sermon . . . Lords . . . the 11ᵗʰ Day of February, 1757* (London 1757), 8ff, 20.

[16] James Johnson, *A Sermon . . . Lords . . . November 29, 1759* (London 1759), 10ff.

in any history. . . . national benefits require us . . . the substantial return of public virtue and national piety.

Around 1760, the history of Israel still provided a relevant source of examples which guided the victorious Britons as a Christian nation on how to live even though no explicit concept of "the British Israel" existed any longer. In Prussia, the Israelite parallels gained quite a different tone.

The Radicalisation of the Idea of Prussian Chosenness

As in all Protestant countries, Israelite parallels played a central role in the descriptions of the political community and absolute monarchy in Prussia ever since the creation of the state in 1701.[17] Israelite parallels were used effectively also by the aged and highly respected Court Preacher Daniel Ernst Jablonski when he spoke in connection with the giving of the oaths of allegiance to Frederick II in July 1740, just a couple of months before Frederick's invasion of Silesia and the start of the Austrian War of Succession. Building on the conventional analogy with the accession of Solomon, Jablonski discussed the special status of the Israelites over other peoples as a chosen people of God. He made the Israelite parallel explicit by using the expressions "our Prussian Israel" and "his Prussian-Markish-Israel" when referring to Prussia to the throne of which Frederick had been sent by God. He carried the identification of Prussia (or its major cities) with Israel even further with his declaration: "Extol the Lord, you Prussian Jerusalem, praise your Lord, you Markish Zion."[18] The expressions referred unquestionably to the Kingdom of Prussia, not just to its public church as a religious community. Prussia, unlike England, thus joined Sweden and the Netherlands in their explicit use of the Israelite parallel in the construction of an identity for the political community, at least in the most traditionalist expressions of the ideology of the state. At the same time, however, Jablonski's use of the concept of a Prussian Israel may

---

[17] At the coronation of Frederick as the King of Prussia in 1701, references were made to him as Solomon, who had inherited the throne of Israel after David. Günther Heiler, *Concio Inauguralis, Frolockende Krönungs-Predigt am 18. Januarii 1701* (Stargardt 1701), 19, appendix.

[18] Daniel Ernst Jablonski, *Huldigungs-Predigt bey geschehener Erb-Huldigung . . . den 31. Julii 1740* (Berlin [1740]), 8–9, 22, 27–28; Jablonski was a supporter of the unity of Protestants, which may have contributed to his ability to see all Prussian Protestants as an Israel of sorts. His expression did not really take into account the increasingly multiterritorial nature of the Hohenzollern state. Rudolf von Thadden, *Fragen an Preußen. Zur Geschichte eines aufgehobenen Staates* (München 1981), 112.

already have been somewhat outdated, as it failed to attract followers among later political preachers.

The preachers of the War of Austrian Succession built the concept of a Prussian Israel with other means. August Friedrich Sack, an orthodox Calvinist churchman and a Court and Cathedral Preacher from 1740, was one of many who applied more implicit expressions. His theory of divine influence on warfare, which was formulated during the First Silesian War, could in principle have been shared by most Protestant clerics of that time, though few would have dared to be so explicit. Sack argued that victories and the capture of countries and cities were all given by God, people being no more than tools in the divine hand as God decided to take and give land to whomever he liked. God knew the misdeeds of countries and judged peoples according to the rules of justice. He had the unconditional power to decide the fates of nations: "He is the Lord who nullifies the councils of nations and turns the thoughts of peoples."[19] Sacks's point was that whatever the results of the Silesian War, they followed from the fair judgement of God between Prussia and Austria. God's choice in favour of Prussia was clear: "You have blessed the arms of your anointed with victory and progress!"[20] The relationship between God and the Prussians–or rather God and the King of the Prussians–was depicted as extremely personal. God was thanked for having looked after the King in a number of dangerous situations: "Your eyes have been open for our King in so numerous and great dangers, your justice has led him, your arm has preserved him, and your mercy has given him back to us again".[21] This certainty that God was an ally of the Prussians was mitigated by a prayer in which the subjects of the King of Prussia confessed that they had not truly deserved the numerous favours and blessings which had been bestowed upon them.[22]

Israelite analogies were also present during the Second Silesian War in 1745, although direct identification of Prussia with Israel was avoided. During the Seven Years' War, on the other hand, Israelite parallels occurred very frequently. They were in no way questioned or modified, but instead *radicalised* for the benefit of the war-faring political community surrounded by enemies from all sides. The notion of a "chosen people" may then have contributed in Prussia to what Hans-Martin Blitz has characterized as a process of making the fatherland appear as unique

---

[19] August Friedrich Sack, *Danck-Predigt . . . Feld-Zugs in Schlesien* (Berlin [1741]), 4, 11, 13.
[20] Sack 1741, 15.
[21] *Idem.*
[22] *Idem.*

and absolute, which later led to the idea of the chosenness of the nation.[23] The idea as such was nothing new, but its application in the context of the Seven Years' War had the potential to result in its secularisation.

The Israelite prototype was in effective use in a number of Prussian sermons. When preaching in a military camp in October 1756, the leading military vicar M. Johann Christoph Decker interpreted the war as one of God in which the Lord had sent his help to the King of Prussia and strengthened his troops "from Zion". Referring to the Prussian troops, he argued: "They were set out with God, now they have also done deeds with God, and this has trampled our enemy."[24] The reference not only to a general Providence but to God's active involvement on the side of the mainly Lutheran Prussians is noteworthy.

The basis of such explicit claims of divine intervention on behalf of Prussia can be found in the prevalent conception of God as actively involved in earthly matters, in the traditional conception of the monarch as a tool in the hand of God, and perhaps also in the Pietistic tradition of personal religion which had a particularly strong hold in Prussia. The rising ideas of the monarch as a servant of the state and as a concrete model combatant ready to sacrifice his life were also united in the formulation of the long-lasting conception of warfare in which the people or the nation did not play any role and within which every subject was expected to sacrifice himself to the abstract state.[25] In the Prussian political community, as viewed by the clerics, it was the person of the monarch through whom the people could enjoy special divine favour during war. Such an idea was held quite independently of the monarch's personal religious scepticism and practical tolerance inspired by the Enlightenment. Paradoxically, Frederick II's tendency to ignore confessional differences in state affairs may have facilitated the personification of the relationship between God and political community

---

[23] Blitz 2000, 179.

[24] M. Johann Christoph Decker, *Danck-Rede . . . im Lager bey Groß-Sedlitz* (Berlin [1756]), 10–11; In contemporary war poetry, too, references to God being with the Prussians were commonplace. Hans Peter Herrmann, "'Fatherland': Patriotism and Nationalism in the Eighteenth Century", *Heimat, Nation, Fatherland: The German Sense of Belonging*, eds. Jost Hermand & James Steakley (New York 1996), 13.

[25] Leonhard 2004, 175–79.

with the monarch and the rise of a non-confessional civil religion which was not, at that stage, yet a secular one.[26]

Sack's sermons to the Cathedral parish of Berlin illustrate these prevalent monarchical conceptions. In 1757, Sack argued that by giving Prussia victories God had done great things "to his anointed, our King and his people".[27] He saw no reason to tone down his use of biblical references when describing Prussia as an Israel-like community which could be considered "your people" or "the people . . . which you have chosen".[28] He did not hesitate to claim that God had been aware of the aims of Prussia's enemies and intentionally fought on the Prussian side in the conflict.[29] During the critical period of the Seven Years' War, Prussian Israelite analogies were carried further than those in most other Protestant countries, particularly England. Rationalism in the sense of distinguishing between religion and earthly politics had not yet entered Prussian war sermons. Intellectual change would take place only after the war, secular patriotism gradually taking the place of the religious construction of political community.[30]

In 1758, for one anonymous preacher,[31] the entire war and victories in its battles still became evidence of the existence of God, which was to be taken seriously by the Prussians: "Let us open our eyes, and recognize the Lord, who is so close to us and who reveals himself so clearly."[32] God's

---

[26] See Thomas Munck, *The Enlightenment: A Comparative Social History 1721–1794* (London 2000), 136, and W.R. Ward, *Christianity under the Ancien Régime 1648–1789* (Cambridge 1999), 182.

[27] August Friedrich Sack, "Dank-Predigt . . . bey Prag" (1757), *Drei Dank-Predigten über die von dem großen Könige Friedrich II. im Jahre 1757 erfochtenen Siege bei Prag, bei Roßbach und bei Leuthen, in demselben Jahre im Dom zu Berlin gehalten* (Berlin 1857), 7; See also Blitz 2000, 176, 179, on references to "his peculiar people" and "his chosen people" and Leonhard 2004, 183, on analogous war songs.

[28] Sack 1757, 8; There was no explicit reference to a "chosen *nation* of Prussia", however, as Blitz has suggested. This conceptual distinction is an important one.

[29] *Ibid.*, 11–12.

[30] See Ward 1999, 183.

[31] The peculiar Prussian manner of printing major political sermons anonymously differs from other Protestant countries and reflects the secondary nature of the person of the preacher in the collective definition of political community. The preacher was merely giving an expression to the official identity of the state as seen by the powers that be, and hence there was no need to mention his name in the publication.

[32] [Anon.], *Danck-Predigt nach dem . . . bey Zorndorf über die Rußen erfochtenen Siege* (Potsdam [ca. 1758]), 5.

personal involvement was manifest in the descriptions of his reaction to the sacrifices which Prussians had made for their fatherland. The preacher maintained that God would repay them generously. The blood shed by the Prussian war heroes had to be avenged, and God recognized that, sending his sword to punish the enemies of Prussia.[33] The Prussian God was a friendly God to the Prussians but revengeful to their enemies. In that sense, the Prussians were still comparable to another rescued people, the people of Israel.

Another anonymous preacher argued that while the troops of the Prussian King had fought bravely, whenever they won a victory, "God won". God did great things for the Prussian King by sending him a guardian angel, and thereby he also did great things for the King's subjects.[34] The preacher described the special, personal and concrete relationship between the Prussians and their God, mediated by the monarch, during the days of the Russian invasion in these terms: "We shouted to you in our fear, and you heard our cries in your great mercy and helped us also this time. You led your servant, our King, by your hand, and you gave him a wonderful victory."[35] The preacher could not but thank God by stating "you have . . . rescued your people in a powerful manner" and "you have made us into your saved ones".[36] It was once again a concrete military victory which was claimed to have delivered the Prussians and allowed them to be saved by God, if not in a spiritual at least in a temporal sense. The Prussians still prayed to God to make them better as Christians and to turn them into "a holy people". The process of the sanctification of the people had clearly begun.[37]

There are numerous instances of claims of God's active involvement on the side of Prussia. According to Adolph Dietrich Ortmann, God profoundly disagreed with the plans of the enemies to destroy "the glory of Prussia and Brandenburg":[38]

> His thoughts are not their thoughts–the plan of His omniscient Providence goes otherwise; and develops into a great scare of our enemies–He does not allow them to beat us in the way they would like to beat us, He does

---

[33] *Ibid.*, 15.

[34] [Anon.], *Die . . . wegen des herrlichen Sieges über das Russische Krieges-Heer gehaltene Predigt* (Berlin [1758]), 11–12, 14.

[35] *Ibid.*, 18.

[36] *Ibid.*, 18–19.

[37] *Ibid.*, 19–20.

[38] Adolph Dietrich Ortmann, *Sieges-Predigt wegen der Schlacht den Lissa* (Berlin 1758), 4.

not admit that they strangle us in the way they would like to strangle us.–
They want to make us small and God makes us great.

So develops the plan which God has made for us. It is a wonder for our
eyes, how God clears the way.–The victory, the unforgettable victory of
Rossbach was the beginning of this way to deliverance.

The Battle of Rossbach was seen as a major turning point in the Seven
Years' War and even European history due to the fact that it proved
Prussia's capability to beat the considerably larger French and allied
forces. It also supported the link between religious and patriotic
understandings of the war.[39] According to Ortmann, the victory showed
that the God of Prussia was consciously fighting on the side of the
Prussians–who had "a just cause"[40]–against their enemies, the enemies of
God. By helping the King as the father of the country, God had delivered
the country and its inhabitants.[41] In Ortmann's sermon, which was given
during the besiegement of the country, the belief in God's involvement in
the fate of Prussia was developing into something more than mere
Christianity; it turned into what might be characterized as a kind of
radicalised Prussian "godly patriotism". No such extensive examples of
the "nationalization" of divinity can be found in any of the other studied
Protestant countries of that time period, which calls for a further analysis
of the peculiar features of the Prussian Protestant conceptions of national
community strengthened by the special circumstances of the threatened
country.[42] At first, however, some further observations on the British case.

Patriotic, Free and Commercial Britain

In Britain, the wars were always fought abroad and often for
commercial and colonial reasons.[43] The traditions of political discourse
were different, too. Thanks to a long tradition of classical humanism in
English education and political discourse, the language of virtue and
patriotism, for instance, had come to play a major role in Anglican
contemplations on the state of the national community by the early 1740s.

---

[39] Leonhard 2004, 183.
[40] Ortmann 1758, 27.
[41] *Ibid.*, 6.
[42] Cf. Leonhard 2004, 249–50, 253, 374 and 757–8, who argues that the German
Sonderweg in the sanctification of the nation through warfare only began after
1810. There may have been a longer tradition of religious community-building in
the background, however.
[43] See Leonhard 2004, 96, 99, 278.

Whig bishops nominated by the Whig oligarchy were particularly keen on vindicating the "correct" vocabulary of patriotism from all abuses. Both consciously and unintentionally, they were introducing the language of virtue and common good into the Anglican version of the ideology of the state.

According to James Tunstall, who spoke in 1746, public prosperity followed from "national piety, virtue, and industry". The Christian religion played a key role in the achievement of such public prosperity, as it "purifies our morality, and carries the duties of love, the love of our neighbour, the love of our country and the love of mankind to their highest perfection" and makes the people "sacrifice . . . to a public good".[44] The ideal of wartime patriotism thus appeared to have Christian roots in the principle of loving one's neighbour. Anglican preachers taught their audience piety, virtue, industry and readiness to sacrifices as essential elements of the love of country. Thomas Rutherforth, in turn, set it as the goal of the nation that "a zeal for liberty and constitution may heighten our devotion, and the calm and gentle spirit of prayer may sanctify the love of our Country".[45] Political and religious values thus appeared to support each other to such an extent that Anglican Protestantism could "sanctify" British patriotism and make people "sacrifice" for the common good. A new kind of holiness that was independent of direct divine involvement was clearly being associated with British patriotism in the days of the Austrian War of Succession.

Such holy links between love of country and true Christianity in the ideology of the British state were carried further during the Seven Years' War. John Hume already saw virtue, truth, conscience, religion, gratitude to King and love of country as forming a "sacred tie" of obligations which united Britons and would enable them to win against their enemies.[46] George Fothergill called for "National Sense, or Feeling for the Community" among all Britons and emphasized "the great Social Duty of Loving our Country".[47] In his fast sermon of 1762, John Ewer derived a Christian concept of patriotism from the concept of charity by stating: "Love of our Country is Charity. It is Charity of a wide Extent, always embracing in its Affection, and often benefiting by actual services, a

---

[44] Tunstall 1746, 8, 14.

[45] Thomas Rutherforth, *A Sermon . . . Commons . . . January 30. 1745–6* (London 1746), 14.

[46] John Hume, *A Sermon . . . Lords . . . January 31, 1757* (London 1757), 26ff.

[47] George Fothergill, *The Duty, Objects and Offices of Love of Our Country. A Sermon . . . Commons* (Oxford 1758), 4, 7.

whole Nation."[48] Christian charity was thus effectively limited to one's own nation rather than extended to all mankind. Though containing an internationalist element, the practice of religious patriotism espoused by Ewer was nation-centred:[49]

> Our Benevolence, our good Wishes, and Prayers can indeed, and ought to extend to the whole Race of Mankind; but the Beneficence, the real and actual Services of so limited a Creature as Man, can very rarely, and very hardly reach beyond the Bounds of one Nation. It is therefore manifest, that national good Deeds are the highest and most diffusive Acts of Charity, that Man ordinarily hath Opportunity and Power to perform.

This was religiously motivated yet simultaneously secular patriotism, with the sense of community focusing primarily on one's own nation and only secondarily on the wider world.

The primary values of the English (and British) nation were also being redefined so that political liberty began increasingly to be considered the major characteristic of Englishness. During the War of Austrian Succession, arguments derived from the concept of political liberty did not yet play a dominant role. By the Seven Years' War, however, the concept of liberty had become central in Anglican descriptions of the national community. Being a Briton appeared as such an obvious synonym for both religious and political liberty that the extensive definition of the term liberty was considered unnecessary. While Protestantism had traditionally been seen as a source of liberty, it became increasingly understood as a religion supporting both spiritual and political liberty. Protestantism itself could even be interpreted as springing from liberty. After the victories of the Seven Years' War, explicit associations between Protestantism and liberty also became rarer. It became more common for preachers to conceptualise the nation in the language of liberty without combining it with a confessional denomination. Liberty in a political sense was taking over while traditional confessional terminology was gradually losing relevance in this context.[50]

A breakthrough in the commercial understanding of national community also seems to have occurred among the Anglican bishops from the 1740s onwards, during a war in which British economic interests took increasingly centre stage. In the eyes of the Whig bishops in particular, trade had become such a significant national interest that it justified its discussion in war sermons. In 1742, Nicholas Clagett talked

---

[48] John Ewer, *A Sermon . . . Lords . . . March 12, 1762* (London 1762), 15–16.
[49] *Ibid.*, 16.
[50] Ihalainen 2005, 505–13.

about "a just and necessary War" against Spain following enemy offences against "our national Rights" and particularly actions hurtful to "our Trade and Commerce". In 1744, Matthew Hutton lauded the way George II had defended "our national Commerce" in his war efforts. When he spoke to the Lords on another occasion in 1746, trade appeared as an integral aspect of British identity that was impossible to distinguish from its older elements, such as religion and liberty.[51] In Anglican formulations of British national identity, Britain was turned into a commercial nation in a temporal sense, which was entirely in tune with the ideology of the political elites of the day. By the Seven Years' War, the advancement of commerce as a national interest had been accepted into the official ideology of the state to such an extent that advocates of a commercial understanding of nation were chosen to speak on several important occasions. William Parker, for instance, praised Britain as a "nation of commerce" in which "every man in his private capacity [may] pursue his own interest in national prosperity".[52] We can conclude that the two wars constituted a watershed both in British colonial expansion and in British conceptions of national community. Increasingly secular patriotism and the language of liberty were taking over the ideology of the British state. Commerce was not claimed to be unproblematic from the point of view of the national community, but it too was understood as a positive phenomenon contributing to progress within the community. In Prussia, which was a much more agrarian kingdom with an absolutist political system, the secularisation of patriotism took another course.

The Radicalisation of Sacrifices for the Fatherland in Prussia

As the members of the Prussian political community were not equally educated and familiar with classical republican thought, Prussian preachers made far less use of the classical vocabulary of patriotism than their English colleagues. Few instances of this language can be found from the sermons given during the War of Austrian Succession. By the Seven Years' War, however, the language of classical patriotism had become

---

[51] Matthew Hutton, *A Sermon ... Commons ... Jan. 30, 1740–41* (London 1741), 19; Hutton 1744, 16; Matthew Hutton, *A Sermon ... Lords ... June 11. 1746* (London 1746), 18.
[52] William Parker, *A Sermon ... Commons ... January 31* (London 1757), 24.

more familiar within the German linguistic sphere,[53] probably as a consequence of the European Enlightenment discourse on patriotism popularised by Montesquieu, other authors and even by King Frederick II himself. During the new conflict, Prussian preachers participated in the propagation, popularisation and intensification of patriotic thought, defining the concept of "patriot" for the purposes of the political education of the state[54] rather than in the spirit of the cosmopolitan patriotism advocated by some Enlightenment philosophers.

In his 1757 sermon, the famous August Friedrich Sack presupposed that everyone in his audience was "a God-fearing patriot".[55] Not unlike England, this Prussian godly patriotism was formulated so that it encouraged the inhabitants to sacrifice their lives for the fatherland. The principle of sacrificing for the fatherland was by no means new, as it derives from antiquity, yet its expressions became increasingly explicit and demanding in Germany during the Seven Years' War, including war sermons. Ancient ideas of classical patriotism were being exploited within a basically religious genre to an extraordinary extent.

Some researchers have suggested that such religious praise of the love of country was related to Pietistic religious zeal.[56] The Pietistic influence on Prussian patriotic thought should not be taken as a universal explanation, but comparisons between Prussian and other Protestant war sermons do suggest that Prussian Protestantism conceptualised love of country more radically than was common elsewhere, particularly in England. Blitz has pointed out that the unconditional identification with the fatherland up to one's heroic death was leading to the secularisation of identity to the extent that not only dying for God but also dying for the fatherland resulted in immortality.[57] Both English and Prussian preachers talked about the sacrifices that were to be made for one's country, but the Prussians more explicitly advocated the politico-religious ideal of *dying*

---

[53]   Rudolf Vierhaus, "'Patriotismus'–Begriff und Realität einer moralisch-politischen Haltung", *Deutschland im 18. Jahrhundert. Politische Verfassung, Soziales Gefüge, Geistige Bewegungen* (Göttingen 1987), 97.

[54] Vierhaus 1987, 100; Herrmann 1996, 4.

[55] Sack 1757, 12.

[56] Dagobert De Levie, "The Patriotic Sermons of Christian Ludewig Hahnzog, Germany 1785", *Journal of Modern History*, Vol. 26, No. 1, 1954, 36; Helga Schultz, "Mythos und Aufklärung. Frühformen des Nationalismus in Deutschland", *Historische Zeitschrift*, Band 263, Heft 1, August 1996, 57–8, 62; For Pietism as the ideology of the Prussian state, see Clark 2000, 84–5, and Richard L. Gawthrop, *Pietism and the Making of Eighteenth-Century Prussia* (Cambridge 1993).

[57] Blitz 2000, 185.

for one's fatherland and promised religious rewards for this ultimate sacrifice.

Instances of this sanctification of sacrifices for the fatherland are easy to find in Prussian war sermons. Sack, among others, argued that the fear of God and love of fatherland led many Prussians to shed their own blood and lose their lives. The memory of these brave men would, however, be preserved by "the grateful fatherland". Sack defined the core of Prussian God-blessed patriotism in terms that were also familiar from contemporary philosophy and poetry: "the ultimate goal of a patriotic wish" of each Prussian was to "win a battle for his King and to die thereafter as a victor".[58] In a thanksgiving sermon given in Potsdam in 1758, the preacher suggested in similar terms that individual soldiers had sacrificed their blood for the fatherland, that the grateful fatherland should remember their great deeds forever, and that they could expect to receive a divine reward for defending the causes of God and fatherland, the two being synonymous. The possibility allowed to individuals to prove their love of fatherland and the holiness awarded to this act are noteworthy here. This militant and state-sponsored Prussian Protestantism, more clearly than war propaganda in other Protestant countries, was opening the way for a secularised civil religion in which sacrifices for the fatherland as such (rather than to God) were seen as holy. By the end of the war, this understanding of patriotism as the willingness to "fight enthusiastically for fatherland, to win or to die" seems to have extended outside of Prussia and into Hanover. The notion that there was nothing greater than to save one's fatherland, by fighting in a war and dying if need be, was becoming a part of the state ideology of the principalities of Northern Germany.[59]

The content of the German concept of fatherland had clearly been radicalised in the discourse of the Seven Years' War.[60] Though similar arguments about the holiness of sacrificing oneself for the fatherland, common good or liberty also appeared in other Protestant war sermons, the Prussian version was by far the most explicit, and at least partly due to the critical state of the country in war. It included a sacred identification with the political community and its leader that would later pave the way

---

[58] Sack 1757, 14; Similar glorification of the noble death for the fatherland as a moral obligation can be found in contemporary drama (1749), war poetry (1758) and philosophy (1761). Johann Wilhelm Gleim wrote in 1758: "Immortal makes a hero's death, a death for the fatherland!". Herrmann 1996, 10–11, 15.

[59] See [Einem Prediger aus dem Zellischen], *Predigt auf das Dankfest, welches wegen des Frieden in den Churhannoverischen Staaten, am 6ten Jan. 1763. gefeyret wurde* (s.l. 1763), 20, 43, 46.

[60] Herrmann 1996, 15.

for secularised patriotism and eventually also for modern nationalism, in which national thought would substitute, at least to a certain extent, for traditional religion as the dominant ideology. As Jörn Leonhard has pointed out, the concepts "people" (*Volk*) and "nation" would be given a sacred status by the early 1810s.[61] Indeed, the Prussian language of political community as formulated by the representatives of the public church seems to have contained elements that sanctified patriotism already in the days of the Seven Years' War.

Two more comparisons illustrate the different stages and directions of development in conceptions of national community in England and Prussia. Firstly, liberty had not yet been considered a relevant theme in the Prussian sermons of the Austrian War of Succession. By the end of the Seven Years' War, however, the attitudes of some members of the leading clergy towards the concept of liberty were beginning to change, not entirely unlike in England. The need to emphasize religious freedom in this military conflict rose from the facts that the monarch favoured the principle and that Prussia was fighting against two Catholic great powers, Austria and France. From the point of view of the traditional discourse of international Protestantism, both countries had considerable records as persecutors of Protestants and violators of the holy principle of the "complete freedom of conscience for everyone," which was supposed to have prevailed in Prussia under Frederick II.[62] Liberty thus constituted a useful concept for war propaganda in Prussia the monarch of which appeared as a defender of both religion and liberty.[63] The concept of liberty, particularly that of political liberty, did not dominate the war sermons of the late 1750s, however. Whenever used, it also carried a sense of liberty secured by an absolutist state rather than one of individual freedom.[64] It was collectivist rather than individual freedom, and passive religious rather than active political freedom that Prussian preachers were talking about. The Lutheran concept of liberty was much more limited than the Anglican one.

Secondly, as data on the state of economic development in Prussia might also suggest, the language of an economically understood political

---

[61] Leonhard 2004, 249–50, 253; Leonhard's point on the religious coding of war only after 1810 should be qualified with references to sermons from the time of the Seven Years' War.

[62] Sack 1757, 16.

[63] Leonhard 2004, 182.

[64] Diethelm Klippel, "The True Concept of Liberty: Political Theory in Germany in the Second Half of the Eighteenth Century", *The Transformation of Political Culture*, 448.

community did not yet play any noteworthy role in the Prussian sermons given during the two wars. Both war sermons and previous research on war propaganda show that, from the clerical and even royal points of view, Prussian warfare was not motivated by economic interests.[65] This does not exclude the contributing role of economic factors in warfare, but it does suggest that conceptions of the Prussian political community were not yet very modern in economic terms. Britain was a commercial state to a much higher extent.

We can conclude that an analysis of English and Prussian war sermons supports much of Anthony D. Smith's thesis on the reformulation of national chosenness in the eighteenth century. British national identity, as constructed by the clergy of the Church of England, was already experiencing fast *modernization* by the early 1760s. This modernization took place rather evolutionarily, as some older notions of an Israel-like community were losing ground and new ones being introduced by leading Whig clerics in particular. Britain was no longer seen merely as an Israel-like sinning nation waiting for divine punishments, but also as a nation working towards the advancement of the common good, liberty and commerce in this world. Ancient myths of chosenness were being secularised in new Christian definitions of patriotism. Conceptions of a more active national community were also introduced.

The conception of political community propagated by the Prussian clergy, in contrast, was *radicalised* during the Seven Years' War to the extent that traditional Israelite parallels were substituted with references to God's personal involvement in battles on the side of Prussia. The modernization of the conceptions of community, though visible in the rise of the vocabulary of fatherland and the sanctification of sacrifices for the fatherland, which were not entirely unlike the English ones, was more modest and led to quite different conclusions about the basic character of the community. In the vulnerable circumstances of a political community fighting on several frontiers, fighting and dying for one's fatherland as such appeared as a holy duty rather than the advancement of liberty, common good or commerce. These conclusions about the duties of ideal citizens would play a role in later conflicts in which Britain and her follower states on the one hand and Germany on the other would be involved. Their long-term effects require analysis elsewhere, perhaps on the basis of later war sermons. All in all, mid-eighteenth-century war sermons not only reinforced traditional religious conceptions of national

---

[65] H.M. Scott, "Prussia's Emergence as a European Great Power, 1740–1763", *The Rise of Prussia*, 164.

communities but also reformulated them in very fundamental and consequential ways.

Works Cited

[Anon.], *Danck-Predigt nach dem . . . bey Zorndorf über die Rußen erfochtenen Siege* (Potsdam [ca. 1758]).

[Anon.], *Die . . . wegen des herrlichen Sieges über das Russische Krieges-Heer gehaltene Predigt* (Berlin [1758]).

Birtsch, Günter, "The Christian Subject: The Worldly Mind of Prussian Protestant Theologians in the Late Enlightenment Period", in Hellmuth, Eckhart (ed.), *The Transformation of Political Culture: England and Germany in the Late Eighteenth Century*, (Oxford 1990).

Blitz, Hans-Martin, *Aus Liebe zum Vaterland. Die deutsche Nation im 18. Jahrhundert* (Hamburg 2000).

Clark, Christopher , "Piety, Politics and Society: Pietism in Eighteenth-Century Prussia", in Dwyer, Philip G. (ed.), *The Rise of Prussia 1700–1830* (Harlow 2000).

Colley, Linda, *Britons: Forging the Nation 1707–1837* (London 1992).

Decker, M. Johann Christoph, *Danck-Rede . . . im Lager bey Groß-Sedlitz* (Berlin [1756]).

De Levie, Dagobert, "The Patriotic Sermons of Christian Ludewig Hahnzog, Germany 1785", *Journal of Modern History*, Vol. 26, No. 1, 1954.

Dwyer, Philip G., "Introduction: The Rise of Prussia", *The Rise of Prussia 1700–1830*, ed. Philip G. Dwyer (Harlow 2000).

Dziembowski, Edmond, *Un nouveau patriotisme français, 1750–1770: la France face à la puissance anglaise à l'époque de la guerre de Sept Ans* (Oxford 1998).

Egerton, John, *A Sermon . . . Lords . . . the 11th Day of February, 1757* (London 1757).

[Einem Prediger aus dem Zellischen], *Predigt auf das Dankfest, welches wegen des Frieden in den Churhannoverischen Staaten, am 6ten Jan. 1763. gefeyret wurde* (s.l. 1763).

Ewer, John, *A Sermon . . . Lords . . . March 12, 1762* (London 1762).

Fothergill, George, *The Duty, Objects and Offices of Love of Our Country. A Sermon . . . Commons* (Oxford 1758).

Gawthrop, Richard L., *Pietism and the Making of Eighteenth-Century Prussia* (Cambridge 1993).

Hayter, Thomas, *A Sermon . . . Commons . . . June 11, 1746* (London 1746).

Heiler, Günther, *Concio Inauguralis, Frolockende Krönungs-Predigt am 18. Januarii 1701* (Stargardt 1701).

Hellmuth, Eckhart (ed.), *The Transformation of Political Culture: England and Germany in the Late Eighteenth Century*, (Oxford 1990).

Hellmuth, Eckhart, "Towards a Comparative Study of Political Culture: The Cases of Late Eighteenth-Century England and Germany", in Hellmuth, Eckhart (ed.), *The Transformation of Political Culture: England and Germany in the Late Eighteenth Century*, (Oxford 1990).

Herrmann, Hans Peter, "'Fatherland': Patriotism and Nationalism in the Eighteenth Century", *Heimat, Nation, Fatherland: The German Sense of Belonging*, eds. Jost Hermand & James Steakley (New York 1996).

Hubatsch, Walther, *Friedrich der Große und die preußische Verwaltung* (Köln 1973).

Hume, John, *A Sermon . . . Lords . . . January 31, 1757* (London 1757).

Hutton, Matthew, *A Sermon . . . Commons . . . Jan. 30, 1740–41* (London 1741).

—. *A Sermon . . . Lords . . . Jan. 30, 1734–44* (London 1744).

—. *A Sermon . . . Lords . . . June 11. 1746* (London 1746).

Ihalainen, Pasi, *Protestant Nations Redefined: Changing Perceptions of National Identity in the Rhetoric of English, Dutch and Swedish Public Churches, 1685–1772* (Leiden 2005).

Jablonski, Daniel Ernst, *Huldigungs-Predigt bey geschehener Erb-Huldigung . . . den 31. Julii 1740* (Berlin [1740]).

Johnson, James, *A Sermon . . . Lords . . . November 29, 1759* (London 1759).

Klippel, Diethelm, "The True Concept of Liberty: Political Theory in Germany in the Second Half of the Eighteenth Century", in Hellmuth, Eckhart (ed.), *The Transformation of Political Culture: England and Germany in the Late Eighteenth Century*, (Oxford 1990).

Leonhard, Jörn, *Bellizismus und Nation. Kriegsdeutung und Nationsbestimmung in Europa und den Vereinigten Staaten 1750–1914* (München 2008).

Lüsebrink, Hans-Jürgen, "Conceptual History and Conceptual Transfer: the Case of 'Nation' in Revolutionary France and Germany", *History of Concepts: Comparative Perspectives*, ed. Ian Hampsher-Monk et al. (Amsterdam 1998).

Maddox, Isaac, *A Sermon . . . Lords . . . May 29. 1742* (London 1742).

Munck, Thomas, *The Enlightenment: A Comparative Social History 1721–1794* (London 2000).

Ortmann, Adolph Dietrich, *Sieges-Predigt wegen der Schlacht den Lissa* (Berlin 1758).

Parker, William, *A Sermon . . . Commons . . . January 31* (London 1757).

Rutherforth, Thomas, *A Sermon . . . Commons . . . January 30. 1745–6* (London 1746).

Sack, August Friedrich, *Danck-Predigt . . . Feld-Zugs in Schlesien* (Berlin [1741]).

—. "Dank-Predigt . . . bey Prag" (1757), in *Drei Dank-Predigten über die von dem großen Könige Friedrich II. im Jahre 1757 erfochtenen Siege bei Prag, bei Roßbach und bei Leuthen, in demselben Jahre im Dom zu Berlin gehalten* (Berlin 1857).

Schultz, Helga, "Mythos und Aufklärung. Frühformen des Nationalismus in Deutschland", *Historische Zeitschrift*, Band 263, Heft 1, August 1996.

Scott, H.M., "Prussia's Emergence as a European Great Power, 1740–1763", in *The Rise of Prussia 1700–1830*, ed. Philip G. Dwyer (Harlow 2000).

Smith, Anthony D., *Chosen Peoples: Sacred Sources of National Identity* (Oxford 2003).

Stukeley, William, *National judgments . . . A Sermon . . . Commons . . . On the 30th Day of January, 1741–2. . .* (London 1742).

Thadden, Rudolf von, *Fragen an Preußen. Zur Geschichte eines aufgehobenen Staates* (München 1981).

Tunstall, James, *A Sermon . . . Commons . . . May 29, 1746* (London 1746).

Vierhaus, Rudolf, "'Patriotismus'–Begriff und Realität einer moralisch-politischen Haltung", *Deutschland im 18. Jahrhundert. Politische Verfassung, Soziales Gefüge, Geistige Bewegungen* (Göttingen 1987).

Ward, W.R., *Christianity under the Ancien Régime 1648–1789* (Cambridge 1999).

Webster, William, *A Sermon . . . Commons . . . May 29. 1742* (London [1742]).

CHAPTER EIGHT

DISSENT AGAINST THE AMERICAN WAR: THE POLITICS OF RICHARD PRICE'S SERMONS

RÉMY DUTHILLE

Richard Price considered himself as a preacher first and foremost. That he has been chiefly remembered for Burke's criticism of his celebration of the French Revolution, should not obscure the fact that Price had used the sermon as a form of political expression in earlier decades. From 1758 to 1783 he preached every Sunday at the Gravel Pit field at Hackney, and in the afternoon at the Presbyterian chapel of Newington Green,[1] a community of prosperous traders and bankers which, in the last three decades of the century, provided a favourable environment for the development of radical ideas by thinkers such as James Burgh and Mary Wollstonecraft.

The War of American Independence gave Price ample occasion for political comment. According to Joseph Priestley, Price's successor at the Gravel Pit:

Dr Price, as well as myself and many other Dissenters, always observed the days appointed for public fasts in the course of the American War, though by no means adopted the language of the prayers published by authority for the use of the clergy on those occasions.[2]

There was indeed a long tradition of political sermons in England, but sermons were criticized for being too "political" when they defended extreme positions or questioned the values of the establishment too directly. As the government proclaimed thanksgiving and fast days to muster public support during wars, fast sermons provided a focus for expressions of loyalty and contestation. Neither government nor Parliament seemed able to control the discourse of the preachers.[3] The fast

---

[1] Price to Benjamin Franklin, 30 September 1772, *Correspondence*, 1:140.
[2] Priestley 1793, 5
[3] Caudle 2000a.

day of 12 December 1776, which marked the recognition by the government that the conflict with the American colonies had grown to a full-scale war, provoked the first protests against the political exploitation of fasts. Burke loudly inveighed against the fast in the House of Commons and even arranged for a friend to host a dinner in Bristol as a protest.[4]

During the American war, Anglican preachers tended to support the government, while Dissenters used fast sermons to express grievances and criticize the government, though there were exceptions.[5] Fast days gave the Dissenting pulpit an importance out of all proportion with the demographic weight of the Dissenters.[6]

Price seems never to have objected to fast days as such, contrary to many Dissenting ministers who considered them as encroachments of the civil power on the religious sphere. Instead, Price chose to use fast sermons as an occasion for criticism of the government's measures, in keeping with his insistence that good citizens should make their opinions known, within the limits prescribed by the law. Price was aware that the context of fast days would give more weight to his political utterances. But of those fast sermons he published only two, those of 1779 and 1781, which I will compare to an earlier thanksgiving sermon, preached in 1759 during the Seven Years War.[7]

It is difficult to determine how well the printed version matched the text Price actually read.[8] The *London Magazine*, commenting on the 1779 sermon, granted that Price had been right to leave "terms . . . perhaps too strong" in the book, so that the readers would not be "biased by misrepresentation."[9] In the absence of any evidence to the contrary, it seems that the printed version of the sermons is not materially different from the sermons as actually preached, although the significance of the

---

[4] Langford 1990, 279; Ippel 1980.

[5] In the Church of England, Jonathan Shipley, bishop of St Asaph, and Richard Watson at Cambridge preached anti-government sermons, Langford 1990, 275-278. For pro-government sermons preached by nonconformists, see Bradley 1990, 123-124.

[6] Ippel 1980, 192.

[7] A Sermon, Delivered to a Congregation of Protestant Dissenters, at Hackney, on the 10th of February Last, Being the Day Appointed for a General Fast, London:Thomas Cadell, 1779, and A Discourse Addressed to a Congregation at Hackney, on February 21, 1781, Being the Day Appointed for a Public Fast, London: Thomas Cadell, 1781. The 1781 sermon is reprinted in Price 1991. See Morgan 1815, 67-68.

[8] Price apparently edited out some critical comments on Charles James Fox when he published his *Discourse on the Love of our Country*, Cookson 1982, 17.

[9] Review of Price's 1779 sermon in *London Magazine* 48, 1779 : 232.

sermons was modified by the addition of footnotes and appendices. This study will examine how the sermons testify to the transformations brought about by the American revolution on Price's views, especially on his judgments on Britain, and on his theory of patriotism and the right of resistance,; it will also offer an analysis of the sermons in the context of the pamphlet wars of the times.

The title of the sermon preached on 29 November 1759: *Britain's Happiness, and the Proper Improvement of It*... reveals a general mood of optimism and satisfaction which is qualified by the consciousness that efforts ought to be made to improve British polity. In this thanksgiving, hints of criticism were already apparent. The government wanted to celebrate "the signal Successes of His Majesty's Arms, both by Sea and Land, particularly by the Defeat of the *French* Army in *Canada*, and the Taking of *Quebec*".[10] Price used the psalm recommended by the Royal Proclamation (Ps. 147.20), which was a way of placing his discourse in keeping with the government's official position.

The fast came at the end of a military *annus mirabilis* marked by victories on three continents, culminating with Hawke's brilliant naval victory over the French at Quiberon Bay on 20 November, which gave the Royal Navy complete command of the sea. Shortly before the fast day the Parliament reassembled in an almost euphoric mood. Pitt governed with a broad coalition of Whigs, which gathered additional support from the king, most tories, and patriotic colonies.

Price was elated by this exceptional, unique political configuration: while "patriotism before 1757 had been the creed of opposition", Pitt tried to apply a "patriotic" programme and he enjoyed the support of Bute and Prince George. Thus the tone of the sermon was tinged by Price's admiration for Pitt. Price extolled Britain to the point of replacing the word "Jerusalem" by "Britain" in the jubilant biblical psalm; this practice was indicative of a strong Protestant patriotism, which could be warlike on occasion if wars could advance the cause of Protestantism against Catholicism.[11] Among Price's writings, the 1759 sermon is what comes closer to the mainstream martial patriotism expounded by Linda Colley.[12] The main ingredients were present in Price's eulogy of Britain. The

---

[10] Church of England 1759, 1.

[11] Earlier in the century, Isaac Watts had already replaced "Jerusalem" with "Britain" in some of his hymns, Colley 1992, 30. Price was conversant with Watts's writings, as one of his uncles was a preacher in Watts's chapel.

[12] Colley 1992.

country was blessed by its insularity: "The ocean is our wall of defence".[13] Thus, Britain was spared the horrors of the war. Price proceeded to conjure up a vision of the horrors of the war, underlining that Britons should be grateful that this carnage is happening in France and Flanders, but not on British soil. Price minimized the effects of the war on Britain, stressing that his congregation experienced the conflict only through newspapers and hardly felt any economic distress. The sermon is remarkable for its reliance on francophobic clichés: the French were presented as "ignoble and miserable slaves" who fought for "their breaden God and their chains". Those xenophobic remarks were unique in Price's writings. From the 1770s on, Price was careful to warn against national prejudices, most famously in his *Discourse on the Love of our Country*. This is revealing of a more general shift in English radicals' attitudes, as some ceased to consider France as the arch-enemy after it had sided with the Americans.[14]

The 1759 sermon, however, noted the defects of the constitution and deplored the shortcomings of the parliamentary representation and the disabilities imposed on Dissenters. In contrast to this particular sermon, the American War sermons reflected a mood both of dissatisfaction with the official policy of coercion of the colonists and of increasing gloominess brought about the military setbacks that begun with the defeat at Saratoga in the autumn of 1777. The form of prayer of the 1779 sermon stated that the fast was ordered "for obtaining pardon of our sins" and to pray for military success.[15] Church of England sermons tended to exonerate the government from responsibility and lay the blame on the sinfulness of the people. Price did consider that Britain needed to obtain pardon for its sins, but he argued that this could be achieved only by opposing the government and adopting measures of conciliation towards the Americans.

For Price, the American War revealed that the patriotic values and the love of liberty were subverted by luxury and by the spread of Tory, anti-liberal opinions. The sermons, as well as the *Observations on Civil Liberty*, presented Britain as the reverse of what it should be, and what it was during the Seven Years' War. Significantly, Price chose for the 1779 sermon the episode in Genesis in which Abraham intercedes with God to spare the city of Sodom (Gen. 18.32). Britain, once an image of the heavenly Jerusalem, was debased by luxury, licentiousness and political waywardness into an accursed city or a god-forsaken island:

---

[13] Price 1991, 2.
[14] Price 1991, 9-11.
[15] Church of England 1779.

In the course of a few years, we have been reduced from the highest
pinnacle of glory to the brink of ruin. A third of the empire is lost; and at
the same time we see powerful enemies combining against us, our
commerce languishing, and our debts and taxes, already insupportable,
increasing fast, and likely soon to crush us. . . . We are indeed forsaken by
Heaven. Nothing has prospered.[16]

The 1781 sermon was even sadder in tone: the situation had become
desperate for the British army in America now that the French had sided
with the Americans and that the prospect of American independence was
looming large. Price was also particularly concerned by the impact of war
on trade, budget, and national debt:

The aspect of public affairs continues darker than I can describe. We see
this nation (lately the first upon earth) reduced to a state of deep
humiliation. Our glory departed — fallen from our high station among the
powers of the world — devastation and bloodshed extending themselves
round us — without colonies — without allies — some of the best
branches of our trade lost — a monstrous burden weighing us down — and
at war with America, with France, with Spain, with Holland, and in danger
of being soon at war with all Europe.[17]

There was more than rhetoric to those complaints: Price was genuinely
distressed and his growing pessimism showed throughout his political
writings and his private correspondence from 1776 on.

Preaching in 1781 on 2 Pet. 3. 13, Price exhorted his congregation to
draw comfort from the prospect of a future life in which injustices would
be redressed and the righteous admitted into the everlasting kingdom of
Christ, as contemporary Britain appeared to drift helplessly into decadence
and away from the model of the heavenly Jerusalem.

Indeed Price believed that the salvation of the country depended on
virtuous men, because they could advocate right measures, and because
God would "direct events for the advantage of the country" where those
righteous men lived.[18] But Price looked around and could not see those
virtuous men: complaining that "there are a smaller number than they
were", he warned that the old Dissenting sects were in danger of being
"ground to death" between Methodist enthusiasm on one side, and
concessions to worldliness ("luxury and fashion") on the other– a
recognition of the dwindling demography of Dissent tinged with wartime

---

[16] Price 1779, 32-34.
[17] Price 1991, 112.
[18] Price 1779, 25-26.

pessimism. These complaints were not unwarranted, since Price sometimes preached to audiences of no more than a dozen of people.[19]

Complaints about the sinfulness of the times and warnings about divine retribution on an irreligious people were conventional in fast sermons. Price's sermons were more original and notable for their reflection on the right of resistance and their concept of patriotism. They did not directly discuss the question of the just war. In the 1759 sermon Price took it for granted that the war was just, because he thought that British victory over Catholic, absolutist, hegemonic France would usher in "a time when Popish darkness and oppression shall be exceeded by universal peace and liberty".[20] This position is at variance, though, with Price's repeated claims that liberal, enlightened principles and true religion should be spread through rational discussion and not imposed by war.

In the 1779 and 1781 sermons there was no necessity to address the issue of the just war, because Price had made it clear in the *Observations on Civil Liberty* that he considered the war was unjust. The pamphlet attacked all the rationales for the American War, but even the section on "the Justice of the War with America" eschewed general discussion on the just war. Price focused instead on the topical debate because he claimed that the American War (a war between colonies and their mother country) was "new in the history of mankind".[21] Price denied Britain's right of taxing the colonies on the principle of "no taxation without representation," but he went further and asserted the Americans' right to self-determination.

During the American war, Price's only statements on the question of the just war are to be found in the *Observations*. He defended the view that only defensive wars were just and offered little justification. In 1789, he stated his position in more detail in *A Discourse on the Love of our Country*:

> When a country is attacked in any of its rights by another country . . . to die for our country is meritorious and noble. These defensive wars are, in my opinion, the only just wars. Offensive wars are always unlawful and to seek the aggrandizement of our country by them . . . to extend dominion, or to gratify avarice, is wicked and detestable.[22]

Price defined the just war in a sermon which was, if anything, a peace sermon, precisely because he hoped that the French Revolution would

---

[19] Seed 1996, 142.
[20] Price 1991, 12.
[21] Price 1991, 37.
[22] Price 1991, 188.

bring peace and prosperity: he was outlining the conditions for securing perpetual peace. Those scattered passages in Price's writings do not amount to a sustained theory of the just war. Price was obviously more interested in questions of sovereignty and legitimate resistance - the central issues of the war, and those that fast sermons discussed in detail.[23] Following the government's position, Church of England sermons indeed branded the Americans as rebels: "Our fellow-subjects, in a distant part of the empire, have exchanged Peace and Order for Anarchy . . . they have renounced the Allegiance due to the British Crown".[24] Preachers favourable to the government did not draw parallels with other wars, but with the "Great Rebellion" of the seventeenth century, and they quoted from 30 January sermons, if not to defend non-resistance and passive obedience, at least to deny that the grievances of the Americans were acute or real enough to justify resistance.

Price harshly criticized those preachers that were too favourable to the doctrine of non-resistance:

> Certain it is, that mankind, instead of being too prone to resistance, have in general been much too tame and passive. Had this not been the case so many oppressive and tyrannical governments which degrade men into beasts, would never have taken place in the world.[25]

Indeed, the 1779 sermon criticized traditional theories that held that resistance was justified only in cases of certain, imminent, serious danger and pointed out a paradox inherent to what Jim Caudle calls "*in extremis* theories of resistance".[26] It would be better, Price argued, if the people reacted as soon as they perceived signs that their rulers were encroaching on their rights; the subjects of Charles I had waited too long out of misplaced caution, so long indeed that they reacted too late and had to engage in full-scale warfare that could have been avoided had they acted sooner. Thus the bloodless character of the revolution of 1688 should be put down to chance more than to the sagacity of the English. In that way, Price replaced the violence involved in resistance theory by a plea for

---

[23] The Whig theory of resistance had already been expounded in sermons earlier in the eighteenth century, especially in times of crisis such as the Jacobite rebellion of 1745, Deconinck-Brossard 1983, 1:269-77; and, more generally, Caudle 1996.

[24] Butler 1777, 6.

[25] Price to William Adams, 11 February 1778, *Correspondence* 1.269, commenting on George Campbell's 12 December 1776 fast sermon. See also Price's critique of Josiah Tucker, *Correspondence* 2.32.

[26] Price 1779, 19; Caudle 2000b, 61.

perpetual vigilance, or in Jim Caudle's words, "refined resistance into reformism".[27]

Price's theory of the necessity of an active role of the people was radical, insofar as it suggested that the whole people (and not just the land-owning élite) ought to engage in politics, and implied that the Commons should be reformed to be more representative. But it was also reminiscent of Commonwealth ideology and its insistence on the jealous vigilance of independent men, since Price also pointed out that economic independence was necessary "to place [the patriot] above temptation".[28]

Those views on resistance were the sermons' major contribution to Price's political philosophy. At first sight, Price's depiction of the patriot as a virtuous, religious man, was rather conventional and certainly did not foreshadow the concept of enlightened patriotism developed in *A Discourse on the Love of our Country*. More interestingly, Price suggested that the righteous (and in particular the Dissenters) should necessarily oppose the American War or at least criticize the government. Patriotism involved "discharging every duty of life and godliness" and warning our countrymen, even admonishing them when "we see our country threatened with calamity" (Price 1991, 112). Thus Price's emphasis on conscience had redefined patriotism and loyalty as dissent from the government: since loyalty was an attachment to the laws, and not to the person of rulers (who are not sacred) it was loyal for a subject to oppose the government when it broke the law.

Price did affirm the doctrine of popular sovereignty but chose not to draw its ultimate consequences – the right to revolution – and merely hinted at the issue of popular representation in parliament (Price 1779, 18, 21). He preferred not to mention the more controversial aspects of his political thought, possibly because he felt that it would be inappropriate in a sermon, but also because the sermons presuppose a previous knowledge of the *Observations on Civil Liberty*. The congregation indeed knew their preacher personally (Price 1991, 113), and the published sermons addressed an educated, informed public that could not fail to know the *Observations*, the best-selling tract of the year 1776 in Britain. Price was aware indeed that there was a demand for the publication of his sermons, which can be understood as episodes in the ongoing controversy sparked off by the *Observations*.

During the American War, sermons, once published, were read, quoted or refuted as though they were just another genre of political literature

---

[27] Caudle 2000b, 63-65.
[28] Price 1779, 22.

(Ippel 1980, 49). Some printed sermons were hardly distinguishable from political treatises. Price's sermons and political pamphlets bear strong resemblance, in style as well as ideology. Using similar rhetorical devices, Price's sermons reiterated and summarized ideas on popular sovereignty and the value of liberty that were already present in the *Observations*:

> Let us remember that we are *men* and not *cattle*; that the sovereignty in every country belongs to the people; and that a righteous man is the best member of every community, and the best friend to his species, by being the most irreconcileable to slavery, the most sensible to every encroachments on the rights of mankind, the most zealous equal and universal liberty, and the most active in endeavouring to propagate just sentiments of religion and government.[29]

Whereas Price's political idiom was thus incorporated into the sermons, conversely some passages in his political pamphlets bore close resemblance to the sermons. The concluding parts of his tracts, so strongly tinged with religious rhetoric castigating the vices of Britain and warning about impending divine retribution would not be out of place in the fast sermons. Price exhorted the reader to prayer and repentance just as a preacher would:

> In this hour of tremendous danger it would become us to turn our thoughts to Heaven. This is what our brethren in the Colonies are doing. From one end of North-America to the other they are fasting and praying. But what are we doing? We are ridiculing them as fanatics, and scoffing at religion, We are running wild after pleasure and forgetting every thing serious and decent at masquerades. We are trafficking for boroughs, perjuring ourselves at elections, and selling ourselves for places. Which side then is Providence likely to favour?... Remember, reader, whoever thou art, that there are no other just causes of war and that blood spilled with any other views must some time or other be accounted for.[30]

The interplay between sermons and political tracts is manifest in the controversies surrounding Price's *Observations*. Several fast sermons concerned with issues of obedience and resistance quoted from or alluded to the *Observations*, in the footnotes or the introduction more often than in the body of the sermon proper. Price's *Observations* had an influence on the ideology of anti-war Dissenting sermons.

Conversely, Price's principles were also attacked in pro-war sermons, often by allusion. A Church of Scotland minister mentioned Price's works

---

[29] Price 1779, 21.
[30] Observations on Civil Liberty, in Price 1991, 69-70.

as an instance of "that unbounded licentiousness which, for a long time, has prevailed in writing and discourse".[31] Price could have no other views than "a revolution" and the overthrow of Church and State. Carlyle cast in doubt the loyalty of Price and other "seditious" pamphleteers to the very polity that gave them freedom of speech. The aptly entitled fast sermon *American Resistance Indefensible* distinguished liberty from licence and turned into an attack on "fanciful Schemes of Government", accompanied by a lengthy footnote on Price's treatise, "so evidently the Work of a Partisan".[32]

Price had to restate his positions several times to answer his critics, especially the Archbishop of York who had denounced his principles in a sermon preached in February 1777.[33] In the introduction to "Two Tracts on Civil Liberty" (1778), Price expressed his dismay at Archbishop Markham's attack on reformers ("the lowest and wickedest combinations" of men in "the last stage of political depravity") and at his wish that bishops might be established in America once "the rebellion [was] crushed".[34]

There is no doubt that Price's reputation (based on his political pamphlets) drew many sympathisers of the radical cause and opponents of the war to attend his fast sermons and "excited an earnestness to peruse [his discourses]",[35] thus encouraging him to publish them. But the sermons also gave rise to strange rumours. Price was apologetic: "This sermon having been misrepresented, I was obliged to publish it." Those complaints do not seem entirely unwarranted, since he had to assure a Dutch correspondent that the sermon "did not at all contribute, as you have been informed, to produce the tumults which attended Admiral Kepple's [sic] acquittal".[36]

Price published the 1779 sermon partly to ward off Bishop Lowth's attacks on the reformers. In a sermon preached at the royal chapel of St James's Palace in 1779, Lowth had quoted extracts from Price's works to refute the doctrine of popular sovereignty; Lowth presented Price as one of those whose "study it has long been to introduce confusion, to encourage

---

[31] Carlyle 1777, 38-39.
[32] American Resistance Indefensible 1776, 9, 22.
[33] Markham 1777.
[34] Price 1991, 16-18. For Price's early reaction, see Price to Benjamin Franklin, 15 June 1777, *Correspondence* 1.257. The controversy spilled into Parliament when Lord Chatham denounced Markham's opinions in a speech to the Lords on 5 December 1777.
[35] Review of Price's 1779 sermon in *London Magazine* 48, 1779 : 231.
[36] Correspondence, 2.42-43.

sedition and to destroy all rule and authority" (Lowth 1779, 25). In the postscript to his 1779 sermon, Price answered the bishop, backing his often repeated arguments with the formidable authority of Locke, Montesquieu and Blackstone, and confronted Lowth with one of his own earlier sermons, to prove that the bishop had once held the opinions he now criticized. Despite Price's claims to the contrary, the attack became both partisan and personal when Price accused Lowth of becoming a Tory (Price 1779, 44). He and Lowth were in conflict over the repeal of the penal statutes on Dissenters and over the issue of American episcopacy. Thus fast sermons could appear as pretexts for settling scores over matters that were not directly linked to the war, but were exacerbated by aspects of it, such as the projects of establishing bishops in America.

Although the practice of publishing sermons to present political views or answer other clergymen's criticism was fairly common in the 18th century (Deconinck-Brossard 1983, 1.24; Ippel 1980, 192), Price was on the defensive and felt obliged to justify his conduct, both in private and in public.[37]

In the "Advertisement" to the 1779 sermon, Price argued that "the present state of the kingdom" made it necessary for his sermon to be political: "This . . . is the first time in which [the author] has entered into politics in the pulpit, and perhaps, it may be the last." Price also took care to insert a note indicating that his views were "general" and that the "candid" reader should not try to decode any personal allusion.[38] But his claims were contradicted throughout the sermon, by his own footnotes (not to mention the postscript attacking Bishop Lowth), in which he praised the virtue and patriotism of the opposition, and attacked the Bishop of Exeter and, again, Archbishop Markham.

Price's temperament and his belief in the virtues of enlightened discussion also account for this attitude. He thought that mankind would reach a "better state" only through free, rational discussion (not invective or violence) and unlimited intellectual enquiry. He soon became weary of political strife; several times during the American war he wished that he had "now done with political publications".[39] Price insisted on his ideal of unbiased "candour" and free, "unfettered", impartial discussion which is characteristic of the enlightened public sphere.[40] Against those who

---

[37] Other anti-war Dissenters, but also preachers defending the government's position, felt compelled to justify their allusions to politics (e.g. *American Resistance Indefensible* 1776, 24).
[38] Price 1779, 25.
[39] *Correspondence* 1.270, 2.43.
[40] Thomas 1977a, 99; Saunders 1996.

suspected him of ulterior motives, he repeatedly argued that he was impelled by conscience.[41] He nevertheless confided to William Adam that the postscript to the 1779 sermon, which contained "some things that are too unsuitable to a sermon," should "be read with a great deal of candour": "But it is out of my hands and now too late to repent".[42]

Price sent his sermons and his *Tracts* to various friends and contacts in America, including governor Jonathan Trumbull (1710-1785) and James Bowdoin (1726-1790). The 1779 and 1781 sermons, along with Price's *Two Tracts on Civil Liberty* offered some comfort to Henry Laurens (1724-1792) during his confinement in the tower of London from October 1780 to December 1781.[43] Price's sermons, which presented the war as unwinnable for the British and suggested that God was on the side of the Americans, were likely to find a more favourable reception among the latter than in Britain.

Price also sent his 1779 sermon to Johann Dirk van der Capellen, a Dutch patriot who had published a spirited pamphlet against Spanish occupation in 1777. Van der Capellen had translated Price's *Observations on Civil Liberty* and *Additional Observations* into Dutch. Price's indictment of British colonial policy and his defence of "self-government" provided the Dutch patriots with rational arguments against Spanish rule. Van der Capellen was delighted by Price's 1779 fast sermon: "Votre sermon sera traduit en Hollandois. Tout ce qui vient de vous est bien reçu ici." There is no evidence that the sermon was ever translated into Dutch though.[44] Van der Capellen's enthusiasm suggests that he considered the sermons might be an effective propaganda tool in a Protestant country such as the Netherlands and that Price's theory of resistance would bolster the case of the Dutch republicans.

Predictably, the reception was more mixed in Britain. Price was criticized in the newspapers for meddling in political affairs which should not concern him, and thus for detracting from the dignity of the preacher. As a Dissenter, he was accused of advancing a "political" agenda of religious toleration and sedition, if not republicanism. The *Gentleman's Magazine* set Price against St Paul:

> While [St Paul] inforces toleration, he insists on submission, and does not, like Dr. Price, preach a fast sermon to lash the Ministry personally. The good apostle was no tool to a party. If he had puzzled his hearers with

---

[41] Price 1991, 113; *Correspondence*, 2.35-36.
[42] *Correspondence*, 2.97-98.
[43] *Correspondence*, 2.80, 2.122-123.
[44] Baron van der Capellen to Price, 1 July 1779, *Correspondence* 2.45.

calculations about the national debt, or spirited up their colonies to independence, they would not have let him "live and preach two whole years in his own hired house."[45]

And yet Price's critics were interested in the political, not the theological content of the sermons;[46] some commentators relished the personal polemics.[47]

Whereas the ministerial *Critical Review* lashed out at Price's theory of popular sovereignty[48], the Whiggish *Monthly Review* was more favourable but nevertheless levelled some criticism at Price. A pamphleteer went as far as to reaffirm the doctrine of divine right kingship; he accused Price of reviling the government out of spite and party spirit, which also allowed him to dismiss Price's grim picture of the moral corruption and financial predicament of England on the same grounds.[49] This led to charges of disloyalty and "abuse of the national character"[50], in keeping with accusations against Dissenters whose loyalty to the Hanoverian dynasty, hitherto unquestioned, came to be suspected.

Price was also frequently criticized for using a language not fit for the pulpit: "you soar above the highest Flight of methodistical Enthusiasm itself".[51] Price, though, mistrusted "enthusiasm" and had no sympathy for Methodism: if Price had been prone to get carried away by his rhetoric, he had soon learned to strike a balance between austerity and enthusiasm. Other pro-American preachers issued much more violent statements, such as George Walker who did not hesitate to exhort the Nottinghamshire militia to consider themselves as "the soldiers of the people more than the

---

[45] *Gentleman's Magazine* 49 (June 1779) : 301.

[46] With the exception of "a Cobler" [sic], who quibbled about Price's non-literal interpretation of the Bible, Cobler 1779.

[47] The *Gentleman's Magazine* was more interested in Price's onslaught on Bishop Lowth than in the ideas expounded in the 1779 sermon proper. *Gentleman's Magazine* 49, (April 1797) : 204. The *Critical Review* reproached Price for preaching a political sermon, but took little notice of the sermon itself and commented at length on the "political" postscript, in the "Controversial" section of the paper, treating the postscript as an independent publication. *Critical Review* 47 (March 1779): 317-318.

[48] *Critical Review* 47 (March 1779): 238. On the editorial code elaborated by the press to criticize sermons, see Langford 1990, 281.

[49] Cobler 1779, 16-17, 35, 33-34. Price's pessimistic accounts of the British finances in *An Appeal to the Public on the Subject of the National Debt* (1772), and in the appendices to *Observations on Civil Liberty*, had already been repeatedly dismissed as exaggerated, fanciful exercises in political denigration.

[50] Cobler 1779, 23.

[51] Cobler 1779, 13.

crown".[52] Price insisted on submission to the law and backed off from such revolutionary implications of the doctrine of popular sovereignty.

Towards the end of the war, when it became obvious that victory was out of reach for Britain, Price's sermons came to be recognized as far-sighted, or even prophetic. In June 1781, Lord Monboddo wrote to Price that he had "written of our affairs with the spirit of Divination" and that his sermons had convinced him that he was not a mere "tool of Party".[53] The *Monthly Review* grudgingly acknowledged that Price's dire predictions had come true, though they had been ridiculed at that time.[54]

Interest in Price's sermons was briefly revived in the early years of the French. Sermons were used as a medium to discuss the events in France and their implications for Britain. The first anti-French sermons were delivered as early as late 1789, but the pace quickened in the winter of 1792-1793, in response to the publication of the second part of Paine's *Rights of Man* and to the war with France.

The issue of "political" sermons came to the fore again, especially after Price's *Discourse on the Love of our Country* expressed vibrant support for the French Revolution and expounded a theory of popular sovereignty and the right of resistance, based on a radical interpretation of the Glorious Revolution. Once more Price was criticized for his intemperate language. Whereas a few critics judged that important political topics were not inappropriate in a sermon, Price's political comments attracted heavy criticism. Even Fox felt compelled to condemn Price for his "political" sermon in a speech to the Commons.[55]

The most devastating criticism came from Burke, who singled out Price as a representative of what he conceived as the ultimately dangerous thought of the Enlightenment. Burke's comparison of Price to Hugh Peters placed the *Discourse* in the context of the "Great Rebellion" of the seventeenth century, which served as a paradigm for discussions of obedience and resistance.[56] Burke's *Reflections* played a crucial role in firmly establishing the reputation of Price as a fierce preacher of seditious doctrines: pamphleteers and caricaturists alike were to take over the image and present Price as a levelling, Puritan, "enthusiastic" preacher.

Price's sermons could thus be exploited for political purposes. A few months after Price's death in 1791, a garbled edition of his 1759 sermon came out. All the critical comments were edited out, leaving the reader

---

[52] Bradley 1990, 133.
[53] Correspondence, 2. 101.
[54] *Monthly Review* for April 1781, 54 (1781) : 315-216.
[55] Fox 1790, 42.
[56] Burke 1987, 10.

with the impression that Price lavished unqualified praise on all the British institutions. Particularly highlighted were the passages in which Price expressed his satisfaction that Dissenters enjoyed toleration, claims that flew in the face of the Dissenters' recent campaign for the repeal of the Test and Corporation Acts. The preface, presenting Price as "a most zealous advocate for the *Rights of Man*", aimed at passing Price off as a Painite radical bent on replacing the constitution by "a government of societies and clubs like those at Paris".[57] The *Gentleman's Magazine* took the hint and affirmed that Price was now "completely convicted of this contradiction" as he had contended in 1759 that Britain was the happiest country on earth.[58] The aim of the reprint was probably to embarrass the reformers by portraying them as self-seeking, unprincipled apostates complaining about imaginary grievances.[59]

In the course of the war against revolutionary France, several fast days were proclaimed, which provided the occasion for pro-war or anti-war sermons and for controversy about royal proclamations. Price's American War sermons were again mentioned, not to praise Price's opposition to the war, but to lament that fasts were the occasion for political discussions which disgraced the pulpit. By the early 1790s, Price had become an object of contempt or ridicule (except in radical or Dissenting circles) and those who wanted to argue again the French Wars did not wish to revive the memory of his opposition to the American War. But on the whole, Price's fast sermons were not much quoted by the loyalists either, because they were dated and too moderate to be used, especially as attention was deflected to Paine's much more extreme statements.

Whereas most parts of Price's fast sermons were conventionally whiggish, the author added his more controversial or political statements into footnotes and various addenda, as other preachers did at that time. This suggests that he delivered rather general statements from the pulpit, and that he chose to tack on more topical material, thus using the publication of the sermon as a pretext for answering critics.

In many ways, Richard Price's fast sermons served to reaffirm positions already stated in his political tracts. This is not to say that the sermons did not offer anything new: they were also occasions for Price to rework some of his central concepts and in particular the theory of the right of resistance, which was at the core of the controversy during the

---

[57] Price 1991, 3, 5.

[58] *Gentleman's Magazine* 68 (1791) : 838.

[59] Price 1791. James (1724-1802) and Charles Rivington (1754-1831) were prominent London publishers; they published the works of many loyalist writers.

American War and again in the early stage of the French Revolution when Price delivered his *Discourse on the Love of our Country*.

Instead of being discussed from a theological point of view, the war served as a catalyst that reactivated long-standing political controversies (parliamentary representation, sectarian conflict, religious toleration, financial crisis). Price's sermons did not convince his opponents; neither could they influence British policies or the course of the war. Towards the end of the war, Price sometimes almost sounded like a Cassandra indulging in a self-righteous attitude and deriving satisfaction from the consciousness of having done his duty and having been justified in his pessimism. The French Revolution briefly revived interest in Price's fast sermons, but Burke's attacks had been so shattering that Price's attitude in the 1770s could not serve as an inspiration.

Works Cited

American Resistance Indefensible. A Sermon, Preached on Friday, December 13, 1776, being the Day Appointed for a General Fast. By a Country Curate. London, 1776.

Bonwick, Colin C. "English Dissenters and the American Revolution" in *Contrast and Connection: Bicentennial Essays in Anglo-American History*, ed. H. C. Allen and Roger Thompson. London: G. Bell. 1976. 88-112.

Bradley, James E. *Religion, Revolution, and English Radicalism*. Cambridge: Cambridge University Press, 1990.

Butler, John. *A Sermon Preached before the Honourable House of Commons, at the Church of St. Margaret's, Westminster, on Friday, December 13, 1776; being the Day Appointed by his Majesty's Royal Proclamation, to be Observed as a Day of Solemn Fasting and Humiliation*. London, 1777.

Burke, Edmund. *Reflections on the Revolution in France*. [1790] ed. J. G. A. Pocock. Indianapolis; Cambridge: Hackett, 1987.

Carlyle, Alexander. *The Justice and Necessity of the War with our American Colonies Examined. A Sermon, Preached at Inveresk, December 12, 1776*. London; Edinburgh, 1777.

Caudle, James. "Measures of Allegiance; Sermon Culture and the Creation of a Public Discourse of Obedience and Resistance in Georgian Britain, 1714-1760." Ph.D. diss, Yale University, 1996.

—. "Preaching in Parliament: Patronage, Publicity and Politics in Britain, 1701-60". In *The English Sermon Revised: Religion, Literature and*

History 1600 -1750, ed. Lori Anne Ferrell and Peter McCullough, 235-263. Manchester; New York: Manchester University Press, 2000a.

—. "Richard Price and the Revolution in Resistance Theory, 1770-1790". In *Consortium on Revolutionary Europe 1750-1850: Select Papers*, 2000b.

Church of England. *Abstract of a Form of Prayer and Thanksgiving to Almighty God; to Be Used in All Churches and Chapels ... on Thursday the 29th of November Instant*. London, 1759.

—. A *Form of Prayer, to Be Used in All Churches and Chapels Throughout that Part of Great Britain Called England, Dominion of Wales, and Town of Berwick upon Tweed, upon Wednesday the Tenth of February Next...* London, 1779.

Cobler. *Three Letters to the Rev. Dr. Price: Containing Remarks upon his Fast-Sermon. By a Cobler*. London, 1779.

Colley, Linda. "Radical Patriotism in Eighteenth-Century England". In *Patriotism: The Making und Unmaking of British National Identity*. Volume I: History and Politics, ed. Raphael Samuel. London; New York: Routledge, 1989.

—. *Britons: Forging the nation 1707-1837*. New Haven, CT; London: Yale University Press, 1992.

Cookson, J. E. *The Friends of Peace. Anti-War Liberalism in England, 1793-1815*. Cambridge: Cambridge University Press, 1982.

Deconinck-Brossard, Françoise. *Vie politique, sociale et religieuse en Grande-Bretagne d'après les sermons prêchés ou publiés dans le Nord de l'Angleterre, 1738-1760*. 2 vols. Paris: Didier, 1983.

Dickinson, H. T. "Richard Price on Reason and Revolution". In *Religion, Politics and Identity, 1660-1832*, ed. William Gibson and Robert G. Ingram. Aldershot: Ashgate, 2005. 231-254.

Fox, Charles James. *The speech of the Right Hon. C. J. Fox, in the House of Commons, on Tuesday, March 2d, 1790, upon his Motion for the Repeal of the Corporation and Test Acts*. London, 1790.

Fox, William. *A Discourse on National Fasts, Particularly in Reference to That of April 19, 1793, on Occasion of the War against France*. 3rd ed. London, 1793.

Gerard, Alexander. D.D. *Liberty the Cloke of Maliciousness, Both in the American Rebellion, and in the Manners of the Time. A Sermon Preached at Old Aberdeen, Feb. 26, 1778. Being the Fast Day*. London,1778.

Hole, Robert. "English Sermons and Tracts as Media of Debate on the French Revolution 1789-99". In *The French Revolution and British*

Popular Politics, ed. Mark Philp, 18-37. Cambridge: Cambridge University Press, 1991.

Ippel, Henry P. "Blow the Trumpet, Sanctify the Fast." Huntington Library Quarterly 44 (1980): 43-60.

Laboucheix, Henri. *Richard Price, théoricien de la Révolution américaine. Le Philosophe et le sociologue, le pamphlétaire et l'orateur.* Paris : Didier, 1970.

Langford, Paul. *The English Clergy and the American Revolution. The Transformation of Political Culture: England and Germany in the Eighteenth Century*, ed. Eckhart Hellmuth. Oxford: Oxford University Press, 1990. 275-308.

Leeb, I. Leonard. *The Ideological Origins of the Batavian Revolution.* The Hague: Martinus Nijhoff, 1973.

Lincoln, Anthony. *Some Political and Social Ideas of English Dissent.* Cambridge: Cambridge University Press, 1938.

Lowth, Robert, bishop of London. *A Sermon Preached at the Chapel Royal, of St James's Palace, on Ash-Wednesday.* London, 1779.

Markham, William. *Sermon Preached before the Incorporated Society for the Propagation of the Gospel in Foreign Parts . . . on Friday February 21, 1777.* By ... William Lord Archbishop of York. London, 1777.

Morgan, William. *Memoirs of the Life of the Rev. Richard Price, D.D. F.R.S.* London, 1815.

Price, Richard. *A Sermon, Delivered to a Congregation of Protestant Dissenters, at Hackney, on the 10th of February Last, Being the Day Appointed for a General Fast.* 2d ed. London, 1779.

—. *Britain's Happiness, and its Full Possession of Civil and Religious Liberty, Briefly Stated and Proved.* By the Late Rev. Dr. Richard Price. With an Introduction by the Editor. London, 1791.

—. *The Correspondence of Richard Price.* 3 vols. Ed. Bernard Peach and D. O. Thomas. Durham, NC: Duke University Press; Cardiff: University of Wales Press, 1983-94.

—. *Political Writings.* Ed. D. O. Thomas. Cambridge: Cambridge University Press, 1991.

Priestley, Joseph. *A Sermon Preached at the Gravel Pit Meeting, in Hackney, April 19th, 1793, Being the Day Appointed for a General Fast.* London, 1793.

—. *The Present State of Europe Compared with Antient Prophecies; a Sermon, Preached at the Gravel Pit Meeting in Hackney, February 28, 1794, Being the Day Appointed for a General Fast.* London, 1794.

Ross, John. *A Sermon Preached before the Lords Spiritual and Temporal, in the Abbey-Church, Westminster; on Saturday, January 30, 1779*: ... By John Lord Bishop of Exeter. London, 1779.

Saunders, Alan. "The State as Highwayman: from candour to rights". In *Enlightenment and Religion. Rational Dissent in Eighteenth Century Britain*, ed. Knud Haakonssen, 241-272. Cambridge: Cambridge University Press, 1996.

Schama, Simon. *Patriots and Liberators: Revolution in the Netherlands 1780-1813*. [1977]. Hammersmith: Fontana, 1992.

Seed, John. "Rational Dissent and Political Opposition 1770-1790". In *Enlightenment and Religion. Rational Dissent in Eighteenth Century Britain*, ed. Knud Haakonssen, 140-168. Cambridge: Cambridge University Press, 1996.

Thomas, D. O. *The Honest Mind*. Oxford: Clarendon, 1977a.

—. "Neither Republican nor Democrat." *The Price-Priestley Newsletter* 1: 49-60, 1977b.

CHAPTER NINE

"THE BATTLE IS GOD'S":
PATRIOTIC SERMONS
DURING THE AMERICAN CIVIL WAR

MASSIMO RUBBOLI

The nation that emerged from the American Revolution possessed a sacred meaning because it was endowed with a divine mission to be an example and a model for the renovation of the world.[1] Since the hopes of humankind rested on its preservation, if this elect nation were destroyed, "crushed and degraded humanity must sink down in despair."[2]

On the eve of the American Civil War, it was quite difficult to accept that the new "chosen people" had divided into two distinct nations. According to a Boston Baptist minister, "We cannot have two or more republics on this soil. God and nature have forbidden it,"[3] but the pastor of St. James' Church in Concord, North Carolina, expressed a different opinion: "Nature and nature's God has marked us out for two nations."[4]

Even more difficult to accept was the fact that these two nations were going to fight not against an external enemy but with each other. If the colonies, as Rev. Ebenezer Baldwin said in November 1775, had been "engaged in a most unhappy War ... a most unnatural War," because

---

[1] A view against the stream was that of Henry J. Van Dyke, who rejected "as blasphemous the sentiment so often uttered by Christian ministers, that God cannot do without the United States, that the Church of Christ is in anywise identified with or dependent upon the national existence." *The Spirituality and Independence of the Church*. New York: n.p., 1864, 3.

[2] Francis Wayland, Francis Wayland, *An Appeal to the Disciples of Christ of Every Denomination in Reference to the Approaching Day of Prayer*, Boston, Mass.: American Tract Society, 1861, 8.

[3] Daniel C. Eddy, *Our Country: Its Pride and Its Peril, or Liberty and the Union* Boston: John M. Hewes, 1861, 19.

[4] Daniel I. Dreher, *A Sermon*. Salisbury, NC: Watchman's Office, 1861, 5.

"those of the same Nation, of the same common Ancestors, of the same language, of the same professed Religion, and heirs of the same Privileges, should be imbuing their hands in each other's Blood,"[5] the new war was again a "most unhappy" and "unnatural war."

From "broken churches" to "broken nation"

It is indeed obvious that the substance of North - South disagreements, and the timing of their eruptions, had most to do with the issues of trade, slavery and state jurisdiction. Yet these apparently self-evident explanations of the conflict of the 1860s were seen at the time as strangely inadequate. People on both sides shared a tragic sense that these ostensible causes of the conflict were insufficient to explain the awesome scale of what was actually happening. They were well aware of the religious dimension of the conflict, a dimension that has been overlooked, if not completely forgotten, by many historians until recent years.[6]

On March 4, 1850, in his last speech to the United States Senate (actually delivered by James Mason because Calhoun was too weak to even read it), John C. Calhoun noted that:

> [t]he cords that bind the States together are not only many, but various in character. Some are spiritual or ecclesiastical; some political; others social. … The strongest of those of a spiritual and ecclesiastical nature, consisted in the unity of the great religious denominations, all of which originally embraced the whole Union. The ties which held each denomination together formed a strong cord to hold the whole Union together; but, powerful as they were, they have not been able to resist the explosive effect of slavery agitation.[7]

---

[5] Ebenezer Baldwin, *The Duty of Rejoicing under Calamities and Afflictions*. New York: Hugh Gaine, 1776, 21-22.

[6] For the influence of religious belief on the South's decision to secede and on the way Northerners and Southerners viewed and conducted the Civil War, see C.C. Goen, *Broken Churches, Broken Nation: Denominational Schism and the Coming of the American Civil War*. Macon, GA: Mercer UP, 1985; Robert M. Calhoon, *Evangelicals and Conservatives in the Early South, 1740-1861*. Columbia, SC: University of South Carolina Press, 1988; Mitchell Snay, *Gospel of Disunion: Religion and Separatism in the Antebellum South*. Cambridge: CUP, 1993.

[7] *The Works of John C. Calhoun*, ed. Richard K. Cralle (New York, 1854), IV, 557-559.

"If the agitation goes on," warned Calhoun, "the same force, acting with increased intensity ... will finally snap every cord, when nothing will be left to hold the States together except force."[8]

In the late 1930s, commenting Calhoun's words, historian William Warren Sweet argued:

> The snapping of the ecclesiastical cords had undoubtedly a large influence in creating the final breach between North and South. Indeed, there are good arguments to support the claim that the split in the churches was not only the first break between the sections, but the chief cause of the final break.[9]

Sweet probably overestimated the role of the churches. However, other historians have argued that both Northern and Southern churches played crucial roles in supplying distorted images and attitudes that inflamed and intensified sectional problems. In the words of historian C.C. Goen, the "broken churches" led to a "broken nation."[10]

Southern churches in particular are said to have sanctioned secular attitudes and prepared the way for secession. Historian John Lee Eighmy coined the phrase "cultural captivity" to suggest that the South's predominant churches reflected a culture of "southernism" shaped by economic and racial elites, but at the same time, churches themselves shaped the institutional and personal development of the South and its people.[11]

The Christian churches – more than other social groups – possessed networks of communication, which influenced their members' vision, and understanding of reality. Preaching was the most important instrument for Northern and Southern churches alike, and ministers devoted the greater part of their time preparing and delivering sermons. Pastors who had charge of one church preached at least two sermons a week. Occasionally they might preach to a group outside the church or deliver a sermon at a funeral or in other special occasion. During the war, they also preached regularly to the troops and, when presidents Davis and Lincoln proclaimed

---

[8] *Ibid.*, 559.

[9] William Warren Sweet, *The Story of Religion in America.* New York: Harper & Brothers, 1939, 448-9.

[10] Goen, Broken *Churches, Broken Nation, 126, 189; John Lee Eighmy, Churches in Cultural Captivity: A History of Social Attitudes of Southern Baptists.* Knoxville: University of Tennessee Press, 1972, 19; James W. Silver, *Confederate Morale and Church Propaganda.* New York: W.W. Norton, 1967, 93.

[11] Charles Reagan Wilson, "Religion and the American South," Southern Spaces, March 16, 2004, http://www.southernspaces.org/contents/2004/wilson/1a.htm.

various days of national thanksgiving and of national fasting and
humiliation, they were called to give thanks for God's help or to
enumerate national failings and to express repentance.

On both sides, Christian ministers found scriptural grounds for ardently
supporting their respective causes, and their sermons could not be other
than central to mobilize popular support and to maintain loyalty. It is
important to note that a large number of sermons were printed and became
widely circulated pamphlets.

Between reluctance and support

When the election of Lincoln in November 1860 prompted Southern
secession, many ministers initially advised caution, being aware of
representing, in the words of one of them, "a class whose opinions in such
a controversy are of cardinal importance."[12] In the North, the more
numerous conservatives, some of whom sympathized with the South,
hoped that a show of forbearance would cause the disunion movement to
collapse and bring the seceded states to their senses. In a sermon preached
on January 4, 1861, at the Madison Square Presbyterian Church in New
York City, the Rev. William Adams made an appeal for peace and
reconciliation between the North and the South.[13] When Confederate
batteries opened fire on Fort Sumter in April 1861, however, reluctance to
coerce the South vanished. The Union had to be preserved.

Lincoln's call for volunteers to suppress the rebellion won nearly
universal backing from ministers.[14] Only a minority opposed the call to
arms and persisted in invoking the end of the armed conflict in order to
allow God to solve the North-South problem.[15] The words of Zachary
Eddy, a Congregational pastor in Northampton, Mass., may well express

---

[12] Benjamin M. Palmer, *The South: Her Peril, and Her Duty. A Discourse
delivered in the First Presbyterian Church, New Orleans, on Thursday, November
29, 1860* . New Orleans: Office of the True Witness and Sentinel, 1860, 4.
[13] William Adams, "Prayer for Rulers, or, Duty of Christian Patriots" in *Fast Day
Sermons: The Pulpit on the State of the Country*, eds. James H. Thornwell et al.
New York: Rudd & Carleton, 1861, 311-36.
[14] James H. Moorhead, *American Apocalypse: Yankee Protestants and the Civil
War, 1860-1869*. Yale: Yale University Press, 1978.
[15] Cf. David Magie, *A Discourse Delivered in the Second Presbyterian Church*.
New York: Francis Hart and Co., 1863.

the position of countless other ministers: "It is the will of God! It is the will of God!"[16]

Before the war, in the South the doctrine of the "spirituality of the church" forbade any hint of political posturing from the realm of the church. At the General Assembly of the Presbyterian Church of 1859, theologian James Henley Thornwell -- the most influential person in Southern Presbyterianism and professor of theology at the denomination's seminary at Columbia[17] -- firmly insisted:

> The church is exclusively a spiritual organization, and possesses none but spiritual power. [...] The Church deals with men as men, as fallen sinners standing in need of salvation [...] Her mission is to bring men to the Cross, to reconcile them to God through the Blood of the Lamb, to imbue them with the Spirit of the Divine Master, and then send them forth to perform their social duties, to manage society, and perform the functions that pertain to their social and civil relations.[18]

While Southern states were discussing the possibility of secession, Thornwell declared:

> The prospect of disunion is one which I cannot contemplate without absolute horror. A peaceful dissolution is utterly impossible ... and a war between the States of this confederacy would, in my opinion, be the bloodiest, most ferocious, and cruel, in the annals of history.[19]

Thornwell maintained his opposition to disunion throughout the 1850s.

The Presbyterian Synod of Virginia, which met shortly before the presidential election, designated the first Sunday in November 1860 as a day of fasting and prayer and suggested that Presbyterian clergymen preach on the duty of Christians as peacemakers.[20] On this occasion

---

[16] Zachary Eddy, "A Discourse on the War" (Northampton, MA: Trumbull and Gere, 1861), in *God Ordained This War: Sermons on the Sectional Crisis, 1830-1865*, ed. David B. Chesebrough. Columbia, SC: University of South Carolina Press, 1991, 313.

[17] Before the outbreak of the war, Thornwell was called "the Calhoun of the Southern Church," see James Oscar Farmer Jr., *The Metaphysical Confederacy: James Henley Thornwell and the Synthesis of Southern Values*. Macon, GA: Mercer University Press, 1986, 39.

[18] J.H. Thornwell, "Speech on African Civilization," *Collected Writings*, 4: 473, quoted in Farmer, *Metaphysical Confederacy*, 188.

[19] J.H. Thornwell to the Rev. Dr. Hooper, March 8, 1850, quoted in Loveland, *Southern Evangelicals*, 257.

[20] The practice of fasting and prayer traced back to the Old Testament prophets and provided a religious frame of reference used in America since colonial times. Cf.

Robert Lewis Dabney, the moderator of the Synod of Virginia destined to become General "Stonewall" Jackson's chief of staff,[21] preached a sermon at College Church in Hampden Sidney, Va., in which he denounced the passionate men who were "stirring" the country and he invited his listeners to pray for peace, vote for virtuous men, and be calm in language and manner.[22]

After Lincoln's election to the presidency in November 1860, but before the secession of South Carolina, some ministers and denominational agencies publicly advocated disunion and played a prominent role in the drive for secession. However, many of Virginia's Baptist clergy wanted nothing to do with the secession movement. They invoked the jeremiad and Fast Day traditions to explain and cope with the secession winter of 1860-61.

When Southern states withdrew from the Union, most ministers accepted the action as part of the providential design and the rhetoric of the cause shifted from civil to religious liberty. The rhetorical transformation is nicely illustrated by the politically charged sermon preached by Thornwell, in response to the Presbyterian synod of South Carolina's declaration of a statewide fast for the nation on November 21, 1860. The text was Isaiah 37:1: "When King Hezekiah heard it, he rent his clothes." Thornwell confessed at the outset of his sermon: "I have never introduced secular politics into the instruction of the pulpit." But with Lincoln headed for the White House, Thornwell was prepared to preach for the first time to what he called "an organized political community," signalling a revolutionary departure from form. He declared that Union, a name "once dear to our hearts, has become intolerable and is now synonymous with oppression, treachery, falsehood, and violence." He denounced Congress as being corrupt and described it as a "den of robbers and bullies."[23] Even before formal independence, it must have appeared to

---

Perry Miller, *The New England Mind, From Colony to Province*. Cambridge, MA: Harvard UP, 1953, 27-39; Sacvan Bercovitch, *The American Jeremiad*. Madison: University of Wisconsin Press, 1978.

[21] On Dabney's relation to General 'Stonewall' Jackson, see Wallace Hettle, "The Minister, the Martyr, and the Maxim: Robert Lewis Dabney and Stonewall Jackson Biography," *Civil War History* 49: 4 (2003): 353-369.

[22] Robert L. Dabney, The Christian Best Motive for Patriotism. A Sermon preached in the College Church, Hampden Sidney, Va., on the 1st of November, 1869. Richmond: Chas.H. Wynne, 1860. Reprinted in Thornwell, *Fast Day Sermons*, 83-96.

[23] James H. Thornwell, "National Sins: A Fast-Day Sermon, Preached in the Presbyterian Church, Columbia, Wednesday, November 21, 1860" in *Fast Day Sermons*, 28, 55.

Thornwell that maybe the South was unique and sacred as Israel was in the Old Testament. There was not yet a new nation to proclaim a public fast, but Thornwell's summons to a rising Christian republic would echo in Richmond's pulpits and throughout the Confederacy in the blood bath to come.[24]

In a sermon delivered a week later, Rev. George Henry Clark, Rector of St. John's in Savannah, Georgia, described fierce civil divisions that had occurred in the world throughout history to show the horrors that could result from the dissolution of the Union, but he concluded that if there were no other solution, he would support secession:

> My hearers, my heart trembles, and the blood thrills through my veins, when I contemplate the dissolution of these States. [...] Men, citizens, Christians, reflect long, labor faithfully, pray earnestly to God for help, before you make your last decision; and then, if there be no remedy, in darkness and in gloom, in sackcloth and in ashes, looking up to heaven for light to guide our sons, for mercy to protect our daughters, we will sing the requiem of these United States.[25]

On November 29, Benjamin Morgan Palmer, pastor of the First Presbyterian Church in New Orleans, preached a Thanksgiving Day sermon. In this widely circulated sermon, Palmer reminded the member of his congregation that until that day he had "never intermeddled with political questions," because he wanted to be "a preacher of righteousness belonging to a kingdom not of this world." But the circumstances had changed, because the Union, which their forefathers had formed no longer, existed and mutual respect and confidence had been destroyed. Therefore, he argued that" secession was the only way the South could carry out its providential task of preserving slavery and "defend the cause of God and religion."[26]

On December 9, the Rev. R.K. Porter of Waynesboro, Georgia, expressed the belief that peace was possible only if the Union was dissolved and he suggested a "speedy dissolution."[27] As late as June 1861,

---

[24] Farmer, *The Metaphysical Confederacy*, 261-263.

[25] George H. Clark, *A Sermon, Delivered in St. John's Church, Savannah, On Fast Day, Nov. 28, 1860.* Savannah: George N. Nichols, 1860, 61-2.

[26] Palmer, *The South: Her Peril, and Her Duty*, 2, 3, 10-11.

[27] R.K. Porter, *Christian Duty in the Present Crisis: The Substance of a Sermon Delivered in the Presbyterian Church, in Waynesboro, Georgia, December 9, 1860.* Savannah: Steam Press of John M. Cooper and Company, 1860, 20.

William Meade, Episcopal bishop of Virginia, called for a peaceful solution of the conflict.[28]

Some scholars have failed to distinguish between the Upper and Lower South Protestants. Robert L. Dabney, for instance, was critical of the secession sentiments of his Presbyterian colleagues in the Deep South and of the precipitate political action of South Carolina. He did not consider the election of Lincoln a cause for secession and he regarded the conduct of South Carolina as unjustifiable and as weakening the position of the South. In March, however, Dabney finally called upon Virginians to leave the Union as soon as possible.[29] Historians have also tended to give more relevance to the Presbyterian and the Episcopal Church, which in terms of membership were quite distant from the Baptists and the Methodists. Stephen Elliot, Episcopal bishop of Georgia, and Presbyterian Palmer and Thornwell were only a part of the whole picture that has been more recently recovered.[30]

Awash in a sea of patriotism

With the firing on Fort Sumter, the initial reluctance of many Northern and Southern ministers to "intermeddle with political questions" gave way to an uncritical support of the war. As the war progressed, in both nations patriotism displaced religious and partisan loyalties and many sermons reveal a lack of moral criticism on either side. "To a high and holy patriotism, we are solemnly called. God summons us to it," declared James H. Appleton, minister of Union Baptist Church in Jersey City, N.J.[31]

It is quite surprising that the author of a study of Civil War preaching could state, "Missing from Union and Confederate sermons were appeals to duty and patriotism that might have motivated men to enlist for military

---

[28] William Meade, *Address on the Day of Fasting and Prayer, June 13, 1861.* Richmond: Enquirer Book & Job Press, 1861.
[29] Haskell Monroe, "Southern Presbyterians and the Secession Crisis," *Civil War History*, 6: 4 (December, 1960): 358.
[30] Charles F. Irons, "Reluctant Protestant Confederates. The Religious Roots of Conditional Unionism," in *Virginia's Civil War*, eds. Wallenstein and B. Wyatt-Brown. Charlottesville, VA: University of Virginia Press, 2005, 72-86.
[31] James H. Appleton, *Piety and Patriotism, the demand of the times, Sanctioned and Enjoined by Christ: a Discourse delivered before the Union Baptist Church, Jersey City, N.J. on Sabbath morning, August 24th, 1862.* New York: C.S. Westcott, 1862, 14. However, most sermons preached during the war continued to deal with spiritual matters and made no reference to the bloodshed and hatred of war.

service."[32] North and South, the clergy urged the people to fight for the defence of their own nation. In fact, "Patriotism" and "Christian Patriotism" were used as the title of several sermons[33] and as the subject of many others by Protestant preachers. Also a Catholic priest pointed out that "patriotism is not only a social virtue, commanding respect, but a Christian virtue, to be rewarded by the blessings of God here and hereafter."[34] And Rabbi Maximilian J. Michelbacher, in a sermon preached in the German synagogue of Richmond, quoted several times the words of Nehemiah 4: 8, "Fight for your brethren, your sons, and your daughters, your wives and your houses."[35] In the concluding prayer, Michelbacher beseeched God's support for the Confederation:

> We believe, O God, that piety cannot subsist apart from patriotism—we love our country, because Thou hast given it unto us as a blessing and a heritage for our children; and, now, O God, we call upon Thee, to bring

[32] Charles Stewart, "Civil War Preaching," in *Preaching in American History*, ed. Dewitte Holland. Nashville: Abingdon Press, 1969, 198.

[33] Orville Dewey, *On Patriotism. The Condition, Prospects, and Duties of the American People. A Sermon Delivered on Fast Day at Church Green, Boston.* Boston: Ticknor and Fields, 1859; Dabney, *The Christian Best Motive for Patriotism; Silas McKeen, Heroic Patriotism. A Sermon delivered at Bradford, Vt., Sabbath afternoon, April 28, 1861, in the presence of the Bradford Guards, when under call to join the First Regiment of the Vermont Volunteers, and go forth in their country's service.* Windsor, VT: Vermont Chronicle Book and Job Office, 1861; Joel F. Bingham, *The Hour of Patriotism.* Buffalo: Franklin Steam, 1862; William Adams, *Christian Patriotism.* New York: Anson D.F. Randolph, 1863; Thomas Brainerd, *Patriotism aiding Piety. A Sermon, preached in the Third Presbyterian Church, Philadelphia, on the 30th of April, 1863, the day appointed by the President of the United States for humiliation, fasting and prayer.* Philadelphia: W.F. Geddes, 1863; Edmund B. Fairfield, *Christian Patriotism: A Sermon Delivered in the Representatives' Hall, Lansing, Michigan, February 22, 1863.* Lansing: John A. Kerr & Co., 1863; Thomas N. Haskell, *Christian Patriotism: A Medium of God's Power and Purpose to Bless Our Land. A Sermon, delivered in the First Presbyterian Church, East Boston, at the United Service, National Fast Day, April 30, 1863.* Boston: Hollis & Gunn, 1863; Joseph Fransioli, *Patriotism, a Christian virtue. A Sermon preached by the Rev. Joseph Fransioli, at St. Peter's (Catholic) Church, Brooklyn, July 26th, 1863*, Pamphlets issued by the Royal Publication Society, from Feb. 1, 1863, to Feb. 1, 1864, no. 24, (New York: Loyal Publication Society, 1864).

[34] Fransioli, *Patriotism*, 2.

[35] Maximilian J. Michelbacher, *A Sermon delivered on the Day of Prayer Recommended by the President of the C.S. of A., the 27th of March, 1863, at the German Hebrew Synagogue "Bayth Ahabah".* Richmond: Macfarlane & Fergusson, 1863, 5, 9, 10, 12.

salvation to the Confederate States of America, and to crown independence with lasting honour and prosperity.[36]

Sometimes, the same biblical text was used for sermons delivered on opposite sides. This is the case, for instance, of II Samuel 10: 12: "Be of good courage, and let us play the men for our people, and for the cities of our God: and the Lord do that which seemeth Him good."
Congregational minister Silas McKeen used this "thrilling charge given by a General, long since, to his officers and soldiers on the eve of battle"[37] in a sermon he delivered at Bradford, VT, on April 28, 1861:

> The impressive address of Joab to his army is entirely appropriate to the loyal citizens of the United States at this tremendous crisis, --especially to the patriotic soldiery, assembling in such great numbers for the support of our Government and national honor. [...] The people of the loyal States are all moved by the same mighty spirit of patriotism, and, without regard to former political divisions, now stand firmly together [...].[38]

Robert Dabney preached on the same text at a funeral service of Lieutenant Abram Carrington held in Richmond, VA, on December 1862. The onetime reluctant Presbyterian minister invited the young men of his congregation to be "ready to sacrifice on [the] country's altar" and "play the men for your people and the cities of your God."[39] Dabney emphatically said that "the blood of our country's martyrs becomes the seed of our new armies,"[40] paraphrasing Tertullian's famous metaphor, semen est sanguis Christianorum (the blood of the martyrs is the seed of new Christians).[41] Another sermon was preached on the parallel passage of I Chronicles 19: 13 by the Rev. Robert N. Sledd in the Methodist Episcopal Church of Petersburg, VA, on September 22, 1861.[42]

---

[36] *Ibid.*, 10.
[37] McKeen, *Heroic Patriotism*, 3.
[38] *Ibid.*, 4.
[39] Robert L. Dabney, *The Christian Soldier: a Sermon commemorative of the death of Abram C. Carrington. Preached and published by order of the session of College Church, Dec., 1862.* Richmond: Presbyterian Committee of Publication, 1863, 13.
[40] *Ibid.*, 8.
[41] *Apologeticum*, 50. Tertullian, however, thought that the Christian can wage war only without the sword, because Christ has abolished the sword (*De corona militis*, 11-12).
[42] Robert N. Sledd, *A Sermon delivered in the Market Street, M.E. Church, Petersburg, VA.* Petersburg: A.F. Crutchfield and Co., 1861.

If patriotism called for a ringing affirmation of hatred and blood revenge, the sense of belonging to the same family of believers in Christ was not completely lost. For example, on May 5, 1861 the Right Rev. Thomas Atkinson, Episcopal Bishop of North Carolina, recommended:

> to check in ourselves and others the growth of rancorous, vindictive, malignant feeling and the use of bitter, scornful opprobrious language concerning those one our brethren, now, alas, it would seem our enemies. For after all we are Christians ...[43]

Two Christian nations

The task of interpreting God's involvement with the conflict and defining the role of the Christian churches in both nations required much more than simply borrowing preconceived theological categories or rhetorical formulas pulled from the Old Testament or the tradition of political preaching in Puritan New England.

In the South, the clergy's new burden of political preaching was made immensely easier by the new Constitution, adopted on March 11, 1861 by seven Confederate States. Many religious leaders rejoiced that the Confederate constitution explicitly recognized the nation's dependence upon God and declared its Christian identity, "invoking the favor and guidance of Almighty God." This invocation of God would not only solidify the South's identity as a Christian republic, but it would also supply a surprisingly powerful critique of the "godless" Northern Constitution that failed to invoke – or even mention – God.

The Federal Constitution, "whether through inadvertence, or, as is unfortunately more probable, from infidel practices imbibed in France by some members of the Convention [...] contained no recognition of God. Our present Constitution opens with a confession of the existence and providence of the Almighty."[44]

The national motto, Deo Vindice ("with God as our defender"), added additional weight to the South's claim to be a uniquely Christian nation. President Davis proclaimed the first national fast for June 13, 1861 to

---

[43] Thomas Atkinson, *Christian Duty in the Present Time of Trouble*. Wilmington, N.C.: Fulton & Price, Steam Power Press Printers, 1861, 12.

[44] Edward Reed, *A People Saved by the Lord*. Charleston: Evans & Cogswell, 1861, 9.

consecrate the new nation and "to recognize [her people's] dependence upon God ... and supplicate His merciful protection for the future."[45]

Richmond's preachers, like clergymen throughout the Confederacy, rallied to make the religious grounds of political union explicit. "The United States Government," declared on the day of the national fast the rector of St. James Church in Warrenton, Va., "ignores God and makes no reference to an overruling Providence!"[46]

A few days after the national fast, on July 21, 1861, God's purposes seemed to be gloriously revealed with the resounding Confederate victory at Manassas Junction (in the North called the First Battle of Bull Run), about thirty-five miles southwest of Washington. Preaching a thanksgiving sermon to commemorate the victory, William C. Butler declared in Richmond's St. John's Episcopal Church that the opportunity to constitute a truly Christian nation amounted to a special calling for the South. The Confederacy did not receive its divine commission from heaven when men ratified the Confederate Constitution: God had to ratify it, and He did so by bestowing the remarkable victory at Manassas. That astounding success proved that the South fought for principles that were fundamental to God's "Divine government":

> God has given us of the South to-day a fresh and golden opportunity – and so a most solemn command – to realize that form of government in which the just, constitutional rights of each and all are guaranteed to each and all. [...] He has placed us in the front rank of the most marked epochs of the world's history. He has placed in our hands a commission which we can faithfully execute only by holy, individual self-consecration to all of God's plans.[47]

Preaching in Savannah one week after the Confederate victory, Stephen Elliott declared that the victory was "the crowning token of his [God's] love—the most wonderful of all the manifestations of his divine presence with us."[48]

---

[45] PROCLAMATION To the People of the Confederate States, *The Charleston Mercury*, May 27, 1861.

[46] O.S. Barten, *Fast Day Sermon*. Richmond: Enquirer Book and Job Press, 1861, 3. Cf. Ferdinand Jacobs, *A Sermon for the Times*. Marion, AL: n.p., 1861, 5.

[47] Quoted in Harry S. Stout and Christopher Grasso, "Civil War, Religion, and Communications," in Randall M. Miller, Harry S. Stout and Charles Reagan Wilson, *Religion and the American Civil War*. Oxford: OUP, 1998), 323.

[48] Stephen Elliott, *God's Presence with Our Army at Manassas!* Savannah: W. Thorne Williams, 1861, 12.

The Rev. T.S. Winn affirmed that God's assistance to the Confederacy was similar to His aiding the Israelites against the Philistines and he compared the victory at Manassas to David slaying the giant Goliath.[49] Through words like those of Butler, Elliott, and Winn, repeated in similar settings throughout the Confederacy, a nation was being born.

Believing the hand of God was in every event, the Northern clergy asserted that through the disastrous defeat of the Union forces, God had punished the United States for slavery. God had thus signalled that the oppressed should go free. However, other Northern ministers explained it as an expression of the wrath of God against the Northern people. For example, influential Congregational pastor Horace Bushnell explored this theme with peculiar force and interpreted the defeat as an instrument used by God to punish the people for their idolatry and sinfulness. He told his parishioners that more reverses were needed:

> There must be reverses and losses, and times of deep concern. There must be tears in the houses, as well as blood in the fields. ... Peace will do for angels, but war is God's ordinance for sinners, and they want the schooling of it often. In a time of war, what a sense of discipline is forced. Here, at last, there must and will be obedience; and the people, outside, get the sense of it about as truly as the army itself [...].[50]

Only through the path of humiliation and suffering could America purge its dross and attain a new, more nearly perfect identity. But once the ordeal had been passed, he prophesied, the United States would become a true "nation – God's own nation."[51]

A few months later, the Northern people had regained their confidence on being on the right side. Many Yankee ministers thought Union soldiers were preparing the way for the kingdom of God on earth. William Buell Sprague, editor of the famed Annals of the American Pulpit, predicted that Northern success would usher in "a flood of millenial [sic] glory," "the great Thanksgiving Day of the World."[52] Julia Ward Howe, a Unitarian

---

[49] T.S. Winn, *The Great Victory at Manassas Junction. God the Arbiter of Battles, A Thanksgiving Sermon preached in the Presbyterian Church at Concord, in Greene County, Alabama, July 28, 1861.* Tuskaloosa, AL: J.F. Warren, 1861, 6.

[50] Horace Bushnell, *Reverses Needed: A Discourse Delivered on the Sunday after the Disaster at Bull Run in the North Church, Hartford.* Hartford: L.E. Hunt, 1861 in Horace Bushnell, *The Spirit in Man: Sermons and Selections.* New York: Charles Scribner's Sons, 1907, 179, 181.

[51] *Ibid.*, 183.

[52] William B. Sprague, *Glorifying God in the fires: a Discourse delivered in the Second Presbyterian Church, Albany, November 28, 1861, the day of the annual thanksgiving, in the state of New York.* Albany: C. Van Benthuysen, 1861. George

abolitionist from Boston, visiting Washington, D.C., in autumn 1861, expressed a widespread faith when her eyes saw "the glory of the coming of the Lord" in the marching ranks of the Union Army.[53]

Like their Northern counterpart, Southern clergy also viewed their cause as just and holy. In their sermons, they assured the people of the South that in the "eyes of God and man" their cause was just, since they were attempting to maintain their institutions against a despotic power, and they were urged to pray for the welfare of the Confederate government and armies.

In May 16, 1862, a Presbyterian minister in Fayetteville, North Carolina, proclaimed:

Our cause is sacred. ... You are fighting for everything that is near and dear, and sacred to you as men, as Christians and as patriots; for country, for home, for property, for the honor of mothers, daughters, wives, sisters, and loved ones. Your cause is the cause of God, of Christ, of humanity. It is a conflict of truth with error – of the Bible with Northern infidelity – of a pure Christianity with Northern fanaticism – of liberty with despotism – of right with might.[54]

The citizens of the new Confederate nation bore a special mission: to set before the world the ideals of ordered liberty, states' rights, and biblical values, all of which Yankees had perverted.

At the outset of the struggle, the North fought to save the Union, not to end slavery. Only those with strong abolitionist convictions argued that departure of the errant states might prove a blessing, freeing the United States from the taint of slavery. In a sermon delivered on Thanksgiving Day 1860, Henry Ward Beecher of Brooklyn's Congregational Church invited the North to act against "the secret intentions of those men who are the chief fomenters of troubles in the South":

What do those men that are really at the bottom of this conspiracy mean? Nothing more or less than this: Southern empire for slavery, and the reopening of the slave-trade as a means by which it shall be fed. ... Their secret purpose is to sweep westward like night, and involve in the cloud of their darkness all Central America, and then make Africa empty into

---

Whitefield (1714-1770) had preached a sermon with a similar title, see "Glorifying God in the Fire" in George Whitefield, *Sermons on Important Subjects*. London: Henry Fisher, Son and P. Jackson, 1836, 83-93.

[53] Julia Ward Howe, "Battle Hymn of the Republic," *Atlantic Monthly* 9: 52 (February 1862): 10.

[54] Joel W. Tucker, *God's Providence in War*. Fayetteville: Presbyterian Office, 1862, 10-11.

Central America, thus changing the moral geography of the globe. ... They mean slavery. They mean an Empire of Slavery. They don't any longer talk of the evil of slavery. It is a virtue, a religion! ...[55]

Throughout 1862 many Northern ministers increasingly indicated the abolition of slavery as the meaning of the war.[56] But on January 1, 1863, Lincoln issued the Emancipation Proclamation and fundamentally altered the character of the war. Northern churches reflected—and, in some cases, promoted—this shift in direction. Initially most ministers were reluctant to support an all-out campaign for abolition, but conversion to this point of view did not proceed at an even rate. Some clergy and church bodies were demanding liberty for the captives in 1861; others did not speak out until well after the Emancipation Proclamation. But early or late, Northern Protestants concluded that God wished slavery to die.

With a few notable exceptions, Southern ministers believed that preserving slavery was an integral part of their nation's mission. God ordained the institution as the most humane means of relating labour to capital, of protecting inferior race, and of introducing that race to the blessings of Christianity.[57] Far from being the oppressors of African-Americans, Southerners were their defenders. "We do not place our cause upon its highest level," wrote Stephen Elliott in 1862, "until we grasp the idea that God has made us the guardians and champions of a people whom he is preparing for his own purposes, and against whom the whole world is banded."[58]

In a sermon before the General Assembly of South Carolina in December 1863, Benjamin Palmer claimed that the Confederate war effort would eventually "enlarge our power to protect and bless the race committed to our trust."[59] Several ministers demanded an end to laws

---

[55] Henry Ward Beecher, *Patriotic Addresses on America and England*. New York: Fords, Howard & Hulbert, 1887, 97.

[56] See William A. Gaylord, *The Soldier God's Minister*. Fitchburg, NH: Rollstone Printing Office, 1862. Cf. James D. Liggett, "Our National Reverses," quoted in Chesebrough, *God Ordained This War*, 325.

[57] Thornton Stringfellow, Scriptural and Statistical Views in Favor of Slavery. Richmond, VA: J. W. Randolph, 1856; Palmer, *The South: Her Peril, and Her Duty*.

[58] *Extract from a Sermon preached by Bishop Elliott, on the 18th September, containing a Tribute to the Privates of the Confederate Army*. Savannah? [s. n.] 1862, 14.

[59] B. M. Palmer, *A Discourse Before the General Assembly of South Carolina, on December 10, 1863: Appointed By the Legislature as a Day of Fasting, Humiliation and Prayer*. Columbia, SC: Charles P. Pelham, 1864, 17.

prohibiting slave literacy and limiting slave preaching, for these kept African-Americans from the gospel. Similarly, reformers desired statutory recognition of slave marriages and families. Although such proposals encountered opposition and were never enacted into law, they did win much favourable comment. Advocates suggested that reform might be necessary to the success of Confederate arms. Southern ministers thundered that God would not bless the Confederacy until it honoured its covenant with God and made bondage fully humane.

National sins and the wrath of God

Throughout the war the hand of God was read into every military victory and defeat. On both sides, ministers presented the war as the expression of the wrath of God and His chastisement for national sins.

In a sermon preached in Baltimore on September 26, 1861, Rev. Richard Fuller – a Baptist raised in South Carolina and educated at Harvard – declared: "as a nation we are guilty, and God is angry with us for our sins."[60] Reflecting on "the reverses which have recently attended our arms," James Thornwell suggested that "the swords of our enemies may be His chosen instruments to execute His wrath. ... We must abandon our sins."[61]

The war was also interpreted as God's method of disciplining His people. Palmer said that God was using the war as a disciplinary action on the Southern people, preparing them "for greatness and for glory."[62] Presbyterian minister Thomas V. Moore of Richmond declared that the war was God's way of disciplining people and nations and of "breaking up mammon worship and effeminacy".[63] A similar view can be found in Northern sermons, for example in the one preached by Thomas Brainerd, a Philadelphia Presbyterian minister:

> ... we are not to interpret any defeats into an impeachment of our natural
> virtue, or our cause; but rather regard them as a moral discipline through

---

[60] Richard Fuller, *Mercy remembered in Wrath. A Sermon preached ... on Thursday, September 26, 1861, Being the Day of National Fasting, Humiliation and Prayer*. Baltimore: Henry Taylor, 1861, 4.

[61] James H. Thornwell, *Our Danger and our Duties*. Columbia, SC: Southern Guardian, 1862, 11, 12.

[62] Palmer, *A Discourse Before the General Assembly of South Carolina*, 23.

[63] Thomas V. Moore, *God our Refuge and Strength in this War. A Discourse before the Congregations of the First and Second Presbyterian Churches, on the Day of Humiliation, Fasting and Prayer, appointed by President Davis, Friday, Nov. 15, 1861*. Richmond. VA: W. Hargrave White, 1861, 9.

which God purifies us from remaining corruptions, to make us "perfect" for our high national mission, "through sufferings."[64]

Although each side reflected on its own transgressions and despite regional differences over the sinfulness of slavery, the transgressions named by the clergy were often surprisingly similar in North and South: intemperance, Sabbath breaking, lack of loyalty to authorities, avarice, bribery, and gaming.[65]

In a sermon delivered before the General Assembly of Alabama, Baptist minister Isaac T. Tichenor denounced: "One of our national sins is the covetousness of our people. ... Another of our national sins has been proud and boastful self-reliance. ... Cotton was our hope, enthroned the god of our confidence, and almost worshipped as our national deliverer."[66]

On March 27, 1863, one of the days appointed for "Humiliation, Fasting and Prayer," Stephen Elliott – at that time Presiding Bishop of the Protestant Episcopal Church in the Confederate States – declared that "God has thought it best for us that this cruel war should endure yet longer and should be waged with an increased ferocity ... Our sins are to be more heavily punished, at the same time that our faith is to be more thoroughly sifted, and our submission to his will made more complete and perfect."[67]

Preaching on August 21, 1863, another Fast Day, John J.D. Renfroe, Baptist chaplain of the 10th Alabama Regiment, ascribed the recent reverses to the lack of trust in God: "We have failed to confide in the God of our mercies, we have trusted in our own strength, and he is subjecting us to severe vicissitudes. ... We need to be deeply convinced that the battle is not ours, but God's."[68]

---

[64] Thomas Brainerd, *Patriotism aiding Piety. A Sermon preached in the Third Presbyterian Church, Philadelphia, on the 30th of April, 1863, the day appointed by the President of the United States for Humiliation, Fasting and Prayer.* Philadelphia: W.F. Geddes, 1863, 17.

[65] For a list of sins or "forms of vice", see Atkinson, *Christian Duty in the Present Time of Trouble*, 9; William Salter, *Our National Sins and Impending Calamities* . Burlington, IA: Hawk-Eye Book Office, 1861, 4-5.

[66] Isaac T. Tichenor, *Sermon delivered ... in the Hall of the House of Representatives of Alabama, on Friday, August 21st, 1863.* Montgomery: Montgomery Advertiser Book and Job Printing Office, 1863, 8, 10.

[67] Stephen Elliott, *"Samson's Riddle." A Sermon Preached in Christ Church, Savannah, on Friday, March 27th, 1863, Being the Day of Humiliation, Fasting and Prayer, Appointed by the President of the Confederate States.* Macon, GA: Burke, Boykin & Co., 1863, 6-7.

[68] John J.D. Renfroe, *The Battle is God's. A Sermon preached before Wilcox's Brigade, Fast Day, the 21st August, 1863, near Orange Court-House, Va..* Richmond: MacFarlane & Fergusson, 1863, 11, 25. Rev. Sylvanus Landrum gave

After the end of the war, Fuller was still convinced that "the chastisements now upon us" were an expression of the wrath of God for the "national sins."[69] A month later, on Independence Day, Rev. James T. Robinson of North Adams, Mass., told the members of his congregation that "the great lesson of this war" was that "it is Punishment, Retribution for National guilt and crime, North and South."[70]

As casualties rose to unimaginable levels, the people felt that something profoundly religious was taking place, a sort of massive "sacrifice on the altar of their country's freedom."[71] Protestants hoped that the Civil War might prove a baptism of blood. As Charles Reagan Wilson has pointed out, that phrase recurred frequently in the utterances of Confederate clergy.[72] Even before the first shot had been fired, Thornwell was warning that "our path to victory may be through a baptism of blood."[73] In 1863 the Episcopal rector B.T. Lacy declared: "A grand responsibility rests upon our young republic. Baptized in its infancy in blood, may it receive the baptism of the Holy Ghost, and be consecrated to its high and holy mission among the nations of the earth."[74] Through the shedding of blood might come atonement for sin and newness of life. It also consecrated the Confederate cause: "Our cause [...] has been consecrated by a holy baptism of fire and blood."[75]

---

the same title to one of his sermons, *The Battle is God's. A Discourse, before the congregation of the Savannah Baptist Church, ... August 21ˢᵗ, 1863.* Savannah: E.J. Purse, 1863.

[69] Richard Fuller, *Wrong and Right Dispositions under National Judgments. A Sermon preached ... on the First Day of June, Being the Day of National Fasting and Humiliation.* Baltimore: J.F. Weishampel, Jr., 1865, 9, 22.

[70] James T. Robinson, *National Anniversary Address, delivered at the Baptist Church, North Adams, Mass. July 4ᵗʰ, 1865.* North Adams: W.H. Phillips, 1865, 4.

[71] Tucker, *God's Providence in War*, 10. Cf. Joseph Fransioli, *Patriotism, a Christian virtue*: "The true Christian patriot brings before the altar of his country, his property and his life cheerfully ready for the sacrifice when it is demanded" (7).

[72] Charles Reagan Wilson, *Baptism in Blood: The Religion of the Lost Cause, 1865-1920.* Athens: University of Georgia Press, 1980.

[73] Thornwell, "National Sins," 57.

[74] B.T. Lacy, *Address Delivered at the General Military Hospital, Winston, N.C.* Fayetteville, NC: n.p., 1863, 7.

[75] Tucker, *God's Providence in War, 10. Cf. Joseph M. Atkinson, God, the Giver of Victory and Peace. A Thanksgiving Sermon, delivered in the Presbyterian Church, September 18, 1862,* Raleigh, N.C.: "A conflict [...] consecrated by the martyr-blood of the best men in these Confederate States" (8).

While Stephen Elliott reminded his listeners that "nations ... must win their way to a place in history through the baptism of blood,"[76] Benjamin Palmer praised the sacrifice of "our martyrs," who were "undergoing the ... baptism of blood."[77]

For Northern clergy, the blood baptism received a final ritual enactment when Abraham Lincoln was assassinated on Good Friday, 1865. The President's death symbolized the expiation of national sins. His shed blood – token of all similar effusions during four years of war – purchased new life for America. As one Presbyterian minister suggested: "The life of the just departed LINCOLN, after having wrought out the painful salvation of the Republic, has been offered, a bloody sacrifice, upon the altar of human freedom and the happiness of his fellow countrymen."[78]

Works Cited

Primary Sources

Adams, William. "Prayer for Rulers, or, Duty of Christian Patriots." In *Fast Day Sermons*. 1861, 311-36.

—. *Christian Patriotism*. New York: Anson D.F. Randolph, 1863.

Atkinson, Joseph M. *God, the Giver of Victory and Peace. A Thanksgiving Sermon, delivered in the Presbyterian Church, September 18, 1862*, Raleigh, N.C.? [n.p.] 1862.

Appleton, James H. *Piety and Patriotism, the demand of the times, Sanctioned and Enjoined by Christ: a discourse delivered before the Union Baptist Church, Jersey City, N.J. on Sabbath morning, August 24th, 1862*, New York: C.S. Westcott, 1862.

Barten, O.S. *Fast Day Sermon*. Richmond, VA: Enquirer Book and Job Press, 1861.

Bingham, Joel F. *The Hour of Patriotism*. Buffalo: Franklin Steam printing house, 1862.

---

[76] Stephen Elliott, *New Wine Not to be Put in Old Bottles*. Savannah: John Cooper & Co., 1862, 4.

[77] Palmer, *A Discourse Before the General Assembly of South Carolina*, 23.

[78] Joel F. Bingham, *National Disappointment: A Discourse occasioned by the assassination of President Lincoln delivered in Westminster Church, Buffalo, Sunday evening, May 7th 1865*. Buffalo: Breed, Butler and Co., 1865, 36.

—. *National disappointment: A discourse occasioned by the assassination of President Lincoln delivered in Westminster Church, Buffalo, Sunday evening, May 7th 1865.* Buffalo: Breed, Butler and Co., 1865.

Brainerd, Thomas. *Patriotism aiding piety. A sermon, preached in the Third Presbyterian Church, Philadelphia, on the 30th of April, 1863, the day appointed by the President of the United States for humiliation, fasting and prayer.* Philadelphia: W.F. Geddes, 1863.

Bushnell, Horace. *Reverses Needed: A Discorse Delivered on the Sunday after the Disaster at Bull Run in the North Church,* Hartford: L.E. Hunt, 1861.

Clark, George H. *A Sermon, Delivered in St. John's Church, Savannah, On Fast Day, Nov. 28, 1860.* Savannah: George N. Nichols, 1860.

Dabney, Robert L. *The Christian Best Motive for Patriotism. A Sermon preached in the College Church, Hampden Sidney, Va., on the 1ˢᵗ of November, 1869.* Richmond: Chas.H. Wynne, 1860.

—. *The Christian Soldier: a sermon commemorative of the death of Abram C. Carrington. Preached and published by order of the session of College Church, Dec., 1862,* Richmond, VA: Presbyterian Committee of Publication, 1863.

Dana, W.C. *A Sermon Delivered in the Central Presbyterian Church, Charleston, South Carolina, November 21, 1860, Being the Day Appointed by State Authority for Fasting, Humiliation, and Prayer.* Charleston: Evans and Cogswell, 1860.

Van Dyke, Henry J. *The Spirituality and Independence of the Church.* New York: n.p. 1864.

Dreher, Daniel I. *A Sermon.* Salisbury, NC: Watchman's Office, 1861.

Eddy, Daniel C. *Our Country: Its Pride and Its Peril, or Liberty and the Union.* Boston: John M. Hewes, 1861.

Eddy, Zachery. *A Discourse on the War.* Northampton, MA: Trumbull and Gere, 1861.

Elliott, Stephen. *God's Presence with Our Army at Manassas!* Savannah: W. Thorne Williams, 1861.

—. *New Wine Not to be Put in Old Bottles.* Savannah: Steam Power Press of John Cooper & Co., 1862.

—. *Extract from a Sermon preached by Bishop Elliott, on the 18th September, containing a Tribute to the Privates of the Confederate Army.* Savannah? [n.p.] 1862.

—. *"Samson's Riddle." A Sermon Preached in Christ Church, Savannah, on Friday, March 27ᵗʰ, 1863, Being the Day of Humiliation, Fasting and Prayer, Appointed by the President of the Confederate States.* Macon, Georgia: Burke, Boykin & Co., 1863.

Fairfield, Edmund B. *Christian Patriotism: A Sermon Delivered in the Representatives' Hall, Lansing, Michigan, February 22, 1863*. Lansing: John A. Kerr & Co., 1863.

Fransioli, Joseph *Patriotism, a Christian virtue. A sermon preached by the Rev. Joseph Fransioli, at St. Peter's (Catholic) Church, Brooklyn, July 26th, 1863*, (Pamphlets issued by the Royal Publication Society, from Feb. 1, 1863, to Feb. 1, 1864, No. 24), New York: Loyal Publication Society, 1864.

Fuller, Richard *Mercy remembered in Wrath. A Sermon preached ... on Thursday, September 26, 1861, Being the Day of National Fasting, Humiliation and Prayer*. Baltimore: Henry Taylor, 1861.

—. *Wrong and Right Dispositions under National Judgments. A Sermon preached ... on the First Day of June, Being the Day of National Fasting and Humiliation*. Baltimore: J.F. Weishampel, Jr., 1865.

Gaylord, William A. *The Soldier God's Minister*. Fitchburg, NH: Rollstone Printing Office, 1862.

Haskell, Thomas N. *Christian Patriotism: A Medium of God's Power and Purpose to Bless Our Lands. A Fast-day Sermon*. Boston: [n.p.] 1863.

Jacobs, Ferdinand. *A Sermon for the Times*. Marion, Alabama: [n.p.], 1861.

Lay, Henry C. *The Devout Soldier. Preached by request to the Powhatan Troop at Emmanuel Church, March 6th 1864*. [n.p.], 1864.

McKeen, Silas *Heroic Patriotism. A Sermon delivered at Bradford, VT., Sabbath afternoon, April 28, 1861, in the presence of the Bradford Guards, when under call to join the First Regiment of the Vermont Volunteers, and go forth in their country's service*. Windsor, VT.: Vermont Chronicle Book and Job Office, 1861.

Magie, David *A Discourse Delivered in the Second Presbyterian Church*. New York: Francis Hart and Co., 1863.

Meade, William. *Address on the Day of Fasting and Prayer*. Richmond: Enquirer Book & Job Press, 1861.

Moore, T.V. *God our Refuge and Strength in this War. A discourse before the Congregations of the First and Second Presbyterian Churches, on the Day of Humiliation, Fasting and Prayer, appointed by President Davis, Friday, Nov. 15, 1861*. Richmond. Va.: W. Hargrave White, 1861.

Palmer, Benjamin Morgan, *The South: Her Peril, and Her Duty. A Discourse delivered in the First Presbyterian Church, New Orlans, on Thursday, November 29, 1860*. New Orleans: Office of the True Witness and Sentinel, 1860.

—. *Slavery A Divine Trust. The Duty of the South to Preserve and Perpetuate the Institution as it Now Exists.* New York: George F. Nesbitt & Co., 1861.

Porter, R.K. *Christian Duty in the Present Crisis: The Substance of a Sermon Delivered in the Presbyterian Church, in Waynesboro, Georgia, December 9, 1860.* Savannah: Steam Press of John M. Cooper and Company, 1860.

Reed, Edward. *A People Saved by the Lord*, Charleston: Steam-Power Press of Evans & Cogswell, 1861.

Renfroe, John J.D. *The Battle is God's. A Sermon preached before Wilcox's Brigade, Fast Day, the 21st August, 1863, near Orange Court-House, Va.* Richmond: MacFarlane & Fergusson, 1863.

Robinson, James T. *National Anniversary Address, deivered at the Baptist Church, North Adams, Mass. July 4th, 1865.* North Adams: W.H. Phillips, 1865.

Salter, William. *Our National Sins and Impending Calamities.* Burlington, IA: Hawk-Eye Book Office, 1861.

Sledd, Robert N. *A Sermon delivered in the Market Street, M.E. Church, Petersburg, VA.* Petersburg: A.F. Crutchfield and Co., 1861.

Sprague, William B. *Glorifying God in the fires : a discourse delivered in the Second Presbyterian Church, Albany, November 28, 1861, the day of the annual thanksgiving, in the state of New York.* Albany: C. Van Benthuysen, 1861.

Stringfellow, Thornton. *Scriptural and Statistical Views in Favor of Slavery.* Richmond, Va.: J. W. Randolph, 1856.

Thornwell, James H. *National Sins: A Fast-Day Sermon, Preached in the Presbyterian Church, Columbia, Wednesday, November 21, 1860.* New York: Rudd & Carleton, 1861.

—. *Our Danger and our Duties.* Columbia, S.C.: Southern Guardian Steam-Power Press, 1862.

Thornwell, James H. and others, *Fast Day Sermons; or, The Pulpit on the State of the Country.* New York: Rudd and Carleton, 1861.

Tichenor, Isaac T. *Sermon delivered ... in the Hall of the House of Representatives of Alabama, on Friday, August 21st, 1863.* Montgomery: Montgomery Advertiser Book and Job Printing Office, 1863.

Trumbull, H. Clay. *Desirableness of Active Service.* Hartford: Case, Lockwood, 1864.

Tucker, Joel W. *God's Providence in War.* Fayetteville: Presbyterian Office, 1862.

Winn, T.S. *The Great Victory at Manassas Junction. God the Arbiter of Battles, A Thanksgiving Sermon preached in the Presbyterian Church at Concord, in Greene County, Alabama, July 28, 1861*. Tuskaloosa, Alabama: J.F. Warren, 1861.

Secondary sources

Bercovitch, Sacvan. *The American Jeremiad*. Madison: University of Wisconsin Press, 1978.

Chesebrough, David B., ed. *"God Ordained This War:" Sermons on the Sectional Crisis, 1830-1865*. Columbia: University of South Carolina Press, 1991.

Eighmy, John Lee. *Churches in Cultural Captivity: A History of Social Attitudes of Southern Baptists*. Knoxville: University of Tennessee Press, 1972.

Farmer, James Oscar, Jr. *The Metaphysical Confederacy: James Henley Thornwell and the Synthesis of Southern Values*. Macon, GA: Mercer University Press, 1986.

Faust, Drew Gilpin *The Creation of Confederate Nationalism: Ideology and Identity in the Civil War South*. Baton Rouge: Louisiana State University Press, 1988.

Fox-Genovese, Elizabeth and Eugene D. Genovese. "The Divine Sanction of Social Order: Religious Foundations of the Southern Slaveholders' World View," *Journal of the American Academy of Religion* 55 (Summer 1987): 211-34.

Fredrickson, George M. *The Inner Civil War: Northern Intellectuals and the Crisis of the Union*, New York: Harper and Row, 1965.

Goen, C.C. *Broken Churches, Broken Nation: Denominational Schism and the Coming of the American Civil War*. Macon, Ga.: Mercer University Press, 1985.

Loveland, Anne C. *Southern Evangelicals an the Social Order, 1800-1860*. Baton Rouge and London: Louisiana State University Press, 1980.

McKivigan, John R. *The War Against Proslavery Religion: Abolitionism and the Northern Churches, 1830-1865*. Ithaca and London: Cornell University Press, 1984.

Miller, Perry. *The New England Mind*, Cambridge, Mass.: Harvard University Press, 1953.

Miller, Randall M., Harry S. Stout, and Charles Reagan Wilson, eds. *Religion and the American Civil War*, New York and Oxford: Oxford University Press, 1998.

Monroe, Haskell. "Southern Presbyterians and the Secession Crisis," *Civil War History* 6 (December, 1960): 351-360.

Moorhead, James H. *American Apocalypse: Yankee Protestants and the Civil War, 1860-1869.* Yale: Yale University Press, 1978.Myers, Robert Manson, ed. *Children of Pride: A True Story of Georgia and the Civil War.* New Haven, Conn.: Yale University Press, 1973.

O'Leary, Cecilia Elizabeth. *To Die For: The Paradox of American Patriotism.* Princeton, NJ: Princeton University Press, 1999.

Silver, James W. *Confederate Morale and Church Propaganda.* New York: W.W. Norton, 1967.

Sweet, William Warren. *The Story of Religion in America*, New York: Harper & Brothers, 1939.

Wallenstein, Peter and Bertram Wyatt-Brown, eds. *Virginia's Civil War.* Charlottesville, VA: University of Virginia Press, 2005.

Wilson, Charles Reagan. *Baptism in Blood: The Religion of the Lost Cause, 1865-1920.* Athens: University of Georgia Press, 1980.

CHAPTER TEN

PREACHING THE AMERICAN NATION AT WAR. A. LINCOLN AND T. W. WILSON'S WAR SERMONS

MARIE BEAUCHAMP-SOW

Abraham Lincoln and Thomas Woodrow Wilson were both elected for two terms as presidents of the United States.[1] They were both in office when, respectively, the Civil War and the First World War broke out. They both delivered speeches at times of national crises.

Even though they occupied the most prominent civil function, they often tapped into the unifying preachers' diction. Two speeches in particular exemplify this more intensely: Lincoln's second inaugural address (March 4, 1865)[2] and Wilson's address to the Senate presenting the Peace Treaty (July 10, 1919).[3] We could have chosen to focus on Wilson's second inaugural address as well. However, the United States had not entered war yet and this speech presenting the Peace Treaty appears to be very "inaugural" in the sense that the Treaty and, with it, the League of Nations, were Wilson's presidency's greatest achievements.

Thus these speeches can be comparatively studied in more than one respect. They were both delivered at the end of the war: a few months before it was over for Lincoln, a few months after the ceasefire was declared for Wilson. And both of them are distinguished from the mass of other speeches by their sermon-like rhetoric. The mere political aspect of the president's authority seems to have been transcended and both men resort to religious turns and references, which at times border prophetical

---

[1] Lincoln was first elected in 1860, and reelected in 1864. As for Wilson, he was first elected in 1912, and reelected in 1916.
[2] Lincoln, Abraham, *Letters and Addresses of Abraham Lincoln*. New York : H.W. Bell, 1903, p. 316-320.
[3] *The Messages and papers of Woodrow Wilson (Vol. I & II)*, introduction de Albert Shaw. New York : George H. Doran, c1924, p. 698-712.

eloquence. This is the reason why Lincoln and Wilson can both be said to have transmuted into priests delivering sermons to their audiences and espousing every aspect of the genre. Yet, the goal of these speeches was not solely to encourage soldierly participation. They served another purpose: a national one. Lincoln and Wilson preached to America, and in attempting to define America, national identity was challenged.

The circumstance in which these two speeches were delivered can be paralleled with that in which sermons are delivered. Lincoln and Wilson, appear before a gathering of people—"fellow countrymen" for Lincoln and "Gentlemen of the Senate" for Wilson. They are in a situation where they represent political authority. Lincoln symbolically derives his authority from the place where he is standing: "While the inaugural address was being delivered from this place…" in the same way as part of the preacher's authority also stems from the pulpit. Wilson, on the other hand, tends to insist on his function as the representative of Americans to assert his authority. Speaking about the soldiers, he claims: "I am proud to have had the privilege of being associated with them and of calling myself their leader." Similarly, preachers' credibility comes from their representing the kingdom of heaven on earth.

However, and this might be of interest for the rest of our study, neither Lincoln nor Wilson make much use of the pronoun "I" (once for Lincoln and twice for Wilson). Despite the authority they embody, they mean to appear before their audiences as mere spokesmen and representatives. They take great care not to speak for themselves only, but rather to voice words and thoughts that are more general and encompassing, even transcendent at times. This ambiguous position both insists on the humility of their role and, at the same time, gives a transcendent and almost omniscient power to their carefully-crafted speeches. This first paradoxical notion of being at the same time in the humblest and most potent of positions as the voice of transcendent words draws them closer to preachers. Furthermore, they structure their speeches like preachers would have. Both speeches start taking stock of the situation, before judging from a moral, sometimes apocalyptic, standpoint for Lincoln and an almost prophetical one for Wilson. Then come their conclusions and the natural consequences of their demonstrations, as well as the path to be followed. Lincoln starts contemplating the four years that just elapsed, before interpreting what happened during those years and reaching a conclusion as to what the future should be. Wilson also begins his speech recalling the American intervention in World War One, before elaborating on

America's new role and responsibility, and concluding with the image of a bright future in the closing lines.

Within that framework, they resort to many images that are part of an American Christian tradition. Lincoln draws on the image of an avenging God. In that, he remains close to his religious upbringing[4] and even borrows from the Old Testament style when he states: "Woe unto the world because of offenses! For it must needs be that offenses come; but woe to that man by whom the offense cometh." And he adds a few lines later: "Yet, if God wills that it continue until all the wealth piled by the bondman's two hundred and fifty years of unrequited toil shall be sunk, and until every drop of blood drawn with the lash shall be paid by another drawn with sword..." This image clearly echoes an apocalyptic vision. However, he does not announce punishment and final destruction, as preachers of the apocalypse would do. Rather he looks back to the years that just elapsed and interprets retrospectively the Civil War as the final destruction of the American sin of slavery, which he alludes to as "offense" or "two hundred and fifty years of unrequited toil", a reference made even more vibrant by the use of the image of "every drop of blood drawn with the lash". His whole speech rests upon this main argument: America sinned by continuing to enslave other human beings. "These slaves constituted a peculiar and powerful interest. All knew that this interest was, somehow the cause of the war. To strengthen, perpetuate, and extend this interest was the object for which the insurgents would rend the Union, even by war..." To make his explanation and his condemnation even clearer, he quotes from the Bible[5], and thus establishes a close connection with his audience. His rhetoric of the divine ordeal sent to the American people resounds with the audience since, being reminiscent of the punishment God sent the chosen people when they broke the Alliance, it also reminds the hearers that, according to America's founding mythology, they are God's new chosen people. Lincoln then inscribes the United States and the Civil War within the long genealogy of people whom God forsook throughout the Old Testament. He recalls this history that goes far back when he speaks of the two hundred and fifty years of slavery as being connected with what was said "three thousand years ago": "as was said three thousand years ago, so still it must be said, 'The judgments of the Lord are true and righteous altogether'". Lincoln's contemporaries are then connected with biblical times. Doing so, he parallels them with Old Testament mythology and implies that the

---

[4] Indeed, Lincoln was raised in a Puritan tradition. However, he never belonged to any Congregation.
[5] Citations from *Matthew* 18 :7 and *Psalm* 19 :9.

punishment was proportionate to the mission God entrusted them with. As preachers would do, then, he resorts to his convictions, based on the Bible's teachings, and applies them to the reality surrounding them: that of a war which tore the country apart. He contemplates reality in the light of these fundamental teachings:

> Both read the same Bible, and pray to the same God; and each invokes his aid against the other. It may seem strange that any men should dare to ask a just God's assistance in wringing their bread from the sweat of other men's faces; but let us judge not, that we be not judged.

Here again he quotes from the Scriptures to explain the realities of the time and draws conclusion from them. He gives out a moralizing approach to war and, from then on, makes recommendations for the path lying ahead, praying: "Fondly do we hope—fervently do we pray—that this mighty scourge of war may speedily pass away", and preaching forgiveness and reconciliation.

Wilson explores other aspects of the American Christian tradition, seemingly taking one step further the image of the chosen people. World War One just ended, a few months after the United States officially entered it, with images of the American intervention on the European front as a Godsend or, more precisely, as a crusade undergone in the name of the transcendent principle all Americans defend and cherish, in Wilson's words, the ideal of democracy. "They [the soldiers] were recognized as crusaders and as their thousands swelled to millions their strength was seen to mean salvation." The tone of his speech is reminiscent of the traditional biblical *topoï* used by war sermons, which oppose the forces of evil to the Kingdom of God and good. Here, the Americans defended the realms of good against evil and they saved the world. Later on, he adds:

> We answered to the call of duty in a way so spirited, so utterly without thought of what we spent of blood or treasure, so effective, so worthy of the admiration of true men everywhere, so wrought out of the stuff of all that was heroic, that the world saw at last, in the flesh, in noble action, a great ideal asserted and vindicated…

Here Wilson indulges in a vibrant eulogy of the American forces, describing their moral and physical superiority, as he accumulates hyperbolic uses of the adverb "so". War is celebrated. If Lincoln looks retrospectively at the Civil War and sees it as a punishment, when Wilson looks back at the First World War, he rather sees the opportunity God sent to the world, first, and, then, to the United States to take on a much more prominent role in the world's affairs as the defenders of democracy and liberty. In this prophetical and missionary perspective, the American soldiers who were drafted to fight in Europe can indeed be called "crusaders". Wilson constantly resorts to that mythology and rhetoric. America embarked on a mission to save oppressed people: "It was our duty to do everything that was within our power to do to make the triumph of freedom and of right a lasting triumph in the assurance of which men might everywhere live without fear." The American soldiers were free men sent overseas to uphold the values best embodied in the United States and free people from their bonds. Soldiers are so numerous they cannot be precisely numbered: they "pour[ed] across the sea" and "as their thousands swelled to millions". In that evokes the cataclysms God sent in the Old Testament to punish Egypt[6]. The American soldiers may be seen as the cataclysm sent to destroy the Central Powers—the enemies of democracy. As God opened the Red Sea to allow the Hebrews to flee Egypt[7], Wilson depicts a movement in reverse, where God opened the sea for the American soldiers to enter Europe and save it. Then, they are painted as almost divine beings insofar as they were endowed with every perfection. Wilson enumerates their qualities and the miraculous effect they immediately produced on the European populations: "The mere sight of our men (…) made everyone who saw them that memorable day realize that something had happened that was much more than a mere incident in the fighting, something very different from the mere arrival of fresh troops". Wilson clearly draws from the image of the Godsend, which he links to the Old Testament story of the chosen people, and applies it to the American intervention. Once he invests the present with this missionary perspective, he goes on drawing conclusions from it and making recommendations for the future. World War One, in Wilson's idea, demonstrated that the United States had a crucial role to play in the world's affairs and the Americans should show themselves worthy of this new responsibility in the future, if his missionary and prophetical voice is to be followed: "The stage is set, the destiny disclosed. It has come about by no plan of our conceiving, but by the hand of God who led us into this way."

Thus, both Lincoln and Wilson borrow from the preachers' words and preach to audiences gathered before them. They turn to a common Christian tradition and use it with different prospects. They can sound sometimes prophetical, sometimes missionary, and tend to read America's recent past in a very providential way. Resorting to Providence, they also

---

[6] *Exodus*, chapters 7 to 12.
[7] *Exodus*, chapters 13 to 15.

legitimate war. And this may remind us that both speeches were conditioned by the wars the country was going through.

This contextualisation is of utmost importance in the perspective of our analysis. Indeed, both Presidents tended to interpret war in religious terms. Both were reelected after having promised that war would either end or be avoided[8]. As a consequence, they were in a position where they had to justify or explain the war. Borrowing from the structure and the rhetoric of sermons, they also attempted to give it meaning. In this respect, both men become interpreters for their audiences. They make use of religious vocabulary and remove the war from its immediate causes to give it a transcendent and providential meaning. War is made legitimate and even necessary.

This is a pattern in military sermons. The conception of the just war rests upon the biblical typology of the warfare of the Kingdom of God against the realms of Satan. Lincoln resorts to this same dichotomy, but in a renewed perspective. In the same way as the war is civil, the forces of good and evil fight within the same country. He insists on the similitude between the two opponents: "Both read the same Bible, and pray to the same God; and each invokes his aid against the other." The evil lies indeed inside the country, and this remark is made even more forceful as it is uttered in the present when the previous lines were in the past. It constitutes a transition between two phases of the speech: one explanatory and the other interpretative. This transition revolves around yet another allusion to slavery: "It may seem strange that any men should dare to ask a just God's assistance in wringing their bread from the sweat of other men's faces". We described this borrowing from the Scriptures in the first part of our analysis. We may add here that Lincoln, emphasizing on God's "just" assistance, clearly distinguishes between the two parties and seems to imply that his party should deserve God's assistance, contrary to the opposed coalition. Yet, he quickly understates what he just suggested underlining the fact that "The prayers of both could not be answered—that of neither has been answered fully." From then on he develops his interpretation of the war, in very religious terms as we saw before, and presents the war as just and even necessary, not in a human perspective but, rather, in a divine one. Warfare could not be avoided. On the contrary, it appears to be providential, in the two senses of the word; it was doomed to happen and it will save the country:

---

[8] "He kept us out of war" was one of Wilson's campaign for reelection's highly popular slogans.

> The Almighty has his own purposes. (...) If we shall suppose that
> American slavery is one of those offenses which, in the providence of God,
> must needs come, but which having continued through his appointed time,
> he now wills to remove, and that he gives to both North and South this
> terrible war, as the woe due to those by whom the offense came, shall we
> discern therein any departure from those divine attributes which the
> believers in a living God always ascribe to him?

In his words then, believers should accept the ordeal sent by God as
just and reviving. In his view, the Americans sinned and God punished
them accordingly. Men's foolishness paved the way for the Civil War and
nothing could have avoided it, as is suggested in the very laconic
expression: "And the war came". War is just from a divine perspective:
"The judgments of the Lord are true and righteous altogether". However,
he does not venture to state explicitly whether it was just from a human
perspective, except for the description of slavery in biblical terms and
references as evil. Lincoln mainly looks back at the founding of the
country, when slavery was first instituted. The particular time when the
speech was delivered, just a few days before the war ceased, may account
for this very cautious tone: it is a time for forgiveness and reconciliation,
rather than for retaliation. In that, the speech is more programmatic than it
seems at first:

> With malice toward none; with charity for all; with firmness in the right, as
> God gives us to see the right, let us strive on to finish the work we are in;
> to bind up the nation's wounds (...) to do all which may achieve and
> cherish a just and lasting peace among ourselves, and with all nations.

Of course, some ambiguities remain as to what "we" exactly includes.
Nevertheless, he clearly states his ambition for reconciliation and
reconstruction. His role as the president of every American is reaffirmed.
This is the reason which leads to argue that war was providential in both
senses of the word.

Similarly, Wilson insists on the justification and necessity of war. At
that point in American history, the war was just and necessary not only for
the United States but also for the whole world. Wilson's missionary
inspiration encompasses the whole world and allows him to justify the war
that is, to demonstrate that it was just to enter the war, as he opens his
speech: "The US entered the war upon a different footing from every other
nation except our associates on this side of the sea." In every speech
delivered during World War One, Wilson never misses an occasion to

stress the American "distinction" in the way Bourdieu defines the term—
different and singular.[9] Wilson proceeds:

> We entered it not because our material interests were directly threatened or
> because any special treaty obligations to which we were parties had been
> violated, but only because we saw the supremacy, and even the validity, of
> right everywhere put in jeopardy and free government likely to be
> everywhere imperiled by the intolerable aggression of a power which
> respected neither right nor obligation...

The president turned into priest by the circumstance immediately
defines the American intervention as more of a spiritual one. What
motivated the country to enter the war were mainly abstract principles:
right and free government. Thus Americans, in Wilson's words, embarked
on a journey to defend these vital principles embodied in the United
States. Warfare was just: it opposed righteous forces defending "free
government" against an evil power "whose very system of government
flouted the right of the citizen..." It was all the more justified as the
American intervention turned the tide:

> The hopes of the nation allied against the Central Powers were at a very
> low ebb when our soldiers began to pour across the sea. There was
> everywhere amongst them, except in their stoutest spirits, a somber
> foreboding of disaster. The war ended in November, eight months ago, but
> you have only to recall what was feared in midsummer last (...) to realize
> what it was that our timely aid accomplished...

Wilson calls the American intervention "our aid", downplaying the
warlike nature of it. We should remember here that he addresses the
Senators, many of whom had opposed the United States' entering the war.
He still needed to defend his decision. Characterizing the aid as "timely",
he suggests that the Americans were providential in the conclusion of the
war. Later, he adds, recalling the "action at Chateau-Thierry", that it began
"the rout that was to save Europe and the world". This use of the turn "was
to"—he resorts to it many throughout his speech—echoes such recurring
expressions as "drawn to it" or "compelled" to do so, which all underline
the fact that the decision was not truly their decision. It was rather God's
decision and they had to accept the mission they were divinely entrusted
with: "It was not an accident or a matter of sudden choice that we are no
longer isolated and devoted to a policy which has only our own interest
and advantage for its object". This is no contingency if they intervened.

---

[9] Bourdieu, Pierre, *La distinction : critique sociale du jugement.* Paris : éditions de
Minuit, 1979, collection "Le sens commun".

On the contrary, "It was our duty to go in, if we were indeed the champions of liberty and of right." The closing lines unveil it even more explicitly: "It has come about by no plan of our conceiving, but by the hand of God who led us into this way". War is dramatized in a very acute way by Wilson when he says in vivid words: "A cry had gone out from every home in every stricken land from which sons and brothers and fathers had gone forth to the great sacrifice..." As a consequence, it demanded the American participation. They were called upon by God and by desperate fellow humans. War then was truly just and necessary, both in a human and in a divine perspective. This justification of warfare, which sometimes verges on propaganda, so characteristic of military sermons also puts forth and is founded on the image of the righteous heroic soldiers. And in that respect too, Lincoln and Wilson can be relevantly compared with ministers delivering war sermons.

Lincoln does not spend so much time on the heroic part of the soldier in the second inaugural address as he did in Gettysburg.[10] Nevertheless, it should be noted that he refers to soldiers as he utters his final words praying for peace and reconciliation. The fact that this reference was placed there is certainly significant. Lincoln seems to be indicating that the soldiers were instrumental in striving for peace. They interceded in the peace process, acting like messengers. Besides, the soldiers are called forth immediately after he pointed to "the nation's wounds". The soldiers bore these stigmas on their bodies. Lincoln seems to imply here that the soldiers actually took on the nation's wounds so as to expiate the national sins. They made this Christ-like sacrifice so that "a just and lasting peace" may be achieved. The soldiers are presented as the embodiment of the nation who accepted to make the ultimate sacrifice for the nation to live on. We can understand from the way Lincoln hints at them that soldiers represent heroes whose death figures heroic martyrdom: "let us strive on...to care for him who shall have borne the battle, and for his widow, and his orphan." Lincoln does not separate the soldier from his family. Here, after the soldier bore the nation, it is the nation's turn to bear the soldier's family. He establishes an underlying, almost physical, relationship between soldiers and the nation, between the soldiers' bodies and that of the nation. The figure of the soldier is set up as an example and as a symbol for the rest of the nation.

Wilson tends to picture the soldier in the same way as well: "They were for all the visible embodiment of America". Just as was suggested through the image of the wounds earlier, Wilson represents the soldiers as

---

[10] Lincoln delivered an acclaimed address at the dedication of the Soldiers' National Cemetery in Gettysburg, on November 19, 1863.

connected to the nation's body. This particular link turns them into indisputable symbols of the nation. In this perspective, it should come as no surprise that Wilson should lay so strong an emphasis on their bodies: "The mere sight of our men,—of their vigor, of the confidence that showed itself in every movement of their stalwart figures and every turn of their swinging march, in their steady comprehending eyes and easy discipline, in the indomitable air that added spirit to everything they did…" But Wilson does not stop here and magnifies their moral qualities, which draw them closer to supernatural beings or saints: "They were recognized as crusaders and as their thousands swelled to millions their strength was seen to mean salvation. (…)" Here the soldier's text espouses the messianic prophecies permeating the Old Testament. "They were terrible in battle, and gentle and helpful out of it, remembering the mothers and the sisters, the wives and the little children at home. They were free men under arms, not forgetting their ideals of duty in the midst of tasks of violence." Just as good and evil are paired in the human, here the "crusaders" demonstrate their fierce side against the enemy and display humanity and grace to the loved ones. This combination of aggressiveness and holiness, exposed in quite a hyperbolic fashion, reminds us of the basic temporal qualities of a Christian soldier, as enumerated by preachers: fortitude, hardness, courage, loyalty and love of their country, as well as prudence and sobriety. Wilson's picture does not differ from that elaborated by ministers delivering war sermons. Soldiers truly become holy models to be emulated: "They were the sort of men America would wish to be represented by, the sort of men every American would wish to claim as fellow-countrymen and comrades in a great cause." Soldiering is justified and honoured, insofar as it is associated with heroic resistance on Wilson's part and with sacrifice, on Lincoln's.

Thus they inscribe themselves in the propaganda of holy warfare, and Wilson even more blatantly so. Both Lincoln and Wilson justify the war, resorting to a providential reading of American history and elaborating on the Christ-like figure of the soldier. These soldiers are represented in close connection with the image of the nation itself. Both preachers weave a national subtext underneath the symbol of a soldier they present to their audiences.

Sacrifice is made for the nation and in the name of the nation. Both speeches put forward the image of a nation crusading against its own evils and for the endurance of the democratic ideal. There are strong ideological, political, even nationalist goals upholding both war sermons, which is why I contend that these speeches delivered by Lincoln and Wilson not only are war sermons but also nationalist speeches. At times of national crises, they preached to America, and in the name of an America they were trying to define, when the nation and the American identity, were challenged.

The position of the men who delivered these addresses should not be overlooked. They led the United States of America at times of great uncertainty and trouble for the country. Evidently, the Civil War constituted a traumatic event in the American nation's history: a period of major unrest, when the nation came close to collapsing and disappearing. During the Civil War, two nationalisms, two visions of the American nation, were confronted. To Lincoln, what was at stake in this war, beyond slavery, was the very representation and existence of the American nation. He exposes it very clearly in the speech under scrutiny recalling:

> On the occasion corresponding to this four years ago, all thoughts were anxiously directed to an impending civil war. All dreaded it—all sought to avert it. While the inaugural address was being delivered from this place, devoted altogether to saving the Union without war, insurgent agents were in the city seeking to destroy it without war—seeking to dissolve the Union, and divide effects, by negotiation. Both parties deprecated war; but one of them would make war rather than let the nation survive; and the other would accept war rather than let it perish.

Lincoln claims here, as he did in other speeches, that soldiers fought to defend the sacred cause of keeping the nation united. Lincoln fiercely opposed secession and he turned war into the necessity to keep the Union alive. He embarked on a political journey to "save the Union", the meaning of which remains rather ambiguous. Indeed, it is sometimes used to encompass the whole nation and sometimes to designate the North. Lincoln accuses the sole Southern states of being responsible for the war, insofar as they perpetuated slavery well past its time. This interpretation participates in a certain effort to rewrite American history. This revision process has nationalist goals since it sets the stage for a particular representation of the nation and a specific image of the "American experience" at the centre of which he places this puzzling paradox: the nation's founders advocated equality and freedom for all human beings and yet slavery was maintained on the territory. This paradox triggered off the war. In the quotation above, he organizes his narrative of the conflicts' origins, in the preterit, around simple sets of opposition. He always refused to envision the nation's division and kept upholding that the Union imagined by the Founding Fathers should be preserved, even through the use of force. His nationalism was rooted in the vision of a united nation, whereas the Southern states advocated secession as the only possible national project that could satisfy every American and guarantee peace to all.

As for World War One, it took place after massive waves of immigration which brought to the American soil millions of men (1880-1914). These new immigrants were more numerous than in the preceding waves. They also came from different national backgrounds: especially from Southern and Eastern Europe. Their cultures had little in common with the first settlers' and immigrants' Protestant anglo-saxon heritage. As migration movements amplified, xenophobia soared again in the United States with one movement in particular: "nativism".[11] Thus the US intervention in the First World War came at a time when national identity was going through a metamorphosis, which considerably scared some. For "Nativists", national identity was nothing less than imperilled. With the Americans' entering the war, part of the population grew even more wary of foreigners and even more so of migrants who came from the countries of the Central Powers. In that context, the Americanisation movement was born, which demanded proofs of their loyalty and patriotism to the immigrants. This preoccupation was not foreign to Wilson who, in addition to that, had to face the people's massive opposition to his decision to send American troops to Europe. Indeed, he had been reelected on a non-interventionist agenda in 1917. In that particular situation, he had to justify his decision, reinvent, and reinterpret old American principles, such as isolationism: "Our isolation was ended twenty years ago; and now fear of us is ended also, our counsel and association sought after and desired. There can be no question of our ceasing to be a world power." Indeed, to Wilson, the United States had to become an outpost for a new world order. Both presidents were thus compelled by the circumstances to define a new or a restored vision of the American nation and present it to the people. War was, evidently so, a time of great questioning and we could argue that tapping into Christian rhetoric constituted the best way for them to articulate this new vision, as it recycled well-known myths and beliefs and could be grasped by most American citizens.

Lincoln and Wilson had to explain the nation to the Americans. They had to redefine the national image and project among violent divergences. And so they did. Lincoln never departs from his view of a united nation. Throughout his second inaugural address, he constantly refers to the nation and "we": "the energies of the nation", "the progress of our arms", "the Union", "we". Perhaps even more revealing is the fact that he translates

---

[11] "Nativism" constitutes a special form of opposition to immigration as it is based on an opposition between American citizens who were born in the United States and citizens who are first-generation immigrants.

the war into an opposition of "parties", between the "insurgents" and the "government". Calling the Southern states "insurgents" amounts to denying any possibility of a division. Indeed, an "insurgent" can be so defined only as long as he belongs to the same country as the person or institution he opposes. He never calls them "belligerents" or "opponents", and the choice of this particular term tells a lot about Lincoln's ambition for the nation. He explains what his ambition is in the last paragraph of his speech:

> With malice toward none; with charity for all; (..) let us strive on to finish the work we are in; to bind up the nation's wounds; to care for him who shall have borne the battle, and for his widow, and his orphan—to do all which may achieve and cherish a just and lasting peace among ourselves and with all nations.

The opposition never ceases to be internal. The nation is wounded but it is not dead in Lincoln's sermon-like rhetoric of conciliation. On the contrary, it can be healed in a reunifying process summed up in the reunion of the antithetic terms "none" and "all" that open the lines. What Lincoln describes here is a whole. He reasserts his role as the president of all Americans. He addresses the nation, in the name of the nation and he constantly praises unity. He invokes the nation in a speech that allows the nation to commune in one republican and democratic rite celebrating its very existence and exposes his vision of a reunified nation in a speech that announces the last public address he delivered: "On Reconstruction." Lincoln develops a powerful rhetoric of conciliation and reconciliation.

Wilson, on the other hand, tends to resort to a rhetoric of moral superiority and lifting in the address he delivered on July 10, 1919, in order to present the Peace Treaty to the Senate. He takes this opportunity, as he is standing before the senators, to define the nation as he imagines it. From the very beginning, he argues that the United States entered the war for ideals, as we demonstrated earlier. He parallels these idealist motivations with the essence of the national spirit. Doing so, he endeavours to project a certain image of the American nation to its citizens but also to the world: "They [the soldiers] were for all the visible embodiment of America. What they did made America and that she stood for a living reality in the thoughts not only of the people of France but also of ten of millions of men and women throughout all the toiling nations of a world standing everywhere in peril of its freedom…" Wilson insists on the large number of people who were affected by the visions of the soldiers: he exposes the width the American influence has reached through a clear gradation, from "people of France" to "tens of millions of men and women" to "throughout all the toiling nations". Not an inch of the globe is spared the true vision of America. This American essence is based on ideals, and especially freedom and free government. He takes on a very prophetical tone and implies that the nation was saved from its long-lived vices. Everything looks as if the nation, through the war, had been redeemed and could now embrace its old native principles and ideals again:

> the whole world saw at last, in the flesh, in noble action, a great ideal asserted and vindicated, by a nation they had deemed material and now found to be compact of the spiritual forces that must free men of every nation from every unworthy bondage. It is thus that a new role and a new responsibility have come to this great nation that we honor and which we would all wish to lift to yet higher levels of service and achievement.

America demonstrated its moral superiority. Now Wilson develops his agenda for the nation. It is now a world power and it should as such take on new responsibilities: "mentors and guides" for the Old World and assume "the moral leadership that is offered to us". Thus Wilson's visionary lines considerably broaden the American perspective for the future. He announces a new American role and responsibility to be played on the world stage. America was revealed to the world, and its essence was revealed to the Americans themselves. Now the country should accept the mission that is offered to them. It is its duty to assume it and lead the world on the path towards liberty and democracy. Saying so he reinterprets the ancient theme of God's elected people. The war, which was so overtly and violently opposed in the country, suddenly becomes through the magic of a discourse a crucial event in America's and the world's history. To convince his audience of this, Wilson using a vocabulary of lifting and transcendence envisions the nation's bright future, making the image he presents to his hearers gleaming with promise. He engages his audience on the road towards the achievement of America's providential destiny:

> The stage is set, the destiny disclosed. It has come about by no plan of our conceiving but by the hand of God who led us into this way. We cannot turn back. We can only go forward, with lifted eyes and freshened spirit, to follow the vision. It was this that we dreamed at our birth. America shall in truth show the way. The light streams upon the path ahead, and nowhere else.

Both presidents define a vision of the American nation and preach it to their audiences through sermon-like rhetoric and inspiration. This well-known preaching rhetoric joins the audience in a moment of national communion as the presidents try to unify the country behind a single cause: the preservation of the Union for Lincoln and American intervention in the world affairs for Wilson. The image of the nation is incarnate in this sacred language, as much as it is invoked and called forth. Both preacher-presidents endeavour to expose their vision of the nation in such words as Americans could appropriate. Here we may quote Wilson's second inaugural address's last lines: "The shadows that now lie dark upon our path will soon be dispelled, and we shall walk with the light all about us if we be but true to ourselves—to ourselves as we have wished to be known in the counsels of the world and in the thought of all those who love liberty and justice and the right exalted.[12]" Both Presidents indeed turned into priests and preached the American nation. They preached it, meaning they addressed the American citizens and they upheld their vision of the nation, exhorting Americans to follow them on the road that unfolded before the country and the world.

Works Cited

Bourdieu, Pierre, *La distinction : critique sociale du jugement*, Paris : éditions de Minuit, 1979, collection "Le sens commun".

Lincoln, Abraham, *Letters and Addresses of Abraham Lincoln*, New York : H.W. Bell, 1903, p. 316-320.

The Holy Bible, King James Version, New York : American Bible Society : 1999 ; Bartleby.com, 2000.

Wilson, Thomas Woodrow, *The Messages and papers of Woodrow Wilson (Vol. I & II)*, introduction de Albert Shaw, New York : George H. Doran, c1924, p. 368-372.

---

[12] *The Messages and papers of Woodrow Wilson (Vol. I & II)*, introduction de Albert Shaw, New York: George H. Doran, c1924, vol. I, p. 368-372.

CHAPTER ELEVEN

CONTENT AND CONTEXT: THE WAR SERMONS OF HERBERT HENSLEY HENSON (1863-1947)

KEITH ROBBINS

When war broke out in 1914, Herbert Hensley Henson was 50. He was perhaps the most celebrated preacher in the Church of England, though it was not a church particularly given to celebrating preachers. Rather, it had been the pulpits of the Free Churches which had been occupied by the most famous preachers of the age. Charles Haddon Spurgeon, a Baptist, had regularly preached before thousands at his Metropolitan Tabernacle in South London. Joseph Parker and R.J. Campbell, successive ministers of the Congregationalist City Temple in Holborn, occupied the "great white pulpit" which famously stood centrally at the front of a church whose seating had been specifically arranged, above all, to ensure that everybody could hear.[1] The "exposition of the Word" was of paramount importance, symbolized by the physical centrality of the pulpit in most Free Churches. The most well-known preachers were, in effect, "celebrities", with their images reproduced on popular picture postcards. There was an element of "entertainment" in their art and in some cases it was not unknown for a would-be audience to have to queue to get in. Sermons were sometimes published by small and specifically religious publishers but mainstream publishers also found them a profitable line of business. It would not be too much of an exaggeration to speak of late Victorian/Edwardian witnessing the hey-day of the sermon and of great preachers. It did have

---

[1] Campbell did not pretend that his sermons – *City Temple Sermons*. London, 1903, *Sermons Addressed to Individuals*. London, 1904 and *New Theology Sermons*. London, 1907 were literature. They were extempore speech addressed, as it were, to one individual. Keith Robbins 'The Spiritual Pilgrimage of the Rev. R.J. Campbell' reprinted in his *History, Religion and Identity in Modern British History*. London, 1993, 133-48.

preachers, but neither architecturally nor theologically, did the Church of England place the same emphasis on "the preaching of the Word".[2] The pulpit was to the side, not in the centre. Even so, Henson had acquired a national reputation. In this, as in many other respects, he was an exceptional man.[3]

He had an extraordinary childhood. His mother died when he was six. He had a grandfather in Devon whom he never met. The household was anarchic and large. His father was wayward, with a strong opinion that the human race was corrupt, which drove him to ever more severe versions of Protestantism, though he never formally ceased to be a member of the Church of England. Later, Hensley came to speak of the Plymouth Brethren as *poisonous schismatics* and to have a horror of over-emotional evangelical preachers. All his life, he hated sectarian religion and believed it had ruined his childhood. Something mysterious happened, though we do not know what, to make that hatred visceral. Even so, it seems that as a child he had an ambition to be a preacher. He found he had a German stepmother who in turn found that he was clever boy. Late, at the age of 14, he attended a school in Kent as a boarder. It was not a great English public (independent) school.[4] He spent his time avoiding playing games, drafting sermons and trying to learn Greek. His father, who had never been to university and was in debt, had the view that Oxford was "a cess-pit". He managed to matriculate and his stepmother persuaded his father to let him go – but he was a non-collegiate student living in cheap lodgings. His train journey to Oxford was the first he ever made. He was an outsider, who devoured books rather than food. He listened to sermons in the university church. He already wrote English of exceptional quality in exceptional handwriting. He did not need tutors, nor did he need friends. Oxford, he wrote subsequently, was a wonderful place for making friends but many of them were not worth making. His religion was in turmoil. He began to be happy only when, thirty years before 1914 he graduated with a First Class in Modern History and was elected a Fellow of All Souls College after competitive examination. It was an institution emerging from a long existence as a refuge for country gentlemen. Electing Henson was a sign of change. He knew that he had got where he was simply by being

---

[2] E.D. Mackerness, *The Heeded Voice*. London, 1959, a study of Anglican sermons between 1830 and 1900.
[3] The details that follow are drawn from Owen Chadwick, *Hensley Henson: A Study in the Friction between Church and State*. Oxford 1983; Norwich, 1994.
[4] Henson therefore stood outside the ethos of 'Anglican public school Christianity' as illustrated in W.J. Reader, *'At Duty's Call' A Study in Obsolete Patriotism*. Manchester, 1988, 92-100.

clever. Into the common room came the most famous men in England, in Church and State. He liked brilliant conversation and repartee. To their amazement, this extraordinary young man could reply in kind. He was surely destined to become a great man – the law or even politics perhaps? But he decided to be a priest, to accept the Christian position and part company with amiable and attractive free-thinkers. He found himself at Barking in Essex, a living in the gift of the College. Here was a preacher not dependent upon his congregation to pay his wages, but he soon knew when people listened to him and when they did not. His church became so full that sometimes people could not get inside. He saw life in the brutal raw. If he did not let his powers of denunciation and sarcasm spoil him, a contemporary observed, he would be a great cleric. He was a professed celibate and sometimes appeared sporting a biretta. He professed himself Catholic and introduced a cross and candlesticks, though was not tempted by incense. He was already a controversialist with a pronounced capacity to "put his foot in it". He flew into "an unspeakable rage" on news of the second verdict of guilty passed on Alfred Dreyfus.

Such a sketch, while summary, may seem excessive. Yet what Henson had to say about the war, and how he said it, cannot be understood without reference to his origins and career– though nothing he ever said was entirely predictable. He had a spectacular capacity for changing his mind, as for example when at the age of 38 this dedicated celibate successfully proposed marriage to a woman four days after meeting her for the first time at a dinner party. In terms of churchmanship he had already moved away from his early Anglo-Catholicism. What he called "Romanism" might seem irresistible at 16, suspicious at 25 but it was impossible at 30. In a celebrated volume published in 1898 he accused ritualists of undermining the principle of church establishment.[5] Church self-government would be a bad thing. So would the separation of Church and State. Whatever form his opinions took, at any given point, they were invariably cogently expressed in a style which no one could ignore.[6] He was rapidly moving up the ecclesiastical ladder. In 1900 he received a letter from the Prime Minister, Lord Salisbury, offering him a vacant canonry at Westminster Abbey, together with being Rector of St. Margaret's, the "parish church" of the House of Commons. He had to conduct fashionable weddings and preach in the knowledge that the Prime Minister or other leading political figures might be in the congregation.

---

[5] H. Hensley Henson, *Cui Bono?* London, 1898.
[6] H. Hensley Henson, *Cross-Bench Views on Current Church Questions*. London, 1902.

He had moved into the heart of "the Establishment" but he was rebellious – in his own way. His biographer characterizes him, if it is not too paradoxical, as "a rebel of the establishment". Reporters asked Henson for his sermon notes at the end of a service. A twenty-five minute sermon was too short, a forty-five minute one too long. He was always in between, with a full text in front of him but he preached as though it were not there. He was not declamatory. His phrases were brilliant. The appeal was to the intelligence. He knew well what challenges there were to Christian belief, for he felt them himself. But he was in the pulpit to declare the Word which was not his own. He saw the danger of trying to please an audience rather than speak the truth – but his understanding of truth changed. He prepared his sermons with the Greek New Testament in front of him. They had to combine interest, intelligibility, relevance and edification. They could not be skimped. There would be nothing worse than to be a windbag. The preacher should not court popularity but he should also be able to sit where his people were sitting. He should remember that *vox populi* was not *vox Dei*. The Gospel had inescapable social implications but it could not be reduced to a Socialist programme and no preacher should abuse the pulpit for party purposes. Henson certainly succeeded in upsetting a good many people, but not always the same people. He found himself in the unusual position of having his sermons cited in the House of Commons.

Reflections of this kind are to be found sprinkled through addresses, sermons and lectures throughout his busy Westminster years. He was always writing letters.[7] His views found fuller expression in lectures on preaching given at Yale in 1909 and published with the title *The Liberty of Prophesying*. He upset high churchmen by now saying that the Church of England should accept the Free Churches as fully Christian. High churchmen were not sure, doctrinally, that Henson was fully Christian. Between 1902 and 1911 he published five short books mainly concerned with what would now be described as ecumenism, at least with Protestant ecumenism. The clergyman who introduced the volume *The National Church* (1908) stated that its general purport was "to protest against the ecclesiastical assumptions which are tending to make the Church of England less National than it has been". The feeling that Henson wished to encourage, he wrote, was that of "a godly English patriotism, which honours the nation as having a Divine calling, and can look upon its

---

[7] Letter-writing was a lifelong enthusiasm. E.F. Braley, ed., *Letters of Herbert Hensley Henson*. London, 1950; E.F. Braley, ed., *More Letters of Herbert Hensley Henson*. London, 1954.

history with pride".[8] He was indeed an Englishman but his wife was a Scot and his reputation had spread beyond England. The University of Glasgow gave him an Honorary DD- something not lightly awarded to Englishmen or Episcopalians. He wanted the Church of England and the Church of Scotland to be in full communion with each other.

In 1912 he preached for the last time in St. Margaret's, Westminster – many hundreds of would-be hearers could not get in. He summoned up his ministry there by stressing a "resolute refusal to accept or respect sectarian categories of Christian membership" and "a deep sense of the actual, and still more of the potential value of the national organization of the Church as secured by the Establishment". He recognized the current mood which appeared to be pulling Church and State apart – as in France – but was convinced that complete separation would be to the detriment of both. The well-being of the whole society would suffer. The "ancient liberties of England, uttered and guarded by the national institutions" were compared to a strong fortress within which, as garrison, were the English people.[9]

In 1905 he had lectured on "Christianity and Politics" before the University of Aberdeen. He claimed there that a perfect society could only be built on the foundation of a perfect individual morality – Jesus Christ. The Founder of Christianity had contributed nothing to political science. The New Testament contained nothing that could be regarded as political doctrine. It had been found to be equally serviceable to political systems as diverse as those of Byzantine Absolutism and American Democracy. His message was simple: there was no quick fix to be found by citing particular biblical texts without regard to context and situation. He does not appear to have preached on the subject of war in peacetime. In his autobiography, *Retrospect of an Unimportant Life* – nevertheless deemed worthy of three substantial volumes – there is no mention of the South African War.[10] He had not felt it his duty at Westminster to provide a running commentary on the state of Anglo-German relations. He was not that kind of preacher. He was very conscious, however, of what he called England's "unique immunity from war" as compared with "the extreme and protracted calamities" which had afflicted her neighbours.[11] It was possible war in Ireland in 1914, rather than in Europe, which filled his mind.

---

[8] H. Hensley Henson, *The National Church*. London, 1908, vii.

[9] H. Hensley Henson, *Christ and the Nation*. London, 1908, 124.

[10] The three volumes were published between 1942 and 1950. The first two were reprinted as one in 1943 and subsequent page references are to that printing.

[11] Henson, *Christ and the Nation*, 121.

By then, Henson was no longer at Westminster at the hub of British politics. In 1912 he had been appointed Dean of Durham, in the North-East of England, living in the shadow of its great cathedral in one of the historic houses of England. He and his wife – they were childless – were supported by a cook, a head parlour maid, a Head Housemaid, a Parlour Maid, a House Maid, two Kitchen Maids and a laundry woman. His dining table could and did comfortably accommodate thirty people. He was much in demand up and down the country and was by no means confined to his northern fastness. He wrote controversially on the Creed. In his autobiography he wrote that all domestic conflicts, however, were driven out of the public mind by the war - which he described (retrospectively, of course) as "not wholly unexpected". However, "still smarting under the losses and humiliations of the South African War", largely "leavened with the perilous sophistries of pacifism", and conscious of its own devotion to peace, the nation had been reluctant to admit the possibility of war between nations so closely linked by ties of interest, culture and traditions.[12]

In fact, (with the exception of the German stepmother to whom he owed so much who happened, worryingly, to be in Göttingen when war broke out) he did not have close personal European ties. He had been to Germany as a boy with his stepmother and, more recently, when in Kiel he had observed "the impudent bellicosity and anti-British tone of the papers and publications exposed for sale".[13] This experience had led him to be part of a delegation to the Prime Minister which warned of this danger. Henson had not studied in a German university. He was not therefore as personally disorientated by going to war with Germany - as many of his leading Nonconformist or Scottish contemporaries were who had studied theology there (and sometimes acquired German wives).[14] He was not, however, in the least attracted by the idea of neutrality. German policy was Machiavellian. There was a moral obligation to resist Germany in her career of cynical and violent aggression. Two days before the British

---

[12] The intellectual context for such a view is explored in Keith Robbins, *British Images of Germany in the First Half of the Twentieth Century and their Historical Legacy.* Göttingen, 1999: Stuart Wallace, *War and the Image of Germany: British Academics 1914-1918.* Edinburgh, 1988; Paul Laity, *The British Peace Movement 1870-1914.* Oxford, 2001.

[13] Henson, *Retrospect*, 175.

[14] Half of the library of the leading Free Church preacher and theologian, P.T. Forsyth – author of *Positive Preaching and the Modern Mind.* London, 1907 for example, was in German and he had studied in Germany. He wrote, however, vigorously in support of *The Christian Ethic of War.* London, 1916.

declaration of war, the veteran Bishop of Durham, Handley Moule, sent a letter to every parish in his diocese stating that it was Britain's "plain duty" to come to the aid of Belgium, even if that meant war with Germany. Henson agreed. On holiday in Scotland when war was declared, he hurried back to Durham. At a hastily-convened meeting in the Town Hall, he added his voice to the call for men to volunteer to fight. He joined with Lord Durham, the Lord Lieutenant (i.e. the King's representative in the county) in a tour to drum up recruits. Henson notes in his autobiography that there were those who held that it was "imprudent and even indecent for a clergyman to advocate so strongly the patriotic duty of military service" but he was unrepentant. It was wrong for someone like himself "who held a prominent position in the hierarchy of the local society" to stand aside in self-isolation at such a juncture.[15] When it became an issue later in the war, Henson strongly supported military conscription.

Historians have frequently drawn attention to the eagerness with which the Bishop of London acted as a recruiting officer. His sermon, "A Call to Arms" had been delivered on 31 August from a wagon at the camp of the London Territorial Rifle Brigade with conspicuous success. In the preface to a volume of his sermons *The Church in Time of War'* (1915) the bishop noted with satisfaction that 'the Church encouraged every young man under its influence to volunteer at once as a duty to God as well as to the country. The exodus from all the Church Choirs, the Church Lads' Brigade, the Church Scouts, and the ranks of the servers, had been enormous'.[16] It is not impossible to locate pulpit orators who spoke like recruiting officers and stoked the fires of hate. In the inter-war period, not least amongst the Anglican clergy themselves, it came to be the accepted view that in 1914-15 in particular, and in relation to the war in general, that this had been generally true but this may be excessive retrospective flagellation. It is of course, true that no Church of England bishop opposed British entry into the war. That was true in the case of even of the Bishops of Hereford and Lincoln who had been most active in the newly-formed Church of England Peace League and who had both been labelled "pro-

---

[15] Henson, *Retrospect,* 174.

[16] Cited in Alan Wilkinson, *The Church of England and the First World War.* London, 1978, 36. The same author has also written *Dissent or Conform? War, Peace and the English Churches, 1900-1945.* London, 1986. See also A. Marrin, *The Last Crusade: The Church of England in the First World War.* Durham, N.C., 1974. *A Call to Arms* was published separately in 1914. Other volumes of his sermons appeared throughout the war. S.C. Carpenter, Winnington-Ingram. London, 1949.

Boer". Only a small minority of Nonconformist ministers preached against the war and those who did frequently found themselves in trouble with their congregations. The majority were anxious to demonstrate that patriotism was not confined to the 'National Church'.[17] What Henson had to say about the war must be seen against this background. However, his sermons must be seen in context. Too often, his remarks, and those of other war-time preachers, have been merely plundered *en passant* as a location for occasional quotations – and it is not too difficult to find examples which might cause one to shudder – without relating content to time and place.

Hensley Henson published with Macmillan (who had become his "normal" publishers) two volumes of wartime sermons. The first, simply called *War-Time Sermons* was published in 1915 and included 21 sermons preached between 9 August 1914 and 3 October 1915. They were not the only sermons he preached between those dates but they were the ones which he selected as presumably embodying what he wanted the general public to read. He dedicated it to the "Faithful Durhams" – that is to say the Durham Light Infantry. The second volume, also published by Macmillan, appeared in 1918, by which date, after much controversy surrounding his appointment, though not occasioned by his views on the war, he had been appointed Bishop of Hereford. *Christian Liberty and other Sermons* covered the period from 12 March 1916 to January 1918. Again, they represent his personal selection. This volume was dedicated to the Mayor and Corporation of the City of Durham. In neither volume, however, were the sermons listed absolutely chronologically. The dedications reflected his strong sense of commitment to the community in which he lived – and in the event he was only to be in Hereford for just over two years before he returned to Durham as bishop

When war broke out he had not ceased to be a national figure – and presumably a factor in publication was the fact that many people who wanted to read what he had to say were not living in "remote" Durham. Only half of the sermons in the first volume had been delivered in the north-east. Of the others, four were preached in London. In Westminster Abbey in February, June and July 1915, in St. Margaret's, Westminster (October 1915) and in the Temple Church (June 1915). The others were preached in Bristol (May 1915), Manchester (October 1914), Carlisle (October 1914), Norwich (twice September 1914) and Oxford, in December 1914. In the north-east, with the exception of two in parish churches in Sunderland, all the sermons were given in Durham Cathedral.

[17] Keith Robbins, *The Abolition of War: The 'Peace Movement' in Britain 1914-1919.* Cardiff, 1976.

Of those delivered outside the north-east, all were given in cathedrals or at Westminster, with the exception of the Temple Church in London and the University Church in Oxford. All were "proper sermons", that is to say each was prefaced by one or more biblical texts and each was given within the context of regular worship. Amongst the 'things which My Soul Hateth', as he recorded late in life, besides people depositing orange peel in the Bishop's Park, were "topical sermons, and disturbances of devotional use and wont incidental thereto" together with the posting of the names of preachers outside the churches, sometimes in gigantic letters'.[18] Preachers had to say what they had to say within the customary pattern of worship, war or no war. To do otherwise was to neglect the fact that while the extraordinary nature of the present could not be denied a preacher always spoke *sub specie aeternitatis.*

In Henson's case too, with his strong historical sense, the fact that in all of the afore-mentioned instances he was preaching in noble and ancient buildings which were redolent of aspects of the nation's past, in their monuments and memorials, was no mere incidental backdrop. It reinforced his sense of time. In Norwich in September 1914, in a sermon on "Change and the Unchanging" with a text from Hebrews which proclaimed that Jesus Christ was the same "yesterday and to-day, yea and for ever" preached at the 813th anniversary of the Consecration of the Church, he was not at all sentimental about the medieval past. Rather, he was "amazed at the chasm which parts the men of the Middle Ages from ourselves".[19] Names of things continued, but their meaning altered, institutions survived, but neither their importance nor their significance stayed the same. Theologies, likewise, were always becoming unsatisfactory and unsatisfying. The bulk of the sermon, nonetheless, is concerned with the ways in which Jesus Christ could be claimed the Lord of life. It is at this point that the war "comes in". The events of the previous few weeks had not demonstrated the bankruptcy of Christianity but rather how a great nation, Germany, had been "blinded by the false glamour of success, and miserably deceived by its leaders in Church and State".[20] His second sermon in that month in Norwich addressed 'Christianity and War' and took as text the injunction in St. Matthew "Love your Enemies". He rejected the notion that Christian morality was

---

[18] Henson, *Retrospect,* 391.

[19] H. Hensley Henson, *War-Time Sermons.* London, 1915, 242-3. The tone of the then Dean of Norwich, in identifying the struggle as one against 'the Dragon and the False Prophet' is stronger than that of the visiting preacher. H.C. Beeching, *Armageddon.* London, 1914.

[20] Henson, *War-Time Sermons,* 252.

simply personal and social and could not be political, but he also rejected "literalism" in the exegesis of any text. Somehow, personal and public duty had to be held together. He considered the testimony of Quakers not without sympathy but nonetheless "reluctantly but decisively" concluded that war was indispensable in the world as it was known.[21] That might not always be so and Britain's reluctance to go to war, as he saw it, was an encouraging indication of the disgust with which the civilized conscience regarded war.[22] But "rational human progress" would take time. It was wrong to suppose that the New Testament offered a simple political and economic prescription. The praise of war to be found in von Bernhardi surprised as much as they shocked Henson. He hoped that in retrospect the war would be seen as a decisive stage along the journey which would lead to "the Final Overthrow of the Theory and Practice of International Violence".[23] The preacher's tone, nearly two months into the war, was sober and subdued.

The tone had not been unreflectively bellicose in sermons preached on "home territory" in Durham even on 9 and 16 August 1914. One of the things which had struck him on coming to Durham was "the intensity of local feeling" which contrasted so sharply with the "cosmopolitan atmosphere of London" with which he had become so familiar. [24] The "Good Soldiers of Jesus Christ" was a sermon given to a packed congregation which was largely made up of Territorial Troops. The war, Henson declared, was different from every war which Englishmen had waged in the past. The nation was fully involved from the outset. Soldiers would also go into action "with a good conscience" but "with no feeling of hatred or bitterness against the German People". They had not had the same freedom of opinion as the English and had been mishandled by their rulers. It was as Christians no less than as Englishmen, that the brutal policy of Germany had to be resisted. Christianity was not merely a religion of peace and gentleness. It spoke of Justice and Sacrifice. He ventured no cheering prospects and did not suggest that war would be over by Christmas. The "Chalice of Human Misery" would be filled to overflowing. On 16 August the Colours of the Durham Local Militia were laid up in the cathedral and Henson reflected on the value of symbols. Patriotism was not a mere submission to authority. It realized a debt and confessed a duty. Citizenship required it. Every young Englishman should brace himself to the personal obligation that rested upon him. Britain was

---

[21] Thomas C. Kennedy, *British Quakerism 1860-1920.* Oxford, 2001.

[22] Henson, *War-Time Sermons,* 22-3.

[23] *Ibid.,* 25.

[24] Henson, *Retrospect,* 393.

not fighting because it hated anybody or coveted territory. It was fighting to break the Empire of Force.[25]

In September he preached on what he saw as a parallel – "Judaea and Belgium". Both were small states placed between mightier rivals. It was about the Belgians that Henson became most emotional and where his sense of shock is most evident. In the deliberate destruction of Louvain, modern civilization had found its Attila. The Garden of Europe was being transformed into a charnel-house by the Armies of the German Emperor, the arrogant Apostle of German Culture.[26] He urged the congregation to give liberally to the Belgian Relief Fund. Further sermons, as the months passed, acknowledged that the conflict was straining the political and social fabric of Europe to breaking point, but there could be no going back. In November, in a sermon before the Mayor and Corporation and in the presence of a contingent of His Majesty's Forces, the emphasis here was understandably civic. The city of Durham was undergoing great change as recruits filled its narrow and winding streets. Henson placed his emphasis on reciprocal obligations. It was a false conception of liberty which refused restraint. Social and political liberty were in the long run conditioned by moral liberty. Christmas Day 1914 found him back in Durham cathedral preaching on "The Paradox of Christianity" taking as text "The foolishness of God is wiser than men". He acknowledged that the singing of Christmas carols could seem "empty and pointless". He again turned to history. What he termed "moral conquest" was gradual, hidden and intermittent but in the end it would be complete. It was a chequered story. He was certain, however, despite natural exasperation and indignation, that it would be right to "trample on the desire for vengeance". [27]

There is nothing, in short, in these 1914 sermons which suggests dissent from the national mission. It is an onerous and costly one, but it could not be shirked. Responsibility is unambiguously placed on the German political/military elite. There are firm injunctions not to seek vengeance and a willingness to believe that the German people have been misled. Gallant little Belgium is singled out but there is no detailed consideration of British pre-war policy or comment on the relationship with France and what that implied by way of "obligations of honour".

While the contrast should not be exaggerated, the sermons delivered in 1915 begin to reflect more widely on the significance of what was happening, for Britain, for Europe, for Christendom and for Christianity.

---

[25] Henson, *War-Time Sermons*, 69.

[26] *Ibid.*, 9.

[27] *Ibid.*, 35.

Henson wrote a preface to his collection one year on from the war's outbreak. He stressed that in his view too many English people had been carried away before 1914 by dreams of universal peace. They had been blinded by a sentimental cosmopolitanism. Empty hopes and theories had been shattered. It was not Christianity which had been undermined but rather what he called "the sentimental misreading of Christianity" in which so many Christians had indulged. He acknowledged that Christian preachers had been taken over by the questions of the war. Their congregations had no ears for "the staple of normal preaching". He was contemptuous of the growth of "spiritualism, occultism, faith-healing and a debased sacramentalism" which he observed. He mocked eminent divines who had credited the now notorious fiction of angelic apparitions to British soldiers and German horses at a critical moment in the Retreat from Mons. He recognized that patriotism was "always rather perilous in the Christian pulpit". Christianity was not a national religion. However, congregations did not help in resisting the distinctive temptations of the patriotic preacher. He had no doubt, however, that Christian Preachers should "keep steadily before their congregations the intrinsic wrongness of mere revenge, the sacred duty of forgiveness". The war would not last for ever and the Christian preacher ought to strive to preach in such a way that he would subsequently be able to recall his words without shame. The Good Friday sermon had as title "The Death of Jesus Exemplary for Us". The reflections on death, which occupy a great part of the sermon, sought a path between morbidity and frivolity. It was necessary to find 'the middle way of a sober remembrance of Death". [28] The Easter Day sermon in Durham proclaimed "that Life, not Death, is the destiny of man; that Death is but an episode of existence, the Gate of Life". [29] Reflecting on the "crowded graves beyond the sea" he acknowledged that the question 'Is it worth while?' was inescapable but he remained certain that the defeat of Wrong was right. Scarcely a sermon passed without the hope being expressed that the German people themselves would pass judgment on the crimes and follies which were deluging Europe with innocent blood. [30] In June, in Bristol, he began to identify "Lessons of the Great War", taking as his text the injunction to 'redeem the time' in Ephesians. He suggested that the war had disclosed the potency of a rival set of principles which were anti-Christian. Germany was an example of a "Christianly civilized nation going away from its principles". [31] He admitted, however, that the "selfish

---

[28] *Ibid.*, 163.
[29] *Ibid.*, 186.
[30] *Ibid.*, 207.
[31] *Ibid.*, 101.

imperialism" which shocked in Berlin was not wholly unknown in
London. Yet, Britons now knew, as never before, what *raison d'être*
patriotism had and were prepared to die for their country. It was no mere
platform orator's point to say that Britain was fighting a war against war.
Never again would people be "cheated by the pageantry and purple
rhetoric of war". Beholding the death of young men, however, it became
apparent that Life could not be measured by years but rather by its power
to fashion men for Duty.[32]

In the same month, in London, preaching on "New Wine and Fresh
Wine-Skins" he pondered on whether the new Europe at the war's end
would emerge more, or less, Christian. He painted an unflattering picture
of "ecclesiastical Christianity". The new standard of judgment which
soldiers had gained in war would shatter denominationalism. The pre-1914
Protestant Agitator would not in future gain a hearing from men who had
received the tender ministries of French Priests and Nuns in hours of
desperate need. The Christianity of the future should not be and could not
be the Christianity of the past. The denominations had quite evidently lost
their religious *raison d'être*. It would be time, too, to accept "the privation
of doctrinal certitude, the burden of reverent agnosticism with respect to
many solemn and infinitely pressing questions". Above all, it was time for
the National Church to give every true and earnest Christian a place within
it.[33] It was in his old church, St. Margaret's Westminster that he expanded
further on what had been a central preoccupation "The Function and
Future of national Christianity". Imperialism, as history had known it, was
no longer compatible with Christianity, but not so the racial and local
loyalties which imperialism overrode. Christianity stimulated individuality
but not individualism. The Christian Englishman should not look forward
to the final disappearance of English Nationality in the triumph of some
universally prevailing type of humanity but rather to a world in which all
national types existed in mutual harmony. The prevailing conflict was both
the vindication and purification of Nationality. Patriotism would cease to
be the spring of international strife and become the grace of mutual
understanding.[34]

The second volume is rather different character. Those selected were
overwhelmingly given in Durham cathedral. The first seven were in a
sequence given there from the first Sunday in Lent (12 March, 1916) to
Easter Day. They can be described as sermons given in time of war rather
than "war sermons" in the sense of those which we have just been

---

[32] *Ibid.*, 109.
[33] *Ibid.*, 224-5.
[34] *Ibid.*, 282-7.

outlining. Collectively, they go under the title "Christian Liberty" and their selection for publication would appear to be not unrelated to the controversy which had surrounded his appointment to the episcopate. The sermons provided, he believed, an effective rebuttal of what had been alleged against him in a sixpenny pamphlet entitled *Dr Hensley Henson's Opinions*. The main body of the reflections on Christian Liberty, one supposes, could have been delivered as much in time of peace as in time of war. By the spring of 1916, the war had become, as it were, "a fact of life" and there was even a sense, in a great northern cathedral, that it was all very remote. "Living here in an island wonderfully protected", Henson admitted, it was only with difficulty that most people could realize what had happened over a great part of Europe.[35] The novel issues which war had posed had already been tackled. Now it was time for a sustained, historically informed, sequence of Lenten sermons delivered before the same congregation. He started with the reply which Cicero had given to the question "What is Liberty?" His own responses consisted of a series of probing reflections on the relationship between Law, Liberty and Licence. European man had suddenly been cast adrift in the world. He had liked to think that he was master of his circumstances. But was this really so? The Easter Sunday sermon, the climax to the series, pointed to "The Eternity in Men's Hearts" though conceding that in the present hour Ecclesiastes rather than St. Paul seemed to set the mood.[36]

He took the opportunity, over the following months, to expose, as he saw it, the limitations of a secularised Christianity as it had often been propounded in England before the war. As a religion, he believed that Christianity could not possibly survive the repudiation of its "otherworldly" hopes. All moral failure was bound up with the spiritual suicide implied in materialism.[37] He was suspicious of the common view that by being a good citizen a man would end by becoming a good Christian. It was the other way round.[38] Such convictions were not irrelevant to the war but neither were they occasioned by it. It was different with the special sermon he gave to mark the second anniversary of the outbreak of the war. Whatever doubts Englishmen might have had about intervention in 1914 had surely been answered by the subsequent revelations of Germany savagery. He praised the "magnanimous valour of France" and the "death-defying devotion" of Russia. After Germany's defeat, he hoped that it

---

[35] H. Hensley Henson, *Christian Liberty*. London, 1918, 53.

[36] *Ibid.*, 79.

[37] *Ibid.*, 94.

[38] *Ibid.*, 105.

would pass through a purgatorial fire.[39] One year later, in another special service, he acknowledged that, with no end to the war in sight, people were writing to him saying that the pursuit of peace was the primary duty of Christians. They had given him anxious thought but he still felt compelled to insist that in the moral order Justice came before Peace. War-weariness was natural but it was to be resisted. It was a time for courage, though hearts were breaking and homes were empty.

He addressed "Religion and Politics" specifically in March 1917 and reiterated his conviction that "We cannot think of peace while the Task is unfounded and we have strength to fight". The magnitude of the task had now been appreciated but it could not be flinched. At the same time, he cautioned against simplicities. Victory would not prove British goodness nor defeat the punishment of British sins. Bishops who said that victory was being delayed because of the sins of the Allied Peoples, sins which were not specified, or who said that victory must come because we are sure that justice is on our side, were simply wrong. He found himself "moved to wonder at the archaic thinking" of those who thought that "the proper consequences of events" could be arrested by repeated petitions. Such views obstructed the road to Faith on the part of thoughtful and educated men.[40] The sermons in 1917 reveal an every deepening consciousness of the disaster that war was. It was "a heart-piercing spectacle, infinitely suggestive. The sheer volume of wretchedness dazes and paralyses us". As a physical tragedy, it took its place alongside the disasters of earthquake, pestilence and flood – catastrophes on which the Gospel cast no light. Even so, in its moral aspect the War was "infinitely consoling". [41] His abhorrence of what he called "the myriad infamies of German warfare" grew stronger, not weaker. It is only rarely that one of the published sermons was given before a special constituency. In Liverpool in October 1917, however, he preached before doctors and nurses. The harrowing work of healing proclaimed to a world in agony the Promise of Redemption.[42] In January 1918 he gave his last sermon in the cathedral as dean. "Change and Continuity" was perhaps an inevitable theme. It was also the annual commemoration of Founders and Benefactors. The time-battered pile, as he called the cathedral, had seen religious fashion change, but not religion; had seen modes of expressing belief change, but not Faith itself.[43] Its glorious nave, now regarded as a

---

[39] *Ibid.*, 145.
[40] *Ibid.*, 134-6.
[41] *Ibid.*, 233.
[42] *Ibid.*, 203.
[43] *Ibid.*, 254.

precious heirloom of the English People in fact perpetuated an epoch of cruel oppression for those who were under the iron heel of hateful foreigners [i.e. the Normans].. So, by analogy, in the retrospect of future generations, the Great War would be seen to be "the travail-pangs of a new Birth in Time".

The "farewell", as has been noted, did not last long. In 1920 he was back as bishop and in as controversial a mode as ever. Yet the characterization of him as a "rebel of the Establishment" remains appropriate. He did not quite fit anywhere – might even be thought the prince-bishop, standing on palatine dignity, which his more distant episcopal ancestors had been. During the war he had scorned the abstinence from alcohol which the King had been persuaded to agree to. He was sceptical of the "National Mission" enthusiastically undertaken by some of his clerical colleagues. He opposed the "Life and Liberty" movement which sought to establish more clear-cut institutions of self-government separate from the State. Yet, when the House of Commons in 1927-8 rejected the Church's Revised Prayer Book, Henson completed his most spectacular somersault. He campaigned vigorously but unsuccessfully for disestablishment. He criticized both "extreme modernism" and "archaic Catholicism". He was unrepentant in his belief that the Church of England and Protestant Nonconformity should be reconciled.[44]

Taking advantage of the seat in the House of Lords which his office gave him, there was scarcely an issue in inter-war Britain on which he did not have an opinion. He also wrote with his customary vigour. He was not persuaded by the pacifism which for a time in the mid-1930s swept through the Church of England and which had been accompanied by the view that the Church and its preachers had "'failed" in 1914-18. He publicized the plight of German Christians and Jews.[45] He became a critic of "appeasement" in British foreign policy. Unlike most of his fellow-bishops, for example, he did not welcome the 1938 Munich Agreement, regarding it as a "grievous injury" to Czechoslovakia and a shameful capitulation to Germany. His new-found enthusiasm for disestablishment moderated as he contrasted the Christianity of the English, albeit often latent, with the paganism of Nazi Germany. On 1 February 1939, however, at the age of 75, he stepped down as Bishop of Durham and went to live in

---

[44] The evolution of his views can be followed in *In Defence of the English Church.* London, 1923, *Quo Tendimus?* London, 1925, *Disestablishment.* London, 1929 and *Ad Clerum.* London, 1937.

[45] *The Yellow Spot: The Extermination of the Jews in Germany: with an introduction by the Bishop of Durham.* London, 1936.

retirement in Suffolk. He found it extremely difficult. "I am no longer Bishop of Durham, taking fourth rank in the Hierarchy. I am not now a spiritual peer having voice and vote in the House of Lords…I am in plain terms just Nobody".[46] There was an autobiography to write and there were old sermons and letters to destroy.

Not quite a Nobody though. When war broke out, he insisted publicly that there should be no compromise or public peace. He published a tract *The Good Fight.* On 17 May 1940, Whit-Sunday, he preached the University Sermon in Cambridge. He returned again to themes with which we are familiar from the First World War. He maintained that the civilisation which had been developed on the soil of Europe, which had indeed become the norm throughout the modern world, could still justly be described as Christian. It was in imminent peril now. He had known Winston Churchill for many years - an unpredictable maverick like himself? In the crisis of May 1940 the King had to choose between Churchill and Lord Halifax, the former at best a "flying buttress" to the Church of England and the latter a devout churchman. Henson privately contrasted the two men: "The one has genius without character, the other has character without genius". Henson thought genius was needed. Winston Churchill, in turn, thought another old genius was needed back in Westminster Abbey and arranged that Henson should take a canonry and preach again. So, for a second time, between September 1940 and the end of April 1941, he was "back home". But it was not a success. He discovered that he was in fact an old man. His eyesight was failing and the wartime blackout of the abbey meant that he could not even see the Bible to read from, or see his sermon notes to preach from – and he had never preached extempore. He felt he could not continue. However, in August 1941, in a London blitzed in a way he could never have imagined when he had first arrived at Westminster in 1900, he published his *Last Words in Westminster Abbey.*[47] In 1900, as in 1940, he declared, Britain was at war, but with a profound difference. Then the nation had been divided but now the people were "united beyond all precedent". The cause of democracy was now also confessedly the cause of Christianity. It comes as no surprise to find that the very last words he uttered 'from this shadowed and shattered Abbey Church' were ones in which he expressed his thanks to God that he was an Englishman. Such enormous wickedness as Hitlerite Germany constituted could not prevail. *Sursum corda.* And so it proved. And he lived to see its defeat. Unsurprisingly, the final volume of Henson's autobiography was fulsomely dedicated to Winston Churchill.

---

[46] Henson, *Retrospect,* 242.
[47] H. Hensley Henson, *Last Words in Westminster Abbey.* London, 1941.

It is scarcely possible to summarize such a lengthy and controversial life in a single paragraph. Nevertheless, a few "Last Words" are appropriate. Henson's "War Sermons" were delivered by a man who had found a niche at the heart of the "Establishment" but was not so comfortable in Auckland Castle, his capacious Durham residence, that he merely echoed "Establishment" wisdom. While we do not know precisely who listened to these sermons, the places in which they were mostly delivered were resonant with the English past and were likely to be directed to men and women who felt the spiritual force around them too. In ways in which he himself might not have been conscious, Henson absorbed his environment. He was, after all, a historian who at one time had thought that he might be a great one. He believed that his nation was right to fight in 1914 and *a fortiori* to being doing so again in 1940. His belief in the justice of this latter conflict perhaps made him unwilling, in an autobiography written during its course, to subject his own earlier remarks to self-criticism. Yet the Church of England, for all its "intimacy" with the English nation, could not be simply national. "The day of Nationalism is over", he wrote in 1939 "…it follows that the epoch of national churches is closed", though he could not say what would take its place in the long human march in which there were no short-cuts or painless solutions.[48] History showed to him that the balance between these two considerations was never stable and, over his long life, had led him to tilt in what were, he acknowledged, contrary directions. Patriotism did not abolish the requirement on a Christian to forgive but neither could a Christian "contract out" from a righteous cause. "Christian civilization" still had meaning.[49] Duty called. There was a good fight to be fought. And it was with words that Hensley Henson fought it.

Works Cited

Beeching, H.C., *Armageddon* (London, 1914).
Braley, E.F., ed., *Letters of Herbert Hensley Henson* (London, 1950).
—. *More Letters of Herbert Hensley Henson* (London, 1954).
Campbell, R.J., *City Temple Sermons* (London, 1903).
—. *Sermons Addressed to Individuals* (London, 1904).
—. *New Theology Sermons* (London, 1907).

---

[48] H. Hensley Henson, *The Church of England.* Cambridge, 1939, 256-7.
[49] Keith Robbins, 'Britain, 1940 and Christian Civilization' reprinted in his *History, Religion and Identity in Modern British History,* 195-214.

Carpenter, S.C., *Winnington-Ingram* (London, 1949).

Chadwick, W.O. *Hensley Henson: A Study in the Friction between Church and State* (Oxford, 1983).

Forsyth, P.T., *Positive Preaching and the Modern Mind* (London, 1907).

—. *The Christian Ethic of War* (London, 1916).

Henson, H. Hensley, *Cui Bono?* (London, 1898).

—. *Cross-Bench Views on Current Church Questions* (London, 1902).

—. *The National Church* (London, 1908).

—. *Christ and the Nation* (London, 1908).

—. *War-Time Sermons* (London, 1915).

—. *Christian Liberty* (London, 1918).

—. *In Defence of the English Church* (London, 1923).

—. *Quo Tendimus?* (London, 1925).

—. *Disestablishment* (London, 1929).

—. (Introduction) *The Yellow Spot: The Extermination of the Jews in German* (London, 1937).

—. *Ad Clerum* (London, 1937).

—. *The Church of England* (Cambridge, 1939).

—. *Last Words in Westminster Abbey* (London, 1941).

—. *Retrospect of an Unimportant Life* (3.vols., Oxford 1942-1950).

Kennedy, Thomas C., *British Quakerism 1860-1920* (Oxford, 2001).

Laity, Paul, *The British Peace Movement 1870-1914* (Oxford, 2001).

Mackerness, E.D., *The Heeded Voice* (London, 1959).

Marrin, Albert, *The Last Crusade: The Church of England in the First World War* (Durham, N.C., 1974).

Reader, W.J., *'At Duty's Call': A Study in Obsolete Patriotism* (Manchester, 1988).

Robbins, Keith, *The Abolition of War: The 'Peace Movement' in Britain 1914-1919* (Cardiff, 1976).

—. *History, Religion and Identity in Modern British History* (London, 1993).

—. *British Images of Germany in the First Half of the Twentieth Century and their Historical Legacy* (Göttingen, 1999).

Wallace, Stuart, *War and the Image of Germany: British Academics 1914-1918* (Edinburgh, 1988).

Wilkinson, Alan, *The Church of England and the First World War* (London, 1978).

—. *Dissent or Conform? War, Peace and the English Churches, 1900-1945* (London, 1986).

Winnington-Ingram, A.F., *A Call to Arms* (London, 1914).

CHAPTER TWELVE

WILLIAM TEMPLE'S BBC RADIO SERMONS DURING WORLD WAR II: BETWEEN POLITICS AND RELIGION

SUZAN BRAY

On September 1 1939 James Welch, recently appointed Director of Religious Broadcasting at the BBC, was recording the daily church service in Studio 3E when a slip of paper was quietly handed to him, saying "Germany invaded Poland this morning".[1] By five o'clock that evening the Religious Broadcasting Department was on its way to its wartime home in Bristol.

All historians agree that the BBC thrived in the wartime years and that it was "a unique institution, uniquely fitted to serve as the official voice of a united people at war".[2] The nine million wireless sets in regular use when war broke out rapidly increased, as the blackout and wartime economy severely restricted all alternative forms of evening entertainment. By the time the war ended, the BBC had over 11,000 staff and broadcast for an average of one hundred and fifty hours per day to destinations all round the world. Religious broadcasting also benefited from a growing audience. Slipped in, as they so often were, between ice hockey from Canada, comedy from Arthur Askey and the news in Gaelic or Norwegian, the religious programmes became more and more popular. Many people would stop what they were doing as they heard on the radio Big Ben strike 9 pm and spend a few moments in "remembrance of God and of our dependence on Him".[3] Official enquiries showed "a definite increase in public approval of broadcast religious services over the first three years of

---

[1] Welch, James W. *"Religious Broadcasting in Wartime"*, *BBC Year Book 1945*, BBC, 1945, 41.
[2] Calder, Angus. *The People's War*. London: Pimlico, 1992, 357.
[3] Temple, William, *The Church Looks Forward*, Macmillan, 1944, 85.

the war". By 1945, Welch felt that his team at the BBC could truthfully cite the famous words of John Wesley: "The world is our parish".[4]

The man in charge of this success story, the Reverend James W. Welch, was perhaps an unusual choice. As well as obtaining a theology degree and then a PhD from Cambridge, Welch had also worked for the Church Missionary Society in Nigeria for six years, organising the primary school system in Isoko. On the evangelical wing of the Church of England, Welch had great missionary zeal, but also a strong ecumenical spirit and maintained excellent relationships with colleagues from other churches. After the war he returned to Africa, first to Tanzania with the abortive groundnut scheme, and then as Professor of Theology at the recently created Ibadan University in Nigeria, where he was an outstanding success. He ran a grammar school in Emevor named after him and influenced many well-known Nigerians, including the writer Chinua Achebe, who referred to him as "an extraordinary man". Welch had got to know William Temple in the late thirties during his time as head of St John's Church of England Teacher Training College in York, while Temple was Archbishop of York. He took over religious broadcasting at the BBC in 1939 from another friend of Temple's, his future biographer F. A. Iremonger. During his time as director he could legitimately claim that "religious broadcasting [had] ceased to be chiefly a Sunday feature, and [had] been more an everyday element in BBC programmes", and also that "the Church [had] begun to learn how to use the medium of radio".[5] For many, he is known as the man who persuaded C. S. Lewis to give the broadcast talks which would later become the best-selling *Mere Christianity*, and who invited Dorothy L. Sayers to write the hugely successful cycle of radio plays known as *The Man Born to be King.* According to a *Daily Telegraph* editorial as recently as 1996: "religious broadcasting never has matched the quality" of such inspired programmes as those produced in the early nineteen forties under Welch's leadership.

Although the success of religious broadcasting during the war has never been in question, at the time it was far from a foregone conclusion and got off to a poor start. The Archbishop of Canterbury, Cosmo Gordon Lang, who had lost a lot of popularity during the abdication crisis three years earlier and gained the nickname "Auld Lang Swine",[6] was invited to Bristol to preach a sermon for the first Sunday of the war. Eric Fenn, Welch's assistant and a Presbyterian clergyman, claimed that "all were

---

[4] Phillips, Justin. *C.S. Lewis at the BBC*, Harper Collins, 2002, 284 and 43.
[5] Welch, *Yearbook*, 42.
[6] Lockhart, J. G. *Cosmo Gordon Lang*, Hodder & Stoughton, 1949, 396.

hoping to hear a message to fit the crisis, one that would lift the spirits".[7] Apparently, all were disappointed as, according to Fenn, the Archbishop's sermon was "completely vapid and totally irrelevant".[8] After this fiasco, the Government, perhaps over cautiously, allowed only Welch, Fenn, the Dean of Bristol cathedral and the Rev. Swann, a local vicar, to preach on the radio. After a month of this rather monotonous regime, Welch gained permission for William Temple, then Archbishop of York and already an experienced broadcaster, to speak, which he did on October 3. For Iremonger, Temple's sermon, entitled "The Spirit & Aims of Britain in the War", was "in every way a memorable utterance" which established Temple as a national leader who could speak "for the conscience of Britain". Temple was a natural broadcaster, with "an effortless delivery well suited to the microphone" and, according to Iremonger, "he became convinced that by broadcasting he could make his greatest personal contribution to the nation's war effort".[9] The BCC obviously agreed as this paper is based on fifty-one radio sermons of Temple's, which were either published or can be found in the archives at Lambeth Palace. This total does not include many sermons from the year 1941, Temple's last year as Archbishop of York before being translated to Canterbury, as the archives at Bishopthorpe in York are currently closed for repairs. As a result of these sermons, Temple emerged as a privileged communicator not only of Christian opinion but "even of public opinion in general", overcoming denominational differences to become in many ways "the spokesman of the whole Church".[10] According to Philip Ziegler, he was also "successful ... at reconciling the demands of church and state".[11]

However, the British authorities were rather wary of Temple. Throughout the war, the Government imposed strict ideological censorship. All known pacifists, including such famous preachers as the Methodist Donald Soper and the Anglican Charles Raven, were not allowed to speak on the radio. Temple was not himself a pacifist, but he was suspect on account of his spirited defence of those who preached conscientious objection, believing that some people had "a special vocation to bear this witness to the unity of all God's family and to the sovereignty of love".[12]

---

[7] Phillips, 24.
[8] Gillard, Frank "Interview with Eric Fenn", BBC Oral History Archive, 4 July 1986. *Hansard*, vol. 370, columns 569-570.
[9] Iremonger, F. A. William Temple, Archbishop of Canterbury, *His Life & Letters*. Oxford University Press, 1948, 540 and 556.
[10] Calder, 482 and 485.
[11] Ziegler, Philip. *London at War*, BCA, 1995, 201.
[12] Temple, William, *Thoughts in Wartime*, Macmillan, 1940, 7.

He was also known for his outspoken presentation of religiously inspired political views and for his leftwing bias. Although these mildly socialist ideas were far from revolutionary, the authorities, particularly after Churchill took over at the helm in May 1940, felt that Temple could not be trusted to keep his political heresies to himself. For example, as recently as August 8 1939, Temple had proclaimed on the radio that: "Christians must try to find their first and deepest fellowship in the great company of believers in Christ, the Christian Church, rather than in their own fellow-countrymen".[13]

This point of view, not surprisingly, did not meet with the Government's approval. Neither did Temple's reminders that Christians are called to love their enemies, nor the call for the "Federal Union of Europe" which he perceived as "the only hope for a permanent settlement"[14] for world peace, and even less the more clearly socialist opinion that "the State ... must undertake the planning of our economic life".[15]

As a result, Churchill's Minister of Information, Duff Cooper, told Parliament that it was "not considered desirable that politics should enter into religious broadcasts".[16] Temple disagreed strongly with this statement. In his sermon "International Justice" in the series *The Hope of a New World*, broadcast in the autumn of 1940 and published a couple of months later, he had already clearly stated that : "... principles of conduct in all departments of life belong to the sphere of religion; for God is supreme over all life and at all points we must obey Him if we have faith in Him".[17] This argument continued for a long time, with Temple seeing the need to remind the BBC Governors again in January 1943 that "neutrality in religion is impossible, because religion covers the whole field of human thought and conduct".[18]

We can assume too that Welch agreed with Temple. He believed that "religion is concerned with man in society, and therefore with politics and economics" and devoted a sermon to this theme at the University of Cambridge in November 1942.[19] He was, however, in a difficult position. Known to be a friend of Temple's, he was employed by the BBC and was obliged to accept and put into practice the directives given him by his superiors.

---

[13] *Ibid.*, p. 5.

[14] *Ibid.*, p. 63.

[15] Temple, William, *The Hope of a New World*, SCM, 1940, 52.

[16] Hansard.

[17] The Hope of a New World, 36.

[18] Letter to BBC.

[19] Welch, Religious Broadcasting.

Long before the argument was over, a compromise was required. The result was somewhat ironically named "The Concordat" and was accepted by the BBC's Central Religious Advisory Committee in October 1941. About ministers of religion, the document stated:

> [they have] no competence to speak on the working out of economic or political issues, but only on the moral and religious principles and criteria by which political and economic situations, proposals and policies should, according to their beliefs, be decided.[20]

A slight concession was made, allowing those religious speakers who were "competent" in politics or economics to make it clear when they spoke on the radio "whether they were speaking as 'experts' or not, and whether their views were 'controversial' or not".[21] It is to be supposed that Temple was included in this category.

In order to enforce this ruling, all sermons or other religious talks had to be submitted in advance, and the speaker was not allowed to deviate from his written text by so much as a word. For example, Welch wrote to William Temple in October 1942 telling him that his Christmas Day sermon would be recorded on December 15 and that the text of "about 800 words" had to be submitted by December 10 at the latest so that the authorities could check its contents. Towards the end of the war, once a positive outcome seemed certain, the Concordat was not always quite so strictly enforced. Temple's D-Day message, directly after the King's speech to the nation, although completely impromptu, was very well received and felt by many to be "a model of what a broadcast address should be".[22]

In spite of these restrictions, it is interesting to note the sheer volume of work Temple agreed to undertake for the BBC, especially after he was enthroned at Canterbury in the spring of 1942. Temple's message to all English-speaking people for Christmas 1942 has already been mentioned. This was broadcast in Britain and in Europe, as well as to the Pacific, African and North American services. At the same time Temple was asked for "a message to the oppressed peoples of Europe", which was to be 400 words long (approximately five minutes) and would be translated into several different languages.[23] He also provided a Christmas address for

---

[20] Phillips, 83.

[21] Briggs, Asa. *The History of Broadcasting in the UK*, vol. 3, The War of Words (1939-45) Oxford University Press, 1970, 623.

[22] Iremonger, 557.

[23] House, Francis. Unpublished letter to William Temple, 23/11/42, Lambeth Palace archives.

"The Church of the Air" on the Canadian Broadcasting network which, at between 1500 and 2000 words, was unusually long for a radio sermon. In addition to these projects for the Religious Broadcasting Department, the Ministry of Information had also asked Temple to write a Christmas message for the British people.

Temple's radio work was not restricted to occasional sermons like these. He also participated in several series of talks by different speakers on political and religious topics, the best known being "The Crisis of the Western World" in July 1943. This series was coordinated by the Master of Balliol, Dr A. D. Lindsay, and included famous speakers from all the main Christian denominations. The Reverend Francis House, another BBC employee, particularly responsible for overseas religious broadcasting, stressed the fact that "each [speaker] was left completely free to treat the subject in accordance with his own convictions". Although this had to be understood in the context of the Concordat, Temple does seem to have been quite outspoken here and even allowed himself to criticise Britain and the United States for their "idolatry of money". [24]

As well as participating with others, Temple also gave several series of talks himself. These varied greatly. The six sermons entitled *The Hope of a New World*, broadcast in September and October 1940, were quite philosophical and applied Christian principles in some detail to the political and ideological problems of the day. On the other hand, the series of eight (possibly nine) five-minute sermons, called "The Archbishop Speaks to the Forces", which were on the air between February and April 1944, were much simpler and more straightforward, not to mention shorter, than those mentioned above. It is interesting to note that the ninth programme in the series, "How a Christian Sees the War", does not appear to have been broadcast. As it contains such controversial statements as "I think the Crusaders were thoroughly wrong" and "You cannot do any positive good by fighting in a war", it is possible that the authorities decided to censor it, although there is no proof of this in the Archbishop's papers. [25] Other, more purely spiritual, series occurred at particular moments in the Church's calendar, like the eight meditations on Christ's words from the cross, delivered every day during Holy Week 1942.

Temple also answered questions sent to the BBC by listeners, particularly from the armed forces and provided particular talks for special occasions, like his commemoration of Abraham Lincoln's birthday for an

---

[24] William,Temple, *The Crisis of the Western World & Other Broadcast Talks*, George Allen & Unwin, 1944. "Good Friday 1944 Postscript", Lambeth Palace archives, vol. 59, 1 and 18.
[25] Lambeth Palace.

American audience in February 1944. He also collaborated with King George VI in the organisation of the various national days of prayer.

Once Temple became Archbishop of Canterbury, and could therefore legitimately claim to be the spokesman of the state Church, it became more difficult for the authorities to censor him. In spite of his official role, the BBC still felt uncomfortable when he advocated particular policies in his talks, even if the policies concerned were entirely inoffensive. The Board of Governors discussed this at their meeting in October 1942, where it was decided that "if this tendency were developed in religious broadcasts, adequate representation should be given to opposite views". Two months later, the Governors indicated that there was a limit to what they would put up with in this domain by vetoing Welch's plans for a series of programmes on religion and politics.[26]

Although the authorities and the press sometimes seemed to believe that Temple spent most of his time talking about politics, Temple always denied this. In answer to a question addressed to him by the Radio Padre, Ronald Selby Wright, Temple insisted: "... five-sixths of my writing and speaking is purely religious, but that doesn't get reported, and when one slips in a solitary political allusion, that is reported by itself as if it were the whole of what one said".[27]

This may have been true of Temple's public speaking in general. However, a considerably higher proportion of his radio sermons refer to political themes, although these always appear in a theological context. The mere fact that Francis House thought it necessary to tell Temple that his Christmas message in 1942 should "be concerned with the religious significance of Christmas rather than any political implications"[28], implies that the BBC were used to Temple mixing religion and politics in his talks. Although he was aware that some people thought that the topics he addressed in his sermons "f[e]ll outside the sphere of religion altogether",[29] he never admitted that any subject at all could do so.

The difficulties in this area seem to come from Temple's own, religiously based, perception of the times he was living in. Soon after his enthronement, he addressed the American people saying that: "The great political issues of our time are in their own nature religious and theological. What this war is really about is the nature and destiny of

---

[26] BBC Board of Governors, *Minutes,* 8/10/42 and 3/12/42.
[27] William Temple, Listener, 20/08/42.
[28] House.
[29] The Hope of a New World, 35.

man".[30] He never changed his mind and, shortly before his death, in a broadcast talk mainly about political freedom, declared that "the reason why power is a problem is to be found not in politics, but in psychology, ethics and theology".[31] The war therefore was, in his opinion, above all "a spiritual war",[32] "a struggle between two incompatible ways of life" and an "opportunity to make a ... Christian civilisation".[33] The reason for this was that the Nazis were not just criminals or ordinary sinners, but idolaters who believed that the State was "an object of supreme allegiance" and therefore "unamenable to any higher authority or law".[34] As a result he considered that "their standards [were] perverted" and, in some issues, "their right [was] our wrong".[35]

If, in Temple's opinion, the war was above all a spiritual conflict, it also had spiritual causes. He wanted his listeners to acknowledge that the war was "a judgement on the Church", showing "how little the Church has penetrated and moulded the civilisation"[36] of Europe over the centuries. It was therefore, to all Christian people, "a call to repent".[37] However, because the spiritual war was started "with an act of aggression", Temple concluded that "earthly weapons [had] to be used".[38] British Christians could be sure of victory, sooner or later, because "it [was] God's cause; and He [would] not let it fail".[39]

In spite of Temple's willingness to sanction the use of armed force, he did not believe that this would ultimately be the deciding factor in the fate of Europe. Most of all, as he saw it, the British people needed "spiritual resources ... to secure the triumph of the cause". From his perspective, the "chief need of England" was to "turn to God".[40] Temple justified this by what he realised would seem to most people "a quite outrageous statement": "This world can be saved from political chaos and collapse by one thing only, and that is worship". [41] He explained this statement by

---

[30] Temple, William, "The Message of the Church Today", 1942, Lambeth Palace archives, vol.59.
[31] Temple, William, "The Pillars of Freedom", recorded on October 8th 1944, Lambeth Palace archives, vol.59.
[32] The Church Looks Forward , 83.
[33] The Hope of a New World, 83 and 65.
[34] Crisis of the Western World, 15.
[35] The Hope of a New World, 11.
[36] Archbishop Speaks to the Forces, 332.
[37] Thoughts in Wartime, 5.
[38] The Church Looks Forward, 83.
[39] The Hope of a New World, 77.
[40] Lambeth Palace Archives, 40 and 340.
[41] The Hope of a New World, 26.

saying that only by worship, spending time in the presence of God, can men and women be changed into the people they need to be to uphold peace, truth and justice in the world. Prayer was also part of this process as, Temple declared: "If those first petitions of the Lord's prayer were fulfilled in Germany today, the war would end tomorrow, for it would involve the renunciation of the whole Nazi philosophy and the aggression which it has inspired".[42]

He made it clear, however, that not only the Nazis would be changed if this prayer were truly answered: "We pray that His Name may be hallowed in all the world – in Russia where men deny it altogether, in Germany where they take it in vain, and in our own country, where our reverence has been half-hearted".[43]

When he was specifically talking about the war, it was quite clear that Temple was applying religious principles to a political situation. However, on several other topics it was not so easy to distinguish the two. Sometimes Temple appeared to be talking about politics when he was in fact explaining a spiritual concept. For example, when Temple said that the Church's "policy looks like appeasement",[44] he was not talking about the British government's attitude to the dictators in the thirties, but was using a political policy that everyone knew about to illustrate the Church's need to fight against the materialistic, compromising attitudes prevalent in society. In the same way, Temple sometimes cited an obvious military truth like this in his sermons:

> ... the amount one English fighting man can do to beat the Germans comes to very little; the amount they can all do if they are unorganised does not come to much; nor acting together if each goes his own way; it is only when we act as an organised body that we can hope to succeed.[45]

His aim, however, was neither political nor military, but religious, as Temple was trying to show how illogical it is for people who claim to be Christian believers not to be active, committed members of the Church.

On the other hand, it is possible to identify several sermons which, at first glance, appear to be wholly religious, but in fact contained political analysis. When talking about Palestine at the time of Christ, Temple pointed out that the Roman empire was bound to fail in the long run as it did "not carry the hearts and will of [its] subjects". He then insisted that

---

[42] *Ibid.*, 35.
[43] The Hope of a New World, 79.
[44] Temple, William, *The Archbishop Speaks to the Forces*, Lambeth Palace archives, vol. 59, 302.
[45] *Ibid.*, 302.

the only type of empire which could ever be indestructible was one which, by love, won "empire over men's hearts and wills".[46] This may be a description of the Kingdom of God, but it was also a clear prediction of the eventual downfall of both the Third Reich and even the British Empire.

Even more subtly, in his series of sermons on Christ's words from the cross, Temple mentioned Israel who "for the sake of its nationalist dream threw away the opportunity of spiritual leadership". He also pointed out that Israel was typical of all civilisations who went "down in ruin when some main feature of [their] life is at variance with the principles of Christ". In the same series, Temple explained that the Romans and Jews of the time "saw no harm" in crucifying Jesus but, on the contrary, "thought it right" to do so. [47] The contemporary political parallels in these and many other examples were not hard to draw, despite the fact that Temple did not once explicitly mention the political situation in this series of sermons.

Although Temple's mix of politics and religion could worry the authorities, there was really very little in what he said that was either original or particularly controversial. He was acceptable to all the different Christian churches, one Free Churchman going so far as to claim that : "… Non-conformists in England do in fact accept you as the spokesman of the whole Church in a way which is quite new in our experience".[48] Although the Roman Catholic authorities could not go quite so far in their acceptance of Temple, he always got on well with them. Cardinal Hinsley was quite happy to share a platform with him or even to issue a joint statement, like for example the open letter they sent to *The Times* in 1941, together with the Archbishop of York and the Moderator of the Free Church Council, entitled "Foundations of Peace – A Christian Basis – Agreement among the Churches".[49] Even politically, nothing Temple said was really new or surprising. Although his ideas were to the left of Churchill's, this was a position Temple shared with the vast majority of the British population at the time, as the 1945 general election would prove. Chips Channon, even further to the right than Churchill, disliked Temple and complained that "he now openly preaches Socialism" (James 337), but friends who were slightly further to the Left, including the Liberal Sir William Beveridge, tended to find his speeches and sermons

---

[46] Temple, William, "Message to English-Speaking People", Christmas 1942, Lambeth Palace archives, vol.59, 132-133.
[47] Temple, William, *Palm Sunday to Easter Day*, SCM Press, London, 1942, 9, 10 and 16.
[48] Calder, 485.
[49] Iremonger, 560.

much too moderate. Angus Calder was undoubtedly right when he referred to Temple's proposals as being, in reality, "the commonplaces of consensus".[50]

Even many of the themes, expressions, images and examples Temple used in his radio sermons did not originate with him. If he presented the war as a spiritual conflict in which the possibility of a Christian civilisation was at stake, Churchill too claimed that "upon this battle depends the survival of Christian civilisation".[51] The King, in his 1939 Christmas broadcast, had also talked about "the cause of Christian civilisation" as that which "binds together my peoples and our gallant and faithful Allies".[52]

Temple also did not hesitate to borrow from other well-known Christian speakers, both in his religious and his political statements. C. S. Lewis, in his famous *Broadcast Talks*, had said of Jesus Christ:

> You must make your choice. Either this man was, and is, the Son of God: or else a madman or something worse. You can shut him up for a fool, you can spit at Him and kill Him as a demon; or you can fall at His feet and call Him Lord and God. But don't let us come with any patronising nonsense about His being a great human teacher. He hasn't left that open to us.[53]

Temple, just over two years later, tackled the same theme in his second series of *The Archbishop Talks to the Forces*, declaring:

> That claim is either true or false. If it is false, he was either a deluded fanatic or else an impostor. He was not a supreme moral and spiritual teacher. If it is true we must serve and worship him as God. The one theory which is contrary to all the evidence is that he was a specifically good man and great religious teacher and no more.[54]

The style was very different, but the argument was obviously the same and there is no doubt that Temple was aware of Lewis's broadcasts and had a copy of the texts in his library.

It is also possible to find similarities between parts of Temple's sermons and the religious speeches and articles of the well-known writer Dorothy L. Sayers. This is all the more surprising as Sayers is known to have voted Conservative. However, on spiritual questions they had very

---

[50] Calder, 482.

[51] Churchill, Winston. "Their Finest Hour", 18/06/40.

[52] Bradford, Sarah. *George VI*. Harper Collins, 1991, 409.

[53] Lewis, C. S. *Broadcast Talks*, Geoffrey Bles, 1942, 51.

[54] The Archbishop Speaks to the Forces, 323.

similar ideas. For instance, Sayers wrote in the Sunday Times in April 1938: "'Why doesn't God smite this dictator dead?' is a question a little remote from us. Why, Madam, did He not strike you dumb and imbecile before you uttered that baseless and unkind slander the day before yesterday?"[55] Six years later, Temple wrote in a script for a broadcast talk: "Why should God intervene to stop [the war] and not intervene to stop anyone of us saying a spiteful thing about our neighbour?"[56]

In the same way, both Temple and Sayers condemned societies which accepted "the authority of Economics as absolute" and spoke in much the same way about original sin and the necessity of dogma. For both, the Nazi ideology was a false religion: "the ancient mystical, persecuting religion of blood and race"[57] otherwise known as "the creed and practice of barbarism", which "has been believed and practised by more persons and over a longer period of time"[58] than any other religion. In the winter of 1939 both were talking about their desire to establish what Sayers calls "a United States of Europe"[59] and Temple "the Federal Union of Europe";[60] but then the ideas of both on this subject can be found in William Beveridge's pamphlet, *Peace by Federation*, which Temple recommended to his listeners in a later radio sermon.[61]

Lewis and Sayers are by no means the only possible sources of ideas for Temple's sermons. Reading through the wartime sermons and writings of Free Churchmen like Nathaniel Micklem, J.H. Oldham or John Whale, as well as Anglicans like Cyril Garbett, Donald MacKinnon and even George Bell, anyone who has studied Temple's radio sermons in detail keeps meeting ideas and expressions he has seen before. Usually the other writer or preacher's contribution pre-dates Temple's.

James Welch claimed that the broadcaster in wartime was faced with a dilemma: "How ...[to] be true to the word of the living God of all the nations and at the same time meet the needs and anxieties of a nation responding to the demands of total war". He was also concerned "not to broadcast anything of which we ... might be ashamed when war passions subside". [62] For Welch, considering the number of times he asked Temple

---

[55] Sayers, Dorothy L. "The Triumph of Easter", *The Sunday Times,* 17/04/38.
[56] The Archbishop Speaks to the Forces, 332.
[57] Sayers, Dorothy L., *Begin Here,* Victor Gollancz, 1940, 73 and 127.
[58] The Crisis of the Western World, 15.
[59] Begin Here, 151.
[60] Thoughts in Wartime, 63.
[61] The Hope of a New World, 45.
[62] Welch, *Year Book,* 41 and 42.

to preach on the radio, and his dependence on him to find the right word in times of crisis like D-Day, Temple could be relied upon to take up that challenge faithfully. But then, Welch and Temple had the same priorities.

It is not, however, surprising that the authorities did not share Dr Welch's enthusiasm, as it was clear from the start that Temple was not going to toe the official line. In a war where the British government was committed to bringing about the total defeat of the enemy, there could not always be a harmonious relationship with a man who showed that he was fighting for even higher stakes, by declaring that:

> The world seeks victories in which one party experiences the bitterness of defeat; but God who is Love can be content only with the victory which wins enemies for friends so that they rejoice in their own defeat.[63]

Yet, Temple succeeded more than most in inspiring his fellow countrymen in the war effort without compromising the Christian message and, according to Iremonger, "from almost every European country messages reached Temple thanking him for his broadcast addresses and prayers" (Iremonger 558). It is certainly at least partly due to these same broadcast sermons that, as Philip Ziegler points out: "... the Church emerged with enhanced credit" (Ziegler 203) from the war. However, if Temple managed to achieve the delicate balance between religion and politics in the difficult years between 1939 and 1944, it could be argued that he completely failed to find another kind of equilibrium. His premature death in October 1944 was undoubtedly hastened by overwork and the peculiar stress of the extremely demanding role he took upon himself at a time of national crisis. His best-selling work today, often referred to as "William Temple's lasting message" (Heath 3) is *Christianity & the Social Order*, a book where politics and religion are inextricably mixed. In Temple's thought, they could never truly be separated.

Works Cited

Achebe, Chinua.
     www.guyanaundersiege.com/Literature/Interview%20with20Achebe.htm
Anon. *The Daily Telegraph*, 12/10/96.
BBC Board of Governors, *Minutes*, 8/10/42.
Bradford, Sarah. *George VI*. Harper Collins, 1991.

---

[63] Palm Sunday to Easter Day, 34.

Briggs, Asa. *The History of Broadcasting in the UK*, vol. 3, The War of Words,(1939-45) Oxford University Press, 1970.

Calder, Angus. *The People's War*. London: Pimlico, 1992.

Churchill, Winston. "Their Finest Hour", 18/06/40, http://www.historyplace.com/speeches/churchill-hour.htm

Gillard, Frank "Interview with Eric Fenn", BBC Oral History Archive, 4 July 1986. *Hansard*, vol. 370, columns 569-570.

Heath, Edward. Foreword to William TEMPLE, *Christianity & the Social Order,* Shepheard-Walwyn, 1976.

House, Francis. Unpublished letter to William Temple, 23/11/42, Lambeth Palace archives.

Iremonger, F. A. William Temple, Archbishop of Canterbury, *His Life & Letters*. Oxford University Press, 1948.

James R. Rhodes (ed.). *The Diaries of Sir Henry Channon,* Weidenfeld & Nicholson, 1967.

Lewis, C. S. *Broadcast Talks*, Geoffrey Bles, 1942.

Lockhart, J. G. *Cosmo Gordon Lang*, Hodder & Stoughton, 1949.

Phillips, Justin. *C.S. Lewis at the BBC*, Harper Collins, 2002.

Sayers, Dorothy L. "The Triumph of Easter", *The Sunday Times,* 17/04/38.

—. *Begin Here*, Victor Gollancz, 1940.

Temple, William. *The Church Looks Forward*, Macmillan, 1944.

—. *Thoughts in Wartime*, Macmillan, 1940.

—. The Hope of a New World, SCM, 1940.

—. Letter to the BBC, 15/01/43.

—. *The Crisis of the Western World & Other Broadcast Talks*, George Allen & Unwin, 1944. "Good Friday 1944 Postscript", Lambeth Palace archives, vol. 59.

—. "Message to English-Speaking People", Christmas 1942, Lambeth Palace archives, vol.59.

—. "Service of Intercession for China" (08/07/42), Lambeth Palace archives, vol. 59.

—. *The Archbishop Speaks to the Forces*, Lambeth Palace archives, vol. 59.

—. "The Message of the Church Today", 1942, Lambeth Palace archives, vol.59.

—. "The Pillars of Freedom", recorded on October 8th 1944, Lambeth Palace archives, vol.59.

—. *Palm Sunday to Easter Day*, SCM Press, London, 1942.

—. The Listener, 20/08/42.

Welch, James W. "Religious Broadcasting in Wartime", *BBC Year Book 1945*, BBC, 1945.

—. unpublished letter to William Temple, 10/10/42, in the Lambeth Palace archives.

—. "Broadcasting Policy", No.6, *Religious Broadcasting*, February 1943.

Ziegler, Philip. *London at War*, BCA, 1995.

CHAPTER THIRTEEN

MINI SERMONS IN A SECULAR WORLD? BBC4 "THOUGHTS FOR THE DAY" AND THE WAR IN IRAQ.

SERGE AUFFRET

A typical "Thought for the Day" on BBC Radio 4 usually lasts about two minutes and forty seconds. This paper will take longer to read, though I, like one of the heroes of *Sense and Sensibility*, appreciate my sermons short. *Thought for the Day*–or *TftD* for short[1]–is meant to be "a moment for inspiration" produced by the Religion and Ethics Department of the BBC, six days a week.[2] Broadcast live both on LW and FM at 7.53 am, a prime time slot within the *Today* programme, *TftD*, though very short, is one of the high profile elements of BBC Radio 4 religious programming, which includes such productions as *Sunday*, the *Sunday Worship*, or the *Daily Service*.

In a recent campaign to open *TftD* to non-religious voices[3], the executive Director of the National Secular Society said:

> The promotion of religion in such a high-profile slot ... is unacceptable on a public broadcasting body that is supposedly serving the entire community. This *TftD* slot ... enjoys a captive peak-time audience far greater than would listen to the programme if it were scheduled away from the popular *Today* programme.

---

[1] The term "Thought" will be used to refer to the individual contributions, while *TftD* will refer to the BBC programme.
[2] Scripts and audio files available at
http://www.bbc.co.uk/religion/programmes/thought/
[3] Conducted by the British Humanist Association, the National Secular Society and the Rationalist Press Association.

The series producer answered "This short strand is unique, offering a faith perspective within a news programme. If we include secular voices, we undermine the slot's very distinctiveness."[4] The controversy raged from August 2002 to July 2003, and resumed in 2005 as the BBC Charter was being reviewed by the House of Lords.[5]

A highly sensitive religious programme on the most sensitive issue of participation in the Iraq war, does *TftD* fall under the category of the editorial, the commentary on a news item? Or can "Thoughts" qualify as sermons? To answer those questions, this study will focus upon both the speakers and the listeners on the *"God slot"*; it will then analyse the messages the speakers convey in relation to war and peace, and finally, how they engage their audience and what techniques they choose to use or not to use, to determine whether the essential features of a sermon can indeed be found in the typical *"Thought."*

The 105 "Thoughts" form two parallel corpora – Corpus 1, 51 "Thoughts" on terrorism, the Middle East, peace and conflict; Corpus 2, 54 "Thoughts" on war and Iraq. The period of reference is August 16, 2002 to June 11, 2003.[6] This spans first the run-up to the war in Iraq; it begins with from the publications in early August of the Bishop of Oxford's article in the *Guardian* (entitled "This war would not be a just war"[7]) and of the pacifist "Christian Declaration"[8] (signed by the Archbishop of Canterbury and stating that "an attack on Iraq would be both immoral and illegal") and ends with the vote in Parliament authorising the use of force on March 18. The period encompasses the war itself, which began on March 20, 2003 and officially ended, according to President George W. Bush, on May 1 when he declared the end of "major combat operations". Finally, it ends with the war's immediate aftermath.

---

[4] http://www.secularism.org.uk/newspress/news05sep02t.htm (accessed April 11, 2005).

[5] House of Lords Select Committee on BBC Charter Review, 2nd Report of Session 2005-06, *Further Issues for BBC Charter Review*, March 3, 2006, HL Paper 128-I, p. 40.

[6] References to individual *"Thoughts"* will therefore only mention the date and the month, 'August' or 'December' necessarily being August and December 2002, and 'January' or 'June,' January and June 2003.

[7] Richard Harries, August 4, 2002:
http://observer.guardian.co.uk/iraq/story0,12239,769010,00.html

[8] "The Morality and Legality of a War against Iraq–A Christian Declaration," Pax Christi, August 6, 2002.

A controversial programme?

Paul Donovan, author of *All our Todays*,[9] in which he reviews the first forty years of the programme, writes of *TftD*: "it is hard to think of any three minutes in the whole of British broadcasting which is more sensitive."[10] There should be nothing controversial about the BBC's Religion and Ethics Department output, if the BBC lives up to its ambitions as expressed in its Religion Editorial Principles:

> The BBC respects the fundamental human right to exercise freedom of thought, conscience and religion, this includes an individual's freedom to worship, teach, practise and observe. At the same time, we recognise our duty to protect the vulnerable and avoid unjustified offence or likely harm. We aim to achieve this by ensuring our output is not used to denigrate the beliefs of others.[11]

We will ensure that the beliefs and practices of the great world faiths are described accurately and impartially. We will ensure the religious views and beliefs of an individual, a religion or religious denomination are not misrepresented, abused or discriminated against, as judged against generally accepted standards.[12]

The study of the formation of public opinion and the nature and extent of the influence of "opinion-makers" admittedly all remain delicate issues. Can the impact of *TftD* on public opinion be measured? No figures for Britain are available, but a comparison with the US, where the place of religion in public and private life is arguably greater than in the UK, may prove enlightening. A nation-wide survey conducted between 13 March and 16 March 2003[13] suggested US media greatly influenced people's opinions on war in Iraq, while religious leaders comparatively did not. What makes *TftD* unique, and such a priority target for secularists–in contrast to other Religion and Ethics Department output–may precisely be

---

[9] Paul Donovan: *All Our Todays: Forty Years of Radio 4's "Today" Programme*, London: Jonathan Cape, 1997; quoted in George Austin "I never listen to Thought for the Day on BBC Radio 4," http://trushare.com/88SEP02/SE02MEDI.htm.

[10] cf *Religion Impartiality Review*
http://www.bbcgovernors.co.uk/docs/reviews/religion_impartiality.html.

[11] http://www.bbc.co.uk/guidelines/editorialguidelines/edguide/religion/index.shtml

[12] http://www.bbc.co.uk/guidelines/editorialguidelines/edguide/religion/religionedit ori.shtml

[13] *"Different Faiths, Different Messages ; Americans Hearing About Iraq from the Pulpit, but Religious Faith not Defining Options,"* March 19, 2003 Pew Forum on Religion in Public Life, Pew Research Center For The People and The Press http://www.pewtrusts.com/pdf/pew_forum_poll_0303.pdf.

the fact that *TftD* contributors, because they are speaking within a prime time news programme, appear to be given enhanced status as "opinion-makers".

The *TftD* speakers

The list of *TftD* contributors reads a little like an excerpt from *"Who's Who in Religion,"* with the Anglican Church contributing its two serving archbishops, Rowan Williams (Canterbury), and David Hope (York),[14] and three serving bishops, Richard Harries (Oxford), Tom Butler (Southwark), and the late Jim Thompson (1936-2003, Bath and Wells); with also one former President of the Methodist Conference, now a member of the House of Lords, Leslie Griffiths; the General Director of the Evangelical Alliance, Joel Edwards; the Chief Rabbi, Jonathan Sacks; and a senior representative of Sikhism, Dr Indarjit Singh. Infrequent *TftD* contributors, the Archbishop of Canterbury, Rowan Williams, and the Archbishop of Westminster, Cardinal Cormac Murphy-O'Connor, both chose to speak and write on Iraq elsewhere, in more official and solemn form.[15]

How are *TftD* speakers chosen? The decision to invite someone to speak on the programme rests solely with the *TftD* editors. Religious credentials come first; non-clerical contributors have either made their names in the media or the world of broadcasting or culture, or achieved recognition in the academic world. Of the 105 "Thoughts" by 31 speakers, 71 were delivered by clerics (72 if one includes in the category US imam Hamza Yusuf), 42 were delivered by speakers with major present or past professional involvement in the world of the media, broadcasting and culture, 37 by speakers with similar involvement in the academic field or the world of education. Two former Heads of BBC Religious Broadcasting, the Reverends Colin Morris and David Winter; one senior BBC Wales presenter and contributor, the Reverend Roy Jenkins; Lavinia Byrne, a BBC Religion presenter of the *Daily Service*, broadcaster and

---

[14] Rowan Williams's only *"Thought"* over the period was delivered on the first anniversary of the September 11, 2001 attacks; David Hope's, on April 17, to advocate the rapid transfer of power to the Iraqis.

[15] See for instance the Catholic and Anglican Archbishops' Joint Statement on Iraq of February 20, 2003:
http://www.rcdow.org.uk/cardinal/default.asp?content_ref=87   and   the   Joint Statement by the Archbishops of Canterbury and York on conflict with Iraq of March 20, 2003,
http://www.archbishopofcanterbury.org/releases/2003/030320.html.

former Roman Catholic sister; the Reverend Angela Tilby, a former broadcaster; or Rabbi Lionel Blue, a popular writer and broadcaster, are regulars on the programme. Some contributors are double-or triple-hatted, like Jonathan Sacks, author, broadcaster and Professor.

TftD was opened to representatives from all the major faiths several years ago. Academic credentials, an especially important sign of success and integration in British society for speakers from religious minorities, account for the selection of Drs Mona Siddiqui, Abdal Hakim Murad, and Jeevan Singh Deol. Speakers Satish Kumar, for Jainism and Buddhism, and Shagufta Yaqub, editor of the Muslim magazine Q-News, and by far the youngest member of the panel–she was 27 in 2003–achieved recognition with the media.

Whether they are young and upcoming or whether they have the benefit of age and experience–the vast majority of the panel–most of the speakers clearly belong to the Establishment, either figuratively or in the proper sense of the word. The proportion of women, or that of speakers under the age of 40, is low, not a surprising finding for a "community" bearing the hallmarks of the Establishment. Several contributors are distinguished citizens, members of various boards or commissions. Whatever one's status, being asked to speak on *TftD* brings social recognition as much as it acknowledges personal success.

How representative are the speakers of religious diversity in Britain? If the results of the April 2001 Census are taken as a reference, with the reservation made by Scotland's Chief Statistician that the single question asked in England and Wales does not make it possible to distinguish between "religion of upbringing" and "religion practised,"[16] the proportions of *"Thoughts"* from Christians and Hindus are in line with the Census figures. The absence of atheist or agnostic speakers on this religious programme means that the Muslim speakers, the Sikhs, the Jews and the Buddhists obtain a much larger share than the proportion they actually represent in the population. Overall, a rather skilful balance is achieved, as the table below suggests. Given the international and religious context, the choices made by the editors seem easy to defend. The *TftD* editors looked for Muslim or non-violent perspectives on potential, then actual war in Iraq. Similarly, regular contributors Lionel Blue and Jonathan Sacks or Jim Thompson were likely to have interesting things to say on the Middle East and the issue of war and peace. On the outbreak of war, it made sense–in the interest of inter-faith harmony–to

---

[16] http://www.scotland.gov.uk/stats/bulletins/00398.pdf.

have representatives of the three major faiths speaking successively on March 21, 22 and 23.

DISTRIBUTION OF "THOUGHTS FOR THE DAY" COMPARED WITH APRIL 2001 CENSUS RELIGION DATA

RELIGION	% of British population	% of total "Thoughts"	Corpus 2 Iraq "Thoughts"		Corpus 1 "Thoughts"		Total
			Number	%	number	%	
Christian	71.6	68.6	37	68.5	35	68.6	72
Church of England	n/a	. . .	24	. . .	22	. . .	46
			2	. . .	1	. . .	3
Church of Scotland	n/a	. . .					
			7	. . .	8	. . .	14
Methodist	n/a	. . .					
Evangelical	n/a	. . .	2	. . .	1	. . .	3
Roman Catholic	n/a	. . .	2	. . .	3	. . .	5
Muslim	2.7	9.5	6	11.1	4	7.8	10
Hindu	1.0	1.9	1	1.8	1	2	2
Sikh	0.6	6.7	4	7.4	3	5.9	7
Jewish	0.5	9.5	3	5.6	7	13.7	10
Buddhist	0.3	3.8	3	5.6	1	2	4
Total	76.7	100	54	100	51	100	105

How representative are the speakers within their own faith group? While the question seems pointless for such eminent clergymen and authors as Richard Harries and Rowan Williams, who additionally have always made defence a special interest, or for Jonathan Sacks, it is worth asking with respect to lay people, or in the case of faith groups with no visible religious hierarchy. The choice as a speaker for Hinduism of Akhandadi Das, a leading member of ISKCON, the International Society for Krishna Consciousness, also known as the Hare Krishna movement, which gained recognition with mainline Hinduism in recent years, may be an indirect statement on British Hinduism. Without prejudging the vexed issue of who is representative of Islam in Britain, invited to speak were two Muslim women, Dr Mona Siddiqui and Shagufta Yaqub, and two converts, Dr Abdal Hakim Murad and American visitor–and adviser to President Bush–Hamza Yusuf, all younger than such senior figures of Islam in Britain as Iqbal Sacranie or Zaki Badawi, frequently interviewed on the BBC, who are not *TftD* contributors.

So who are the panel's *TftD* contributors ultimately? In keeping with BBC Religion editorial principles, all *TftD* participants share the conviction that inter-faith and ecumenical dialogue in the United Kingdom is an essential value. Though one should be wary of "pigeon-holing" people and exaggerating the "political" type approach to religious matters, the speakers also share a predominantly "liberal" rather than "orthodox" or "conservative" brand of religion. This is true across the board for all faith groups concerned, from the largest, the Church of England, to the smallest, the Buddhists and Hindus. The Roman Catholic speakers, lay people Clifford Longley and Dr Lavinia Byrne, a former sister, are both critical of their Church's positions and authorities. Lionel Blue described himself as "a very reformed Rabbi". The Muslim, Buddhist or Hindu speakers are also mainly "liberal" as opposed to "orthodox," or, at least, their "Britishness" means that they do not subscribe to the more radical version of their religions.

The *TftD* audience

What can we know about the *Today* programme's audience, and therefore *TftD* listeners? According to the radio ratings operation RAJAR study[17] whose data is relevant to our period, the 5-million listener average audience is a good cross section of British society and opinion, with 13% of *Guardian* readers, 17% of *Daily Telegraph* readers, 14% of *Daily Mail* readers, except that it only includes under 4% of readers of *the Sun*. *Today* programme listeners look for serious comment and reliable information. They are often difficult to please and eager for quality reporting and

---

[17] Quoted in the *New Statesman*, January 12, 2004.
http://www.newstatesman.com/People/200401120019

analysis. Sample comments from the period 3 November 2004 to 4 April 2005 show that they often listen to, or read, the "Thoughts" with attention, and react critically or appreciatively.[18] Main criticisms depict the latest "Thought" as "arrogant"–often for daring to say "we" and to speak in the listeners' names; "patronising", "tedious", or possibly "pompous". But overall, reactions are positive and even grateful–the "Thought" was "brilliant", "penetrating", "timely," "relevant". It "helped [the listener] take a few moments respite from a very busy day"; was "well thought out", "helpful", "memorable", "powerful", "passionate"; its "punchline was brilliant". And sometimes it met its ultimate goal–it was "thought-provoking", "inspiring", "uplifting" and "heartwarming"–"a breath of fresh air" which "stayed with [the listener] all day".

Producing the programme

In what conditions is the programme produced? The conditions in which "Thoughts" are prepared have an impact on the content. Speakers often have little time to prepare. This reduces the risk that their "Thought" might be "stale like the proverbial 'yesterday's newspaper'," a risk associated with recording in advance. But the days seem to be gone when a "Thought" could literally have been written on the back of an envelope on board a taxi to BBC studios after the papers were read on the way.

The conditions in which a "Thought" is preserved today on the BBC's web site, with the sound file made available almost immediately, and the script five days later, may induce an enhanced sense of responsibility, and the feeling that *TftD* contributions could no longer be so ephemeral as they used to be.

Once the speakers have prepared their script, they submit their "Thought" in advance, but the only advice they get from BBC staff will normally concern delivery, not content. The BBC supposedly does not edit what it broadcasts, though claims of attempts at "blue-pencilling" have occasionally been made.[19] The most spectacular episode was the removal (after a vigorous protest campaign) from the BBC's web site, with apologies, of the script and sound file of a controversial "Thought" by John Bell on Israel which included factual errors with serious deontological implications.[20]

---

[18] http://www.bbc.co.uk/religion/programmes/thought/comments.shtml; the blog goes back about six months.
[19] George Austin "I never listen ..." *idem.*
[20] http://www.bbc.co.uk/religion/programmes/thought/documents/t20030222.shtml.

Typical challenges for *TftD* contributors

They are essentially of two types of challenges for *TftD* contributors. First, did the speaker maintain the appropriate distance with events, while at the same time establishing a credible connection with the news? Are religious people in a position to speak on world events, foreign policy and defence issues? The concept underlying a *"Thought"* is that a connection should be established between what is happening, what will shortly happen, or, more frequently, what has just happened, and a deeper understanding of, or perspective on, events. It is standard practice for speakers to start with a reference to a recent development in the news and to establish a connection with a given passage from their religious tradition's sacred texts.

Second, did the speaker find the appropriate ways and means in terms of content, and language and rhetoric used? The final result should be neither of the proselytising or controversial type; nor should it resort to the "bland," facile, "smallest common denominator" approach that shocks nobody but bores everybody. More than a few *"Thoughts"* do not rise to the occasion in this respect.

The claim that too many *"Thoughts"* border on the "trite",[21] are "utterly predictable" and "Religion Lite" is sometimes heard; some even claim that "no slot on the BBC does a better job of taking God out of religion."[22] But criticism of *TftD* also comes from opposite quarters, as George Austin mentions "'religious absolutists' objecting to what they see as [*TftD's*] 'soggy liberal propaganda'".[23]

The speakers definitely find themselves between a rock and a hard place, for if they adopt a consensual, smallest common denominator approach, they will be blamed for being predictable, bland, boring, or even for betraying their ministry: "Message to Joel Edwards, leader of Britain's evangelical Christians: 2 thoughts for the day in 2 weeks– and not a word about Jesus! 2 missed opportunities!" a listener protested on 12 January 2005. Either secularists find fault with them, arguing that a humanist point of view might as well have been presented by humanists themselves. Or, if the religious speakers adopt a more challenging or outspoken approach, they run the risk of being denounced as proselytising or intolerant. And

---

[21] Leader, *The Independent*, quoted on
http://www.secularism.org.uk/newspress/news05sep02t.htm.
[22] Editorial, *The Daily Telegraph, op. cit.*
[23] "I never listen ..." *idem.*

indeed the secularists talk of "the Radio 4 homily slot" featuring "religionists" pouring out their "religious propaganda".[24]

Unsurprisingly, speakers from traditions other than Christianity benefit from their "otherness" in this respect, with the advantage they have of bringing to the slot "fresh" spiritual or cultural elements unknown to a British audience. For them, the challenge lies elsewhere, as in their effort to reconcile their religion and Britishness, they may displease their original "religious constituency," or become no longer representative. Alternatively, they may fail to connect with a wider audience if they remain too "parochial".

Key concepts in Corpus 1 *"Thoughts"*: a doctrine of unanimous British religion?

It should be noted that, though the speakers and listeners may feel directly concerned, Britain was not directly involved as a nation here. In dealing with terrorism, the Middle East, peace and conflict in the world, the focus was on what the religions have in common, what they share. The use of the words "we", "our", "us" is central and refers to the alleged common approach, or purpose, of the various religions, including also the common humanity shared with non-believers. One could term this kind of deliberate respect for another religious tradition's values and heritage the "spirit of Assisi." Initiated, but not claimed exclusively, by the Roman Catholic Church, the "spirit of Assisi" can best be defined by the search for peace, and the generous mutual respect witnessed in the three inter-religious meetings that took place there on three occasions (1986, 1999 and 2002). In a sense, to paraphrase what was said of Assisi and prayer, it could be argued that *TftD* is a forum where the various speakers "do not teach together, but are together to teach."

Two conflicting views of religion are identified: religions may insist on enmity, or they may adopt a positive attitude[25] As Alan Billings put it, "It is possible to find in all the great religious traditions, resources that encourage inclusiveness and reaching out, or intolerance and turning in."[26] This was most forcefully expressed by Jonathan Sacks on November 29:

> You can see religion as a battle, a holy war, in which you win a victory for your faith by force or fear. Or you can see it as a candle you light to drive away some of the darkness of the world. The difference is that the first sees

---

[24] http://www.secularism.org.uk/newspress/news18aug2t.htm.
[25] August 20; November 29.
[26] May 5.

other religions as the enemy. The second sees them as other candles, not threatening mine, but adding to the light we share.

Mona Siddiqui agreed: "I very much believe faith speaks to faith, that people of different religions do not have to agree with each other but still possess the sensibilities for genuine mutual respect."[27]

Solidarity among men and women of good will is seen as having immense value. Highly symbolic gestures are made in highly symbolic places, like "Ground Zero" in New York:

> Earlier this year, writes Jonathan Sacks, I stood at Ground Zero, together with leaders of the world's great faiths. The Archbishop of Canterbury said a prayer. So did a Muslim imam. The Chief Rabbi of Israel read a reflection. A Hindu sprinkled holy water from the Ganges. And I was struck by the sheer dissonance between this coming together of faiths in peace and the terrible religious extremism that stalks our world. Religion, I knew then, is like fire. It warms, but it also burns, and we are the guardians of the flame.

He goes on to say: "God has made many faiths and many civilisations but only one world in which to live together". Equally emblematic was the meeting at Jerusalem's *Dominus Flevit* (the Lord wept) church between three friends, a Palestinian Anglican from East Jerusalem, a Jew, and the Reverend Rob Marshall, giving rise to an "epiphany": "Standing and looking out over the Holy City with my two friends at *Dominus Flevit* – taking in the Golden Dome mosque, the spire of the Holy Sepulchre Church, the Western Wall, it was a moment of intense solidarity".[28]

The various religions share essential values on the best way to achieve peace, and trust these values are universal and acceptable by humanists. For Akhandadi Das, there is an element of the divine in every man.[29] The Christians and Jews agree, seeing this as the result of man's being created in God's image. David Winter insists this very dignity of man should be an obstacle to mindless violence.[30] As Indarjit Singh put it, following the police raid on the fundamentalist Finsbury Park mosque: "Today, it is more important than ever before to ensure that our holy places of worship are used positively to teach us the need for responsibility, tolerance and sensitivity to our fellow beings, of all faiths and persuasions."[31] Tellingly, in many cases, it would be impossible to guess to which religion the

---

[27] August 13.
[28] January 30.
[29] October 29.
[30] December 21.
[31] January 21.

author of the quotation belongs. To promote peace and understanding, an essential value on which *TftD* contributors agree is humility.[32]

One may wonder whether this picture of present relations between religions is not somewhat idyllic or irenical. But all disagreement did not disappear, though it was a rare occurrence. Roy Jenkins used a very strong word, blasphemy, "the blasphemy that this [a suicide operation by Chechen rebels] was being done 'for the sake of God' ".[33] On May 14, following suicide bomb attacks in Riyadh, Jim Thompson stressed the difference: "But suicide is not martyrdom, nor is killing innocent people a true sign of any faith. The contrast with Jesus is striking–he entered the cauldron, refused armed help, died in gentleness of spirit, giving his life for humankind–a true martyr for God".

In conclusion, several caveats are useful. Unanimity does not necessarily make for interesting dialogue; the speakers may only be representative of a certain elite; depending on which religion, culture or country is involved, words like "tolerance" or "freedom of religion" may be misnomers. Having said that, it seems that rather than seeking the smallest common denominator–a reductionist and impoverishing approach–*TftD* contributors search for consensus, diversity and complementary points of view, "candles adding to the light we share", in the words of the Chief Rabbi. The consensus is on traditional Christian virtues like hope, humility, love of neighbour, selflessness, justice, goodness, compassion, trust, mercy, forgiveness, patience, restraint, moderation, loyalty, obedience, sharing, the belief in a merciful God, the importance of prayer. Values important for humanists are also seen as essential, like solidarity, faith in progress, the belief in human rights, the refusal to read sacred texts in a narrow-minded or "fundamentalist" way, the idea that freedom of conscience is essential, that the truth cannot be imposed, and that religious pluralism and multiculturalism are good things. Arrogance, self-righteousness, theocracy, the holding of Manichean views of the world and the belief in "holy" war typify what *TftD* speakers reject. While much of this makes *TftD* speakers predictable, the virtual community that they form, the assumptions that they agree to share are typical of a kind of new vulgate, a joint interpretation of how religions can live together in secularised Western European societies.

---

[32] *eg* Mona Siddiqui, August 20; Roy Jenkins, October 26; Jim Thompson, November 19.
[33] October 26.

Corpus 2– Iraq "Thoughts" in context

The impression that Saddam Hussein was constantly playing for time, and would only cooperate when the credible threat of the use of force was wielded, led some *TftD* contributors opposed to a potential war to have doubts and lend a more welcoming ear to the arguments of the government. Key elements in the developing debate however were the negative impression produced by the government's September 2002 dossier on Iraqi weapons of mass destruction; the unconvincing nature of the evidence presented by Secretary of State Powell to the United Nations; the massive demonstrations on 15 February; the controversy surrounding the necessity or absence of necessity of a second UN resolution; and the resignation of the Leader of the House of Commons, Robin Cook on the eve of the vote of 396/217 in favour of the government's policy in the House of Commons on March 18. Operations *Iraqi Freedom*, for the Americans, and *Telic 1*, for the British side, started two days later.

Over the period, the Anglican and the Roman Catholic Church leaders increasingly acknowledged the fact that the decision ultimately rested with the executive, that "the moral alternative to military action [could not] be inaction, passivity, appeasement or indifference". They also insisted on the necessary role of the United Nations and expressed hopes for "peace with justice [in] Iraq and the Middle East". The non-violent, pacifist, or anti-war movements had clearly been unable to win the public opinion war.

There was a direct correlation between how events unfolded on the international scene and how often Iraq was the main subject of a *"Thought"*, with a peak in the three months of February, March and April 2003. The Iraq war greatly strained community relations in Britain, and the necessity to think rapidly posed a specific challenge to the contributor trying to find the correct distance with events. The Archbishop of Canterbury did not speak on *TftD,* but took the time to ponder the new situation, and then, after producing a joint statement with the Archbishop of York on March 20 and a solemn Joint Statement by Religious Leaders on conflict with Iraq the next day, he wrote in the *Times* the important article entitled "Weaknesses and moral inconsistency led us to war".[34]

---

[34] March 25, 2003;
http://www.archbishopofcanterbury.org/sermons_speeches/2003/030325.html.

Key concepts in Corpus 2 *"Thoughts"*

Given the highly sensitive nature of the issue of war with Iraq, was there a search for consensus similar to the one witnessed on general issues of war, peace and terrorism? Cross-religious references, with a speaker quoting from another culture or religion, virtually disappeared, a sign that in times of extreme tension one tends to turn to one's own tradition and identity. In this grave context, *TftD* speakers did not use words lightly. Dr Charles Reed, the International Policy Advisor for the Church of England's Archbishop's Council distinguishes two roles: the advisory role, which the Anglican and Catholic Churches tried to assume; and the campaigning, or protest, role.[35] Diversity within the Church of England was reflected early on by Elaine Storkey's eloquent advocacy of peace from a non-violent, possibly pacifist perspective and her rejection of "enlisting God": "'Before God the nations are like a drop in a bucket... Before him, they are as nothing.' God is not on any nation's side, however big it is, or however much it thinks it has God in its pocket".[36] But the pronouncements made on *TftD* were consistent with the "main line" held by the Church or faith group to which the speaker belonged. Campaigning was not acceptable under the BBC's editorial guidelines, and Professor Schmidt-Leukel and his colleagues remind us that "just war" theory exists in virtually all the major religions.[37] So, except in the case of Satish Kumar, it was the just war criteria that shaped the debate, not pacifism or non-violence. Initially, almost every speaker opposed the war or expressed serious reservations based on the fact that just war criteria were not met. All the major questions, reservations, or nuances expressed by civil society at the time, whether in Parliament or in the media, found an echo on *TftD*. The "pacificist" approach identified by Professor Martin Ceadel invokes just war criteria, but insists that just war requirements cannot be met in today's world. Can the majority of *TftD* contributors be called pacifists? Probably not; rather, prudence and restraint were the norm, with several speakers expressing how difficult it was for them to decide which attitude to adopt.

Any significant departure from the overall consensus or BBC guidelines is of particular interest. *TftD* contributors rarely ever made openly political pronouncements. It was generally assumed that trusting the government was both a necessary premise in a democracy, and a

---

[35] *Just War?*, London: SPCK, 2004.
[36] Elaine Storkey, August 16 and 30, quoting Isaiah, 40, 15; March 17.
[37] cf *War and Peace in World Religions*, Perry Schmidt-Leukel ed., London: SCM Press, 2004.

religious requirement. But Indarjit Singh wrote: "It's no secret that leading members of President Bush's cabinet, including the President himself, have extensive personal interests in the oil industry." On February 15, in a rare call to demonstrate, Satish Kumar said: "Those who are walking today can be proud that they are following a great tradition of peace-makers".

As war was becoming imminent, consensus was put to the test. In two successive "Thoughts" on March 17, on the eve of the vote in the Commons, and March 18, a few hours before the Commons debate and vote, Elaine Storkey's call to patience was directly answered by Alan Billings's "The time for patience has simply run out". It was only from then on that voices clearly in favour of war began to be heard on the programme.

To act as bridge-builders, Abdal Hakim Murad and Shagufta Yaqub attempted to be true to the strong feelings of British Muslims; one controversially suggested on February 12 that the victorious West may be converted by the vanquished, as when Baghdad was invaded by the Moghol, while the other, insisting on her British education, warned on March 12 against a possible backlash in the British Muslim community, and, drawing a parallel with the battle of Karbala, added that in case of injustice "the collective Muslim conscience [would] never forget." When on the first three days of the war,[38] the Bishop of Oxford, the Chief Rabbi and Abdal Hakim Murad successively issued a solemn call to prayer, Abdal Hakim Murad's "Thought," uncharacteristically starting with the words "What is it like to be licensed to kill?" and bluntly talking of "the young people, cast like dice by distant politicians," ended on the prayerful demand, which sounded like a warning, that the war might bring "healing, instead of more rancour and division". In a later "Thought" on September 1, 2003, he put this into context, explaining "When the war began, I mounted the pulpit of my local mosque and preached the most difficult sermon of my career... to heal the anger of my congregation, newly united in its resentment of the war".

Equally unique was the tone and language used by former SAS Chaplain Jimmy Morrison on March 25, resorting to the brutal metaphor of "ethical surgery— ... cutting the cancer of a corrupt and murderous regime from the body of Iraq." His "Thought" was often quoted by people who left out the nuances, retaining only the "sound bite". But the punch line did include the language of apparent demonisation of the enemy.

---

[38] March 20, 21 and 22.

"Thoughts for the Day" as "mini-sermons"

The concept of a "thought for the day" is commonly used outside the BBC in a religious context. A very good description of the challenges inherent to the writing of fifty five "Thoughts" on Operation Telic 1 is provided in an article entitled "The Prophetic Role of the Chaplain: Experiences with a daily 'Thought for the Day'"[39] by a Church of Scotland military chaplain, the Reverend S P Swinn. A "Thought" should proclaim and apply the word of God; teach; exhort, or warn. The main demands identified which can also apply to a Radio 4 "Thought" are the following: the "mini-sermon" should not take "unfair advantage of a captive audience, ... different to a church audience and [having] to be treated differently;" "in effect, to say something relevant, meaningful and fresh require[s] just as much thought and preparation as if [one was] preparing a full sermon a day". He outlines seven lessons in homiletics from his experience in the Gulf which may be relevant: the importance of preliminary prayer; the use of Scripture; true brevity–"mak[ing] every word count"; clarity; currency; sincerity and purpose; and being natural.

Ascertaining whether prayer was involved in the preparation of the various "Thoughts" is not feasible. Concerning the use of scripture, of the 105 "Thoughts," only 33 (Corpus 1: 19; Corpus 2: 14) do not involve a *verbatim* quotation from sacred texts –with length and role varying greatly. But only 14 (Corpus 1: 11; Corpus 2: 3) do not include a direct reference to scripture, its spirit, or later religious writings. How often true brevity was achieved is open to debate, but a "Thought"–typically four hundred to five hundred words long–is between two and a half and five times as short as sermons from a control sample delivered between 2001 and 2004.[40] The choice of the word "mini-sermon" to qualify a "Thought" seems fully appropriate. Clarity is obtained thanks to the adoption of a clear structure or thread, and the use of simple language, but parallels or multiple references sometimes obscure the structure and the message. Currency is usually achieved by a direct reference to a recent or ongoing event, or the religious festival of the day. A "Thought" should indeed be a "dish best served hot". Sincerity means there is little room for brilliance for brilliance's sake or irony in a typical "Thought". Alongside the many quotes from the various religions' sacred texts, this clearly distinguishes a "Thought" from editorials or "Op-Eds". Given the subject and the

---

[39] In Operation Telic 2003 Chaplaincy Reflections, p. 25-43, unpublished document.
[40] For online Anglican and Roman Catholic sermon archives on war in Iraq, September 11, 2001, terrorism, see for instance http://www.westminster-abbey.org/voice/sermon/archives/ and http://rcdow.org.uk/

circumstances, how could *TftD* contributors joke about war? There is therefore little recourse to the kind of humour for which contributors like Lionel Blue are rightly famous, contrary to the trend witnessed in contemporary parish or even University chaplaincy preaching, where resorting to humour often seems to have replaced traditional eloquence and rhetoric. To establish rapport with the audience, give a conversational character to a "Thought", or liven it up", humour is replaced by the use of informal or colloquial expressions.[41]

Apart from the use of rhetorical questions, a basic technique, there are very few visible rhetorical devices employed, and virtually no metaphor or anaphora. The tone is never grandiloquent. The general trend is to use conversational, homely, unadorned, language, and there is a three-to-one ratio between informal language–146 occurrences, frequently involving long phrases– and formal language –50 occurrences, mainly of isolated words. Colin Morris's use of the "God forefend" archaism on April 14 is a rare exception. The "bureaucratic slang and jolly jargon", the language of "spin" –"systems", "assets", "collateral damage", "breaking the china", "the Mother of all bombs", "friendly fire", "party lackeys", "smart bombs", "roadmap to peace", "taking out Saddam Hussein", " 'doing' God"–are debunked by Colin Morris, Rhidian Brook, Huw Spanner and Clifford Longley. Informal language is often used to suggest you don't take yourself too seriously, you are not sanctimonious. Thus, we hear of "Jesus turn[ing] up"; of his "inner cabinet of disciples"; of "the parable of the England cricket team"; of an "enthusiastic celebrity spotter" listening to Jesus; of "being always ready to give an answer to every man that asketh you a reason of the hope that is in you, with meekness and fear"– explained as follows "The last bit means don't boast about it, stay cool"

In times of wars and rumours of war, the purpose was to be a witness by being profoundly human rather than brilliant, avoiding sensationalism and aggressive or emotional language. Interestingly–the tradition of British understatement?– sincerity meant scant recourse to emotional language, with few speakers employing words like "awesome", "agonising", "terrifying", "horrendous"; from March 24, the pity and the horror of war made their way into *TftD*, with "wounded civilian children sobbing in hospital beds" (Elaine Storkey), "the hideous paraphernalia of mechanised hatred" and "ruined houses, their windows gaping empty like long dead skulls" (David Winter), "A mother screaming in inexpressible

---

[41] The *Collins Cobuild English Language Dictionary*, London: Harper Collins, 1987 and *Webster's Encyclopedic Unabridged Dictionary of the English Language*, New York: Gramercy Books, 1989 were used as references to categorise register.

anguish; two dead siblings side by side; and a dead man without a name face down in the gutter". (Joel Edwards), "the corpses of women and children as well as men and boys summarily shot" and "weeping women cradling bags of rotten bones" (John Bell). But there was no sensationalism.

Virtually no exclamation marks to express indignation are used in the corpuses. Vehement language is almost never featured; invective, controversial language, pandering to jingoistic feelings or the use of facile jokes are banned. Saddam Hussein is rarely called "Saddam". Several contributors occasionally departed from the guidelines; but paradoxically, it was the contributors closest to non-violence, John Bell, associated with the Iona Community, and Elaine Storkey, who provided the few instances of the use of adversarial language. In a context of anti-French feelings in certain tabloids or government circles, John Bell wrote on February 20 "To love the neighbour doesn't require our leaders to French-kiss their Iraqi or Zimbabwean counterparts"; Elaine Storkey's anger at the war surfaced in her use of "Bush and Blair" (March 17) or "Saddam, Bush and Rumsfeld" (March 24).

On the whole, *TftD* style is rarely "defeated expectancy"; rather, it illustrates the famous Buffon phrase "Style is the man himself." Irony is mainly used by the two Catholic speakers; Mona Siddiqui, Abdal Hakim Murad and Hamza Yusuf all use rather formal language. Full of images and energy, Joel Edwards's style uses the language of emotions in combination with informal and sustained language. His are "the adrenaline of freedom", "the womb of antiquity, a cradle of ancient biblical history", "a self-rape of its own cultural wealth", "drawn to Iraq like a helpless hypnotic", "an image from the Bible has been spliced into my mind"–a uniquely charismatic Evangelical remark; "a Palestinian bomber self-destructed on a Tel Aviv bus" and "scattered among his bewilderment are the basic answers". Like Colin Morris's, Leslie Griffiths's "Thoughts" typically juxtapose formal and informal language; his October 30 "Thought" on conflict over the Common Agricultural Policy between President Chirac and Prime Minister Tony Blair uses a wide variety of formal and informal phrases–"almighty row", "what a to-do!", "a quiet chat together", "stitched up a deal", "pretty much in place", "St Paul ... St Peter, two other larger-than-life figures", "You can't have it both ways," "the poor who are being sold down the river".

Tone and delivery are characterised by the search for measure and restraint. The average pace–around 2.5 words per second–contrasts with that of the *Today* programme reports, ranging from 2.8 to 3 words per second, with a maximum of 3.3 words per second, based on the study of a

sample of reports and interviews of comparable duration recorded on the
BBC between 1999 and 2005. A difference of 0.3 word per second is
readily perceptible. In the hurly-burly of the news, no wonder then the
serenity of a good "Thought" should provide a welcome respite, in terms
of content and style.

In conclusion, while the typical "Thought for the Day", written to be
listened to rather than read, certainly belongs to the minor arts in so far as
rhetoric is concerned, a few "Thoughts" perhaps transcend the ephemeral
genre. But all good "Thoughts" are far more than mere comments on the
news with a religious varnish. Given the current trend towards shorter
sermons and away from oratory, given also the religious content,
references and vision of the world the "Thoughts" convey, they cannot be
subsumed within the convenient category of the "religious editorial". The
occasional calls to prayer; the frequent references to God; the sometimes
awkward "preaching"; the quotations from sacred texts; the identity of
most of the speakers; the way the secularists oppose the slot in its present
form all point to the specificity of those "mini-sermons" written for and in
a secular, multi-faith, world. Filled with a genuine longing for peace and
inter-faith harmony, typifying a certain "inclusive" attitude to religion
common to a number of Western European countries, the "Thoughts"
promote a specific set of values, and to do so, most of them resort to
techniques characteristic of the short parish sermon and consistent with the
content preached. Because they were concerned with serious matters of
peace, war, terrorism, certain "tools in the preacher's toolbox" like
humour could not be used. But the fact that these "Thoughts" were
essentially serious, reflective occasion pieces fundamentally answered one
of the main requirements of listeners to the *Today* programme–to be given
"food for thought" at the start of the day.

Postscript, January 2009: Since our conference took place, the TftD
slot now takes place a few minutes earlier, so that a listener joining early
because he wishes to listen to the main headlines (and the weather report!)
will no longer have to listen to *Thought for the Day*. This is probably a
direct result of the campaign by the NSS and others. The wave of
successive leaks, revelations and investigations over the past few years
concerning the use (and abuse) of intelligence by the Prime Minister might
lead one to think that the speakers on *TftD* failed in their 'prophetic'
mission. While the criticism that the contributions were occasionally too
bland has a degree of truth, one should beware of the 'malefit' of hindsight.
It should be remembered that *TftD* aims precisely at providing a spiritual
pause in a programme which in essence is political, and that much that is
today thought of as 'fact' was at the time a subject of polemic.

Works Cited

Ceadel, Martin *Thinking about Peace and War*, Oxford: Oxford University Press, (1987) 1989.

—. *Pacifism in Britain 1914-1945: The Defining of a Faith*, Oxford: Clarendon Press, 1980.

Donovan, Paul, *All our Todays*, London: Random House, 1998.

Riccardi, Andrea, *La paix préventive. Raisons d'espérer dans un monde de conflits*, Paris: Salvator, (2004) 2005.

Sacks, Jonathan, *The Dignity of Difference How to Avoid the Clash of Civilizations*, (2002, 2003) 2005.

Schmidt-leukel, Perry, *War and Peace in World Religions. The Gerald Weisfeld Lectures 2003*, London: SCM Press, 2004.

Sinclair, John, ed., *Collins Cobuild Learner's Dictionary*, London: HarperCollins, 1987.

Webster's *Encyclopedic Unabridged Dictionary of the English Language*, New York: Gramercy Books, 1989.

References

Bainton, Roland H. *Christian Attitudes Toward War and Peace. A Historical Survey and Critical Re-evaluation*, London: Hodder and Stoughton, (1960) 1961.

Bonhoeffer, Dietrich, *The Cost of Discipleship*, London: SCM Press, (1948, 1959) 2001.

Bierley, Peter, *The Tide is Running Out. What the English Church Attendance Survey reveals*, London: Christian Research, 2000.

Brown, Callum G., *The Death of Christian Britain. Understanding Secularisation* London: Routledge, 2001.

Davie, Grace, *Religion in Britain since 1945. Believing without Belonging* Oxford: Blackwell, 1994.

Durand, Jean-Dominique, *L'esprit d'Assise*, Paris: Editions du Cerf, 2005

Gauchet, Marcel, *La religion dans la démocratie*, Paris: Gallimard, 1998.

Harries, Richard, ed. , *Reinhold Niebuhr and the Issues of our Time,* Oxford: Mowbray, 1986.

D'Haussy, Christiane ed., *English Sermons : Mirrors of Society,* Toulouse : Presses Universitaires du Mirail, 1995.

Huntington, Samuel P., *The Clash of Civilizations and the Remaking of World Order*. New York: Simon and Schuster, (1996) 2002.

Martin, David, *A Sociology of English Religion*, London: Heinemann, 1967.

—. Does Christianity Cause War? Oxford: Oxford University Press (1997) 2006.

—. *Pacifism. An Historical and Sociological Study*, New York: Schocken Books, 1965.

—. *On Secularization. Towards a Revised General Theory*, London : Ashgate, 2005.

McLeod, Hugh, MEWS, Stuart et d'HAUSSY, Christiane (dir.)., *Histoire religieuse de la Grande-Bretagne*, Paris, Cerf, 1997.

Merton, Thomas, *Peace in the Post-Christian Era*, New York: Orbis Books, 2004.

Minois, Georges. *L'Église et la guerre: de la Bible à l'ère atomique*. Paris : Librairie Arthème Fayard, 1994.

Nhat Hahn, Thich, *Peace Is Every Step: The Path of Mindfulness in Everyday Life*, New York: Random House, 1992.

O'Donovan, Oliver, *The Just War Revisited* Cambridge: Cambridge University Press, 2003 .

Ramsey, Paul, *War and the Christian Conscience*, Durham: Duke University Press (1961) 1967.

Welsby, Paul A., *Sermons and Society. An Anglican Anthology*, London: Penguin Books, 1970.

Wilkinson, Alan, *Dissent or Conform? War, Peace and the English Churches*, London: SCM Press, 1986.

Williams, Rowan *The truce of God. Peacemaking in troubled times*, Norwich: Canterbury Press, 2005.

Wolfe, Kenneth M. *The Churches and the BBC 1922-1956. The politics of Broadcast Religion*, London: SCM Press, 1984.

CHAPTER FOURTEEN

AMERICAN CATHOLICS' SERMONS AND GEORGE W. BUSH'S "JUST CAUSE" DURING THE WAR IN IRAQ

ANNE DEBRAY

The Roman Catholic Church in America is a very strong and diverse Church: it is served by over 500 religious orders and has been the largest American denomination since the 1860s when large numbers of Irish and Germans immigrated. Today, strengthened by immigrants from Latin America, South-east Asia and Africa, they number 65 million, comprising nearly a quarter of the American population.[1] In the 20th century, Catholics fully emerged and participated in mainstream cultural and political life as they consider that grace and salvation come through visible signs and symbolic actions. Many active Catholics used Vatican II conciliar reforms—promoting openness to the world and popular participation—to push for participatory democracy.

Catholic Chaplains have become more visible and now serve a variety of communities, from school and universities, military installations to political institutions: the current Chaplain of the House of Representatives is a Catholic, a first since Chaplains were assigned to Congress in 1799, most having been Protestant. Reverend Daniel P. Caughlin opens each day's proceedings with a prayer, offers counsel and celebrates Sunday services with the Senate Chaplain. Today, American Catholics experience the diversity and greater political participation that characterized other denominations before.

---

[1] Since 1936, figures based on each Church declarations. For Catholics, it includes all baptised individuals. The next largest denomination is the Southern Baptist Convention with 16 million members. *Yearbook of American & Canadian Churches,* 2003 in www.infoplease.com.

The September 11, 2001 terrorist attacks on New York, the Pentagon and Pennsylvania affected the whole world and led to immediate US government action and military intervention. Faced with the threat of war, spiritual leaders of all religious denominations and faiths took a stand. The purpose of this study is to analyze the sermons delivered by Catholic priests, first when facing a potential war and afterward living in a time of war. It will address the dilemma experienced by priests caught between the authority of their Church—embodied by the Vatican and, at home, by the United States Conference of Catholic Bishops—and their allegiance to their country's leaders. This paper will examine more specifically the stances of prominent and vocal Catholic pacifist priests and of the sermons from Archbishop Edwin O'Brien, head of the Archdiocese for the Military Services, a unique Catholic institution.

Fighting terrorism: political actions and military interventions

Within days after the terrorist attacks, the Bush Administration had fixed blame for the attacks on Osama Bin Laden and his Al Qaeda network and spurred the drafting of several Congressional Resolutions launching the Administration's "war on terror". Members of Congress voted House Joint Resolution 64 on September 14, 2001 to authorize the use of United States Armed Forces against those responsible for the attacks launched against the United States, namely to track Al Qaeda and the Taliban terrorists in Afghanistan. It authorized the invasion of Afghanistan under the name "Operation Enduring Freedom". The resolution gathered unanimous backing from all Congress members, except one Democrat, a Representative from California, Barbara Lee, who cast the only vote against the measure. The immediate invasion was seen as a self-defensive counter-attack and drew enormous public backing as well.

As the United States continued "fighting terrorism" and "preventing future attacks", Saddam Hussein's regime, defying United Nations authority, became identified as a major threat to U.S. security, and Congress debated on the next steps to take. House Resolution 118, voted on 11 October 2002, amounted to giving President Bush *carte blanche* to invade Iraq and overthrow Saddam Hussein. The measure authorized "Operation Iraqi Freedom": it included the invasion of Iraq -mounted five months later- nd subsequent operations in Iraq. This time, the resolution showed some division among Congress members, mostly along partisan lines: it was backed by 69 percent of the House members and 77 percent of the Senators and it was much less popular among Americans than the September 2001 resolution. To many, imminent danger from Saddam Hussein was not obvious. Intense debate took place with numerous groups and organizations pleading against going to war.

Churches around the world debated the issue and lively discussions pitted many American church leaders and divided members of the same religious affiliation, conservative "hawks" against liberal peaceful "doves". The Southern Baptist Convention -the most conservative dynamic and largest protestant denomination- was the only Church to support the war from the start. Other denominations originally opposed the war and issued official statements in that sense, as when the liberal United Methodist Church opposed the war in Iraq and very openly criticized its most prominent member, namely the President of the United States. But George W. Bush, raised as a Methodist, has since been "born again". And the Bush Administration has nourished close links with the Baptist Convention: Franklin Graham, Billy's son and successor, delivered the Republican Convention invocation, blessed President Bush's 2000 inauguration and has given the Pentagon Holy Friday's prayers.

To refer to post 9/11 military Operations, President Bush often used the phrase "Just Cause" as an echo to the religious concept of "Just War" defined among others by the Catechism of the Catholic Church, "the fundamental Christian truths" expressed by the Holy See to the attention of Catholics around the globe (see *infra*). The phrase was actually borrowed from a military operation launched by George H. W. Bush's Administration in December 1989 which sent American troops into Panama and captured General Noriega. "Just Cause" first appeared in the current President's remarks and speeches as the Administration was preparing to invade Iraq. Invading Afghanistan had met no public opposition; the invasion of Iraq however met obstacles and forced the Bush Administration to polish its rhetoric. Invading Iraq constituted the first pre-emptive war in recent history.

Religious overtones or rhetorical labels have always played a meaningful part in President Bush's public speaking. In his speeches, he consistently presented invasions of Afghanistan and Iraq as necessary responses to the terrorist attacks: "None of us asked for this war. None of us wished that what happened on September the 11th happened".[2] He told American citizens that they were on a moral journey, all united in this

---

[2] "President's Remarks at 'Congress of Tomorrow' Lunch" (Republican retreat), Feb. 1, 2002.

"fight for freedom": "We have a just cause to guide us".[3] Like a
charismatic religious leader resorting to sermonic and prophetic tones,
George W. Bush pictured himself as a leader endowed with a holy
mission. The mission was to defend freedom in the U.S. and in the
Middle-East. By stressing, in the fashion of the millenarian movements, a
dualism between good and evil, often resorting to the "axis of evil" phrase
crafted for the 2002 "State of the Union Message", he wished to turn his
citizens' anger after the attacks into support of his policies, and in fact to
forge their anger into zeal for their mission.[4] There is therefore a clear
appeal to religious themes and rhetoric in President Bush's public
addresses.

Catholics response to post 9/11 military operations

The authority of the American Catholic Church is embodied in the
United States Conference of Catholic Bishops, an assembly "working
together to unify, coordinate, promote, and carry on Catholic activities in
the United States".[5] The nation's Bishops meet yearly and issue pastoral
letters and position papers. The most extensive pastorals are probably the
1983 *Challenge of Peace: God's Promise and Our Response*, the 1986
Economic Justice for All and the 1993 *Harvest of Justice is Sown in
Peace.* They state the ideals to which the American Catholic Church
aspires. Since the 1980s, American Bishops have focused on political
issues with moral implications: nuclear strategy, U.S. policy in Central
America, negotiation against the war in the Gulf and have made their
voice heard in the political arena, often testifying at Congressional
Hearings, for instance. The position of the U.S. Catholic Church on war is
articulated in two documents: the Catechism of the Catholic Church, last
revised by the Vatican in 1990, and the 1993 *Harvest of Justice is Sown in
Peace* pastoral. Part III, Section 2 of the Catechism, entitled "Life in
Christ", is devoted to the Ten Commandments.[6] Article 5, "The Fifth
Commandment—You shall not kill", includes several sections on
safeguarding peace and the Just War doctrine. The concept was first
developed by Saint Augustine (354-430): a Bishop in Northern Africa, he

---

[3] Remarks by the President at the Port of Philadelphia United Coast Guard, March
31, 2003.
[4] Several members of his Administration indeed belong to the millenarian
movement: his private counsel Karl Rove, first Attorney General John Ashcroft,
first Secretary of the Interior Gale Norton.
[5] USCCB website, www.usccb.org.
[6] www.vatican.va/archive/index.htm.

attempted to reconcile violence with the Scriptural prohibition of it. Faced with the danger of barbaric invasions, he legitimated war as a way to achieve peace, under the authority of the Prince who himself was under the authority of God. In the XXth century, Catholics define Just War as the right to self-defense after all peace efforts have failed. The concept is specifically detailed in Section 2309 of the Catechism:

> The strict conditions for legitimate defense by military force require rigorous consideration. The gravity of such a decision makes it subject to rigorous conditions of moral legitimacy. At one and the same time: the damage inflicted by the aggressor on the nation or community of nations must be lasting, grave, and certain; all other means of putting an end to it must have been shown to be impractical or ineffective; there must be serious prospects of success; the use of arms must not produce evils and disorders graver than the evil to be eliminated. The power of modern means of destruction weighs very heavily in evaluating this condition. These are the traditional elements enumerated in what is called the "Just War" doctrine. The evaluation of these conditions for moral legitimacy belongs to the prudential judgment of those who have responsibility for the common good.

The last sentence stresses that the government is the final interpreter and bears the ultimate responsibility in deciding to wage a war. The government has information that the public does not have; citizens must trust their leaders and help them decide through public debate. The chapter ends with Section 2330: "Blessed are the peacemakers, for they shall be called sons of God" (Matthew 5:9). As Saint Augustine pointed out, the peacemakers are those working to establish peace and this might not exclude resorting to war to achieve that goal. Sermons in time of war offer, as we shall see, a wide range of interpretations of that term alone.

The Second Vatican Ecumenical Council (1962-65) had reflected on universal threat of war and the justification of war: "insofar as men are sinful, the threat of war hangs over them, and hang over them it will until the return of Christ" (*Gaudium Et Spes* § 78). It added that the ultimate destination is peace, to fulfil the words of the prophet, according to which the nations "shall beat their swords into plowshares, and their spears into pruning hooks; nation shall not lift up sword against nation, neither shall they learn war any more" (Isaiah 2:4).

Following what Americans now call the First Gulf War, the 1993 *Harvest of Justice is Sown in Peace* pastoral provides a moral framework to the Catholic Just War doctrine.[7] It updates the conditions that must all be met to justify the use of force (*jus ad bellum*), namely:

> *Just Cause:* force may be used only to correct a grave, public evil, i.e., aggression or massive violation of the basic rights of whole populations; *Comparative Justice:* while there may be rights and wrongs on all sides of a conflict, to override the presumption against the use of force the injustice suffered by one party must significantly outweigh that suffered by the other; *Legitimate Authority:* only duly constituted public authorities may use deadly force or wage war; *Right Intention:* force may be used only in a truly just cause and solely for that purpose; *Probability of Success:* arms may not be used in a futile cause or in a case where disproportionate measures are required to achieve success; *Proportionality:* the overall destruction expected from the use of force must be outweighed by the good to be achieved; *Last Resort:* force may be used only after all peaceful alternatives have been seriously tried and exhausted.

In the chapter entitled "Agenda for Peacemaking", the Bishops already stressed the need to strengthen international institutions, especially the United Nations, in particular to help the oppressed people of Iraq. In 2001, the Bishops viewed the Bush Administration's operation in Afghanistan as a just response to terrorism and, following massive American public support, never questioned the moral legitimacy of the invasion. Shortly after, the Conference issued a pastoral message entitled *Living with Faith and Hope After September 11* where it stressed that this "legitimate use of force" must be accompanied with non-military measures as well as reflections on the roots of terrorism and the need to reach out to other "faith communities", specifically Muslims.[8] Here, the criteria for Just War were discussed not as tests for the right to proceed to a war but as measures for the "just" conduct of war (*in bello*). In 2002, however, the looming invasion of Iraq brought expressions of serious moral reservations, as the Bishops saw no evident sign of an imminent attack from Iraq and therefore no legitimacy for a pre-emptive war. In a September 17, 2002 letter, Bishop Wilton D. Gregory, President of the Conference, urged President Bush to step back from war and instead to help lead a global response with the United Nations.

Thus, the threat of war in Iraq united American Catholics, the Vatican and most other national Catholic Churches behind a strong will to pursue

---

[7] The Harvest of Peace is Sown in Justice, A Reflection of the NCCB on the Tenth Anniversary of The Challenge of Peace, Nov. 17, 1993.

[8] A Pastoral Message: Living with Faith and Hope After September 11, U.S. Conference of Catholic Bishops, Nov. 14, 2001, p. 2.

disarmament and peace and to petition the Bush Administration not to initiate war. In September 2002, Cardinal Ratzinger—now Pope Benedict XVI, but then prefect of the Vatican Congregation for the Doctrine of the Faith—acknowledged that political questions were not within his competence, but suggested it was the responsibility of the United Nations, thereby making a political statement.[9] Cardinals and Bishops discussed the notion of "preventive war" on various occasions. Cardinal Angelo Sodano, Vatican Secretary of State, declared: "We are against the war. That is a moral position, and there's not much that needs to be said about whether [the war] is 'preventive' or 'nonpreventive'. It's an ambiguous term. Certainly the war is not defensive."[10] In March 2003, as the war seemed certain, Pope John Paul II sent a special envoy to deliver a personal message to President Bush stressing that military force could only be used within the framework of the United Nations and emphasizing the unity of the Holy See and of Catholics over the world on that issue.[11] A war without UN approval would be "immoral, illegal, unjust".[12] And Cardinal Ratzinger further confirmed that the "concept of a preventive 'war' did not appear in the Catechism of the Catholic Church".[13] However, once the conflict started on March 20, 2003, the US Conference of Catholic Bishops then remained silent on the issue, respecting their government's choice, acknowledging the superiority of the government over civilians to gather intelligence, tacitly confirming the legitimacy of "the Prince" and his prerogatives, as in Section 2310 of the Catechism.

The American Catholic Church is built on powerful institutions; it both answers to its assembly—the Conference of Bishops—and to the Vatican with its papal magisterial structure. Strong traditions and high respect for the creed and the sacrament result in a Church with probably less independence and freedom than in most other American Churches, especially Protestant denominations. To remain silent after the war had started was the softest form of dissent American Bishops could send to the rest of the Roman Catholic Churches who did not experience the political dilemma of their American brothers. In the parishes, many American Catholics developed their Church's anti-war position; some expressed their vocal and physical opposition to the war and were put into US custody for that offense. Others, including conservative Catholics,

---

[9] In *Zenit*, Vatican Information Service, Catholic World News, Sept. 24, 2002.
[10] Interview with Italian reporters, Jan. 29, 2003.
[11] "Statement of Cardinal Pio Laghi", March 5, 2003, Vatican News Service.
[12] Stephen Steele, "Papa Envoy Meets Bush", *Catholic News Service, U.S. Conference of Catholic Bishops*, March 5, 2003.
[13] Sept. 24, 2002 in www.catholicpeacefelllowship.com.

disagreed upon which road to take to achieve lasting peace and favored military intervention.

Modern Catholic pacifism developed with the Catholic Movement that emerged in the depression years. The Movement was concerned with social justice and pushed for Catholic radical views. It included Dorothy Day and the movement she founded, *The Catholic Workers*. During the Second World War, her group was the sole pacifist voice in the largely isolated and anti-communist Catholic community. In 1958, a pastoral letter detailed social Catholicism and its commitment to fight discrimination and racism. The focus on justice opened up to international responsibility for justice worldwide. Today, a number of peaceful Catholic groups and publications gather thousands of active American Catholics. To defend peace, Catholic pacifists refer to the numerous Church teachings on peace and war, including canonical reference texts, words from the Saints and from the Holy Fathers. *The Catholic Peace Fellowship*, for example, defends the right of conscientious objectors clearly stated in Section 2311 of the Catechism of the Catholic Church and *Pax Christi* offers an Ambassadors of Peace Program.

The war sermons noted here begin with pacifist voices from the Catholic Church, particularly from weekly Sunday sermons of two prominent and vocal figures from the Catholic Peace Movement—Jesuit John Dear and Bishop Thomas Gumbleton are well-respected and often-quoted pacifists and they make their sermons easily available to the public. Father Dear headed the *Fellowship of Reconciliation*, the largest interfaith peace organization in the United States, based in New York, and has extensively worked, lectured and spoken on peace and justice. He is a *Pax Christi* Ambassador of Peace; he was assigned to a parish in New Mexico in 2002.[14] Bishop Gumbleton is the Auxiliary Bishop of the Archdiocese of Detroit.[15]

The second set of sermons exampled were given by Archbishop Edwin O'Brien heading the US Archdiocese for the Military Services, which has a unique congregation of Catholics on active duty in the U.S. military services.[16] The status of military Chaplains was drafted at the time of the Declaration of Independence; in 1775, the second article of Navy Regulations set up the Chaplain Corp and enumerated the duties of Navy Chaplains: to provide divine services twice a day and preach a sermon on

---

[14] Transcripts of his weekly Sunday sermons: www.johndear.org.
[15] Transcripts of his weekly Sunday sermons:
www.nationalcatholicreporter.org/peace/archives1.htm
[16] Archbishop O'Brien's sermons are available at www.kofc.org and www.catholicmil.org.

Sunday. The first Chaplain was assigned in 1799 and the Archdiocese took its modern shape in 1939.[17] Today, it provides spiritual and pastoral services and support to American military personnel and their families. Catholic Chaplains, who serve 375,000 active duty Catholics, are largely underrepresented in the fields: 28 percent of active duty personnel are Catholics and the 500 Catholic Chaplains represent 8 percent of all military Chaplains. US Chaplains now come from about 220 different denominations and faith groups and the first female Muslim Chaplain was assigned in December 2001.[18] Unlike traditional Archdioceses, the Archdiocese for the Military Services does not own properties and it solely relies on donations. Their largest provider is the conservative and patriotic Knights of Columbus organization, "the world's largest Catholic fraternal service organization with 1.7 million members".[19] Apart from offering insurance and annuities to their members, the Knights support military personnel and in 2003 and 2004, together with the Archdiocese for the Military Services, the Order produced and distributed 200,000 *Armed with the Faith* spiritual handbooks for the troops stationed in the Middle-East.

Catholic pacifist and military sermons in a time of war

The war sermons of this study were given by Catholics who, following the words from the Holy See and the pacifist voice of their national leaders, opposed the Bush Administration's desire to go to war in Iraq. However, the three clergymen hold very different occupations and Church statuses that might interfere with their commitment to their Church and influence the content of their sermons. They offer diverging interpretations and representations; the same excerpts from the Scriptures as well as the same religious concepts are quoted, but they are given different meanings and connotations. For instance, Military Archbishop O'Brien uses the concept of evil to identify the enemies of the United States that must be fought:

> May [the Lord] bring swift and decisive judgement to those evil forces responsible for the sacrilege we have witnessed [...] In our new world order, Americans and other free people are being asked to sacrifice conveniences, leisure and luxuries, financial and other material resources and even our very lives to excise an aggressive, cancerous evil. That evil

---

[17] www.milarch.org.
[18] National Conference on Ministry to the Armed Forces, www.ncmaf.org.
[19] www.kofc.org.

mocks and mars the biblical belief that each of us is made to the image and likeness of God, each of us a sacred reflection of the divinity.[20]

However, Bishop Gumbleton and Father Dear see the roots of evil in the sin that is in men's hearts. Going to war against what President Bush identified as the "axis of evil" will not destroy evil but produce more evil. The answer is in love, in the way of love shown by Jesus (Feb. 9, 2003). The Archbishop was preaching just after the 9/11 attacks and Bishop Gumbleton in the tense pre-war days; the difference in focus—evil versus love—is emblematic of their personal attitude.

Then they offer different visions of what a soldier is. Whatever the Catholic Church's position on the legitimacy of a conflict, the men and women serving their country and engaged in battle hold a special place in the Catechism as well as in preachers' hearts. Vatican II spoke of military personnel in the following terms:

> Those [...] who devote themselves to the military service of their country should regard themselves as the agents of security and freedom of peoples. As long as they fulfil this role properly, they are making a genuine contribution to the establishment of peace.[21]

In Archbishop O'Brien's sermons, the soldier is described as a "sentinel", a safeguard working for the establishment of peace. The soldier is said to defend a noble cause, which echoes President Bush's "Just Cause". Soldiers are "freedom-loving, uniformed Americans", a phrase reminiscent of the "freedom fighters", a term Ronald Reagan had used to describe the Contras who opposed the Sandinista government in Nicaragua.[22] Archbishop O'Brien commends the strong sense of a mission, the vocation soldiers live through (Oct. 11, 2001). The choice of a powerful term—vocation—referring both to their military carrier and to their faith is no coincidence:

> You, our service men and women and their families, are responding, sometimes heroically, to that [baptismal] call [to follow Christ]. It is indeed a noble vocation to give one's life even in death that our neighbor

---

[20] Archbishop O'Brien, "Homily at the Basilica of the National Shrine of the Immaculate Conception: Mass for the Nation in a Moment of Tragedy and a Time of Hope", Sept. 16, 2001 and "Months Mind Mass", Basilica of the National Shrine of the Immaculate Conception, Oct. 11, 2001.

[21] *Gaudiu Et Spes*, Section 1: Avoidance of War, § 79.

[22] Archbishop O'Brien, "Homily for the Mass Honoring WWII Chaplains", Saint Patrick's Catholic Church, June 27, 2004.

might enjoy the justice and peace so often threatened by the despot and the terrorist. (May 23, 2004)

The terms vocation, call and mission have both strong spiritual and professional meanings. None of these terms are used by Bishop Gumbleton or Father Dear in that context. Archbishop O'Brien sermons have a heavy military and political tone that is explained by the very nature of his audience.

The peacemaker is a concept taken from the Bible which is recurrently used by Catholic hawks and doves alike: "Blessed are the peacemakers, for they shall be called sons of God. Blessed are those who are persecuted because of righteousness, for theirs is the kingdom of heaven".(Matthew 5:9-10). The term appears in the Catechism (Section 2330) and is used by American Bishops in their September 11, 2001 pastoral letter to promote peace through peaceful means. Father Dear, quoting the Pope, tells his church followers that the true peacemakers are those working to avoid war. (March 5, 2003). For Catholics in the Military, the interpretation is different: in their definition of Just War, the term embodies the soldier. They complete their definition with quotes from Bishop Sheen's sermon given on the eve of the U.S. entry into World War II: "Peace is not a passive but an active virtue. Our Lord never said 'blessed are the peaceful'. But he did say, 'blessed are the peacemakers'".[23] In the same vein, Archbishop O'Brien tells soldiers they are "defenders of the peace" or "promoters of the peace" (Christmas 2001). He enlarges the concept to the Pentagon when referring to the victims of the September 11 attacks: "We present their souls to God the Most High as innocent martyrs, sacrifices to the Lord for the cause of peace to which your Pentagon family is dedicated" (Sept. 11, 2002). These words echo President Bush's rhetoric—or is it the reverse?—when he declared: "Defending freedom is a noble cause and it is a just cause [...] The fight against terror is noble and it's just".[24] He consistently repeats the verb "to serve" when addressing military audiences, to honor fallen soldiers and appease the families which have lost them, he often says, "The nation is grateful for their service".

Bishop Gumbleton and Father Dear for their part build their sermons both into a spiritual message and a strong political statement. They consider it a moral duty to discuss and question the government for "everyone of us has a responsibility to make sure we are not simply taking

---

[23] In www.catholicmil.org/html/justwar.html#others.
[24] "President Launches Quality Teacher initiative", March 4, 2002 in www.whitehouse.gov and "State of the Union Message", Jan. 28, 2003.

what our government says as the word we must accept and follow. Only God gives us the word that we must follow." (March 23, 2003) Or: "We have to question [the government] at times, even act against the authorities" (March 23, 2003). Pope John Paul II said "human justice is always fragile and imperfect [...] The natural law [is] the source of inspiration for the right of nations and for the formulations of international law".[25] From there, Father Dear argues that men must follow the eternal law, the Law of God Moses held to lead Jesus on his way to Jerusalem into non-violent resistance (March 16, 2003). Christians have a moral duty to oppose their government when the decisions are immoral and unjust. The interpretation of the Just War theory set in the Catechism, Section 2309, is at the heart of dissent and all the sermons studied here stress the authority of the Church over the state before the war started. For the supreme law is the law of God. Father Dear and Bishop Gumbleton present Jesus as an outlaw. Using modern language, they picture Jesus breaking the civil law in Capernaum (Feb. 9, 2003) or touching a man suffering from leprosy (Feb 16, 2003). Father Dear refers twice to the Temple when Jesus overturns the tables of injustice as an "act of peaceful civil disobedience" to urge his followers to peaceful action.[26] For the law of God's love is the only law.

As the threat of war looms, Father Dear's exhortations become more direct, angry in tone and highly critical of the Bush Administration. He openly calls for civil disobedience:

> And finally, the Gospel calls us to let Jesus preach to us and announce God's reign in our midst, and then, like Jesus to be people who welcome God's reign of non-violence and peace and justice and love, people who proclaim reign of peace to one another and everywhere. Our allegiance is to God's reign of peace and non-violence, not America's tyranny of war, nuclear weapons, killing Iraqis and global domination for corporate billionaires. (Feb. 9, 2003)

A few weeks later, he develops:

> So I invite you to spend the next few days preparing for Lent and what you are going to do this Lent for Jesus [...] You can study Gospel non-violence and get involved in the Catholic peace movement and speak out against war and nuclear weapons. (March 2, 2003)

---

[25] Pope John Paul II, "Address to the Diplomatic Corps", Jan. 13, 2003 and "No Peace without Justice, No Justice without Forgiveness", World Day of Peace, Jan. 1, 2002.
[26] Father Dear, Sep. 1, 2002 and Feb.2, 2003.

Once the war started in March 2003, he makes direct accusations and voices strong criticisms of the American system he equates with the Temple:

> We have a lot of voices that we listen to today. Maybe you listen to CNN or Dan Rather or Tom Brokaw. Maybe you listen to the President or Chaney or Powell or Rumsfield or the other warmakers. But today God commands us to listen to Jesus [...] The Temple system was the ultimate imperial and religious institution of injustice; a huge building like the Pentagon, U.S. Capitol, White House, and National Cathedral all rolled into one. (March 16 and 23, 2003)

Bishop Gumbleton, somewhat softer in his accusation—maybe mindful of his position—refers to the "propaganda that our government sets forth to try to justify this war" (Feb. 16, 2003) Yet the next month he goes further, saying: "[The war in Iraq] wouldn't happen to us if it weren't for the oil." (March 23, 2003). Father Dear and Bishop Gumbleton bring a historical dimension to the conflict and evoke warfare, weapons, the destructive power of nuclear weapons, the Holocaust or Hiroshima. In the same vein of social criticism, Bishop Gumbleton concludes his post 9/11 sermon with a condemnation of social injustice which he says is at the root of violence and fanaticism: "It's time for us to close the gap between the rich and the poor. And this will bring us peace in the world" (Sep. 30, 2001).

These sermons are structured more like homilies: each final paragraph exhorts the audience to act and change. Here is an example: "When the authorities start objecting to Jesus, he alludes to the resurrection [...] That should be our attitude too as we follow him in seeking an end to this war and every form of injustice anywhere and everywhere." (March 23, 2003). In most sermons, two or three keywords dominate, with sometimes one running on to the following Sunday. Dominating keywords show a strong attachment to Christian virtues. Here is a selection of Father Dear's associations: injustice and war as opposed to justice and peace (Sep. 1, 2002)—love, compassion and forgiveness as opposed to vengeance, bombings and war (Sep. 8, 2002)—love and justice (Feb. 2, 2003)—nonviolence, love and peace (Feb. 9, 2003)—change (March 2, 2003)—troublemaker and civil disobedience (March 23, 2003). At the start of the war in Iraq, he illustrates the dilemma Christians face, concluding his sermon with pairs of alternatives: "So as always, the scriptures say we have a choice: between light or darkness, truth or lies, love or hate, nonviolence or violence, peace or war, life or death". (March 30, 2003). Bishop Gumbleton's choices of keywords seem more traditional in contrast: foolishness (Sep. 30, 2001) – evil, sin, violence and love (Feb. 9,

2003) – evil, violence and love (Feb. 16, 2003) – sin and temptation (March 9, 2003) – change and love (March 16, 2003).

The sermons given by the Archbishop for the Military Service offer a different Catholic voice emblematic of the institution he belongs to. The Archdiocese for the Military Services and the Chaplains it oversees experienced indeed a dual status and held an ambiguous position: while their Church adopted a pro-peace stance, their base is made up of active duty members whose commander-in-chief is the President of the United States. Chaplains and soldiers respond both to the nation's secular leader—the President—and to God. They serve both God and their country: this double allegiance is very well expressed by Archbishop O'Brien: "In serving you, O Lord, may our Sailors serve their country; through Jesus Christ, our Lord."[27] Or, as he put it in a talk honouring World War II Chaplains:

> No priest lives more in the midst of his people than the Chaplain. His is a vocation within a vocation, a truly missionary vocation, trusted, even revered by Catholic and non-Catholic alike. He embraces every hardship and sacrifice inherent in military life, claiming no self-defense, and assuring one and all of God's presence, even in the most violent of strife [...] For being a soldier is a true calling from God. A true vocation.[28]

However, religion comes always first, military call second or third. Sr. Maria Magdalena C. Alamares from the Department of Pastoral Support in Washington, D.C. defines the Chaplaincy: "We are a community without walls, no building, yet connected through our faith, our heart, our military." Similarly, in the "Call for Vocation" posted on their website, the questions addressed to potential Chaplain recruits are in the following order:

Do you have...
1 A passion for your faith?
2. A deep love of ministry?
3. A calling to support the needs of the military and their families with the sacraments?
4. A desire to try something new in your ministry?
5. A strong sense of creativity in your ministry?

---

[27] www.milarch.org/Chaplains/index.html.
[28] Archbishop O'Brien, "Homily for the Mass Honoring WWII Chaplains", June 27, 2004 and "Address to the sailors board the USS Abraham Lincoln", Christmas 2001.

Archbishop O'Brien's sermons prove also to be at the crossroad between Catholic faith and service to the country. He often stresses this dual obedience: "[We live] renewed lives of selfless service to God and Country" (Sep. 11, 2002) and an ensuing potential dilemma pervades his words over time. The choice of dominating powerful words in Military Archbishop O'Brien's sermons brings a focus different from the focus of the pacifist sermons: evil (Sep. 16, 2001)—hope (Oct. 7, 2001) – burden and sacrifice (Oct. 11, 2002) – sacrifice and gift (Sep. 11, 2002) – faith, vocation and freedom (June 27, 2004). Catholic Bishops and the military Archdiocese never questioned post-9/11 "Operation Enduring Freedom"'s invasion of Afghanistan; indeed the Bishops stated the use of force against Afghanistan followed Just War norms. The language used by Military Bishops at the time reveals a strong connection with the Bush Administration's rhetoric and style. In his September 16, 2001 sermon, Archbishop O'Brien's words echo the Congressional Resolution's aggressive style:

> May our Nation's response to this dark day be all, but no more, than it must be: to seek out and visit appropriate retribution upon all who in any way have planned and carried out this attack [...] May [the Lord] bring swift and decisive judgement to those evil forces responsible for the sacrilege we have witnessed.[29]

He is confident that the resort to arms was of last resort and in self-defense. (Oct. 11, 2001). He develops: "We do have confidence and trust in our Nation's leadership—its integrity, its resolve, its dedication." (Oct. 11, 2001). In contrast, Bishop Gumbleton's reference to the attacks as a "terrible accident" (Sep. 30, 2001) seems unwarrantedly soft and Father Dear's answer to the attacks is reconciliation and non-violence: "I think Jesus would certainly want us to respond with love, compassion and forgiveness to September 11th, instead of with vengeance, bombings and war" (Sep. 8, 2001).

Later however, Archbishop O'Brien, together with mild conservative Catholics, actually expressed doubts concerning the war in Iraq. But he did not voice this questioning in the sermons intended to support the troops and their family, he published them in remarks or interviews. Indeed, as early as September 2002, he challenged the moral justification of a pre-emptive war and prayed that the war would not be necessary. He did so in

---

[29] Archbishop O'Brien, "Homily at the Basilica of the National Shrine of the Immaculate Conception: Mass for the Nation in a Moment of Tragedy and a Time of Hope", Sep. 16, 2001.

a statement published by a Catholic peace group.[30] In late 2004, even the Knights of Columbus acknowledged too the limits of the Just War doctrine applied to pre-emptive self-defense. Then, Archbishop O'Brien recognized the Church's moral duty: "We have every right and obligation to present moral questions to the Administration to either make them refine their decisions, change their decisions, or incorporate these moral questions as they go on with their decisions", thereby approaching the calls to action voiced by Father Dear and Bishop Gumbleton.[31] But again, he did so in a statement, not in a sermon. This critical stand might be the reason why he was not allowed to repeat his visit to the troops stationed in the Middle-East for Christmas 2002. The invasion of Iraq seems to have retrospectively shed a different light on the past event he did not question first. In a May 2004 Sunday sermon, he prayed for the military community and added: "As a result of the September 11th terrorist attacks, our nation and its allies have taken bold and controversial steps in Afghanistan and Iraq."[32] Or in a July 2004 sermon, he commends Saint Thomas's reluctance to believe in the resurrection and quotes Pope St Gregory: "More does the doubt of Thomas help us to believe than the faith of the disciples who did believe."[33]

To Archbishop O'Brien, sermons serve a specific purpose. Fighting soldiers deserve the unconditional respect, admiration and gratitude of their Archdiocese and must be given spiritual support and help—no matter the moral questioning of their mission. In his sermon honouring World War II Chaplains, he concludes with the following words:

> Can one not hate war—as we all must—and still glow with admiration and gratitude for the courage of those of the Greatest Generation, and generations of Americans before and since, willing to leave family and farm behind and pay with their very lives the costly price of freedom.[34]

Prior to the war's beginning, American Bishops followed the Pope, condemning and speaking out against it. Once the war had begun, however, they focused on the troops and on the need for a moral conduct

---

[30] "Statement by Archbishop Edwin O'Brien on the Current Threat of an Iraqi Invasion", Sep. 30, 2002, published in www.catholicpeacefellowship.org.
[31] In www.catholicmil.org/html/justwar.html#others.
[32] Archbishop O'Brien, "Ascension Sunday Homily, Military Pilgrimage", Basilica of the National Shrine, May 23, 2004.
[33] Archbishop O'Brien, "Homily for the Episcopal Ordination of Bishops Higgins and Estabrook", July 3, 2004.
[34] Archbishop O'Brien, "Homily for the Mass Honoring WWII Chaplains", June 27, 2004.

of the war, a view clearly stated by the President of the Bishops' Conference:

> Our nation is on the brink of war. We worked and prayed and hoped that war would be avoided. The task now is to work and pray and hope that war's deadly consequences will be limited, that civilian life will be protected, that weapons of mass destruction will be eliminated, and that the people of Iraq soon will enjoy a peace with freedom and justice.[35]

Pacifist Catholic priests were consistently vocal and highly critical of their Administration while the Military Archdiocese remained caught in the dilemma inherent in its role: serving Catholics themselves serving their country in uniform. It nonetheless did not stop Military Archbishop O'Brien from expressing doubts to reporters. The recent military interventions launched by the U.S. government led Catholics to confront their spiritual and political beliefs. Their reactions very clearly showed that they consider public affairs as having moral and religious dimensions and added fuel to the long fight of their leaders against secularism. It shed a modern light on common grounds and divisions that emphasize the very complex and "spiritual mosaic" that American Catholics form today.

Works Cited

Blaser, Klauspeter, *Les Théologies Nord-Américaines*. Genève : Labor et Fides, 1995.

Bureau of the Census, *Statistical Abstract of the United States*. Washington, D.C.: Government Printing Office, 1878.

Casey, Patrick W., "Catholicism" in *Encyclopedia of the U.S. in the XXth Century*, Stanley Kutler ed., Vol. IV, New York: Charles Scribner's Sons, 1996 : 1511-37.

Crepon, Pierre, *Les religions et la guerre*, Paris: Albin Michel, 2nd ed., 1991.

Debray, Anne, "Vote et action des femmes élues à la Chambre des Représentants", *Cycnos*, vol. 21, n°2 : *Les Etats-Unis et la guerre, les Etats-Unis en guerre*, (2004) : 213-27.

Froehle, Brian T. and Mary L. Gautier, Catholicism USA: A Portrait of the Catholic Church in the United States. New York: Orbis, 2000.

Gleason, Philip, *Keeping the Faith: American Catholicism Past and Present*. Notre Dame: University of Notre Dame Press, 1987.

---

[35] Most Reverend Wilton D. Gregory, President, United States Conference of Catholic Bishops, "Statement on War with Iraq", March 19, 2003.

Martin, Jean-Pierre, *La religion aux Etats-Unis*. Nancy: Presses Universitaires de Nancy, 1989.

McMartin, James P., "The Waning of the 'Catholic Other' and Catholicism in American Life After 1965", RFEA, n°95: *Le fait religieux aux Etats-Unis : approches culturelles et cultuelles*, Belin, (février 2003) : 7-29.

McNeal, Patricia, *Harder than War: Catholic Peacemaking in Twentieth-Century America*. New Brunswick, N.J.: Rutgers University Press, 1992.

Nolan, Hugh. J. ed., *Pastoral Letters of United States Catholic Bishops*, 5 vol. (1984-1989), Washington, D.C.: National Conference of Catholic Bishops.

The Official Catholic Directory (1900-2005), New York: P. J. Kennedy & Sons.

CONTRIBUTORS

Leticia ÁLVAREZ-RECIO is a Junior Lecturer in English Literature at the University of Seville (Spain). Her publications include *Rameras de Babilonia. Historia cultural del anti-catolicismo en la Inglaterra Tudor* (Salamanca, 2006) and a number of articles and chapters on sixteenth and seventeenth-century English literature and history. She is a member of a research team that works on the printed history of Middle English verse romances. This project has been subsidized by a Spanish government grant.

Serge AUFFRET, a graduate of the École Normale Supérieure (Rue d'Ulm), has been teaching English and British and American civilization at the French Military Academy of Saint Cyr since 1987. A member of the Centre for Military Ethics, he is currently working on a doctorate on '*The Churches in Great Britain and the two Gulf Wars (1991-2003) : Ethics, Politics and Society*' at the Sorbonne University in Paris.

Marie BEAUCHAMP-SOW is a former *élève* of the École Normale Supérieure – Lettres Sciences Humaines (Lyon). She is now at the University Paris Diderot – Paris 7, where she is working on her doctorate under the supervision of Professor Mark Meigs. She is writing about the representation of the American nation through the commemorative speeches delivered in honour of the soldiers who fought during the Civil War, the Spanish-American War, and the First World War. While writing her dissertation, she teaches at the University Paris 7 (Department of English Studies). Her recent publications include *Politique d'aménagement linguistique et identité en Louisiane* (Presses Universitaires de Limoges, 2006).

Suzan BRAY is Professor in the English Department at Lille Catholic University. She specializes in literature and theology in twentieth-century Britain and has published extensively on C. S. Lewis, Charles Williams, and Dorothy L. Sayers. Her most recent publication is an edition of the (previously unpublished) talks delivered by Dorothy L. Sayers on the BBC during the Second World War, *The Christ of the Creeds.*

Anne DEBRAY is an Assistant Professor at the University of Nice-Sophia Antipolis in the English Department (since 2001). She defended her PhD thesis on *'The Work of Congresswomen elected between 1990 and 1996'*. Her research focuses on American institutions and on the notion of political representation, both locally and on the federal level.

Rémy DUTHILLE is completing his PhD thesis on universalism and patriotism in late-18th century British radical discourse, at the Universities of Paris III – Sorbonne nouvelle and Edinburgh. He currently holds a teaching and research position at University Paris – Diderot.

Pasi IHALAINEN Ph.D. (1999), is a Professor of General History at the University of Jyväskylä, Finland. He has published widely on political discourse on parties, modernizing notions of national identity and the redefinition of the political role of the people and democracy in the eighteenth century, applying often a comparative perspective. His published books include *The Discourse on Political Pluralism in Early Eighteenth-Century England* (Finnish Historical Society: Helsinki 1999), *Protestant Nations Redefined : Changing Perceptions of National Identity in the Rhetoric of English, Dutch and Swedish Public Churches, 1685-1772* (Brill: Leiden & Boston 2005) and *Agents of the People: Democracy and Popular Sovereignty in British and Swedish Parliamentary and Public Debates, 1734-1800* (forthcoming Brill: Leiden & Boston 2009). His extensive article on " The Enlightenment Sermon: Towards Practical Religion and a Sacred National Community " can be found in *Preaching, Sermon and Cultural Change in the Long Eighteenth Century*, ed. Joris van Eijnatten (Brill: Leiden & Boston 2008), 219-260. Ihalainen is currently writing a book on Swedish and German long-term influence on Finnish political culture.

Marie-Christine MUNOZ is a Senior Lecturer in the English Department of Montpellier III University, and a permanent member of the I.R.C.L. (Institut de Recherches sur la Renaissance, l'Age Classique et les Lumières, UMR 5043). She holds an M.A. (Birmingham University) and a PhD (Montpellier III) in Shakespeare Studies. She is currently writing a book about the figure of Venus and the representations of female desire in Early Modern Drama. She is also engaged in a collaborative edition of penitential Psalms rewritings by major Renaissance poets (Wyatt, Sidney, Harrington, etc...). She has recently published an article on King Lear for 'Les éditions du Temps'. She is engaged in collective programs from

IRCL, such as a dictionary of mythological allusions in Shakespeare's plays or a data bank of allusions to Shakespeare's plays in French cinema.

Keith ROBBINS is Vice-Chancellor Emeritus of the University of Wales, Lampeter. He was a lecturer at the University of York, and professor, successively, at the University of Wales, Bangor and at the University of Glasgow. He has held visiting posts in Canada and Australia. He has lectured in China, the United States and many European countries. He has been editor of the journal *History* and President of the Historical Association. He was concurrently Senior Vice-Chancellor of the Federal University of Wales (1995-2001). He is a Fellow of the Royal Society of Edinburgh and has been a Vice-President of the Royal Historical Society. He has served on the *Beirat* of the German Historical Institute in London and on that of the *Institut fur Zeitgeschichte* in Munich. He holds honorary degrees from the universities of Wales and the West of England, Bristol. He has written widely on modern British/European political, diplomatic and religious history, including the following books: *Munich 1938, Sir Edward Grey, Winston Churchill, The Eclipse of a Great Power: Modern Britain 1870-1992, Nineteenth-Century Britain: Integration and Diversity, Great Britain: Identities, Institutions and the Idea of Britishness, History, Religion and Identity in Modern Britain, Politicians, Diplomacy and War in Modern British History, Bibliography of British History 1914-1989, The First World War, The World since 1945, Past and Present: British Images of Germany* and *Britain and Europe, 1789-2005*. His latest book is *England, Ireland, Scotland, Wales: The Christian Church 1900-2000* (Oxford University Press, 2008). He has contributed to many other books and written a large number of articles. He edits the following series: (1) *Profiles in Power*,(2) *Turning Points,* (3) *Inventing the Nation,* (4) *Religion, Society and Politics in Britain,* (5) *Britain and Europe,* (6) *The Wiley/Blackwell History of the Contemporary World* for various British publishers. Some of his books have been translated into German, Italian, Russian, Polish, Hungarian, Latvian, Turkish, Portuguese and Spanish. He is editing two forthcoming publications on *Religion and Diplomacy in modern British foreign policy* and *The Dynamics of Religious Reform in Northern Europe 1780-1920*.

Christine RONCHAIL holds a Master's Degree in theology from the Protestant Faculty of Theology of Montpellier (France). Her dissertation was on *'Devotion in Charenton in the XVIIth Century: Du Moulin, Drelincourt, Claude'*. She is completing a PhD Thesis on the French Reformed Church of Paris under the personal reign of Louis XIV through the correspondence of pastor Jean Claude, at the University of Montpellier. Her fields of interest range from the study of the Reformed Church in Paris under the Edict of Nantes, to the relations of the Parisian pastors with foreign countries (England, the United Provinces, Switzerland) and the theological debates that they triggered.

Michael ROTENBERG-SCHWARTZ is an Assistant Professor of English at New Jersey City University. He has published or has forthcoming articles on Milton's Psalm translations, the war imagery in Laurence Sterne's sermons, Pope's "Windsor-Forest," eighteenth-century georgic poetry, the use of gore in Romantic poetry, the war poetry of Brian Turner and David Harsent, and the phrase "Go to Jericho." He is also the editor of Global Economies, Cultural Currencies of the Eighteenth Century, forthcoming from AMS Press.

Catherine ROYER-HEMET teaches the Civilisation of the British Isles at the University in Le Havre, France. She is currently completing a thesis at La Sorbonne in Paris, the title of which is *'Sermons & Propaganda during the Hundred Years War'*. She has already published a number of articles about various aspects of her research in different French scholarly magazines. She also wrote an article entitled "The lords in the *Lord of the Rings*", in which she investigates the concept of lordship in Tolkien's novel in a book entitled *Tolkien and the Middle Ages,* published by the CNRS.

Massimo RUBBOLI is a professor of North American history at the University of Genoa, Italy. He has published books and articles on many topics in American and Canadian history, including *Politica e religione negli USA* [Politics and Religion in the USA] (1986), *Religione alle urne* [Religion at the Ballot Box] (1988) and *Dio sta marciando* [God is Marching On] (2003).

Waltraud VERLAGUET studied medicine in Germany and Switzerland. She became a doctor in Medicine in 1974. She practiced medicine from 1978 until 1993. She studied theology at the Protestant Faculty of Theology in Montpellier (France). Her PhD thesis, which she defended in 2003 was on the Medieval mystic Mechthild of Magdeburg. She is a member of Pro-Fil and editor of "Point théo" and "La Lettre de Pro-Fil". Her publications include: *Comment suivre Dieu, quand Dieu n'est pas là ? La spiritualité de Mechthild de Magdebourg*, Paris, Cerf, 2006; *L'« éloignance ». La théologie de Mechthild de Magdebourg (XIIIe siècle)*, Bern etc., Peter Lang, 2005. She also translated with an introduction: *Mechthild de Magdebourg, La Lumière fluente de la Divinité*, Grenoble, Jérôme Millon, 2001.